# Phenomenology of Sociality

"Szanto's and Moran's volume is a veritable treasure trove that amply documents the fertility and richness of the phenomenological tradition. Containing contributions on both familiar and lesser well known phenomenologists, *Phenomenology of Sociality: Discovering the 'We'* is mandatory reading for anybody working on sociality and collective intentionality."
—*Dan Zahavi, University of Copenhagen*

"This book is essential reading for anyone interested in the phenomenological foundations of the social mind and our experience of living together in a common world of the 'We.' It brings together eminent scholars and talented young researchers to evaluate the relevance of a phenomenological theory of sociality in contemporary philosophical and interdisciplinary discussions, thereby revitalizing lesser-known voices from the tradition as well as exploring new directions of phenomenological research."
—*Thiemo Breyer, University of Cologne*

"A groundbreaking collection of fresh insights into the nature of the social self."
—*James Mensch, Charles University, Prague*

Phenomenological accounts of sociality in Husserl, Heidegger, Merleau-Ponty, Sartre, Scheler, Schütz, Stein, and many others offer powerful lines of arguments to recast current, predominantly analytic, discussions on collective intentionality and social cognition. Against this background, the aim of this volume is to reevaluate, critically and in contemporary terms, the rich phenomenological resources regarding social reality: the interpersonal, collective, and communal aspects of the life-world (*Lebenswelt*). Specifically, the book pursues three interrelated objectives: it aims 1.) to systematically explore the key phenomenological aspects of social reality; 2.) to offer novel, state-of-the-art assessments of both central and lesser-known proponents of the phenomenology of sociality (Gurwitsch, Löwith, von Hildebrand, and Walther), and 3.) to contextualize this elaborate body of work in light of contemporary social cognition research, the growing literature in analytic social ontology, and current trends in moral psychology, moral phenomenology, and social and political philosophy. The collection brings together original work by a host of prominent scholars and upcoming young talents to provide a comprehensive and up-to-date treatment of the topic. It will be essential reading for those studying phenomenological accounts of intersubjectivity, empathy, and community, including analytic, social, moral, and political philosophers, and will also be of interest for social scientists and social psychologists.

**Thomas Szanto** is a Postdoctoral Research Fellow at the Center for Subjectivity Research (CFS), at the University of Copenhagen, Denmark.

**Dermot Moran** is Professor of Philosophy at University College Dublin, Ireland and Sir Walter Murdoch Adjunct Professor in the Humanities at Murdoch University, Australia.

# Routledge Research in Phenomenology

Edited by Søren Overgaard, *University of Copenhagen, Denmark*, Komarine Romdenh-Romluc, *University of Nottingham, UK*, and David Cerbone, *West Virginia University, USA*

1 **Phenomenology and the Transcendental**
   *Edited by Sara Heinämaa, Mirja Hartimo and Timo Miettinen*

2 **Philosophy of Mind and Phenomenology**
   Conceptual and Empirical Approaches
   *Edited by Daniel O. Dahlstrom, Andreas Elpidorou, and Walter Hopp*

3 **Phenomenology of Sociality**
   Discovering the 'We'
   *Edited by Thomas Szanto and Dermot Moran*

# Phenomenology of Sociality
Discovering the 'We'

**Edited by Thomas Szanto and
Dermot Moran**

NEW YORK AND LONDON

First published 2016
by Routledge
711 Third Avenue, New York, NY 10017

and by Routledge
2 Park Square, Milton Park, Abingdon, Oxon OX14 4RN

First issued in paperback 2017

*Routledge is an imprint of the Taylor & Francis Group, an informa business*

© 2016 Taylor & Francis

The right of the editors to be identified as the author of the editorial material, and of the authors for their individual chapters, has been asserted in accordance with sections 77 and 78 of the Copyright, Designs and Patents Act 1988.

All rights reserved. No part of this book may be reprinted or reproduced or utilised in any form or by any electronic, mechanical, or other means, now known or hereafter invented, including photocopying and recording, or in any information storage or retrieval system, without permission in writing from the publishers.

*Trademark notice*: Product or corporate names may be trademarks or registered trademarks, and are used only for identification and explanation without intent to infringe.

*Library of Congress Cataloging-in-Publication Data*
Phenomenology of sociality : discovering the we / edited by Thomas Szanto and Dermot Moran. — 1st [edition].
    pages cm. — (Routledge research in phenomenology ; 3)
Includes bibliographical references and index.
1. Intersubjectivity.  2. Phenomenology.  I. Szanto, Thomas, editor.
B824.18.P44 2015
142'.7—dc23         2015031324

ISBN 13: 978-1-138-49902-7 (pbk)
ISBN 13: 978-1-138-91879-5 (hbk)

Typeset in Sabon
by Apex CoVantage, LLC

# Contents

Introduction: Phenomenological Discoveries Concerning
the 'We': Mapping the Terrain  1
THOMAS SZANTO AND DERMOT MORAN

## PART I
## Historical and Methodological Issues

1 Locating Shared Life in the 'Thou': Some
   Historical and Thematic Considerations  29
   JAMES RISSER

2 Hannah Arendt's Conception of Actualized Plurality  42
   SOPHIE LOIDOLT

3 Habermas and Hermeneutics: From *Verstehen* to *Lebenswelt*  56
   RICHARD WOLIN

4 Second-Person Phenomenology  70
   STEVEN CROWELL

## PART II
## Intersubjectivity, the "We-World," and Objectivity

5 Concrete Interpersonal Encounters or Sharing a
   Common World: Which Is More Fundamental
   in Phenomenological Approaches to Sociality?  93
   JO-JO KOO

6 *Ineinandersein* and *L'interlacs*: The Constitution of
   the Social World or "We-World" (*Wir-Welt*) in
   Edmund Husserl and Maurice Merleau-Ponty  107
   DERMOT MORAN

7  Davidson and Husserl on the Social Origin
    of Our Concept of Objectivity                                127
    CATHAL O'MADAGAIN

## PART III
## Social Cognition, Embodiment, and Social Emotions

8  From Types to Tokens: Empathy and Typification              143
    JOONA TAIPALE

9  An Interactionist Approach to Shared Cognition:
    Some Prospects and Challenges                               159
    FELIPE LEÓN

10 "If I had to live like you, I think I'd kill myself":
    Social Dimensions of the Experience of Illness              173
    HAVI CAREL

11 Shame as a Fellow Feeling                                   187
    CHRISTIAN SKIRKE

12 Relating to the Dead: Social Cognition and
    the Phenomenology of Grief                                  202
    MATTHEW RATCLIFFE

## PART IV
## Collective Intentionality and Affectivity

13 Affective Intentionality: Early Phenomenological
    Contributions to a New Phenomenological Sociology           219
    ÍNGRID VENDRELL FERRAN

14 Love and Other Social Stances in Early Phenomenology        234
    ALESSANDRO SALICE

15 Gurwitsch and the Role of Emotion in Collective Intentionality  248
    ERIC CHELSTROM

16 The Affective 'We': Self-Regulation and Shared Emotions     263
    JOEL KRUEGER

## PART V
## Collective Agency and Group Personhood

17 Husserl on Groupings: Social Ontology and
   the Phenomenology of We-Intentionality                    281
   EMANUELE CAMINADA

18 Collectivizing Persons and Personifying Collectives:
   Reassessing Scheler on Group Personhood                   296
   THOMAS SZANTO

19 Brothers in Arms: Fraternity-Terror in Sartre's
   Social Ontology                                           313
   NICOLAS DE WARREN

   *Contributors*                                            327
   *Index*                                                   333

# Introduction
# Phenomenological Discoveries Concerning the 'We'
## Mapping the Terrain

*Thomas Szanto and Dermot Moran*

> "[. . .] I, we, and world belong together."
> (Husserl, *Ideen II*, 288)

> "Even the Being-alone of *Dasein* is Being-with in the world."
> (Heidegger, *Sein und Zeit*, 120)

> "[. . .] the I is but a 'part' of the We, and the We an essential part of the I."
> (Scheler, *Wesen und Formen der Sympathie*, 225)

## I  FROM THE SECOND-PERSON PERSPECTIVE TO THE FIRST-PERSON PLURAL (AND BACK)

What is it to belong to a 'We' or an 'Us'? What is the nature of interpersonal understanding, social interaction, and social participation? For instance, is sharing a common socio-cultural environment, a common history, or a common life-world, prior to, or even a necessary condition for, such understanding, interaction, or participation, or, rather, a result of them? How can *we* collectively—rather than just *you* and *me*, and *others*—constitute and share norms, experiences, or even emotions? Are there any other 'proprietors' of the social domain? Is social reality composed entirely of individuals, or are there also irreducibly plural subjects or 'We' agents?

Curiously, the nature of social and collective identity or plural agency has not been at the forefront of philosophy over the past hundred years, although it has been treated in sociology and in those social sciences inspired by Marxism and, in some more restricted circles, by Hegelianism. As a matter of fact, the issue of collectivity has only relatively recently been given serious attention in analytic philosophy, especially in the work of Michael Bratman, Margaret Gilbert, Philip Pettit, Carol Rovane, John Searle, and Raimo Tuomela. There is an older tradition especially stemming from the work of Peter Winch, and Georg Henrik von Wright, which was, in turn, inspired by Wittgenstein and Collingwood, but this tended towards the philosophical critique of sociological explanation rather than an examination of the nature and varieties of togetherness.

Arguably, however, when looking back over the last century of thinking about sociality, there seems to be no other single intellectual tradition within philosophy, or even in neighboring disciplines in the humanities and social sciences, including sociology, other than phenomenology, that has endeavored to address the issue of interpersonal understanding, collectivity, and togetherness with such rigor and detail. Phenomenology, from its very inception and for systematic reasons, was always synonymous with the phenomenology of sociality, the careful descriptive elucidation of the layers and strata of both social and collective life. Moreover, as the epigraphs of this introduction vividly illustrate, a great number of phenomenologists, even if certainly not all, would concur with the idea that sociality is not only a matter of *intersubjectivity*, of relations between subjects, in the sense of *you* and *me* appropriately interacting, but also of me, or me *and* you, relating to a 'We,' or forming an *us*, which may or may not be formed against a *them*. The different forms of 'We' may eventually be more or less rationally or normatively coherent, more or less emotionally cohesive, or more or less diachronically or institutionally robust, and may, in different contexts, be formed out of very different reasons, or pursue, as group agents, very different goals. To be sure, the very notion of an irreducible collective subject, or group agent, is controversial, and it is one of the themes explored in this book.

All the contributions of the present volume share the conviction that phenomenology is always a phenomenology of sociality. They also agree that phenomenologists of the social have to endorse, or at least critically confront, not only the second-person perspective, but also the first-person perspective plural. Although phenomenology has always insisted on the first- as well as the second-person (singular) perspective regarding consciousness, subjectivity, and intersubjectivity, there is also a first- and indeed second-person plural. This recognition of the need for singularity, for alterity, as well as for plurality in the understanding of subjectivity is, incidentally, a perspective that Husserl famously invoked when he expressed the need for a methodological shift from the *ego cogito* to a *nos cogitamus* (Husserl 1959, 316; cf. Carr 1986).

In fact—and contrary to still widespread prejudices—it is entirely wrong to conceive of phenomenology as practicing any form of methodological individualism, let alone solipsism. Rather, phenomenology has always recognized that humans come to develop their intentional, meaningful, and meaning-constituting lives always and only in the context of a given socio-historical context, a common background, or a set of shared habits, and embedded in a world in which they participate, and which they possibly aim to individually or collectively transform. Thus, phenomenologists, however much they differ in degree and commitment, all agree on the basic idea that humans are intrinsically social beings, acting within specific historical and cultural contexts, and embedded in a shared life-world. Phenomenologists of all traditions and hues have sought to analyze the complex network of social relations and social acts, constitutive of values, norms, communities, and social or institutional facts. Phenomenological conceptions of sociality, moreover, are expressed in a particularly rich range of notions. For example, virtually all phenomenologists, including above all Max Scheler, Edith Stein, Edmund Husserl, Alfred Schütz, and Maurice Merleau-Ponty, have elaborated on the core notion of the intersubjective encounter, 'empathy' (*Einfühlung*), while others have employed cognate conceptions of 'Being-with-others' (Heidegger's 'Being-with' or Sartre's 'Being-for-Others'). But beyond this fairly well-known conceptual territory, most phenomenologists have also referred to vocabulary that points not only to *interpersonal* but to *collective* or genuinely *communal* engagements, such as 'consociality' (Schütz), 'common minds' and 'higher order persons,' the "We-world," 'communalization,' and 'socialization' (Husserl), 'communal persons' (Scheler), and 'Being-for-groups' and 'Being-in-groups' (Sartre), to name just a few. Many of these concepts are explored in the contributions in this volume.

In a remarkable historical turn, these very phenomenological notions can also be found re-expressed in somewhat different technical terms in contemporary analytic 'social ontology'—indeed, it is notable that the very term 'social ontology' was first coined by Husserl more than a hundred years ago (Husserl 1973, 102; cf. also Salice 2013; Caminada 2011; Szanto 2015). Current social ontology studies collective practices, social institutions, and cultural products that are, in some sense or another, dependent on what has been called collective intentionality, shared goals, collective agreements, or joint commitment. Searle, for example, claims that "social ontology is both created by human actions and attitudes but at the same time has an epistemically objective existence and is part of the natural world" (Searle 2006, 12). Phenomenology has long understood and analyzed such 'creation' as a genuinely *social constitution*, without, to be sure, simply confusing the (social) constitution of social reality with the social construction of reality (cf. Berger & Luckmann 1966; Collin 1997, 110–121). Very few contemporary analytic social ontologists are familiar with the phenomenological tradition (e.g., Schmid 2009), and most simply ignore it. On the other hand, many phenomenologists offer powerful lines of argument that challenge the hitherto predominantly analytical discussions, which often all-too-narrowly focus on team reasoning, joint commitments, or shared agency. Current social ontology could greatly benefit from reintegrating the respective phenomenological insights concerning, for instance, the role of affectivity, habituality, or embodiment in collective intentionality, as could, conversely, the phenomenology of sociality benefit from such a contemporary reassessment. Thus, by setting its methods and vocabulary in the context of current research, this book aims to eventually transform the understanding and reception of social phenomenology as well as to contribute to the contemporary debates in social philosophy, social cognition, and social ontology.

The same applies to social cognition as to social ontology: philosophical work on what is now the rapidly growing area of social cognition—our ability to interpret and understand others—is also in the process of 'rediscovering' core conceptions of the phenomenology of sociality, such as empathy (Stueber 2006), or the affective and embodied nature of socio-cognitive engagements, which were long emphasized and extensively studied by phenomenologists (cf. Taipale 2014; Jensen & Moran 2013). The chapters in this book will discuss and develop these insights in articulating, for a new era, phenomenology's contribution to the social cognition literature.

Let us now outline in more detail some of the main issues that have dominated the philosophy of sociality over the past two decades. In doing so, we will point to some important, but hitherto underexposed, connections between social cognition research, social ontology, and social philosophy more broadly conceived, and notably to those desiderata that will be addressed in this volume.

Consider first interpersonal relations, which have been the object of much scrutiny lately within the social cognition paradigm. One of the core, and still largely unsettled, issues here is how to explain our psychological, epistemic, or emotional access to other minds. This debate has become known as the 'theory of mind' or the 'mindreading' debate (Davies & Stone 1995a, 1995b; Coplan & Goldie 2011; Decety 2012; Baron-Cohen et al. 2013, Stueber 2013; Michael 2014; Zahavi 2014). Is social cognition grounded in explicitly or non-inferentially simulating or imitating (e.g., Heal 1995; Stueber 2006; Gordon 2008) or sub-personally mirroring (Gallese 2001) others' experiences in oneself, or in adapting others' first-person perspectives? Or is it rather to be conceived of as engaging in a conceptual, inferential, and interpretative activity of mindreading, by applying a folk-psychological theory of mind to oneself and others (Leslie 1987; Gopnik & Wellman 1992; Meltzoff & Gopnik 1993; Baron-Cohen 1995; Leslie et al. 2004)? Alternatively, others suggest that we should employ a so-called 'hybrid' strategy, and conceive of social cognition in terms of simulating-*cum*-projecting mental models (Nichols & Stich 2003; Goldman 2006). Meanwhile, and as the debate between theory theorists and simulation theorists (and hybrid theorists) has already become somewhat deadlocked, phenomenologically inspired theorists have put much pressure on both camps, and argued for novel ways to conceptualize what they would usually refer to as 'empathy' (*Einfühlung*). They argue that our ability to experience and understand others rests on a specific form of 'direct perception' of others' expressions and their social context, or is a '*sui generis* experience' of the embodied mind of others (Ratcliffe 2007; Gallagher 2008a, 2008b; Krueger & Overgaard 2012; cf. Jensen & Moran 2012, 2013, and, critically, Jacob 2011, and Zahavi 2014).

The social cognition debate is very active, but, curiously, it has not attended properly to what phenomenologists have long acknowledged as the passive, habitualized, affective, or embodied nature of social interaction. The social cognition debate has also largely ignored the role of a common background of shared values, habits, or perspectives, the role of social typification, or the role of a shared and essentially social life-world, sometimes called a "We-world" (Husserl) (cf., however, De Jaegher & Di Paolo 2007; Gallagher 2008a, 2008b; De Jaegher et al. 2010).

Furthermore, one of the fault lines in the discussion opens up around the question as to whether some form of sharing of experiences, and of affective states in particular, between an empathizer and the target subject is necessary for empathy to succeed and, if so, what this sharing precisely amounts to (Jacob 2011; Michael & Fardo 2014; Zahavi 2011, 2014).

The issue of 'sharing,' and especially the sharing of mental properties or actions, has been recently addressed by a number of analytic philosophers of action working on collective intentionality and joint agency. They have investigated how it is possible for two or more individuals to intend to do something, or to cooperate in doing what they intend. Discussions in this area have typically focused on the question of whether collective intentions and agency are reducible to an aggregation of individual agents and, if not, whether we would then need to postulate some supra-individual bearer, some group mind, group person, or group agent, of the collective intentionality (cf. Rupert 2005, 2011; Chant et al. 2014; Huebner 2014; Szanto 2014; Tollefsen 2015). More specifically, philosophers of action dwelled upon the question of where to 'tie in,' as it were, the 'jointness' in collective engagements: in the intentional object, or the 'interlocking' of interdependent intentional plans and shared goals (Bratman 1992, 1993, 2014), the 'we-mode' (e.g., Searle 1995, 2010; Tuomela 2007, 2013), the 'plural subject' (Gilbert 1989, 2013) of collective intentions, or some other form of the 'rational integration' of individuals (Rovane 1998, 2014; Pettit 2003; List & Pettit 2011; cf. Chant et al. 2014).

When it comes to broader ontological issues concerning social reality, analytic social ontology also differs from earlier debates in the philosophy of the social sciences. Earlier debates have largely focused on the issue of methodological individualism versus holism understood as an explanatory program (cf. O'Neill 1973; Udehn 2002; Zahle & Collin 2014), or on the issue of explanation vs. understanding (e.g., in the work of G. H. von Wright and Karl-Otto Apel; see *Richard Wolin's* contribution in this volume). In contrast, the current social ontology typically proceeds by reflecting on the related but different metaphysical and normative issues concerning the relation between individuals and social entities and the proper ontological status of the latter (cf. Ruben 1985 and Epstein 2015). To get a fair idea of what is at stake here, consider three doctrines, which, in one form or another and even if sometimes under different headings, can be encountered in most contemporary social ontologies (e.g., Gilbert 1989; Pettit 1993, 2014):

> *Intentional-Psychological and Social Holism*: the conditions of the individuation of a subject S's conscious intentional states and its (objective

and/or phenomenal) contents are fixed by (i.) the intra-subjective relations that those states have vis-à-vis other intentional states of S, and (ii.) by the inter-subjective and social relations that S bears to other subjects (S* . . . S*n) (and their intentional states).

*Socio-Ontological Anti-Singularism*: social reality comprises not only individuals, but also social entities and collectives and, possibly, higher-order or supra-individual entities or properties (possibly with their own laws and systemic, normative, etc. structures governing them), which are not reducible to, but may be founded, or supervene, upon, individuals.

*Ontological and Normative Anti-Collectivism*: neither (a) individual intentional psychology, nor (b) individual personhood (including its ontological and moral properties, such as autonomous agency, volition, spontaneity, moral accountability, dignity, etc.), are compromised, 'outflanked,' or 'overridden' (Pettit 1993) by an individual's membership in collectives and the (intentional or normative) laws governing such collectives.

On the face of it, it seems as if these claims run counter to one another. In particular, the third doctrine, anti-collectivism, seems to be incompatible, or, at least, in serious tension, with the first two. As a number of contributions in this volume powerfully demonstrate, however, most phenomenological versions of social ontology can accommodate all three sets of claims without encountering a contradiction (cf. esp. the chapters by *Caminada, O'Madagain, Szanto*, and *Vendrell Ferran* in this volume).

It is surely the case that social cognition, social ontology, and collective intentionality do not represent opposing lines of research, and that the respective issues should be dealt with side by side. This, however, is still far from the current situation. Only in very recent times can one witness a growing but still rather underdeveloped tendency to link the issues in social *cognition* to social *interaction*, sometimes referred to as 'interaction theory' (De Jaegher & Di Paolo 2007; De Jaegher et al. 2010; Gallagher & Varga 2013; Schilbach et al. 2013; Satne & Roepstorff 2015; cf., critically, Herschbach 2012; Michael et al. 2014; Overgaard & Michael 2015). Notwithstanding some recent attempts, research relating social cognition to collective intentionality and shared agency is still in its infancy (Hobson & Hobson 2007; Butterfill 2013; Gallotti & Frith 2013; Tomasello 2014; Zahavi 2014, 2015a, 2015b; Abramova & Slors 2015; cf. Szanto & Moran 2015; Bianchin forthcoming, and *Felipe León's* contribution in this volume). Among the issues dealt with within this paradigm, the phenomenon of joint attention (Eilan et al. 2005; Seemann 2012; cf. Baron-Cohen 1995) figures predominantly. Given the crucial developmental role of this form of social cognition (Tomasello 2014), this is a little surprising. But, again, what is indeed surprising, especially when viewed from a phenomenological perspective, is the almost complete ignorance within the collective intentionality debate of the single most basic form of social cognition, to wit, empathy.

This lacuna is all the more apparent given that, in sociology, social psychology, and the collective intentionality debate, there has recently been a very lively debate on shared affectivity and collective emotions (e.g., Parkinson et al. 2005; von Scheve & Salmela 2014; Stets & Turner 2014). Given that empathy is the primary access to emotions and affective states—though empathy is surely not restricted to such states—the absence of research on the matter is somewhat puzzling.

Social relations are, almost always, emotionally charged, and have some affective dimension. Sociality has not only its *ontology* and *epistemology*, therefore, but also its specific and often richly differentiated *phenomenology*. Other individuals and groups *matter* to us, or *concern* us; some matter to us more, some less. Accordingly, our empathic access, too, will vary, based typically on our social typification, identification and our social distinctions (cf. Eres & Molenberghs 2013). Social cognition is typically not *just* cognition but, rather, *affective* and *embodied interaction*. Similarly, collective intentionality and group agency involve not just coordination, team reasoning, and rational agency, but may also involve shared emotions and values. And some would even go so far as to attribute collective or corporate emotions to whole groups.

Within the collective intentionality debate, the focus has specifically been on the sense and feeling of sharedness, and their role in joint commitments and shared agency (Michael 2011), as well as on socially extended or distributed emotions (Krueger 2015) and genuinely collective or group-level emotions (Gilbert 2002, 2014; Helm 2008, 2014; Schmid 2009, 2014; Konzelmann Ziv 2007, 2009; Huebner 2011; Salmela 2012, 2014; Guerrero 2014; Schützeichel 2014).

Phenomenologists have long recognized affectivity and emotions as the integral building blocks of social reality. As many of the contributions to this volume demonstrate, we can find the most elaborate analyses of shared affectivity and social emotions (such as grief, shame, etc.) in the work of the so-called 'early' or 'realist' phenomenologists from the Munich and Göttingen Circles, such as Max Scheler, Gerda Walther, Edith Stein, or Dietrich von Hildebrand, but such analyses may also be found in the work of such figures as Gurwitsch or Merleau-Ponty (see esp. the contributions in Part III and Part IV of this volume; cf. Szanto forthcoming).

In this connection, phenomenologists have argued for the following claims, though with quite different emphases:[1]

> *Socio-Normative Embeddedness of Emotions*: a subject's emotional directedness towards objects and persons, i.e., his 'affective intentionality,' is deeply embedded in our social environment, and our shared (aesthetic and moral) norms and values.
>
> *Social Holism Regarding Emotions*: given the socio-normative embeddedness of emotions, but also moving beyond that, a subject's

experience, expression and/or regulation of her (social or non-social) emotions is socially modulated or co-constituted by her interpersonal relationships, her social identity, or her membership in certain groups.

*Anti-Singularism Regarding Emotions*: emotions, or some aspects of emotions (e.g., their expression or regulation), are not, as it were, bound to their typical phenomenal locus of instantiation, namely individuals. Rather, under certain conditions, in certain types of communities, and in some sense or another (e.g., in terms of 'joint ownership,' synchronous 'entrainment,' 'social appraisal'), emotions can be shared among or across individuals, or may even be attributed to collectives as such, which can then be said to have an emotional life of their own.

Notice that, if these claims go through, they will not only hold for distinctively social, or other-directed emotions, such as resentment, betrayal, or grief, but rather quite generally for all kinds of affective states and emotions. Given that there has been quite some confusion about this (cf. Darwall 1998; Zahavi 2014, 2015a, 2015b), it is also worth mentioning that none of these claims entail any equivalence between empathy and shared emotions. Since, phenomenologically viewed at least, empathy is neither necessarily an affective state, nor presupposes any interpersonal similarity between the affective sates of empathizer and target (cf. Jacob 2011 *versus* Zahavi 2011), the fact that virtually all phenomenologists stress the relevance of empathy for interpersonal engagements has nothing to do with any of their arguments for the above three claims. Quite the contrary, phenomenologists from the outset have been adamant in emphasizing the difference between empathy and emotional sharing. For a striking example, just think of Scheler's (1926a, 1926b) fine-grained conceptual distinctions that disambiguate between 'empathy' (*Nachfühlen*), 'feeling-with' (*Mitfühlen, Sympathie*), and joint and shared feelings (*Einsfühlung, Miteinanderfühlen*) (see also Stein 1917, 1920, and Walther 1923; Konzelman Ziv 2007; Zahavi 2015a, 2015b).

There are two further reasons why phenomenological accounts can contribute to moving towards a more adequate and more comprehensive theory of shared affectivity: (1) first, phenomenological accounts may help to circumvent problems associated with both phenomenal token-identity construal of shared emotions, on the one hand, and cognitivist-*cum*-normativist accounts, on the other hand. According to the phenomenalist account, collective emotions entail a "phenomenological fusion" of emotions, such that "there is one token affective state in which many individuals take part," and which has its own "phenomenological subject" (Schmid 2014, 9; cf. Schmid 2009); meanwhile, according to cognitivist-*cum*-normativist accounts, collective emotions are a matter of "joint commitments to feel" (Gilbert 2002, 2014; cf. Helm 2014). From a phenomenological point of view, both accounts are, however, seriously limited (see the contributions in *Part IV* of this volume; cf. Salmela 2012; and Szanto forthcoming).

(2) Secondly, phenomenological accounts of emotions emphasize the intentional (object-related), cognitive, evaluative, and normative, but also the passive, affective, and embodied aspects of emotions (Vendrell Ferran 2008). And since, arguably, both cognitive and non-cognitive components are at play in sharing emotions, the phenomenological approach is best suited to addressing this issue.

Beyond the discussion on shared and collective emotions, phenomenologists offer uniquely rich ways to address distinctively other-directed, or social, emotions, such as shame or grief (see esp. the contributions of *Steven Crowell*, *Matthew Ratcliffe*, and *Christian Skirke* in this volume; cf. also León 2013; Zahavi 2014). Moreover, given many phenomenologists' insistence on the intrinsic relation between emotions and (shared) norms and values—think of the theory of "value-ception" (*Wertnehmen*) in Scheler, Stein, or Husserl—phenomenologists are particularly well prepared to contribute to the moral psychology of social emotions such as guilt or forgiveness (Rinofner-Kreidl 2013, 2014; Steinbock 2014).

Finally, this brings us to yet another important avenue upon which phenomenologists and their 'offspring' have embarked in elucidating social reality—an avenue, for one, that has been endorsed only by strikingly few authors within contemporary social phenomenology, or even social philosophy in general: namely the moral, normative, and especially the political dimensions of the 'We.'

Phenomenologists are generally not only opposed to any form of solipsism and individualism but, moreover—and in stark contrast to the much more restricted focus of standard contemporary social ontology (cf., however, Pettit 1997, and Gilbert 2006)—their contribution to the analysis of social reality was never purely an ontological, epistemological, or, for that matter, purely philosophical or *phenomenological*, enterprise. Thus, from Husserl, to Scheler, Stein, Schütz, and Arendt, and from Merleau-Ponty to Sartre, virtually all of the thinkers of the phenomenological movement were deeply interested in contemporary sociological, social, and political thought, and many typically also engaged directly in the concrete social movements of their times: these included educational reform (e.g., Stein), the Catholic 'communitarianism' *avant-la-lettre* of the interwar period (e.g., Scheler, Stein, and Hildebrand), post-war Marxism (Sartre, Merleau-Ponty, Paci, and Trân Duc Thao), and post-war anti-(Soviet) Communism (Merleau-Ponty and Patočka), just to name a few (cf. Waldenfels et al. 1977ff.). Thus, we fully endorse Michael Gubser's recent corrective to this narrative:

> When future historians chronicle the twentieth century, they will see phenomenology as one of the preeminent social and ethical philosophies of its age. [. . .] Central to the tradition from the start [. . .] was a preoccupation with ethics and social renewal—at times overt, often implicit—that inspired not only second-generation phenomenologists *engagé*, but also the founders.
>
> (Gubser 2014, 1)

Consequently, the book shall also contribute to restoring and recasting certain normative conceptions of sociality as discussed in the post-war and post-Frankfurt School moral, social, and political philosophy, and especially in the work of authors like Hannah Arendt, Jürgen Habermas, Axel Honneth, and Stephen Darwall.

We hope, then, to have made a clear enough case for why phenomenology is a most suitable candidate for making an impact on the contemporary landscape in regard to social ontology, social cognition, and the philosophical study of sociality generally. But, surely, one might still wonder whether we need *another* phenomenologically oriented collection of essays on this topic. If we look at the English, German, or French contemporary literature on the subject, though, we take the answer to be clearly positive. For one, notwithstanding lively debates and an ever-growing interest in phenomenology in the English-speaking world, which is also reflected in an increasing number of edited volumes, companions, and handbooks (Moran 2000; Dreyfus & Wrathall 2009; Luft & Overgaard 2012; Zahavi 2012), somewhat surprisingly, there is yet no single comparable account of the phenomenology of sociality available. To be sure, a fair number of monographs have been devoted to 'second-person phenomenology,' or the phenomenology of interpersonal relations and intersubjectivity (Theunissen 1965; Waldenfels 1971; Steinbock 1995; Haney 1994; Zahavi 2001, 2014; Schmid 2000; Overgaard 2007). However, with very few exceptions (Theunissen 1965; McMullin 2013), they have typically restricted their focus to Husserl or broadly Husserlian phenomenology. Moreover, 'discovering the "We"' means, as we have seen, essentially moving beyond the merely interpersonal domain, and incorporating investigations of the first-person plural, or "we-mode" (Tuomela 2007), as well as the broader socio-normative contexts arising from such we-intentionality (cf. Chelstrom 2013). This is the distinctively novel focus of the present volume.[2]

In addition, the phenomenological contributions to the philosophy of the social sciences and sociology have more often than not been restricted to work on Schütz's (and Luckmann's; e.g., Schütz & Luckmann 2003) arguably seminal analysis of social reality. Thus, Schützian sociology of knowledge and interpretative sociology (the so-called *Wissenssoziologie*, or *Verstehende Soziologie*) have hitherto either been the dominant paradigms for phenomenology's contribution to the philosophy of the social sciences (Natanson 1970, 1973; Barber & Dreher 2014; cf. Collin 1997),[3] or else social sciences-oriented phenomenology was confined to broadly Marxist publications, entitled, for example, *Phenomenology and Marxism* (Waldenfels et al. 1977ff.), however valuable these indeed were for the early reception of a phenomenology of sociality (cf. Thonhauser & Schmid forthcoming).[4] Yet, we believe that such limitations must once and for all be overcome, as there is much more to phenomenology's contribution to the social sciences than interpretative sociology or Marxism, just as there are many more phenomenologists than Schütz to lend themselves for such contributions (see also *Vendrell Ferran's* contribution in this volume). Thus, there is a whole series of other positions, in particular within the so-called 'early,' or 'realist,' phenomenological movement, but also within the work of the movement's founding fathers, Husserl and Scheler, and its French and American (e.g., Gurwitsch) avenues and crossings, to be rediscovered for social philosophy—as well as for, it's fair to say, most social *phenomenologists* working today. Accordingly, in contrast to the standard accounts, one of the special features of this volume is that a number of chapters will critically engage with lesser known but still important authors of the phenomenological movement. Thus, the volume will focus not only on the work of the most influential German and post-war French phenomenologists of sociality (notably Edmund Husserl, Martin Heidegger, Max Scheler, Alfred Schütz, Jean-Paul Sartre, Maurice Merleau-Ponty, and Emmanuel Levinas), but will also cover relevant topics in the highly sophisticated social ontologies of such lesser-known figures as Adolf Reinach, Edith Stein, Gerda Walther, Dietrich von Hildebrand, Karl Löwith, and Aron Gurwitsch. Furthermore, a number of chapters will deal with prominent philosophers who, though not part of the phenomenological movement strictly speaking, have sympathetically or critically engaged with or have been strongly influenced by phenomenological thought, viz. Martin Buber, Hans-Georg Gadamer, Jürgen Habermas, Hannah Arendt, and Jean-François Lyotard.[5]

In summary, then, the ambition of the volume is to reevaluate, critically and in contemporary terms, the unprecedentedly rich phenomenological resources regarding social reality on the level of interpersonal, collective, and communal engagements. In doing so, the book pursues three objectives: first, it aims to systematically explore all the key phenomenological aspects of social reality, ranging from its cognitive, intentional, agential, and affective to its normative and political dimensions; secondly, to offer novel assessments of the central but also the lesser-known proponents of the phenomenology of sociality; and, finally, to contextualize this elaborate body of work within contemporary trends in social philosophy, including social cognition research and the ever-growing literature on analytic social ontology, as well as the philosophy of emotions and embodiment and the broader spectrum of contemporary social and political philosophy.

## II  AN OVERVIEW OF THE VOLUME

The volume is divided into five variously interconnected parts. All center on systematic and thematic rather than purely historical or methodological considerations. To be sure, however, one cannot go about (re-)discovering collectivity in phenomenological thought by means of phenomenological analysis in ignorance of the socio-historical context and without dwelling upon the key methodological, meta-theoretical, or foundational issues of such an endeavor. After all, and in a rather obvious sense, neither early nor post-Husserlian phenomenologists devised their conceptions of sociality in a conceptual or socio-cultural void. Setting the historical and methodological stage, then, and elaborating on the most salient normative aspects, ethical motives, and the broader political-philosophical background is the task of the opening part of the volume.

## Part I: Historical and Methodological Issues

A central question in the phenomenology of sociality is whether I-Thou relations, i.e. dyadic, interpersonal relations between subjects who directly address one another, are to be given priority over the standpoint of individuals.

In the opening chapter, *James Risser* addresses this issue from a historical perspective. The chapter follows the complex trail of thinking about the relation between I and Thou from such diverse, early phenomenological voices as Stein, Buber, and Löwith up to Gadamer's hermeneutical version of being- and speaking-with-one-another and Heidegger's Being-with.

Closely related to the issue of the priority of I-Thou relations over the individual's first-person perspective is what *Steven Crowell* calls 'second-person phenomenology,' i.e. the reflection on experiencing oneself 'in the accusative.' Crowell asks whether such experience is constitutive of a shared world, and of such essentially normative concepts as responsibility, accountability, self-identity, and rationality. Following a broadly Levinasian path, and critically examining Stephen Darwall's contemporary construal of the second-person perspective, Crowell argues that this is indeed so. Moreover, he shows that the second-person perspective, in turn, is not a constituted stance, to wit, not constituted by empathy, but precisely a constitutive phenomenon. In particular, it constitutes both the other, understood as another rational and normatively responsive being, and, at the same time, via the experience of a feeling of obligation towards those others, one's own responsiveness to others' normative claims.

Beyond such foundational issues, *Part I* also probes phenomenology's contribution to pre- and post-war (and post-Marxist), as well as contemporary social and political, philosophy.

Accordingly, *Richard Wolin's* chapter investigates the status of phenomenology vis-à-vis the hermeneutical analysis of the lifeworld and sociality, and in particular against the debate on explanation versus understanding in the philosophy of the social sciences. Furthermore, the chapter elaborates critically on Habermas's communicative and normative reappropriation of the transcendental-phenomenological idea of a social lifeworld.

*Sophie Loidolt* reexamines the work of one of the eminent figures of post-war social and political thought, Hannah Arendt, a thinker who is often sidelined in phenomenological scholarship, to be sure, unjustly so. In her chapter, Loidolt focuses on Arendt's phenomenologically inspired conception of 'actualized plurality' and reconstructs this notion as a specific form of being and living together, that is, as a practical enactment of we-intentionality that is not purpose-bound. Importantly, the chapter demonstrates how Arendt's social ontology is essentially political, without necessarily converging to standard notions of politics.

## Part II: Intersubjectivity, the "We-World," and Objectivity

A central issue of any phenomenology of sociality is the question of the priority of I-Thou relations over sharedness and collectivity, or the priority of the second-person singular over the first-person plural perspective. This issue is canvassed under a historical and meta-theoretical angle in *Part I*, and is taken up again and expanded on by the contributions in *Part II*. This part, then, revolves around the conceptual triad of intersubjectivity, the notion of a "We-world," and objectivity.

The first chapter in this section, by *Jo-Jo Koo*, addresses the foundational issue of the commonality of the life-world versus dyadic encounters head-on. Koo argues—siding with the early Heidegger and Merleau-Ponty, and in opposition to phenomenologists such as Buber, Sartre, Theunissen, and Levinas—that an adequate phenomenology of social reality should grant primacy to the explanation of our already sharing a common world. At the same time, he maintains that we should not lose sight of the importance of our embodied, interpersonal encounters with one another as a crucial explanandum of any phenomenology of sociality worth its salt.

Taking up this lead, *Dermot Moran* elaborates in more detail on the role that embodiment, mutual recognition, and the interpenetration of subjective consciousnesses play in the constitution of the intrinsically social life-world. Specifically, Moran traces the relations between the embodied self-experience, experience of others, and experience of the world in Merleau-Ponty and in the later Husserl, and explores their notions of "We-world," 'inter-corporeality,' and 'interpenetration' (*Ineinandersein*).

Finally, in his chapter on the intersubjective constitution of objectivity, *Cathal O'Madagain* argues that combining Husserl's intersubjective theory of the constitution of intentional objects with Davidson's theory of the triangulation of subjectivity, objectivity, and intersubjectivity yields a novel argument to the effect that our very concept of a mind-independent objectivity depends on our interaction with others. In doing so, the chapter forcefully shows how one may productively bridge the gap between analytic and phenomenological thought on sociality, instead of engaging in mere turf wars.

Social interaction, including social cognition, not only amounts to specific intentional, epistemic, or agential relations between intrinsically embodied agents, but is typically an emotional affair; often, collective intentionality and agency, too, are laden with affectivity. This is the issue that the following two thematically interlinked sections of the volume address. Accordingly, the contributions in *Part III* and *IV* are devoted to the complex web of embodied, affective, and emotional underpinnings of social interaction, social cognition, and collective intentionality. The chapters here resume and reformulate, yet again, the question of whether dyadic or collective forms of social relations are constituents of our social reality. Thus, a number of chapters deal with social emotions and social typification in the context of social cognition and collective intentionality (see esp. the contributions of *Christian Skirke, Matthew Ratcliffe, Eric Chelstrom*, and *Joona Taipale* in this volume), as well as with the hitherto largely missing link between research on social cognition and collective intentionality (*Felipe Léon*). Importantly, the topics covered in these two parts straddle a number of philosophical sub-disciplines and neighboring fields of empirical research, such as social, developmental, and moral psychology (esp. *Joel Krueger, Joona Taipale*), moral phenomenology (*Alessandro Salice, Vendrell Ferran*), the philosophy of psychiatry (esp. *Matthew Ratcliffe*), and health care (*Havi Carel*).

## Part III: Social Cognition, Embodiment, and Social Emotions

Against the backdrop of these historical, methodological, and conceptual foundations, *Part III* develops the phenomenology of *interpersonal* encounters. Here, the contributions lay particular stress on the pathological and non-pathological aspects of empathy and embodied social interaction. Thus, a number of chapters from quite different perspectives elaborate on the core phenomenological concept of social cognition, to wit, empathy. Unlike standard accounts, however, these chapters deal with empathy not only within the context of ordinary dyadic encounters, but also in the context of non-dyadic, collective, or social interaction, social emotions (esp. shame and grief), or non-ordinary interpersonal relations, for instance, in our relations to the dead, or the chronically ill.

*Joona Taipale* examines the extent to which we always build on assumptions concerning general typicalities when experiencing others. He argues that, in empathic encounters, we never meet some wholly unknown, or 'mysterious' others, but already take others as often predictable representatives of more or less distinct social groups. Such tacit assumptions point to what Taipale describes as 'empathic typification.' Specifically, Taipale shows how empathy is initially 'type-oriented,' and only gradually develops into a 'token-oriented' experience of concrete others. It is worth pointing out in this connection that this issue of social typification represents a central desideratum for both contemporary social ontology and social philosophy, and notably one that a number of classical phenomenologists have long tackled successfully. Incidentally, this is also shown in *Eric Chelstrom*'s contribution, which deals, among others, with this very concept of typification in Gurwitsch.

*Felipe Léon*, too, addresses the question of how to best conceive of social cognition. Léon concentrates on the most recent trend in social cognition research, in which social cognition is viewed as a specific form of embodied interaction. Drawing on a paradigmatic experimental setting (the 'perceptual crossing' paradigm), he argues that this theory of social cognition, viz.

'interaction theory,' is best understood as a theory of distinctively *shared* cognition—without, to be sure, eliminating any self/other differentiation, which, rather, is necessary for any *inter*personal understanding. Consequently, the chapter suggests that interaction theory provides interesting insights for current discussions of collective intentionality.

*Christian Skirke's* contribution presents another angle on the phenomenological concept of empathy by relating the issue of social emotions to social cognition. Skirke argues for a strong parallelism, or structural isomorphism, between shame and empathic fellow feeling. He claims that both are intentionally directed at, or present in, the experiences of others that are not originally experienced, or 'lived through,' by the subject of those social experiences. (For a related but different analysis of shame, see also the contribution of *Steven Crowell*).

*Matthew Ratcliffe* starts from the critical observations that work on social cognition, and specifically those relying on standard belief-desire psychology that restrict their focus to interpersonal relations with the living, and, hence tend to overlook our often deeply charged emotional relations with the dead. Against this, and drawing on both empirical and literary descriptions of the phenomenon, Ratcliffe directly addresses the phenomenology of experiences of grief. In an original take, Ratcliffe proposes to view grief as a genuinely second-personal experience of absence, rather than as the absence of a second-person experience. Consequently, he claims that this stance is firmly embedded in the social life-world and dynamically intermeshed with our other, more 'ordinary' interpersonal relations.

Finally, *Havi Carel* confronts another form of the disruption of ordinary embodied interaction by engaging in a phenomenological analysis of the social experience of illness and its normative implications. She argues that, with the impediment or breakdown of our embodied social encounters, i.e., our 'bodily empathy' in illness, a certain distance or asymmetry between the being-in-the-world of the ill person and that of her healthy counterparts is established. Carel then shows that what ultimately gets reconfigured, and often truncated, in illness is not only the ill person's relationship to her environment, but also the social norms that usually underpin such a relationship.

## Part IV: Collective Intentionality and Affectivity

What role do emotional and affective components, or a 'sense of togetherness,' play in collective intentionality, especially—though certainly not exclusively—in such highly cohesive or 'fused' I-Thou relations as love, friendship, or infant-caretaker relationships? What effect do social roles, types and functions have on such relations? What is the role of emotions in empathy, sympathy, and emotional contagion, and what role do they play for the understanding of intersubjectivity, and for participation in the social world? Are early, so-called 'realist,' phenomenological accounts of social emotions better geared to explaining social reality than, for example, Schützian phenomenological sociology? And how is (the sociality of) affectivity related to normativity and values?

In the first, programmatic, chapter of this part, *Íngrid Vendrell Ferran* pleads for an alternative construal of a phenomenological sociology, one that puts feelings, emotions, sentiments, and values, or so-called 'affective intentionality,' center stage. By bringing into play the resources offered by key representatives of the early phenomenological movement of the Munich and Göttingen Circles (and esp. Scheler, Stein, Walther, and Hildebrand), she argues that we need to distinguish between different ways of being-together, according essentially to different levels and dimensions of emotional bonding, as well as different possibilities of grasping and sharing values.

*Alessandro Salice*'s contribution can be seen as a prime example of precisely such an alternative approach, as he is homing in on early phenomenology's contributions to a social phenomenology of emotions. In particular, Salice dwells upon the similarities and differences between the epistemology and phenomenology of genuine 'social acts' (Reinach), such as promises or orders, on the one hand, and affective or emotional 'social stances' (Hildebrand), such as romantic love or Scheler's 'vicarious feeling' (*Nachfühlen*), on the other. By doing so, the chapter, again, successfully testifies that early phenomenologists have the most sophisticated resources to analyze both the normative as well as the affective 'glue' that binds individuals together.

In a similar vein, *Eric Chelstrom* also takes up the challenge of contributing to a novel phenomenological sociology, and traces the development of a theory of shared emotions in Aron Gurwitsch, an eminent social phenomenologist who has, however, hitherto been overshadowed by his colleague and close friend, Alfred Schütz, the founding father of phenomenological sociology. Critically, and with respect to the current treatments of collective intentionality (esp. by Gilbert and Bratman), Chelstrom fleshes out the intricate distinctions that Gurwitsch draws between different types of social connections (i.e., societal, or instrumental, 'partnerships,' membership-based affective communities, and still more affectively charged interpersonal and collective bonds, so-called 'fusions'). In particular, he discusses the different functions that affectivity plays in those social relationships, which, in turn, largely depend on the symmetrical or asymmetrical distribution of the participants' social roles.

In the last chapter of this part, while still investigating the nature and structure of emotional sharing, *Joel Krueger* suggests looking more closely at the way emotions may be jointly regulated by two or more subjects, in order to get a grip on the idea that, numerically, the same emotions can be given or experienced by more than one subject. Building on both phenomenology as well as developmental and social psychology, Krueger then argues that the very phenomenology of (shared) emotions is modulated by embodied processes of emotion regulation, processes, that is, that may indeed be distributed across subjects. This, as Krueger demonstrates, happens essentially through the 'co-regulation' of emotions by 'off-loading' self-regulative processes to others, as is characteristic, for example, in infant-caretaker situations, or parental grieving, or by means of mutual affective 'entrainment,' for instance, jointly attending to music.

## Part V: Collective Agency and Group Personhood

The chapters in the final part of the volume pick up the main issues of the debate on collective intentionality discussed from the perspective of affectivity and emotions in *Part IV*. Here, the contributors focus more on agential, practical, and normative aspects, and embark on reassessing three major figures of phenomenological social ontology. The three chapters in this section are tightly interconnected, though each deals with thinkers of the phenomenological movement who could hardly be more different in philosophical, but also socio-political, temperament (Sartre, Scheler, and Husserl). While the first chapter examines in more general ontological terms the emergence or genetic constitution of social groupings (*Emanuele Caminada*), and the second chapter engages in a structural as well as a normative evaluation of the issue of collectivism in phenomenology, the third and final chapter concentrates, from a socio-political and moral-philosophical angle, on practical 'groups-in-action,' as it were (*Nicolas de Warren*).

The main questions guiding these spotlights on the ontological and normative fabric of social reality can be summarized as followed: what individuates different types of social formations, or 'groupings' of individuals? Put differently: what kinds of 'forms of togetherness' correspond to various levels of robustness of collective intentionality (e.g., 'fused groups,' 'serialized collectives,' 'communal persons,' 'plural agents,' etc.)? What is the phenomenological structure of practical and theoretical forms of collective intentionality, or collective agency, and how do they emerge genetically, or come to be constituted? What is the role of habit and habituality in collective engagements? Do we need to postulate some supra-individual 'bearer' of collective intentionality? In particular, can and *should* we posit any group persons in our social ontology?

*Emanuele Caminada* addresses these questions by couching Husserl's 'intentional' or 'transcendental sociology' within the framework set by contemporary social ontology. He focuses specifically on the structural and genetic elements in the constitution of always and already 'socialized' individuals as well as of 'higher-order,' or 'supra-individual,' socialities (e.g., the role of embodied or communal habitualities, or shared background beliefs). In doing so, Caminada critically launches a two-fold challenge: the challenge that 'discovering the We' poses for the classical transcendental-phenomenological project, and, conversely, the challenge that phenomenologically and genetically 'enriched' forms of the 'We' might pose for those social ontologists who typically abstract from the concrete life-world in which such communities are embedded.

Expounding the discussion of higher-order persons, which is briefly discussed in the previous chapter, *Thomas Szanto* tackles the question of whether there are, in the face of contemporary metaphysical and normative accounts of group personhood (e.g., by Philip Pettit or Carol Rovane), any viable, i.e., non-collectivist, conceptions of group personhood in phenomenological thought. Along the lines of a critical, yet ultimately favorable, reassessment of Scheler's notoriously ambiguous conception of communal persons (*Gesamtpersonen*), Szanto investigates the normative, rational, and phenomenological properties of corporate personhood. In order to safeguard this conception from normative distortions, he then suggests distinguishing different versions of collectivist claims, and argues that Scheler can, in fact, accommodate these distinctions.

In the final chapter of this volume, *Nicolas de Warren* touches on the political dimensions of the 'We' by reintroducing a highly intriguing but much-neglected major work in phenomenological social ontology, namely the late Sartre's *Critique of Dialectical Reason*, to contemporary readership. This seems all the more pertinent as ignorance of this work, even among otherwise avid readers of Sartre, is prevailing, which is, arguably, due to the work's unflinching adherence to a radical form of (Soviet) Marxism. The article revolves around the Sartrean notion of 'fraternity' and its group membership-based distortion in acts of terror against traitors. The group paradigm, here, is comprised of such highly cohesive and essentially 'practical' groups that emerge out of, often implicit, 'pledges' (*le serments*, which are notably, Sartre's version of what, in Margaret Gilbert's influential terminology, would today be labeled 'joint commitments'). In elucidating these notions, de Warren unearths Sartre's distinctively political version of social ontology, and hence demonstrates how it is amenable to current discourses on terrorism, social identity, or political movements.

## NOTES

1 Notice that these claims, which are left deliberately vague at some junctures so as to accommodate the different stances different phenomenologists would take on them, partly mirror the above-stated socio-ontological claims. For the different weighing and emphasis of each of these claims, see again the articles in Part III and Part IV, and especially Vendrell Ferran's contribution.

2 Here, it should not go unnoticed that there are in fact a number of more specific, and almost exclusively Husserlian, works focused on elaborating on a phenomenological social ontology, often with quite domain-specific analyses (e.g., pertaining to the specific types of collectives, the state, etc.) (e.g., Toulemont 1962, Schuhmann 1988, Perreau 2013); for an interesting, Husserlian inspired but highly original account of social ontology, see also Hart 1992, and Spiegelberg 1973; for more literature regarding this line of research, see also Szanto 2015.

3 Introductory textbooks or collected volumes on (again, mostly Schützian) *phenomenological sociology* abound, to be sure; see, e.g., Psathas 1973; Wagner 1983; Grathoff 1995; Benoist & Karsenti 2001; Ferguson 2006; Bühl 2007;

Fischer 2012. To be sure, Berger & Luckmann 1966 duly credit Scheler's pioneering work on the sociology of knowledge (Scheler 1926c), but note also that it has been—to wit, already in the 1960s—almost completely forgotten or overshadowed by others, such Karl Mannheim.

4 Think also of the by now largely forgotten, but at the time highly influential, works of Trân Duc Thao (esp. 1951), or Enzo Paci (esp. 1963); cf. also Smart 1976.

5 Three even lesser-known figures of the early phenomenological movement are Tomoo Otaka, Kurt Stavenhagen, and Felix Kaufman, who have each contributed highly intriguing work to the phenomenology of sociality and collectivity (Otaka 1932; Stavenhagen 1933; and Kaufman 1944). Though they are not explicitly dealt with within this volume, they should certainly not go missing from this list. Incidentally, Otaka and Kaufmann both had an intensive critical exchange with Schütz.

## REFERENCES

Abramova, Ekaterina, & Slors, Marc (2015). "Social Cognition in Simple Action Coordination: A Case for Direct Perception." *Consciousness and Cognition.* http://dx.doi.org/10.1016/j.concog.2015.04.013.

Barber, Michael, & Dreher, Jochen (Eds.) (2014). *The Interrelation of Phenomenology, Social Sciences and the Arts.* Dordrecht: Springer.

Baron-Cohen, Simon (1995). *Mindblindness: An Essay on Autism and Theory of Mind.* Cambridge, MA/London: MIT Press.

Baron-Cohen, Simon, Lombardo, Michael, & Tager-Flusberg, Helen. (Eds.) (2013). *Understanding Other Minds. Perspectives from Developmental Social Neuroscience.* Oxford: Oxford University Press.

Benoist, Jocelyn, & Karsenti, Bruno (Eds.) (2001). *Phénoménologie et sociologie.* Paris: Presses Universitaires de France.

Berger, Peter L., & Luckmann, Thomas (1966). *The Social Construction of Reality: A Treatise in the Sociology of Knowledge.* New York: Anchor.

Bianchin, Matteo (forthcoming). "Simulation and the We-Mode. A Cognitive Account of Plural First Persons." *Philosophy of the Social Sciences*, doi: 10.1177/0048393115580267.

Bratman, Michael (1992). "Shared Cooperative Activity." *Philosophical Review* 101 (2), 327–341.

——— (1993). "Shared Intention." *Ethics* 104 (1), 97–113.

——— (2014). *Shared Agency: A Planning Theory of Acting Together.* Oxford: Oxford University Press.

Bühl, Walter (2007). *Phänomenologische Soziologie. Ein kritischer Überblick.* Konstanz: UVK Verlagsgesellschaft.

Butterfill, Stephen (2013). "Interacting Mindreaders." *Philosophical Studies* 165 (3), 841–863.

Caminada, Emanuele (2011). Husserls intentionale Soziologie. In: V. Mayer, C. Erhard & M. Scherini (Eds.). *Die Aktualität Husserls.* Freiburg/München: Alber, 56–85.

Carr, David (1986). "Cogitamus Ergo Sumus: The Intentionality of the First-Person Plural." *The Monist* 69 (4), 521–533.

Chant, Sarah Rachel, Hindriks, Frank, & Preyer, Gerhard (Eds.) (2014). *From Individual to Collective Intentionality: New Essays.* Oxford: Oxford University Press.

Chelstrom, Eric (2013). *Social Phenomenology: Husserl, Intersubjectivity, and Collective Intentionality.* Lanham: Lexington.

Collin, Finn (1997). *Social Reality.* London/New York: Routledge.

Coplan, Amy, & Goldie, Peter (Eds.) (2011). *Empathy: Philosophical and Psychological Perspectives*. Oxford: Oxford University Press.
Darwall, Stephen (1998) Empathy, Sympathy, Care. *Philosophical Studies* 89 (2–3), 261–282.
Davies, Martin, & Stone, Tony (Eds.) (1995a). *Folk Psychology: The Theory of Mind Debate*. Oxford: Blackwell.
Davies, Martin, & Stone, Tony (Eds.) (1995b). *Mental Simulation: Evaluations and Applications*. Oxford: Blackwell.
Decety, Jean (2012) (Eds.). *Empathy: From Bench to Bedside*. Cambridge, MA/London: MIT Press.
De Jaegher, Hanne, & Di Paolo, Ezequiel (2007). "Participatory Sense-Making." *Phenomenology and the Cognitive Sciences* 6 (4), 485–507.
De Jaegher, Hanne, Di Paolo, Ezequiel, & Gallagher, Shaun (2010). "Can Social Interaction Constitute Social Cognition?" *Trends in Cognitive Sciences* 14 (10), 441–447.
Dreyfus, Hubert L., & Wrathall, Mark A. (2009). *A Companion to Phenomenology and Existentialism*. Chichester: Wiley-Blackwell.
Eilan, Naomi, Hoerl, Christoph, & Roessler, Johannes (Eds.) (2005). *Joint Attention: Communication and Other Minds*. Oxford: Oxford University Press.
Epstein, Brian (2015). *The Ant Trap: Rebuilding the Foundations of the Social Sciences*. Oxford: Oxford University Press.
Eres, Robert, & Molenberghs, Pascal (2013). "The Influence of Group Membership on the Neural Correlates Involved in Empathy." *Frontiers in Human Neuroscience* 7, 176.
Ferguson, Harvie (2006). *Phenomenological Sociology: Insight and Experience in Modern Society: Experience and Insight in Modern Society*. London: Sage.
Fischer, Peter (2012). *Phänomenologische Soziologie*. Bielefeld: Transcript.
Gallagher, Shaun (2008a). "Direct Perception in the Intersubjective Context." *Consciousness and Cognition* 17 (2), 535–543.
——— (2008b). "Inference or Interaction: Social Cognition without Precursors", *Philosophical Explorations* 11 (3), 163–174.
Gallagher, Shaun, & Varga, Somogy (2013). "Social Constraints on the Direct Perception of Emotions and Intentions." *Topoi* 33 (1), 185–199.
Gallese, Vittorio (2001). "The 'Shared Manifold' Hypothesis: From Mirror Neurons to Empathy." *Journal of Consciousness Studies* 8 (5–7), 33–50.
Gallotti, Mattia, & Frith, Chris D. (2013). "Social Cognition in the We-Mode." *Trends in Cognitive Sciences* 17 (4), 160–165.
Gilbert, Margaret (1989). *On Social Facts*. London/New York: Routledge.
——— (2002). "Collective Guilt and Collective Guilt Feelings." *The Journal of Ethics* 6 (2), 115–143.
——— (2006). *A Theory of Political Obligation: Membership, Commitment, and the Bonds of Society*. Oxford: Oxford University Press.
——— (2013). *Joint Commitment: How We Make the Social World*. Oxford: Oxford University Press.
——— (2014). "How We Feel: Understanding Everyday Collective Emotion Ascription." In: C. von Scheve, & M. Salmela (Eds.). *Collective Emotions*. Oxford: Oxford University Press.
Goldman, Alvin I. (2006). *Simulating Minds: The Philosophy, Psychology, and Neuroscience of Mindreading*. Oxford: Oxford University Press.
Gopnik, Alison, & Wellman, Henry M. (1992) "Why the Child's Theory of Mind Really *Is* a Theory." *Mind & Language* 7 (1–2), 145–171.
Gordon, Robert M. (2008). "Beyond Mindreading." *Philosophical Explorations* 11 (3), 219–222.

Gubser, Michael (2014). *The Far Reaches. Phenomenology, Ethics and Social Renewal in Central Europe*. Stanford: Stanford University Press.
Guerrero, Sánchez H. A. (2014). "Feelings of Being-Together and Caring-With." In: A. Konzelmann Ziv, & H. B. Schmid (Eds.). *Institutions, Emotions, and Group Agents*. Dordrecht: Springer.
Grathoff, Michael (1995). *Milieu und Lebenswelt. Einführung in die phänomenologische Soziologie und die sozialphänomenologische Forschung*. Frankfurt a.M.: Suhrkamp.
Haney, Kathleen M. (1994). *Intersubjectivity Revisited: Phenomenology and the Other*. Athens, OH: Ohio University Press.
Hart, James G. (1992). *The Person and the Common Life. Studies in a Husserlian Social Ethics*. Dordrecht: Kluwer.
Heal, Jane (1995). "How to Think about Thinking." In: M. Davies, & T. Stone (Eds.). *Mental Simulation*. Oxford: Blackwell, 33–52.
Heidegger, Martin (1927). *Sein und Zeit*. Tübingen: Niemeyer 1967. [Engl.: *Being and Time*. Transl. by J. Macquarrie, & E. Robinson. Oxford: Blackwell.]
Helm, Bennett (2008). "Plural Agents." *Noûs* 42 (1), 17–49.
—— (2014). "Emotional Communities of Respect." In: C. v. Scheve, & M. Salmela (Eds.). *Collective Emotions*. Oxford: Oxford University Press.
Herschbach, Mitchell (2012). "On the Role of Social Interaction in Social Cognition: A Mechanistic Alternative to Enactivism." *Phenomenology and the Cognitive Sciences* 11 (4), 467–486.
Hobson, Jessica A., & Hobson, Peter R. (2007). "Identification: The Missing Link Between Joint Attention and Imitation?" *Development and Psychopathology* 19 (2), 411–431.
Huebner, Bryce (2011). "Genuinely Collective Emotions." *European Journal for Philosophy of Science* 1 (1), 89–118.
—— (2014). *Macrocognition: A Theory of Distributed Minds and Collective Intentionality*. Oxford: Oxford University Press.
Husserl, Edmund (1952) [=Hua 4]. *Ideen zu einer reinen Phänomenologie und phänomenologischen Philosophie. Buch II: Phänomenologische Untersuchungen zur Konstitution*. Ed. by M. Biemel. The Hague: Nijhoff. [Engl.: (1989). *Ideas Pertaining to a Pure Phenomenology and to a Phenomenological Philosophy. Second Book. Studies in the Phenomenology of Constitution*. Transl. by R. Rojcewicz, & A. Schuwer. Dordrecht: Kluwer.]
—— (1959) [=Hua 8]. *Erste Philosophie. Zweiter Teil. Theorie der phänomenologischen Reduktion*. Ed. by Rudolf Boehm. Den Haag: Nijhoff.
—— (1973) [=Hua 13]. *Zur Phänomenologie der Intersubjektivität. Texte aus dem Nachlaß. Erster Teil: 1905–1920*. Ed. by Iso Kern. Den Haag: Nijhoff.
Jacob, Pierre (2011). "The Direct-Perception Model of Empathy: A Critique." *Review of Philosophy and Psychology* 2 (3), 519–540.
Jensen, Rasmus T., & Moran, Dermot (2012). "Introduction: Intersubjectivity and Empathy." *Phenomenology and the Cognitive Sciences* 11 (2), 125–133.
Jensen, Rasmus T., & Moran, Dermot (Eds.) (2013). *The Phenomenology of Embodied Subjectivity*. Dordrecht: Springer.
Kaufmann, Felix (1944). *Methodology of the Social Sciences*. Oxford: Oxford University Press.
Konzelmann Ziv, Anita (2007). "Collective Guilt Feeling Revisited." *Dialectica* 61 (3), 467–493.
—— (2009). "The Semantics of Shared Emotion." *Universitas Philosophica* 26 (52), 81–106.
Krueger, Joel (2015). "Varieties of Extended Emotions." *Phenomenology and the Cognitive Sciences*, doi: 10.1007/s11097-014-9363-1.

Krueger, Joel, & Overgaard, Søren (2012). "Seeing Subjectivity: Defending a Perceptual Account of Other Minds." *ProtoSociology* 47, 239–262.
León, Felipe (2013). "Shame and Selfhood." *Phänomenologische Forschungen* 2013, 193–211.
León, Felipe, & Zahavi, Dan (2015). "Phenomenology of Experiential Sharing: The Contribution of Schutz and Walther." In: A. Salice, & H. B. Schmid (Eds.). *Social Reality: The Phenomenological Approach*. Dordrecht: Springer.
Leslie, Alan M. (1987). "Pretense and Representation: The Origins of 'Theory of Mind'." *Psychological Review* 94 (4), 412–426.
Leslie, Alan M., Friedman, Ori, & German, Tim P. (2004). "Core Mechanisms in 'Theory of Mind'." *Trends in Cognitive Sciences* 8 (12), 528–533.
List, Christian, & Pettit, Philip (2011). *Group Agency. The Possibility, Design, and Status of Corporate Agents*. Oxford: Oxford University Press.
Lohmar, Dieter, & Fonfara, Dirk (Eds.) (2013). *Soziale Erfahrung. Phänomenologische Forschungen* 2013.
Luft, Sebastian, & Overgaard, Søren (Eds.) (2012). *The Routledge Companion to Phenomenology*. London/New York: Routledge.
McMullin, Irene (2013). *Time and the Shared World: Heidegger on Social Relations*. Evanston, IL: Northwestern University Press.
Meltzoff, Andrew N., & Gopnik, Alison (1993). "The Role of Imitation in Understanding Persons and Developing Theories of Mind." In: S. Baron-Cohen, & H. Tager-Flusberg (Eds.) (1993). *Understanding Other Minds: Perspectives from Autism*. Oxford: Oxford University Press.
Michael, John (2011). "Shared Emotions and Joint Action." *Review of Philosophy and Psychology* 2 (2), 355–373.
——— (2014). "Towards a Consensus about the Role of Empathy in Interpersonal Understanding." *Topoi* 33 (1), 157–172.
Michael, John, & Fardo, Francesca (2014). "What (If Anything) Is Shared in Pain Empathy? A Critical Discussion of De Vignemont and Jacob's Theory of the Neural Substrate of Pain Empathy." *Philosophy of Science* 81 (1), 154–160.
Michael, John, Christensen, Wayne, & Overgaard, Søren (2014). "Mindreading as Social Expertise." *Synthese* 191 (5), 817–840.
Moran, Dermot (2000). *Introduction to Phenomenology*. London/New York: Routledge.
Natanson, Maurice (Ed.) (1970). *Phenomenology and Social Reality. Essays in Memory of Alfred Schutz*. Den Haag: Nijhoff.
——— (1973). *Phenomenology and the Social Sciences*. Volume 1 & 2. Evanston, IL: Northwestern University Press.
Nichols, Shaun, & Stich, Stephen P. (2003). *Mindreading. An Integrated Account of Pretence, Self-Awareness, and Understanding Other Minds*. Oxford: Oxford University Press.
O'Neill, John (Ed.) (1973). *Modes of Individualism and Collectivism*. London: Heineman.
Otaka, Tomoo (1932). *Grundlegungen der Lehre vom sozialen Verband*. Wien: Julius Springer.
Overgaard, Søren (2007). *Wittgenstein and Other Minds: Rethinking Subjectivity and Intersubjectivity with Wittgenstein, Levinas, and Husserl*. London/New York: Routledge.
Overgaard, Søren, & Michael, John (2015). "The Interactive Turn in Social Cognition Research: A Critique." *Philosophical Psychology* 28 (2), 160–183.
Owens, Thomas J. (1970). *Phenomenology and Intersubjectivity: Contemporary Interpretations of the Interpersonal Situation*. Den Haag: Nijhoff.
Paci, Enzo (1972 [1963]). *The Function of the Sciences and the Meaning of Man*. Transl. by P. Piccone, & J. E. Hansen. Evanston, IL: Northwestern University Press.

Parkinson, Brian, Fischer, Agneta H., & Manstead, Antony S. R. (2005). *Emotion in Social Relations: Cultural, Group, and Interpersonal Processes*. New York: Psychology Press.
Perreau, Laurent (2013). *Le monde social selon Husserl*. Dordrecht: Springer.
Pettit, Philip (1993). *The Common Mind. An Essay on Psychology, Society and Politics*. Oxford: Oxford University Press.
——— (1997). *Republicanism. A Theory of Freedom and Government*. Oxford: Oxford University Press.
——— (2003). "Groups with Minds of Their Own." In: F. Schmitt (Ed.). *Socializing Metaphysics*. New York: Rowman & Littlefield.
——— (2014). "Three Issues in Social Ontology." In: J. Zahle, & F. Collin (Eds.). *Rethinking the Individualism-Holism Debate*. Cham: Springer.
Psathas, George (Ed.) (1973). *Phenomenological Sociology. Issues and Applications*. New York: Wiley.
Ratcliffe, Matthew (2007). *Rethinking Commonsense Psychology: A Critique of Folk Psychology, Theory of Mind and Simulation*. London: Palgrave Macmillan.
Rinofner-Kreidl, Sonja (2013). "Zwischen 'cheap grace' und Rachsucht: Zu Reichweite und ambivalenter Bewertung von (Selbst-)Vergebung". *Phänomenologische Forschungen* 2013, 197–235.
——— (2014). "Neid und Ressentiment. Zur Phänomenologie negativer sozialer Gefühle." In: K. Mertens, & J. Müller (Eds.). *Die Dimension des Sozialen. Neue philosophische Zugänge zu Fühlen, Wollen und Handeln*. Berlin/Boston: de Gruyter.
Rovane, Carol (1998). *The Bounds of Agency. An Essay in Revisionary Metaphysics*. Princeton: Princeton University Press.
——— (2014). "Group Agency and Individualism." *Erkenntnis* 79 (9), 1663–1684.
Ruben, David-Hillel (1985). *The Metaphysics of the Social World*. London: Routledge.
Rupert, Robert D. (2005). "Minding One's Cognitive Systems: When Does a Group of Minds Constitute a Single Cognitive Unit?" In: *Episteme* 1 (3), 177–188.
——— (2011). "Empirical Arguments for Group Minds: A Critical Appraisal." In: *Philosophy Compass* 6 (9), 630–639.
Salice, Alessandro (2013). "Social Ontology as Embedded in the Tradition of Realist Phenomenology." In: M. Schmitz, B. Kobow, & H. B. Schmid (Eds.). *The Background of Social Reality*. Dordrecht: Springer.
Salmela, Mikko (2012). "Shared Emotions." *Philosophical Explorations* 15 (1), 33–46.
——— (2014). "The Functions of Collective Emotions in Social Groups." In: A. Konzelmann Ziv, & H. B. Schmid (Eds.). *Institutions, Emotions, and Group Agents*. Dordrecht: Springer.
Satne, Glenda, & Roepstorff, Andreas (Eds.) (2015). "Introduction from Interacting Agents to Engaging Persons." *Journal of Consciousness Studies* 22 (1–2), 9–23.
Scheler, Max (1926a). *Der Formalismus in der Ethik und die material Wertethik. Neuer Versuch der Grundlegung eines ethischen Personalismus*. Bern: Francke 1980. [Engl.: *Formalism in Ethics and Non-Formal Ethics of Values: A New Attempt Toward the Foundation of an Ethical Personalism*. Transl. by M. S. Frings, & R. L. Funk. Evanston, IL: Northwestern University Press, 1973.]
——— (1926b). *Wesen und Formen der Sympathie*. Bonn: Bouvier 2005. [Engl.: *The Nature of Sympathy*. Transl. by P. Heath. London: Routledge & Kegan Paul, 1954.]
——— (1926c). *Probleme einer Soziologie des Wissens*. In: *Die Wissensformen und die Gesellschaft. Gesammelte Werke*. Bern: Francke 1982, 15–190. [Engl.: *Problem of a Sociology of Knowledge*. Transl. by M. S. Frings. London: Routledge & Kegan Paul, 1980.]

Schilbach, Leonhard, Timmermans, Bert, Reddy, Vasudevi, Costall, Alan Bente, Gary, Schlicht, Tobias, & Vogeley, Kai (2013). "Toward a Second-Person Neuroscience." *Behavioral and Brain Sciences* 36 (4), 393–414.
Schmid, Hans Bernhard (2000). *Subjekt, System, Diskurs: Edmund Husserls Begriff transzendentaler Subjektivität in sozialtheoretischen Bezügen*. Dordrecht: Kluwer.
—— (2009). *Plural Action. Essays in Philosophy and Social Science*. Dordrecht: Springer.
—— (2014). "The Feeling of Being a Group. Corporate Emotions and Collective Consciousness." In: C. von Scheve, & M. Salmela (Eds.), *Collective Emotions*. Oxford: Oxford University Press.
Schuhmann, Karl (1988). *Husserls Staatsphilosophie*. Freiburg/München: Alber.
Schütz, Alfred (1932). *Der sinnhafte Aufbau der sozialen Welt. Eine Einleitung in die verstehende Soziologie*. Wien: Springer. [Engl.: *The Phenomenology of the Social World*. Tansl. by G. Walsh, & F. Lehnert. Evanston, IL. Northwestern University Press 1967.]
Schütz, Alfred, & Luckmann, Thomas (2003). *Strukturen der Lebenswelt*. Konstanz: UVK Verlagsgesellschaft.
Schützeichel, Rainer (2014). "Fühlen als ein soziales Phänomen: Über responsive und reflexive, geteilte und kollektive Emotionen." In: K. Mertens, & J. Müller (Eds.). *Die Dimension des Sozialen. Neue philosophische Zugänge zu Fühlen, Wollen und Handeln*. Berlin/Boston: de Gruyter.
Searle, John R. (1995). *The Construction of Social Reality*. London: Penguin.
—— (2006). "Social Ontology. Some Basic Principles." *Anthropological Theory* 6 (1), 12–29.
—— (2010). *Making the Social World. The Structure of Human Civilization*. Oxford: Oxford University Press.
Seemann, Axel (Ed.) (2012). *Joint Attention: New Developments in Psychology, Philosophy of Mind, and Social Neuroscience*. Cambridge, MA/London: MIT Press.
Smart, Barry (1976). *Sociology, Phenomenology and Marxian Analysis: A Critical Discussion of the Theory and Practice of a Science of Society*. London: Routledge & Kegan Paul.
Spiegelberg, Herbert (1973). "On the Right to Say 'We': A Linguistic and Phenomenological Analysis." In: George Psathas (Ed.). *Phenomenological Sociology. Issues and Applications*. New York: Wiley.
Stavenhagen, Kurt (1933). "Charismatische Persönlichkeitseinungen." In: E. Heller & F. Löw (Eds.). *Neue Münchener Philosophische Abhandlungen. Alexander Pfänder zu seinem sechzigsten Geburtstag gewidmet von Freunden und Schülern*. Leipzig: Johann Ambrosius Barth.
Stein, Edith (2008 [1917]). *Zum Problem der Einfühlung*. Wien/Basel/Köln: Herder. [Engl.: *On the Problem of Empathy*. Transl. by W. Stein. Washington, DC: ICS Publication, 1989.]
—— (2010 [1920]). *Beiträge zur philosophischen Begründung der Psychologie und der Geisteswissenschaften*. Wien/Basel/Köln: Herder. [Engl.: *Philosophy of Psychology and the Humanities*. Transl. by M. C. Baseheart and M. Sawicki. Washington, D.C.: ICS Publication 2000.]
Steinbock, Anthony (1995). *Home and Beyond. Generative Phenomenology after Husserl*. Evanston, Ill.: Northwestern University Press.
—— (2014). *Moral Emotions. Reclaiming the Evidence of the Heart*. Evanston, IL: Northwestern University Press.
Stets, Jan E., & Turner, Jonathan H. (Eds.) (2014). *Handbook of the Sociology of Emotions, Vol. II*. Dordrecht: Springer.
Stueber, Karsten (2006). *Rediscovering Empathy: Agency, Folk Psychology, and the Human Sciences*. Cambridge, MA/London: MIT Press.

—— (2013). "Empathy." In: E.N. Zalta (Ed.). *The Stanford Encyclopedia of Philosophy*. (Spring 2013 Edition). http://plato.stanford.edu/archives/win2014/entries/empathy/.
Szanto, Thomas (2014). "How to Share a Mind: Reconsidering the Group Mind Thesis." *Phenomenology and the Cognitive Sciences* 13 (1), 99–120.
—— (2015). "Husserl on Collective Intentionality." In: A. Salice, & H. B. Schmid (Eds.). *Social Reality: The Phenomenological Approach*. Dordrecht: Springer.
—— (forthcoming). "Collective Emotions, Normativity, and Empathy: A Steinian Account." *Human Studies*, doi. 10.1007/s10746-015-9350-8.
Szanto, Thomas, & Moran, Dermot (Eds.) (forthcoming). *Empathy and Collective Intentionality. The Social Philosophy of Edith Stein*. Special Issue: *Human Studies*.
Taipale, Joona (2014). *Phenomenology and Embodiment: Husserl and the Constitution of Subjectivity*. Evanston, IL: Northwestern University Press.
Theunissen, Michael (1965). *Der Andere. Studien zur Sozialontologie der Gegenwart*. Berlin/New York: de Gruyter.
Thonhauser, Gerhard, & Schmid, Hans Bernhard (forthcoming). "Existenzialistischer Marxismus." In: M. Quante & D. Schweikard (Eds.). *Marx Handbuch*. Stuttgart: Metzler.
Tollefsen, Deborah P. (2015). *Groups as Agents*. Cambridge: Polity.
Tomasello, Michael (2014). *A Natural History of Human Thinking*. Cambridge, MA: Harvard University Press.
Toulemont, René (1962). *L'Essence de la société selon Husserl*. Paris: Presses Universitaires de France.
Trân Duc Thao (1951). *Phénoménologie et matérialisme dialectique*. Paris: Editions Minh Tan. [Engl.: *Phenomenology and Dialectical Materialism*. Transl. by D. J. Herman, & D. V. Morano. Dordrecht: Reidel, 1986.]
Tuomela, Raimo (2007). *The Philosophy of Sociality. The Shared Point of View*. Oxford: Oxford University Press.
—— (2013). *Social Ontology: Collective Intentionality and Group Agents*. Oxford: Oxford University Press.
Udehn, Lars (2002). "The Changing Face of Methodological Individualism." *Annual Review of Sociology* 28, 479–507.
Vendrell Ferran, Ingrid (2008). *Die Emotionen. Gefühle in der realistischen Phänomenologie*. Berlin: Akademie.
von Scheve, Christian, & Salmela, Mikko (Eds.) (2014). *Collective Emotions*. Oxford: Oxford University Press.
Wagner, Helmut R. (1983). *Phenomenology of Consciousness and Sociology of the Life-World. An Introductory Study*. Edmonton: University of Alberta Press.
Waldenfels, Bernard (1971). *Das Zwischenreich des Dialogs: Sozialphilosophische Untersuchungen in Anschluss an Edmund Husserl*. Dordrecht: Springer.
Waldenfels, Bernard, Broekman, Jan M., & Pažanin, Ante (Eds.) (1977ff.). *Phänomenologie und Marxismus*. Vols. 1–4. Frankfurt a.M.: Suhrkamp. [Engl. (Selection). Waldenfels, Bernhard, & Broekman, Jan M. (Eds.). *Phenomenology and Marxism*. Transl. by J. C. Evans, Jr. London: Routledge, 1984.]
Walther, Gerda (1923). "Zur Ontologie der sozialen Gemeinschaften." *Jahrbuch für Philosophie und phänomenologische Forschung* 6, 1–158.
Zahavi, Dan (2001 [1988]). *Husserl and Transcendental Intersubjectivity. A Response to the Linguistic-Pragmatic Critique*. Transl. by E. A. Behnke. Athens, OH: Ohio University Press.
—— (2011). "Empathy and Direct Social Perception: A Phenomenological Proposal." *Review of Philosophy and Psychology* 2 (3), 541–558.
—— (Ed). (2012) *The Oxford Handbook of Contemporary Phenomenology*. Oxford: Oxford University Press.

——— (2014). *Self and Other: Exploring Subjectivity, Empathy, and Shame*. Oxford: Oxford University Press.

——— (2015a). "You, Me, and We. The Sharing of Emotional Experiences." *Journal of Consciousness Studies* 22 (1–2), 84–101.

——— (2015b). "Self and Other: From Pure Ego to Co-Constituted We." *Continental Philosophy Review* 48 (2), 143–160.

Zahle, Julie, & Collin, Finn (Eds.) (2014). *Rethinking the Individualism-Holism Debate: Essays in the Philosophy of Social Science*. Cham: Springer.

# Part I
# Historical and Methodological Issues

# 1 Locating Shared Life in the 'Thou'
## Some Historical and Thematic Considerations

*James Risser*

1

In this chapter, I want to explore the issue of the sociality of existence under the heading 'shared life,' first historically, then thematically, with a specific focus on Gadamer's contribution to the issue. The key development in this exploration is the point of difference that emerges between Gadamer and Karl Löwith in their respective projects in the 1920s.

For phenomenology, the issue of sociality came to prominence in the early part of the 20th century. When Edith Stein published *Philosophy of Psychology and the Human Sciences* in *Husserl's Yearbook* in 1922, she had already made great inroads to surpass the prevailing idea that the relating of one to another resided in analogical presentation—the form of presentation in which one apprehends the other by comparison with oneself. As we learn from her earlier dissertation work under Husserl on the problem of empathy, Stein thought that the experience of relating to another was a form of intentionality directed towards the experience of others. The experience of empathy, which she took to be comparable to an act of perception, is for her an experience of foreign consciousness in general (Stein 1989, 11). It is an encounter with the foreign other in which the ego sees both identity and difference, in effect allowing the ego to become more aware of itself through the encounter. While Stein's understanding of empathy ultimately preserves the experience of the non-identical in the relating of one to another, it remains configured through perceptual presentation and the starting point of the conscious subject. What is different in *Philosophy of Psychology and the Human Sciences* is Stein's extension of her analysis of relating to another through a consideration of the various forms of living together. At the center of this investigation is the specific living together of community, understood as the organic union of individuals. But here too, despite the fact that she introduces the notions of solidarity and being-*with*-one-another, she continues to frame her analysis in the language of consciousness. And here too, the starting point is the subject, as if community were simply a plurality of subjects in a relation of reciprocity. More to the point, Stein does not appear to thematize the relation as such, but only takes note that there is evidence to account for an orientation of individuals to one another, thereby constituting an idea of sharing in a broad sense. The broader with-one-another of community is simply "out there in life" (Stein 2000, 197). In the end, Stein's analysis of the relation of one to another is insufficient for coming to terms with more fundamental aspects of the with-one-another of shared life.[1]

When Martin Buber publishes *I and Thou* in 1923, we have what could be considered the first attempt to explicitly thematize the relation of one to another *as* a relation. For Buber, the I-Thou relation precedes any self-recognition of an I. The relation occurs "in the beginning," which means that there are not first two terms, the I and the you, which are subsequently placed in a relation. What is first is the "genuine originality, the lived relationship," as the immediate encounter (Buber 1970, 69).

In looking closely at the historical context, we know that Buber does not invent the terms I and Thou. As he tells us in "The History of the Dialogical Principle," the expression I-Thou occurs first in a 1785 writing of Friedrich Jacobi, and is later used by Ludwig Feuerbach in his *Principles of the Philosophy of the Future* from 1843 (Buber 1972, 209f). Buber's reference to Feuerbach is not at all a passing one. Buber had read Feuerbach intensively in his youth, finding there not just the mention of the I-Thou, but a philosophical anthropology centered on the dialogical relation of the I-Thou.[2] We also know that in the years immediately prior to the publication of *I and Thou*, the neo-Kantian Hermann Cohen had used the expression in his religious writings, speaking of a correlation rather than a relation (*Beziehung*) (Cohen 1995). The expression was also familiar to Buber's friend and collaborator, Franz Rosenzweig, who contested Buber's account of the I-Thou prior to the publication of the book. Rosenzweig thought that Buber's presentation of the I-Thou relation was too narrow, that he had compressed all of authentic life into his I-Thou, ignoring other possible relations in the basic relation of one to another (Buber 1996, 280). Ironically, it was Rosenzweig's influence that provoked Buber to amend his text as it was going to print. The idea of dialogical speech as not simply an immediate relation of self-realization was now seen by Buber to be an essential component of the I-Thou relation.

When Karl Löwith then publishes his *Habilitationsschrift*, *Das Individuum in der Rolle des Mitmenschen*, under Martin Heidegger in 1928—the same year that Hans-Georg Gadamer was completing his *Habilitationsschrift* under Heidegger—he was well aware of these earlier developments on the sociality of the I-Thou. In his work, Löwith not only devotes the opening section to a brief summary of Feuerbach's *Principles of the Philosophy of the Future*, but also makes the same argument for the I-Thou relation as Buber, viz., that the relation has priority over the *relata*. More importantly, Löwith sees his work as an attempt to supplement Heidegger's analysis of intersubjectivity in *Being and Time* (1927). Despite Heidegger's own insistence that the possibility of an I-Thou encounter must be grounded on the more basic being of *Dasein* as transcendence in which we live first from a shared being (*Mitsein*) in the world, Löwith thinks he can articulate a basic sociality of being-with-one-another (*Miteinandersein*) not erected from the fundamental ontology of *Dasein* in which the *Mitsein* of *Dasein* is determined. For Löwith, this will entail putting forth a concept of person within intersubjectivity drawn along Kantian lines. With Heidegger's protest to the contrary—a protest repeatedly made in his lecture courses during this time, no doubt in direct response to Löwith's work—it would appear that the real merit of Löwith's argument was to exhibit the being-with-one-another as the primary and decisive feature of our being in relation, against what one could consider Heidegger's insistence on having it both ways: *Dasein* as the original co-being and at the same time, in each case, mine.[3]

Regarding Löwith's contribution to the issue of shared life, two features deserve comment here. First, Löwith's argument for the primacy of the with-one-another entails a primacy of social practices over individual activity, thereby giving greater weight to the sociality of existence than Heidegger does with his analysis of *Dasein* in its everydayness, where a commonly held world effectively disappears. Moreover, Löwith regards these social practices not as something an individual makes by him or herself, but as pre-existing the individual in their particularity of time and place. That is to say, Löwith wants to hold to a "formally concrete" ontic anthropology rather than to the formal ontology of the "existentials" of *Dasein*'s being (Heidegger 2007, 290). It is precisely this difference that allows Löwith to start from what he calls *menschliches Dasein* and not simply *Dasein*. And Heidegger, for his part, is willing to see this as an ontic supplement to his fundamental ontology, which we can see mitigates somewhat Heidegger's initial protest against Löwith's position. His protest, after all, could not have been so strong, since Löwith did in fact habilitate under Heidegger.

The second feature of Löwith's position pertains to the point of intersection between Löwith and Gadamer that emerges in Löwith's emphasis on being-with-one-another and the essential role played by dialogue. In the section titled, "*Miteinandersein als Miteinandersprechen*," Löwith claims that the with-one-another of conversation binds the speakers such that there can be communication. Löwith writes:

> That which is communicated is there in an original way only in communication. In the communication (*Mitteilung*) that communicates something one shares (*teilt*) oneself with another at the same time. The authentic meaning of the 'with' of sharing ('*mit*' *der Teilung*) is found in the one-another (*Ein-ander*).
>
> (Löwith 1928, 20)

When Gadamer then writes his *Habilitationsschrift* on Plato, he too will thematize the being-with-one-another in conversation, but not without some criticism of Löwith's position.[4] In his preliminary discussion of the nature of Socratic conversation and the ability to bring about a shared understanding

(*Verständigung*), Gadamer first notes how the matter to be understood is taken up in speech and is thus understood through its expression: beyond the words spoken, the speaker's intonation and gestures express the disposition and inner state of the speaker. The pattern of mutual self-expression will then constitute a specific possible way of being with another (*Miteinandersein*). Gadamer then adds that this would seem to imply that the shared understanding guiding this activity is not necessarily one in which agreement is reached, but simply what enables "the participants themselves to become manifest to each other in speaking about it" (Gadamer 1991, 37).

The question for Gadamer is "whether this way of understanding the other person represents a genuine way of being with one another," for every response is to the speaker's self-expression (Gadamer 1991, 37). What is behind this question is Gadamer's concern that understanding others through self-expression about something is made possible by *self-reflection* and, if so, this would be a degenerate form of being with one another.[5] In this early text, Gadamer is framing what he will later call, in *Truth and Method*, the second form of the I-Thou relation, in which the relation is inadequate for understanding, precisely because it is reflective and does not express a shared world (*mitweltlichen*) in any real sense. In this relation, a person reflects him or herself out of the mutuality of the relation, thus changing the relation and destroying its moral bond in the process. Despite having the character of a 'We'-relation, it is the form of understanding oneself by contrast with others, and, as such, Gadamer insists, it actually pushes the other away. A real conversation attends only to the substantive intention of what is said and not what the speech expresses, and in real conversation with an other, which can even occur in one's own thinking, the distinction (and separation) between I and the other can break down. It is at this point in Gadamer's text that a small critique of Löwith's position appears in a small footnote. According to Gadamer, Löwith understood thinking in a one-sided way, as dealing with fixed cognitive assumptions, which loses sight of a more encompassing thinking and reasoning that Gadamer wants to argue for. While the critique is minor (for at the end of his note, Gadamer says that what he is arguing for is "in keeping with the deeper coherence of Löwith's analysis"), it opens for us the context for yet another version of a shared world in which the Thou is a focal point (Gadamer 1991, 43).[6]

## 2

Let me begin here to make my argument for this other version of shared life. Gadamer's distancing from Löwith does indeed pertain in part to his rejection of the privileged place of reflection operative in speaking-with-one-another. It is not that Gadamer is opposed to reflection, since it is undoubtedly an essential dimension of thinking and the ability to make something present to oneself. His reservation is pointed at the difference between the thinking of thought, which holds to reflection, and the more primary thinking of something. The reflexivity of reflection amounts to a "secondary phenomenon, compared to turning directly to some object" (Gadamer 2000c, 277f). Gadamer insists that this non-reflective orientation has its own way of carrying out the necessary critical function achieved in reflection, namely, through the dynamic of question and response that occurs in dialogical conversation. But this is not to suggest that for Gadamer, dialogical conversation is oriented to agreement over statements.

The difference here pertains to the enlarged sense that Gadamer gives to being-with-one-another and to the way in which the Thou in the relation of one to another has priority. We can describe this enlarged sense by saying that the fundamental relation for Gadamer is the with-one-another of human experiencing in the life of language. This experiencing, which comprises for the most part the intentional life in human living, is, from the outset, sharing—an idea that Gadamer finds first in Aristotle.[7] As outlined in the *Rhetoric*, Aristotle thinks that humans achieve a sense of community among themselves because they are capable of mutual understanding through speech (Aristotle (1967 [1253a], 15–18). Gadamer will translate this basic idea into the linguisticality of understanding as a participatory act of encounter and event. We understand in relation to someone saying something about something; we understand by responding to what the other has to say, and are drawn into an experience of meaning that goes beyond the initial intentions in speaking (the event character of understanding). And here, language is understood broadly as the very bond that makes possible the relation between understanding and life in general. Very explicitly, Gadamer writes, "Who thinks language already moves beyond subjectivity" (Gadamer 2000c, 286). Language is thus the condition for sharing in its purest form. And with a slight variation from Löwith, Gadamer writes, "'Communication' (*Mitteilung*)—what a beautiful word! It involves the idea that we share (*teilen*) something with one another (*miteinander*), that does not become less in the sharing but perhaps even grows" (Gadamer 1983, 15). Gadamer's variation pertains to the idea of becoming more, i.e., in sharing there is an opening, presumably between one and another, where the world becomes larger, not smaller. The difference between community, with its overtones of formation, and mere association may very well lie within this idea.

But the exact sense of encounter and event in shared life is yet to be seen. When Gadamer speaks of this encounter in the language of I and Thou, it is of critical importance for Gadamer that this relation should not be taken as one of intersubjectivity.[8] In a 1993 interview with Gadamer, Carsten Dutt quotes Gadamer's own text on the nature of conversation in order to solicit a response from Gadamer. The text reads, "Conversation with another person, whatever the objections or disagreements, whatever the understandings or misunderstandings, means a kind of expansion of our individuality and a probing of the possible commonality we have to which reason encourages us" (Gadamer 2001, 59). Dutt then poses the question of whether his philosophy thematizes conversation as our capacity for rational intersubjectivity, and Gadamer responds, "Oh, please spare me that completely misleading concept of intersubjectivity, of a subjectivism doubled! In the passage you quoted I did not make any clever theoretical constructions at all: I said a conversation is something one gets caught up in, in which one gets involved" (Gadamer 2001, 59). What Gadamer objects to is framing conversation in terms of the priority of a "subject," and a doubling of the subject, no less. In different words—and this is the key—through such framing, the very commonality that subtends subjectivity, namely, the shared common world of language to which we first belong as the condition for sharing, is lost.

Yet despite this reservation towards intersubjectivity, Gadamer employs a very rich account of the I-Thou encounter in *Truth and Method*, an account that we now know has very little to do with Buber, but almost everything to do with Löwith.[9] That account emerges in *Truth and Method* in connection with Gadamer's analysis of the concept of experience (*Erfahrung*), which is introduced as a way of articulating how a historically effected consciousness operates in the interpretation of historical tradition. As he explains it, experience is a process involving a knowing in which one's expectations are not always confirmed, so that experiential knowing entails not only an openness to new experience, but more importantly, a negativity, in the sense that something otherwise is encountered in experiencing. That is to say, experience involves a reversal in the experiencing of consciousness constituting what we ordinarily call learning. This learning is, effectively, an experience of limitation, and broadly considered, amounts to the experience of finitude. Gadamer then applies this concept of experience to the historically effected consciousness, i.e., to hermeneutic experience concerned with historical tradition, by characterizing it through three versions of the I-Thou relation. The first version has little to do with a Thou and relationality as such, since it is described as the mastery of historical tradition by method. The second version corresponds to an I-Thou that approximates a bad form of intersubjectivity, for it is described along the lines of Hegel's dialectic of recognition where one does not want to cede to the other. As previously noted, it is a form of self-relatedness: one claims to know the other from one's own point of view, and thus, according to Gadamer, the "thou loses the immediacy with which it makes its claim." In being understood, the Thou is "preempted reflectively from the standpoint of the other person" (Gadamer 1989a, 359). The third form of the I-Thou is the only one that captures the full import of a historically effected consciousness. Gadamer writes:

> In human relations the important thing is, as we have seen, to experience the Thou truly as a thou—i.e., not to overlook his claim but to let him really say something to us. Here is where openness belongs [. . .]. Without such openness to one another there is no genuine human

bond. Belonging together always also means being able to listen to one another [. . .]. When two people understand each other, this does not mean that one person 'understands' the other. Openness to the other, then, involves recognizing that I myself must accept some things that are against me, even though no one else forces me to do so.

(Gadamer 1989a, 361)

In characterizing shared life in this way, Gadamer is effectively pointing to the danger in configuring shared life in terms of a doubling of the subject. It is the danger of destroying the very possibility of sharing as a genuine participation with the other.

If the I-Thou is not a relation of intersubjectivity for Gadamer, it remains nevertheless a relation, for the Thou is what we are in relation to, as a partner in dialogue, and as such, the relation constitutes shared life. But while shared life is coextensive with the opening of a world, it is also marked by a certain deficiency. The problem in the relating that is shared life is not that we do not understand the other person, "but that we don't understand ourselves." In the task of understanding, Gadamer contends that "we must break down resistance in ourselves if we wish to hear the other as other" (Gadamer 2007, 371). That is why Gadamer gives priority to the Thou, for by strengthening the other against oneself, one not only allows one "to recognize in principle the limitation of one's own framework," but also "allows one to go beyond one's own possibilities" (Gadamer 2000c, 284). And it is here that we can also see why Gadamer would rather use the word "other" in place of the 'Thou.' While Gadamer acknowledges the philosophical importance that the I-Thou problem served in the 1920s, he also acknowledges that such speech "hides a mystifying substantiation" that blocks us from getting at the real problems. To say "the other" in place of 'the Thou' changes the perspective, for "every other is at the same time the other of the other" (Gadamer 2000c, 282).

But as yet, we have not shown how this relating of one to the other actually characterizes our sociality. In pursing this, we cannot move too quickly away from the issue of language, for, as Gadamer writes, "language intends the other." Such a claim makes little sense, of course, if we confine language to merely making statements in which the directions of meaning in language that arise in speaking to another are removed. Gadamer regards language as a unique life process where world is disclosed, "uniting all who talk with one another" (Gadamer 1989a, 446). So Gadamer would insist, along this Aristotelian line, that being-with-one-another "develops in the true life of language," which we find in conversation. Conversation, in turn, is the word seeking an answer; i.e., while there are the intentions of meaning from the speakers in dialogue, in a genuine dialogue, words are given their play, which means that "the one-another of word and answer has its own entitlement." This entitlement is what Gadamer describes in *Truth and Method* as the self-presentation of meaning in language. And this is to say that the with-one-another that develops in the true life of language is enactment (*Vollzug*), and a sharing in its fundamental sense of participation. The word is not just seeking an answer: it is seeking the right word that enables one to hear the other. In his late essay, "Towards a Phenomenology of Ritual and Language," Gadamer describes this interaction as partnership, which, he says, "reminds us of the Greek concept of *mexthexis*—participation," which in turn requires taking part in something larger than oneself (Gadamer 2000b, 46). With this slight variation in the description of sharing, Gadamer is able to link language and ritual.[10] For both, there is an enactment through mutual agreements, and for ritual in particular, it is an enactment in which the correctness is not supported by the rule of law, but by the *ethos* in living together. Rituals pertain to those forms of human living that "carry and support us," but then the same can be said with respect to speaking-with-one-another.

This idea of partnership can also be characterized by what Leo Strauss considered to be the form of the I-Thou relation in classical Greek philosophy, namely friendship—an idea that Gadamer will follow in his own way (Gadamer 1989a, 535).[11] This is the friendship that Gadamer sees in the "friendly questioning" of Socratic *elenchus*, namely, as a favorable putting forth of questions to call for further statements, or, as Gadamer says in his reply to Derrida in 1981, a good will to see that the other is right (Gadamer 1989b, 55). This is also, and preeminently so, the friendship of goodwill and mutuality that we find in Aristotle's ethics. But Gadamer is not suggesting here that the friendship in which the communality of life is lived out is a simple friendship among those who are like in virtue or as a general love of one's neighbor. Here, too, it is a matter of participation. For Gadamer, Aristotelian friendship is that distinctive relation with another—the "stream of self-forming commonalities"—in which one begins to feel and recognize oneself. It is an orientation toward fulfillment against the cognizance of one's own limitations. And it is this same element of "living with" that enters all forms of human cognition for Aristotle.[12]

In this regard, it is interesting to see how Gadamer describes the associated Aristotelian virtue of *sunesis* in ethical life in his discussion of *phronesis* in *Truth and Method*. The word *sunesis* is actually related to a cluster of words connoting a kind of intelligence directed toward and intimately related to others. It is often translated as good intelligence, but this does not adequately convey its intended sense. In Aristotle, the word is used to name the capacity to discern what is to be done in relation to the council of others, conveying more precisely the sense of conscientious apprehension. Gadamer will translate *sunesis* as sympathetic understanding (*Verständnis*) in practical matters, adding, "someone's sympathetic understanding is praised, of course, when in order to judge he transposes himself fully into the concrete situation of the person who has to act" (Gadamer 1989a, 323). This transposition, though, should not be confused with empathy. It is simply that the one who is understanding "does not know and judge as one who stands apart and unaffected but rather he thinks along with the other from the perspective of a special bond of belonging, as if he too were affected" (Gadamer 1989a, 323). *Sunesis* is thus not so much an individual's ability to be united with the other through sympathetic knowing; *sunesis* is not an understanding *of* the situation of the other in which the subject can say, "I can understand the other, the other is like me." *Sunesis* is rather understanding *for* the view of someone else, which is possible only if one and the other are bound together from the outset (Smith 1991, 86).

And finally, this partnership, this practice with respect to life in common, is given one other formulation by Gadamer that deserves comment. Gadamer has often used the term "solidarity" for this practice to describe the co-existence of differences in contemporary social life. Such attending to one another should not be taken to mean that Gadamer is advocating for a vague notion of humanity that would make an appeal to an equally vague notion of tolerance towards others. Certainly, it is the case that Gadamer sets the notion of solidarity against the ever-increasing uniformity of life brought about by a globalized, technological society, and in this context, he worries about the possibilities for our humanity.[13] But equally so, he worries about the other extreme, namely, a public life that places "too much emphasis on the different and disputed" in which what unites us, however minimal that may be, is without a voice (Gadamer 1992d, 192). Solidarity is indeed about the humanism of life, and this will require the "self-evident communality which alone allows for the common establishment of decisions which each considers to be correct in the areas of moral, social, and political life" (Gadamer 1992a, 218). In this common establishment, there is not simply the common as a substantialized entity that robs sociality of its differences, but a relation to the other in which "one is risking one's own in relation to the recognition of the other" (Gadamer 1992c, 207).[14] For Gadamer, the humanism of life entails the need to live with an other, to live as the other of the other. In fact, this is precisely what he regards as being at stake in the humanism of life. At one place, Gadamer writes, "We may perhaps survive as a humanity if we [. . .] learn to stop and respect the other as an other [. . .]; and if we would be able to learn to experience the other and others, as the other of our self, in order to participate with one another" (Gadamer 1992b, 235–6).

What we see in Gadamer's version of shared life, then, is a distinctive form of relation and encounter, certainly when compared with Löwith, with whom he shared the same impetus to think more deeply the character of Heidegger's *Mitsein*. Perhaps it would be against Heidegger more so than Löwith to say that for Gadamer, the with-one-another of shared life is such that we are to see ourselves put into question, as we attempt to hear what the other has to say. For Gadamer, this sharing cannot come about by either reflection or Heidegger's positive determination of *Mitsein* as leaping ahead for the other, but only in the mediation of the rationality of the practice of sharing that remains its own constant.

## NOTES

1 In relation to a critique of the priority of the subject and its presumed encapsulation, Heidegger will be dismissive of the claims of empathy: "'Empathy' does not first constitute being-with, but is first possible on its basis, and is motivated by the prevailing deficient modes of being-with in their inevitability" (Heidegger 2010a, 121). For Heidegger, empathy leaves unexplained how this alter ego is first manifested into an ego. The critics of Heidegger, who insist there is a solipsistic element of *Dasein*, seem to fly in the face of Heidegger's own insistence that *Dasein* is fundamentally a being-with-others and that as being-in-the-world, *Dasein* is fundamentally a relationality. However, that there are different modalities of being-with will undoubtedly complicate the issue, as is the case with Heidegger's insistence that Dasein is inseparable from a notion of selfhood. See below, note 5.

2 Feuerbach writes, "The single man in isolation possesses in himself the essence of man neither as a moral nor as a thinking being. The essence of man is contained only in the community, in the unity of man with man, a unity that rests on the reality of the distinction between 'I' and 'You'" (Feuerbach 1986, 71).

3 From a 1925–26 lecture course, Heidegger writes, "In interpreting the phenomenon of being-with and as being-unto-an-other never forget that we never experience other people as some indeterminate mental 'centers,' floating around in an empty 'over-against-us.' We experience each other person as an existence, a being-with, a being-with-one-another in a world. Even being-with-another lives first of all from a shared-being [*Mitsein*] with him in a world. Thus, the other is, in principle, uncovered for others in his very existence. So it is a mistake to interpret the other phenomenally as a second ego, and it is absurd to pose the problem of co-being with others in such a way that one posits the constructivistic presupposition that first I am given only to myself–and then how does this *solus ipse* manage to reach out to a thou?" (Heidegger, 2010b, 197). What is more interesting are Heidegger's similar statements made in lecture courses after the publication of *Being and Time*. They can be found in his 1927–28 winter semester course, his 1928 summer semester course, and his 1928–29 winter semester course. A similar statement also appears in his essay "On the Essence of Ground," written in 1928 and published in 1929. All of these explicitly refer to the I-Thou relation. Two deserve citation. From his 1928–29 lecture course, Heidegger writes, "The With-one-another (*Miteinander*) cannot be explained through the I-Thou relation, but rather conversely: this I-Thou relation presupposes for its inner possibility that Dasein functioning as I and also as Thou, is determined as with-one-another; indeed even more: even the self-comprehension of an I and the concept of I-ness (*Ichheit*) arise only on the basis of the with-one-another, not from the I-Thou relation" (Heidegger 2001, 145f). Heidegger is even more explicit in "On the Essence of Ground": "The statement: *Dasein exists for the sake of itself*, does not contain the positing of an egoistic or ontic end for some blind narcissism on the part of the factical human being in each case [. . .] The statement in question contains neither a solipsistic isolation of Dasein nor an egoistic intensification thereof. By contrast, it presumably gives the condition of possibility of the human being's being able to compart 'himself' *either* 'egoistically' *or* 'altruistically.' Only because Dasein as such is determined by selfhood can an I-self comport itself toward a you-self. Selfhood is the presupposition for the possibility of being an 'I,' the latter only ever being disclosed in the 'you.' Never, however, is selfhood relative to a 'you,' but rather—because it first makes it possible—is neutral with respect to being an 'I' and being a 'you' [. . .] (Heidegger 1998, 122). (See also, Heidegger 1997, 214, and Heidegger 1984, 187.)

4 In his *Habilitationsschrift*, "*Platos dialektische Ethik*", which was accepted in February of 1929 and published in 1931, Gadamer discusses in one section the notion of a shared world, which is necessary for dialogical conversation. He not only references Löwith's work, but also points to his review of Löwith's work, which was published in 1929. See Gadamer 1987.
5 The emphasis on reflection by Löwith is apparent from the quote from Schelling which makes up the opening lines of *Das Individuum in der Rolle des Mitmenschen*: "We awake through reflection, through coerced turning back to ourselves. Without opposition there is no turning back" (Löwith 1928, 1).
6 Gadamer states basically this same criticism in his review; see Gadamer 1987, 238.
7 Commenting on the passage in Aristotle's *Politics*, Gadamer refers to the concept of *syntheke*, which he claims is misleadingly translated as "convention." "In truth, the complete sense of language and the whole sense of the humanity of life are determined through this expression [. . .]. The concept 'syntheke,' mutual agreement, implies first that language constitutes itself in the with-one-another (*Miteinander*), to the extent that understanding develops by means of which one can come to agreements" (Gadamer 2000a, 11–12).
8 In Axel Honneth's "On the destructive power of the third," Honneth critiques what he considers Gadamer's position on intersubjectivity, citing Löwith against Gadamer because of Löwith's retention of the element of reflection. But in failing to see that conversation for Gadamer is not a matter of intersubjectivity, Honneth's criticism of Gadamer is misplaced. See Honneth 2003.
9 After noting the second of the three versions of the I-Thou, Gadamer references this "reflective" dialectic of the I-Thou in Löwith's *Das Individuum in der Rolle des Mitmenschen* (Gadamer 1989a, 359).
10 The idea of ritual also approximates the idea of festival that Gadamer discusses in relation to the concept of play in *Truth and Method* (Gadamer 1989a, 122f).
11 The connection of Gadamer's notion of sociality with friendship is discussed elsewhere. See Vessey 2005, and Risser 2011.
12 "The wisdom of Aristotle recognizes in all human cognition—as in the *sumpatheia*—an element of the 'with': perceiving-with, knowing-with, thinking-with—that is, living with and being with (*Mitsein*)" (Gadamer 1999, 139f).
13 Solidarity is also set within the relation to modern science in general, and can be seen as Gadamer's version of the life world. What is at stake in this relation then is "a critical effort which shares the modern ideal of method and yet which does not lose the condition of solidarity with and justification of our practical living" (Gadamer 1975, 311).
14 David Vessey (2011) argues that Gadamer gives up the dialectic of recognition in his later writings for the idea of friendship as the proper mode of being with others. While I am sympathetic to his argument, I do think Gadamer holds to a notion of recognition even within friendship. Formally, Gadamer seems to hold to a complementary double emphasis in friendship, namely, the self-recognition through the other and the recognition of the other as encounter.

# REFERENCES

Aristotle (1967). *Rhetoric*. Transl. by J. H. Freese. Cambridge, MA: Harvard University Press.
Buber, Martin (1970). *I and Thou*. Transl. by W. Kaufmann. New York: Charles Scribner's Sons.
——— (1972). "The History of the Dialogical Principle." In: *Between Man and Man*. Transl. by R. G. Smith. New York: Macmillan.

——— (1996). *The Letters of Martin Buber: A Life of Dialogue*. Ed. by N. Glatzer, & P. Mendes-Flohr. Syracuse: Syracuse University Press.
Cohen, Hermann (1995). *Reason in Religion*. Transl. by S. Kaplan. New York: Oxford University Press.
Feuerbach, Ludwig (1986). *The Principles of the Philosophy of the Future*. Transl. by M. Vogel. Indianapolis: Hackett.
Gadamer, Hans-Georg (1975). "Hermeneutics and Social Science." *Cultural Hermeneutics* 2.
——— (1983). "Die Kultur und das Wort." In: *Lob der Theorie*. Frankfurt a.M.: Suhrkamp.
——— (1987). "Ich und Du (Karl Löwith)." In: *Neuere Philosophie II, Gesammelte Werke*, Bd. 4. Tübingen: Mohr/Siebeck.
——— (1989a). *Truth and Method*. Transl. by J. Weinsheimer, & D. Marshall. New York: Continuum.
——— (1989b). "Reply to Jacques Derrida." In: D. Michelfelder, & R.E. Palmer (Eds.). *Dialogue and Dialectic*. Albany: SUNY Press.
——— (1991). *Plato's Dialectical Ethics*. Transl. by Robert Wallace. New Haven: Yale University Press.
——— (1992a). "Citizen of Two World." In: D. Misgeld, & G. Nicholson (Eds.). *Hans-Georg Gadamer on Education, Poetry, and History: Applied Hermeneutics*. Albany: SUNY Press.
——— (1992b). "The Diversity of Europe." In: D. Misgeld, & G. Nicholson (Eds.). *Hans-Georg Gadamer on Education, Poetry, and History: Applied Hermeneutics*. Albany: SUNY Press.
——— (1992c). "The Future of European Humanities." In: D. Misgeld, & G. Nicholson (Eds.). *Hans-Georg Gadamer on Education, Poetry, and History: Applied Hermeneutics*. Albany: SUNY Press.
——— (1992d). "The Limitations of the Expert." In: D. Misgeld, & G. Nicholson (Eds.). *Hans-Georg Gadamer on Education, Poetry, and History: Applied Hermeneutics*. Albany: SUNY Press.
——— (1999). "Friendship and Self-Knowledge." In: *Hermeneutics, Religion and Ethics*. Transl. by J. Weinsheimer. New Haven: Yale University Press.
——— (2000a). "Boundaries of Language." In: L.K. Schmidt (Ed.). *Language and Linguisticality in Gadamer's Hermeneutics*. Lanham, MD: Lexington Books.
——— (2000b). "Towards a Phenomenology of Ritual and Language." In: L.K. Schmidt (Ed.). *Language and Linguisticality in Gadamer's Hermeneutics*. Lanham, MD: Lexington Books.
——— (2000c). "Subjectivity and Intersubjectivity, Subject and Person." Transl. by P. Adamson, & D. Vessey. *Continental Philosophy Review* 33 (3), 275–287.
——— (2001). *Gadamer in Conversation*. Ed. & Transl. by R. Palmer. New Haven: Yale University Press.
——— (2007). "Hermeneutics and the Ontological Difference." In: R. Palmer (Ed.). *The Gadamer Reader*. Evanston: Northwestern University Press.
Heidegger, Martin (1984). *The Metaphysical Foundations of Logic*. Transl. by M. Heim. Bloomington: Indiana University Press.
——— (1997). *Phenomenological Interpretation of Kant's Critique of Pure Reason*. Transl. by S. Emad, & K. Maly. Bloomington: Indiana University Press.
——— (1998). "On the Essence of Ground." In: *Pathmarks*. Ed. & Transl. by W. McNeill. Bloomington: Indiana University Press.
——— (2001). *Einleitung in die Philosophie, Gesamtausgabe 27*. Frankfurt: Vittorio Klostermann.
——— (2007). "Letter Exchange with Karl Löwith on *Being and Time*." In: T. Kisiel, & T. Sheehan (Eds.). *Becoming Heidegger: On the Trail of His Occasional Writings, 1910–1927*. Evanston: Northwestern University Press.

——— (2010a). *Being and Time*. Transl. by J. Stambaugh, rev. by D.J. Schmidt. Albany: SUNY Press.

——— (2010b). *Logic, the Question of Truth*. Transl. by T. Sheehan. Bloomington: Indiana University Press.

Honneth, Axel (2003). "On the Destructive Power of the Third: Gadamer and Heidegger's Doctrine of Intersubjectivity." *Philosophy and Social Criticism* 29 (1), 5–21.

Löwith, Karl (1928). *Das Individuum in der Rolle des Mitmenschen*. München: Drei Masken Verlag.

Risser, James (2011). "Shared Life." In: B. Weber et. al. (Eds.). *Cultural Politics and Identity*. Berlin: LIT Verlag, 49–60.

Smith, P. Christopher (1991). *Hermeneutics and Human Finitude*. New York: Fordham University Press.

Stein, Edith (1989). *The Problem of Empathy*. Transl. by W. Stein. Washington, DC: ICS Publications.

——— (2000). *Philosophy of Psychology and the Humanities*. Transl. by M. Baseheart and M. Sawicki. Washington, DC: ICS Publications.

Vessey, David (2005). "Gadamer's Theory of Friendship as an Alternative to Intersubjectivity." *Philosophy Today* 49, 61–67.

——— (2011). "Paul Ricoeur's and Hans-Georg Gadamer's Diverging Reflections on Recognition." In: F. Mootz, & G. Taylor (Eds.). *Gadamer and Ricoeur*. New York: Continuum.

# 2 Hannah Arendt's Conception of Actualized Plurality

*Sophie Loidolt*

Philosophical debates of the last century have shown a strong tendency to deconstruct and reconceptualize the classic picture of an atomistic Hobbesian or Cartesian subject that sovereignly constitutes a world and only retroactively forms a society. A variety of theories that conceive of the intersubjective as primordial have proposed new foundations not only for ethics, society, and politics, but also for transcendental philosophy, metaphysics, and ontology. With her concept of plurality, Hannah Arendt makes an important contribution to these "intersubjective transformations" (Apel 1999), which has also been acknowledged in numerous commentaries, especially in political theory.[1] I want to argue, however, that these accounts often remain on the level of a "standard interpretation," which fails to capture the radicality of Arendt's ontological commitment to plurality. Thereby, the more profound philosophical consequences of Arendt's approach, which conceive of the political realm not as one "regional ontology" among others, but instead *reconceptualize the whole ontological order from the departing point of plurality*, are left unexplored and sometimes even become obscured. I aim to show that Arendt's notion of plurality needs a phenomenological underpinning in order to be fully understood: Arendt's famous notion of "the political," far from being equivalent to some ordinary notion of politics, can only be properly understood when explained as a phenomenology of plurality. In this chapter, I shall assess the phenomenological lineage and methodology inherent in Arendt's notion of plurality, which is not a plurality of properties (a "what"), but a plurality of first-person perspectives (a "who"). Moreover, I will give an account of how, in "actualized plurality," we may phenomenologically discover the 'We.'

## 1 "STANDARD INTERPRETATIONS" OF PLURALITY

Almost every existing commentary on Arendt recognizes plurality as "the most politically relevant characteristic of human beings" (Canovan 1992, 130) and, consequently, as a "concept for political life" (Schott 2010, 56). Yet, most authors are interested in the concrete *political consequences* that follow from "the political principle par excellence" (Passerin d'Entrèves 1994, 176; Benhabib 2003, 190; cf. also Bernstein 1996, Dossa 1988, Dietz 2002). In contrast to these controversial debates on a "politics of plurality"—be they republican (Canovan 1992, 204–8), radical democratic (Honig 1993/1995), agonistic (Honig 1993, Villa 1996, 52–61), or narrative (Benhabib 2003)—I will engage in an explicitly phenomenological interpretation of Arendt's core phenomenon of "actualized plurality." The heritage of the phenomenological notions of "intersubjectivity" and *Mitsein* is obvious in the development of the phenomenon of actualized plurality, as is its transformation of the classic Husserlian or Heideggerian phenomenology.

My aim here is to promote a new understanding of plurality as something that not simply factually exists, but as something that has to be actualized in certain modes of being together. Thereby, I wish to contest standard interpretations of plurality as an "anthropological" feature (Gerhardt 1991, Passerin d'Entrèves 1994, Jaeggi 1997), as a value (Klockars 2008, Moran 2000, 316), as a simple empirical fact (Dossa 1988, 74, McGowan 1998), or even as the mere biological fact "that all human beings are of the same species" (Canovan 1974, 59; cf. also Passerin d'Entrèves 1994, 70). In contrast, I would like to phenomenologically expand upon some observations made by Canovan, Benhabib, and Hinchman and Hinchman to the effect that plurality is an "*experience* [my italics, S.L.] of equality and distinction" (Canovan 1992, 206) and "a fundamental existential condition" (Benhabib 2003, 50; cf. also Hinchman & Hinchman 1994; Bickford 1995). Also, I want to focus on Cavarero's important remark that most theories dealing with pluralism (communitarian or liberal) maintain "the ontology of the individual" and therefore miss Arendt's point. This argument stands in need of further support from a phenomenological investigation—all the more so, since, as Cavarero states, "Arendt's plurality is, first of all, [. . .] the incontrovertible fact of an elementary ontology, or, perhaps, a radical phenomenology" (Cavarero 2005, 191).

## 2 A PHENOMENOLOGICAL INTERPRETATION OF ARENDT'S CONCEPT OF PLURALITY

Arendt's phenomenology is rooted in the facticity, the *Urfaktum* (Husserl), of plurality. Arendt simply calls it a "fact" (*HC* 7; *VA* 17, 213) and the "basic condition" (*HC* 175) of action and speech. But it would be misleading to think of it merely as an empirical fact that conditions other empirical facts, like temperatures below zero are the condition for snow. For a phenomenological interpretation, it is important to understand that the notion of plurality exceeds the sheer aggregation of empirically existing humans. What Arendt has in mind as a "fact" and "condition" for action and speech is rather that we, *as first-person perspectives*, exist in the plural. This is something that can be articulated, realized or not. The realization or non-realization of plurality does not change anything about the sheer quantity or aggregation of humans. But it makes individual "whos" appear. Plurality is thus *more* than a fact—it is an actualization and only in this case does it function as a condition. The full-fledged "who" that Arendt talks about occurs in actualization together with others, as a certain 'We,' and within a "web of relationships."

## 2.1 The Basic Ontological Condition of Plurality

By "plurality," Arendt neither means a mere quantitative multiplicity nor a quantitative or qualitative differentiation within a multiplicity, like unique genetic codes, different socialization processes, or multiculturally understood "diversity." Plurality is not a matter of fact that is just "there," or "present at hand" (*vorhanden*), like trees or tables. To be sure, there is a quantitative multiplicity of humans, who are "just there," but sheer "present-at-hand" quantity would not result in plurality. The proper perspective for understanding the aims of the notion of plurality is phenomenological. This interpretation takes its point of departure from first-person experience instead of conceiving of the multiplicity of humans "from the outside," in their quantity or in their qualities and properties from a third-person perspective. Arendt approaches the issue of plurality from "within" by addressing this multiplicity from a first-person perspective. This is why she distinguishes between (1) "otherness" (*alteritas*), which pertains to "everything that is" because "we are unable to say what anything is without distinguishing it from something else," (2) "distinctness," which emerges with the variations of organic life, and (3) "uniqueness," which is the capacity to "express this distinction and distinguish [one]self," to "communicate [one]self and not merely something"(*HC* 176). While "otherness" is an abstract universal property of every being (the scholastic *alteritas*), and "distinctness" is an unconscious variation of life in living beings, "uniqueness" implies living and self-aware beings who are able to express their stances. The latter is therefore a concept that involves an articulate first-person perspective, as well as other first-person perspectives that are receptive of the stance expressed.

If one chooses the view from "outside" (third-person perspective), there are, as indicated, quantitative and qualitative aspects of human plurality that become visible and accessible—as "present-at-hand" properties (this can also include descriptions of differences in interest and opinion, self-understanding, cultural background, etc.). All of these approaches would make "uniqueness" and "distinction and equality" (two further fundamental characteristics of plurality that Arendt lists) conceivable through observation. Arendt's answer to the question of what makes us unique, however, reads quite differently:

> The manifestation of who the speaker and doer unexchangeably is, though it is plainly visible, retains a curious intangibility that confounds

all efforts toward unequivocal verbal expression. The moment we want to say *who* somebody is, our very vocabulary leads us astray into saying *what* he is; we get entangled in a description of qualities he necessarily shares with others like him; we begin to describe a type or a 'character' in the old meaning of the word, with the result that his specific uniqueness escapes us. (HC 181)

The fact that Arendt emphasizes the "who" as opposed to the "what" speaks directly to her phenomenological approach. The "what" denotes a describable quantitative and/or qualitative quasi-uniqueness through the ever-different combination of accessible properties. The unique "who," however, remains "curiously intangible," in that it can neither be captured by an observational description, nor by a character description. What resonates here in particular is Heidegger's distinction between a "who" of *Dasein* and a "what" of *Vorhandensein* (cf. Heidegger 1927/1962, §§15–24). The Being of *Dasein* is not exhausted in being a sheer objective presence, like other beings. *Dasein* actualizes itself (*vollzieht sich*) and its "being there" as a special perspective on the world. It is "open" to the world, which it experiences. It is—to put it in Husserlian terms (and thus to insist on a fundamental commonality in their phenomenological approaches)—consciousness. This being-a-perspective is being a bodily locus of experience in the world to which the world is given. Only "within" this world is there a "what" describable from a third-person perspective. The access, the experiencing itself, is not another "what": if we understood and described it in terms of a "what," we would confront it like an object. Yet, my being conscious always eludes full objectification, and thus it cannot be treated like an object in the world. This insight unites not only Husserl and Heidegger, but all kinds of phenomenological approaches that reflect upon the world-disclosing dimension, a reflection that differs from the observation of inner-worldly objects. Insofar as experiencing/*Dasein*/consciousness does not allow for a reification without disappearing as what it is (the access to objects and the world), it cannot be addressed as a "what." This is why Heidegger, and, following him, Arendt, speaks of a "who." It is exactly this dimension of "who" or "whoness" that Arendt is interested in in her phenomenological conception of plurality. The fact of plurality concerns the plurality of "who" and not of "what." And this being a "who" precisely accounts for the singularity that is disclosed in a phenomenologically understood plurality. Thus, plurality, taken in a strictly phenomenological sense, is a plurality of the "who," understood as a plurality of perspectives.

Essentially, this underlying ontological structure, disclosed by a phenomenological approach, touches upon the same topic as Husserl's fundamental conception of a "plurality of monads" (Husserl 1973, 355); however, it is recast in the existential manner of Heidegger's analytic of *Dasein* and *Mitsein*. And yet, plurality is not a structure *of Dasein* like *Mitsein*; rather, it addresses the factuality of *Miteinandersein* (Being-with-others) as an ontico-ontological structure of worldly existence: Being-in-the-world (an ontological structure) thus is equivalent to being with (ontic) others, "*inter homines esse*." This is why I characterized ontological plurality as an *Urfaktum*, a term Husserl uses to indicate a fact that precedes and makes possible all imagination: "I cannot transcend my factical Being, and, therewith, neither the intentionally implied *Mitsein* of others, i.e. absolute reality [my translation]" (Hua 15, 386).[2]

Plurality qua "basic condition" (*HC* 175), "the fact that men, not Man, live on the earth and inhabit the world" (*HC* 7), is thus taken as an ontological and existential fact. Such a fact can only be disclosed by reflecting on experience. Instead of the rather unsupported claim that we are unique simply because we belong to the human species, it turns out that "uniqueness" is the result of an active encounter of singular accesses in the plural, by speaking with one another and by acting together. This goes far beyond merely stating an existence (*Vorhandensein*) of plurality and politically appreciating it. Yet, this is precisely what most interpreters suggest when they take plurality as simply referring to Arendt's indeed important appreciation of the diversity of people's different lifestyles and opinions. What these interpretations miss, however, is Arendt's specific usage of the concept of "point of view," namely, as a phenomenological concept of perspective that avoids any empirical or metaphysical "theories" about the "uniqueness" of persons—a construal that one may all too quickly read into Arendt's texts if one ignores the specifically phenomenological angle.

Now, Arendt's notion of the uniqueness of the "who" has important consequences not only for a concept of the self, but also for the relation between self and other. Just as my own access to the world cannot be articulated in objectifying, third-person-perspective terminology, so does the other's being-an-access elude this grasp. I encounter others in the world as living bodies with objective properties. But what makes them truly unique is not the possible uniqueness of these properties or of a combination of properties, but rather that each of them is a singular access to the world and presence of the world, which is neither reducible to an inner-worldly object nor directly accessible to me (if it were, we would simply share or rather *be* one consciousness). Arendt speaks of a "curious intangibility" (*HC* 181), which, certainly not accidentally, calls to mind Husserl's "original inaccessibility" (cf. Husserl 1950, 143). Furthermore, a certain notion of "alterity" resonates here, which arguably gives Arendt's thought its ethical character, beyond any value theories or rational and moral foundations of plurality.

Yet, even if it eludes descriptive, objectifying, and even narrative language, this being-an-access can, according to Arendt, in a specific sense, *appear in the world* and it can be experienced by me, namely through the actualities of speech and action. And this is something that neither Husserl nor Heidegger recognized, or something that they did not find important enough to explore. Hence, Arendt's original phenomenological approach investigates this specific form of the non-objectifying experience of others in speech and action, and, correlatively, the appearance of a "who" in the world. Moreover, what is distinctive about Arendt's approach, in contrast to other phenomenological accounts, is that she is explicitly interested in a 'We' that is composed of the "paradoxical plurality of unique beings" (*HC* 176), and which can be actualized by acting, speaking, and judging "in concert." This is also the way in which the initial first-person perspective in the singular can achieve a plural state—which can, I contend, only be a state of actualization. Plurality is something that has to be achieved, it is not simply a matter of fact with a quasi-transcendental function. It must be realized as a possibility of existence: for Arendt, this is "the political," the basic structure of political intersubjectivity.

## 2.2 Actualizing Plurality

"Actualizing plurality," for Arendt, is not a static or a substantial concept, but instead describes something that happens, like an activity, e.g., the activity of dancing or of conducting a conversation. This points to an operative concept in Arendt's thought that is crucial for an adequate understanding of the phenomenological approach in general: appearance, which is equivalent to the intentional presence of the world, is not to be understood as a functional or causal relation between two pregiven substances, subject and object. Instead, appearance is the basic event, a state of actuality, from which subjectivity, world, and intersubjectivity emerge as interrelated elements. I want to argue that without recognizing the concept of *Vollzug* (actualization or performance) as an operative element in Arendt's thought, we cannot properly understand how she conceives of world relation as well as intersubjective relation. It is crucial for Arendt's approach that she regards the activities of speaking, acting, and judging, as well as a space of visibility ("the public") as being necessary for *actualizing* plural uniqueness—which otherwise would remain unarticulated, a mere difference in properties and not in perspectives. These activities actualize a respectively different plural 'We.' Acting and speaking form the closely intertwined ontological core domain of plurality, while judging expands its horizon to the dimension of spectators who judge actors and thereby form a community.

Here, Arendt points to the existential possibility of becoming a self by articulating one's perspective on the world, in the face of and together with others. By taking Being-with-others (*Miteinandersein*) as the source for realizing and articulating my specific *Jemeinigkeit* (mineness), she inverts an essential movement of *Being and Time*, in which being an authentic self tends to exceed social forms of being together, notably those that are "public." More specifically, by transferring the dimension of authenticity (*Eigentlichkeit*) from being a self on my own to being a self amongst others, Arendt radically rethinks the concept of Being-with. The practices of acting, speaking, and judging that she analyzes, constitute a certain 'We'—as opposed, for example, to the instinctively constituted 'We'—that discloses the distinctiveness of singular world accesses. Arendt explicitly describes different phenomena of actualized plurality, of which the most recognized is *power*, which "exists only in its actualization" (*HC* 200) and therefore cannot be "stored up and kept in reserve for emergencies, like the instruments of violence" (*HC* 200). The other well-known "product" of actualization is a "space of appearance" (*HC* 199): acting and speaking establish "a space between the participants which can find its proper location almost any time and anywhere" (*HC* 198). In the following short analysis, I want to address the concept of actualizing plurality and how it not only yields theories concerning power and the public sphere, but also concerning the emergence of "who one is" (cf. Hart 2009, 271). This emergence is conditioned and accompanied by a special form of *Miteinander* (a term Arendt uses frequently in the German-language version of *HC*, cf. *VA* 220, 221, 225, 249, 253, 256, 264, 265, 279, 305, 315, etc.). Both topics are of vital interest for a phenomenology of intersubjectivity.

## 2.3 Who One Is: Self-Appearance, Anarchic Appearance, Narrativity, and the Web of Relationships

I believe that Arendt offers us valuable reflections on the worldly appearance of the self that are not exhausted by standard conceptions of a "narrative self" (cf. Schechtmann 2011, for an account on Arendt, see Benhabib 2003). Arendt addresses an interpersonal self from the viewpoint of appearance, which also goes beyond narration. This self is essentially intersubjectively "exposed." Yet, in contrast to many phenomenological approaches, it is not so much conceived in its affectivity or basic emotional exposedness of the self (as, for example, with shame). Instead of being reduced to the objectifying appearance of my body (as Sartre describes it in his analyses of shame; cf. Sartre 2003, 375), Arendt points to a sort of self-appearance (mostly in speaking and acting) that does not objectify me, but is the appearance of my very unique subjectivity in the face of others, as an *intersubjective* event. This experience of worldly self-appearance before others allows the acquisition of self-experience and knowledge of oneself as an appearing self. This relates me to others and the world as a shared space of appearance. It opens up the view for a basic form of political intersubjectivity that can complement existing accounts, focusing on affective forms of the interpersonal self.

In the following, I would like to present six basic theses I take to be vital for Arendt's notion of "who one is" as well as for the fundamental features of political intersubjectivity—and thus a possible form of the 'We':

(1) "Who one is" appears and develops only together with others (thesis of self-appearance-in-togetherness).
(2) What appears is not controllable. It might reveal itself better to others than to ourselves (thesis of anarchic appearance; *daimonion* thesis).

(3) The appearance of the "who" is at the same time a withdrawal with respect to propositional and narrative language (withdrawal thesis).
(4) Still, speaking and acting leave something behind that can be woven into a story (narrativity thesis).
(5) The appearance of the "who" needs and sustains a space of appearance. Its medium of appearance is a web of relationships (thesis of the second in-between).
(6) The appearance of the "who" together with others is experienced as an end-in-itself and creates a shared reality (end-in-itself and reality thesis).

Ad (1) *The Thesis of Self-Appearance-in-Togetherness*: "who one is" for Arendt is not a question of one's intentions or will, of one's plans, wishes, or inner feelings, or one's picture of a real, inner self. It is a question of *appearance*. And it is a matter of intersubjectivity. Appearance of objectivity is, as Husserl has already argued, intersubjective. This also holds for the appearance of subjectivity, although its mode of appearance significantly differs from that of objects. The mode in which the "who" shows itself—and, at the same time, eludes the fixation of the "what"—is that of acting and speaking: it is an intersubjective interaction. The "who" that appears in this interaction is not a representative or a reflection of an already full-fledged substantial "inner self"; as an appearance it " 'expresses' nothing but itself, that is, it exhibits or displays" (Arendt 1977, 30). Thus, "who one is" only develops in actualization with others. The self is given as self-appearance in the face of others, which, however, does not mean that it is originally individuated by others. Instead of the classical "dative of appearance" that remains in itself, Arendt's brand of subjectivity is turned "inside out" and enacts itself in the world.

Ad (2) *The Thesis of Anarchic Appearance; The Daimonion Thesis*: since Arendt thinks of *self-appearance as the appearance of a unique world access in the world before others*, it is not surprising that she sometimes speaks about the world in terms of the metaphor of a "stage" (cf. *"die Bühne der Welt"* (VA 219)). To this, she additionally emphasizes that the appearance of the self is not under my control—in contrast to my intentions, which I might or might not want to display. Like all appearances, the appearance of the self is a public event. So, paradoxically, it is precisely the "who I am" that is not fully at my disposal, but given to others in the space of appearance. To put it more precisely: what is at my disposal and characterized by my exclusive first-person access are the intentions of my actions—but *how I appear* in the course of realizing my intentions in acting and speaking is not. It is a worldly, intersubjective event and, thus a "risk." Arendt wants to capture the intersubjective appearance of the first-person perspective *in the world*. It is a "surplus" in acting and speaking that inevitably discloses "who one is": the *daimon*[3] that is originally not available to me but to others in the mode of "sheer togetherness." "This revelatory quality of speech and action comes to the fore where people are *with* others and neither for nor against them—that is, in sheer human togetherness. Although nobody knows whom he reveals when he discloses himself in deed or word, he must be willing to risk the disclosure [. . .]" (*HC* 180). Since for Arendt, co-appearance is not an intentional act, it is not at the disposal of the speaking subject. Instead of conceiving of social acts mainly through an "intentional interpenetration" (Husserl), Arendt conceptualizes an openness of appearance far surpassing my intentionality (and my involvements with other intentionalities, e.g., in pursuing a common goal). The intersubjective space of appearance is hence an "anarchic" space. It lies beyond sovereignty and control, since appearance cannot simply be controlled. It is a space in which I am, to put it negatively, wholly at the mercy of the uncontrollable. On the other hand, this is the only space in which something "real" can happen, something that entangles me with the world.

Ad (3) *The Withdrawal Thesis*: it is important to note, however, that the mode of givenness of the "who" is as much a disclosure as it is a withdrawal. Arendt describes the "frustration of language" qua propositional, "apophantic" language when it wants to capture the "who": "The moment we want to say *who* somebody is, our very vocabulary leads us astray into saying *what* he is" (*HC* 181). She compares this to the "well-known philosophic impossibility to arrive at a definition of man," which tries to state "what" man is; yet, she adds, the specific difference of man is that he is a "who," (in the German version: *ein Jemand* [*VA* 223]) and "that this being a who is indefinable [. . .] and incomparable [. . .] [my translation]" *(VA* 223)[4].

Ad (4) *The Narrativity Thesis*: "[the] living flux of action and speech" discloses an unobjectifiable "who," but it also has a product: stories. Arendt opens up an unusual view: "The most original product of acting is not [as one would assume, S.L.] the realization of intended goals and aims but it is the stories that initially were not at all intended and that come about when certain goals are pursued. For the agent, these stories might at first seem like accidental by-products of his actions. However, what is eventually left behind in the world by his actions, are not the impulses that set himself in motion, but the stories he caused or provoked [my translation]" (*VA* 226 f.). These stories are not "made" or "fabricated" like invented stories who have an author, but they are generated in the openness of plurality. "The real story in which we are engaged as long as we live has no visible or invisible maker because it is not made" (*HC* 186). Again, Arendt speaks of an "originally intangible manifestation of a uniquely distinct 'who'" that "can become tangible *ex post facto* through action and speech" (*HC* 186). When someone has "left behind a story," the "who" comes to the fore with a certain clarity, because the story is concluded and there are no more possibilities to be engaged in. Yet, this relative clarity and tangibility is paid for with the price of death—the disappearing of a living presence of the world in the world. The "who" is now transformed into a different phenomenon: from an appearance that resembles "the notoriously unreliable manifestations of ancient oracles" because its living spontaneity " 'neither reveal[s] nor hide[s] in words, but give[s] manifest signs' "⁵ (*HC* 181), it is transformed into a manageable piece of meaning that is interwoven with other stories, and that sustains its existence in circulating within the texture of plurality.

Ad (5) *The Thesis of the Second In-Between*: in the space of appearance, "the space where I appear to others as others appear to me, [. . .] men exist not merely like other living or inanimate things but make their appearance explicitly" (*HC* 198 f.). This explicit appearance does not happen in a void. This takes us to the medium of disclosure, the "texture" in which all individual disclosures of the "who" take place: the web of relationships. The web of relationships "consists of deeds and words and owes its origin exclusively to men's acting and speaking directly *to* one another" (*HC* 183). Again, the givenness of this sphere, being a "background" and "medium," differs from an objective appearance in the world: Arendt here describes the specific constitution of an intersubjective world that emerges through interaction. What is created in speaking and acting is nothing tangible like objects are, but rather the intersubjective relation itself, which she also characterizes with the metaphor of the "fabric." "We call this [. . .] the 'web' of human relationships, indicating by the metaphor its somewhat intangible quality" (*HC* 183). This web has a temporal and historic dimension and it is just as much in need of constant actualization as is every phenomenon of plurality.

Ad (6) *The End-in-Itself and Reality Thesis*: in actualized plurality, Arendt sees a non-purpose-bound activity that finds its end in itself. This is how she translates the Aristotelian notion of *praxis* into a meaningful experience of intersubjectivity or intersubjective co-existence. The second criterion by which the actualization of plurality can be differentiated from other forms of social interaction is its effect on *reality*, which, phenomenologically put, "is guaranteed only by the presence of a with-world, in which one and the same world appears in different perspectives [my translation]" (*VA* 251). For Arendt, reality, just like Husserl's objectivity, can only be constituted by others. However, Arendt goes further. She urges us to recognize a form of worldly reality other than merely objective reality: the reality of first-personal intersubjective encounters in which we need to trust, so that we eventually can establish the reality of our own selves and identities. "[F]or without a space of appearance and without trusting in action and speech as a mode of being together, neither the reality of one's self, of one's own identity, nor the reality of the surrounding world can be established beyond doubt" (*HC* 208).

## 3 FORMATIONS AND DEFORMATIONS OF THE PLURAL 'WE'

It is through the activities of speech, action, and judgment that Arendt characterizes the emergence of actualized plurality, which consists in a certain togetherness (*Miteinander*) of a 'We' revealing unique "whos." It must be noted that Arendt does not thematize the emergence of a 'We' in general but, rather, privileges certain forms of 'We.' Considering Arendt's remarks in *HC*, different activities form different modes of 'We,' as well as states in which a possible 'We' is either absorbed, obstructed, or destroyed. This is most obvious in her famous analyses of the activity modes of "labor" and "work" as well as in her critical assessments of the modern age, totalitarianism, and consumerist mass society. Accordingly, Arendt can be read as arguing for a specific development of a 'We' that allows for a distinctly human and humane existence. This involves a strong thesis concerning the constitution, the reality, and the nature of a 'We,' what actually is a "real We" and what is not, as well as a thesis as to how it comes about. For Arendt, an authentic form of 'We' does not dissolve the uniqueness of the "I's". Quite the contrary, it is the necessary medium of their distinct articulation and appearance. The fully developed and most authentic form of 'We' is thus the most fully developed and most authentic form of I and vice versa. Therefore, the highest possible form of a We-community is that which is dedicated to this task of articulating individuality in togetherness (which Arendt calls "the political"), or, at least, which is aware of its vital importance for a human community.

This is crucial, because there are, as Arendt shows with great insistence, also other forms of the 'We' that can form strong groups, but tend to level down the uniqueness of the subjectivities involved. Where "anonymous interest"—e.g., the logic of production and consumption, or the necessities of the life process—dominates, the 'We' assumes an "inauthentic" form; thus, it becomes deformed. The reason for this is that domination either subordinates people to the structure of *one* organism, or apprehends them only as regards their sameness and not as regards their actual distinctness. Arendt's claim of inauthenticity and deformation of the 'We' can indeed be backed up by plausible reasons, for how can *one* organism speak in the first person plural? The 'We' that would be uttered here is, in fact, only one voice, instead of a plurality constituted by singularities. Or, as Arendt puts it, "this unitedness of many into one is basically antipolitical" (*HC* 214)[6], i.e., it is *not* a form of actualized plurality. Joint activities that belong to the logic of life and the body (like exercising, or being engaged in rhythmically organized labor processes) have the force of *merging* the members who engage in it—which can also be a source of pleasure. Arendt does not deny this; but it is clear that she does not value these activities and their correlated 'We's' as high as 'We'-groups emerging from activities directed to the common world, simply because they do not seize the human possibility for activating and showing their distinctness in being together. This establishes a certain "ranking" of the different modes of intersubjectivity according to the different logics of life (labor), worldliness (work), and plurality (action/speech).

Yet, there has to be made another distinction between authentic and inauthentic forms. Speech, as Arendt writes, can easily become "idle talk" (*Gerede*), and action can be degraded to mere accomplishment, which also constitutes a distorted 'We' and obscures or abolishes the appearing "who." So the 'We' does not only depend on the activity, but also on *how* it is realized. And this again depends on the space of meaning in which this actualization takes place. Under the conditions of totalitarianism and, in a different sense, those of consumerist mass society, the dangers are high that every form of the 'We' is either deformed, absorbed, or destroyed. The concentration camps, which, as Arendt claims, systematically sought to annihilate *plurality and natality* (the power to be together and to begin something new) represent the ultimate form of this destruction of the 'We' as well as of the "who." But Arendt was equally skeptical with respect to the sterility of the job holder society, with its streamlined interests, as being able to form a we-community strong enough to counter the menace of totalitarianism. Where all are "imprisoned in the subjectivity of their own singular experience, which does not cease to be singular if the same experience is multiplied innumerable times" (*HC* 58), no 'We' in the Arendtian sense of distinct and different experiences is possible.

To summarize: I have claimed that the condition of plurality and the possibility of its realization lies in unique world accesses, streams of consciousness in the plural for whom one and the same world appears. This is the basis for being a "who" and not being reducible to an inner-worldly "what." What is unique about Arendt is that she reflects on the *worldly self-appearance of the who*, on its *givenness* and on its *conditions of givenness*. These appearance conditions are constituted by a plural togetherness (*Miteinander*) that establishes a space of appearance. Actualized plurality, explicated phenomenologically, means the plurality of irreducible perspectives on a common world as the interacting articulation and disclosure of each one's being-a-perspective, and at the same time, the constant actualization and establishment of a space of appearance and, thus, of a common world, which is the medium and background of this disclosure. The "content" of this space of appearance that lends it a temporal, genetic/generative or historic component is the "web of relationships" or the "second in-between," which consists of stories. Stories are the "products" that action and speech leave behind. The "web of relationships" or "second in-between" is as important in constituting our *reality* as the objective world. However, acting and speaking are actualizations of a plurality that need *not necessarily be actualized*. (In order to live or just to survive, I am not dependent on this kind of actualization, whereas I am highly dependent on my bodily actualizations of life.) The space of appearance and the web of relationships, which are the medium of the first-personal intersubjective disclosure of the "who," are dependent on the constant actualizations of acting and speaking through which they not only emerge, but are continuously sustained in their existence.

Hannah Arendt thus points to a fragile dimension of the 'We,' for which we are responsible for the formation of our communities. This yields not only political but also ethical consequences. Arendt "discovered the 'We'" in this special form of actualized plurality: not just as an additional mode to being an 'I,' but as the essential way in which our existence unfolds in the world and how it can meaningfully unfold as an experience of uniqueness in being together.

## NOTES

1. E.g., Canovan 1992, Honig 1995, Passerin d'Entrèves 1994, Bernstein 1996, Benhabib 2003, Villa 1996, Kateb 2006, etc.; for an overall view, consider May/Kohn 1996 and the collected essays in Williams 2006 (including pieces by Habermas, Lefort, Ricoeur, and many others).
2. For Husserl, this is the *Ur*-facticity by which all reflections on eidetic possibilities are made possible in the first place (cf. also Tengelyi 2007, 149).
3. "In acting and speaking, men show who they are, reveal actively their unique personal identities and thus make their appearance in the human world [. . .] It is more than likely that the 'who,' which appears so clearly and unmistakably to others, remains hidden from the person himself, like the *daimon* in Greek religion which accompanies each man throughout his life, always looking over his shoulder from behind and thus visible only to those he encounters" (*HC* 179f).
4. I will quote several passages from the German version of *HC* in my own translation, which are only to be found there (the English and German version of the book differ frequently, especially with respect to phenomenological vocabulary).
5. Arendt quotes Heraclitus in this passage. In German, the translation from the ancient Greek reminds one of Wittgenstein: "der weder sagt noch verbirgt, aber zeigt" (*VA* 223), or "The who is thus not expressible by "saying," but it "shows" itself."
6. The German version states additionally "Verschmelzung der Vielen in ein Kollektiv, also die Aufhebung der Pluralität" (*VA* 272).

## REFERENCES

Apel, Karl-Otto (1999). *Transformation der Philosophie, Vol. 2*. Frankfurt a.M.: Suhrkamp.
Arendt, Hannah (1977). *The Life of the Mind. Vol. One: Thinking. Vol. Two: Willing*. New York: Harcourt Brace Jovanovich.
―――― (1981) [=VA]. *Vita activa oder vom tätigen Leben*. München/Zürich: Piper.
―――― (1998) [=HC]. *The Human Condition*. Chicago: University of Chicago Press.
Benhabib, Seyla (2003). *The Reluctant Modernism of Hannah Arendt. New Edition*. Lanham: Rowman and Littlefield.
Bernstein, Richard J. (1996). *Hannah Arendt and the Jewish Question*. Cambridge: Polity Press.
Bickford, Susan (1995). "In the Presence of Others: Arendt and Anzaldúa on the Paradox of Public Appearance." In: B. Honig (Ed.). *Feminist Interpretations of Hannah Arendt*. University Park, PA: Pennsylvania State University Press.
Canovan, Margaret (1974). *The Political Thought of Hannah Arendt*. New York: Harcourt Brace Jovanovich.
―――― (1992). *Hannah Arendt: A Reinterpretation of her Political Thought*. Cambridge: Cambridge University Press.
Cavarero, Adriana (2005). *For More than One Voice: Toward a Philosophy of Vocal Expression*. Stanford: Stanford University Press.

Dietz, Mary G. (2002). *Turning Operations: Feminism, Arendt, and Politics.* London/New York: Routledge.
Dossa, Shiraz (1988). *The Public Realm and the Public Self: The Political Theory of Hannah Arendt.* Waterloo, Ontario: Wilfred Laurier University Press.
Gerhardt, Volker (1991). "Vernunft und Urteilskraft. Politische Philosophie und Anthropologie im Anschluß an Kant und Arendt." In: M.P. Thompson (Ed.). *J. Locke und/and I. Kant.* Berlin: Duncker & Humblot, 316–333.
Hart, James G. (2009). *Who One Is. Book 1. Meontology of the "I": A Transcendental Phenomenology.* Dordrecht: Springer.
Heidegger, Martin (1927/Engl. 1962). *Being and Time.* Transl. by J. Macquarrie and E. Robinson. Oxford: Basil Blackwell.
Hinchman, Lewis P. & Hinchman, Sandra K. (Eds.) (1994). *Hannah Arendt: Critical Essays.* Albany, NY: State University of New York Press.
Honig, Bonnie (1993). "The Politics of Agonism." *Political Theory* 21 (3), 528–533.
——— (Ed.) (1995). *Feminist Interpretations of Hannah Arendt.* University Park, PA: Pennsylvania State University Press.
Husserl, Edmund (1950) [=Hua 1]. *Cartesianische Meditationen und Pariser Vorträge.* Ed. by S. Strasser. Den Haag: Nijhoff.
——— (1973) [=Hua 15]. *Zur Phänomenologie der Intersubjektivität III.* Ed. by I. Kern. Den Haag: Nijhoff.
Jaeggi, Rachel (1997). *Welt und Person. Zum anthropologischen Hintergrund der Gesellschaftskritik Hannah Arendts.* Berlin: Lukas.
Kateb, George (1984). *Hannah Arendt: Politics, Conscience, Evil.* Oxford: Robertson.
——— (2006). "The judgment of Arendt." In: G. Williams (Ed.). *Hannah Arendt. Critical Assessments of Leading Political Philosophers. Vol.4: Arendt and Philosophy.* London/New York: Routledge, 265–282.
Klockars, Kristian (2008). "Plurality as a Value in Arendt's Political Philosophy." *Topos: Journal for Philosophical and Cultural Studies* 2 (19), 62–70.
May, Larry, & Kohn, Jerome (Eds.) (1996). *Hannah Arendt. Twenty Years later.* Cambridge MA/London: MIT Press.
Moran, Dermot (2000). *Introduction to Phenomenology.* London/New York: Routledge.
McGowan, John (1998). *Hannah Arendt: An Introduction.* Minneapolis: University of Minnesota Press.
Passerin d'Entrèves, Maurizio (1994). *The Political Philosophy of Hannah Arendt.* London/New York: Routledge.
Sartre, Jean-Paul (2003). *Being and Nothingness: An Essay in Phenomenological Ontology.* Transl. by H. E. Barnes, revised edition. London/New York: Routledge.
Schechtmann, Marya (2011). "The Narrative Self." In: S. Gallagher (Ed.). *The Oxford Handbook of the Self.* Oxford: Oxford University Press, 394–418.
Schott, Robin M. (2010). "Natality and Destruction." In: R.M. Schott (Ed.). *Birth, Death and Femininity. Philosophies of Embodiment.* Bloomington: Indiana University Press, 49–71.
Tengelyi, László (2007). *Erfahrung und Ausdruck. Phänomenologie im Umbruch bei Husserl und seinen Nachfolgern.* Dordrecht: Springer.
Villa, Dana R. (1996). *Arendt and Heidegger: The Fate of the Political.* Princeton: Princeton University Press.
Williams, Garrath (Ed.) (2006). *Hannah Arendt. Critical Assessments of Leading Political Philosophers. 4 volumes: Vol. 1: Arendt and political events. Vol. 2: Arendt and political philosophy. Vol.3: The Human Condition. Vol. 4: Arendt and Philosophy.* London/New York: Routledge.

# 3 Habermas and Hermeneutics
## From *Verstehen* to *Lebenswelt*
### Richard Wolin

Husserl came to his social phenomenology of the *Lebenswelt* relatively late in life, with his 1936 manuscript on the *Crisis of the European Sciences and Transcendental Phenomenology*.[1] Two decades later, its reception helped to inspire the emergence of phenomenological Marxism. In central Europe, this paradigm stood as a reflexive alternative to official Marxism qua "diamat" (dialectical materialism), which, in the lands of "really existing socialism," had congealed into a dogmatic and repressive "science of legitimation." Phenomenological Marxism's leading representatives were Sartre, Maurice Merleau-Ponty, Karel Kosík, Tran Duc Thao, and Enzo Paci. In the Czech context, given Kosík's prominence, it played an important role in the Renaissance of Marxist humanism that culminated in the notion of "Socialism with a Human Face" and the Prague Spring.

The crisis of Marxism was reflected in Marxism's objectivistic self-understanding as "scientific socialism": an approach that downplayed subjectivity and thus seemed indifferent to the demands of human freedom. Husserl's notion of intentionality offered a compelling alternative to the prevailing scientism, and it was this aspect that was embraced by phenomenological Marxists in their search for a philosophical orientation that could counter the reigning methodological determinism. Insofar as the concept of intentionality identified the constitutive function of the transcendental ego as a sine qua non for experience and cognition, it represented a thoroughgoing challenge of positivism in all its variants.

These preoccupations are central to Husserl's *Crisis of the European Sciences*, in which he identifies the "mathematicization of nature" as the orientation responsible for European decline. Thus, Husserl understood the crisis in, primarily, intellectual and spiritual terms:

> The exclusiveness with which the total worldview of modern man, in the second half of the nineteenth century, let itself be determined by the positive sciences and be blinded by the 'prosperity' they produced, meant an indifferent turning-away form the questions which are decisive for a genuine humanity. Merely fact-minded sciences make merely fact-minded people [. . .] It excludes in principle precisely the questions

which man, given over in our unhappy times to the most portentous upheavals, finds the most burning: questions of the meaning or meaninglessness of the whole of this human existence.

(Husserl 1970, 6)

For Habermas, who throughout his career remained faithful to the idea of Marxism as a "critique," the reception of the later Husserl's notion of the lifeworld would play a key role in surmounting the well-entrenched scientistic biases of philosophy and social science. In his pivotal Frankfurt University inaugural lecture, "Knowledge and Human Interests" (1965), Habermas relied extensively on Husserl's approach. Fifteen years later, in his *Theory of Communicative Action* (1981), the lifeworld, as an inexhaustible repository of non-thetic, implicit meanings, assumed an even more important role as a reservoir of semantic resistance vis-à-vis the predatory subsystems of money and power that, under late capitalism, increasingly become hegemonic. It is in this vein that he spoke of the "colonization of the lifeworld" to characterize the process whereby informal spheres of life are increasingly subjected to regulation and control by superordinate instrumental and bureaucratic structures. In this respect, the discourse of "social phenomenology," as it derived from Husserl and the work of Alfred Schütz, came to supplant the role that hermeneutics had formerly played in his work as a methodological alternative to the objectivating approach of the social sciences.

In this regard, it is important to keep in mind that, for Habermas, as for Husserl during the 1930s, the attempt to remedy philosophy's positivistic self-misunderstanding signified more than a merely abstract, theoretical concern. Also at stake was what Habermas referred to as the growing "scientific-technical organization of the lifeworld"; hence, the practical consequences were potentially immense. It is in this vein, perhaps, that in *Theory and Practice* Habermas memorably characterized his own methodological approach as "Critical Theory with a practical intent" (see Habermas 1973, 1).

## HERMENEUTICS

Underlying Habermas's Dilthey reception during the 1960s was a scholarly context as well as a political context. The scholarly context pertained to the revival of turn-of-the-century debates concerning "explanation vs. understanding" (*Erklären* vs. *Verstehen*) in the human sciences, a controversy that had been addressed in important books by Georg Henrik von Wright (1971) and Habermas's Frankfurt colleague, Karl-Otto Apel (1984).

Whereas the empirical sciences seek to *explain* social phenomena and historical events by subjecting them to causal-nomological accounts, the *Geisteswissenschaften* conversely seek to *interpret* them via the non-objectivating technique of understanding (*Verstehen*). As an interpretive practice, understanding seeks to heed the motivations and intentions of historical actors. In Dilthey's rendition of *Verstehen*, the technique of "empathy," or *Einfühlen*, was also paramount, an approach that it was necessary for the historian or interpreter to intuit or identify with the mindset of the actors whose motivations s/he was trying to comprehend.

As a philosopher of culture, Dilthey was also the foremost generational representative of *Lebensphilosophie*, displaying all of the limitations and idiosyncrasies of that perspective. Foremost among these limitations was *Lebensphilosophie*'s rather frank devaluation of ratiocination and conceptualization. Bluntly put, in Dilthey's view, intellection, in all its guises and manifestations, constituted a falsification of the vibrant immediacy of "life" (*Leben*). As a philosopher of cognition, or *Erkenntnistheoretiker*, Dilthey viewed it as his task to de-transcendentalize the transcendental subject that had been epistemologically venerated by Descartes and Kant. He vigorously contested the transcendental ego's *material impoverishment*, which he interpreted, correspondingly, as a denigration of *Erlebnis* or "lived experience"—a condition that he associated with the experiential vacuity of a hyper-rationalized, Western *Zivilisation*. As Dilthey remarked in seminal passage from *Einführung in die Geisteswissenschaften*, "No real blood flows in the veins of the knowing subject constructed by Locke, Hume, and Kant; it is only the diluted juice of reason, a mere process of thought" (Dilthey 1976, 162).[2]

Dilthey viewed the very act of cognitive apprehension as a betrayal of "life." Yet how could one in good conscience aspire to "science" or "knowledge," if all theory were, as Dilthey claimed, intrinsically an act of betrayal or falsification? In his critique of historical reason, Dilthey sought to formulate objective concepts that would make historical life intelligible. Yet, was not this very act of subsuming the singularity of lived experience under general concepts such as "life," "expression," and "experience" itself a violation of Dilthey's own hermeneutics—and, as such, a falsification in its own right? Moreover, even if hermeneutics' claims concerning the epistemological superiority of "life" over "ratiocination" were true, from a normative perspective, we would remain simply perplexed, awash in the flux of pre-cognitive *Erlebnis* (experience), and thus lacking a trustworthy and reliable point of orientation to guide us (Schnädelbach 1984, 145). In this respect, the shortcoming of the hermeneutical approach foreshadowed the impending "crisis of historicism," as thematized by Friedrich Meinecke and others.

Subtending such contentions and criticisms, it was not difficult to discern the distinctive echoes of German *Zivilisationskritik*—i.e., the anti-Western, anti-civilizational ethos that would rise to a fever pitch during the 1920s with the work of Spengler, Arthur Moeller van den Bruck, and Martin Heidegger. Like other representatives of historicism, Dilthey was a cultural relativist. Late in life, he elaborated his doctrine of *Weltanschauungen* or worldviews, the mental parameters that defined a given period or epoch. According to this perspective, "values" were intrinsically arbitrary and could never be objectively grounded or justified.

Nevertheless, for Habermas during the 1960s, Dilthey's hermeneutics represented something like a usable past. By emphasizing the specificity and irreducibility of *Verstehen*, Habermas believed that hermeneutics could be enlisted in the methodological struggle against scientism, which had sought to extend its instrumental attitude toward physical nature to the domain of human social action. According to Habermas, "Whereas the empirical-analytical methods aim at disclosing and comprehending under the transcendental viewpoint of technical control, *hermeneutic methods aim at mutual understanding in ordinary language communication and in action according to common norms*" (Schnädelbach 1984, 176).

Surprisingly, the ideological objections that the Critical Theory tradition had frequently raised about Dilthey's work—objections that had called into question hermeneutics' "conventionalism," or over-identification with tradition, as well as its agnosticism about ultimate ends or values—were absent in Habermas's account. Instead, Habermas's criticism of Dilthey paralleled his critique of the other intellectual protagonists discussed in *Knowledge and Human Interest*: Marx, Peirce, and Freud. It was in this vein that Habermas suggested that, like these other thinkers, Dilthey's approach had succumbed to a "scientistic self-misunderstanding." Thus, despite his penetrating insights concerning the methodological limitations of the natural sciences, Dilthey ultimately succumbed to the illusions of the age and sought to legitimate the practice of hermeneutics in the language of scientific objectivity. Paradoxically, Dilthey suggested that hermeneutics' methodological superiority derived from the fact that its results guaranteed a greater measure of "objectivity" than could the competing, "naturalizing" approaches that had been borrowed from the *Naturwissenschaften*. Habermas refers to this peculiar methodological blind spot as Dilthey's "covert positivism" (cf. Schnädelbach 1984, 179).

In *Truth and Method*, Hans-Georg Gadamer—Habermas's colleague at Heidelberg from 1963–65—went far toward redressing one of the major drawbacks of Dilthey's hermeneutics: its objectivism or latent positivism. Thus, Gadamer countered Dilthey's scientistic self-misunderstanding by rejecting the methodological ideal of finality or completion—the Rankean notion that one should interpret historical events "as they really were" through the eyes of the actors themselves—in favor of a more open-ended, dialogical, and hermeneutically situated model of understanding. Nevertheless, in his critique of Gadamer, Habermas sought to demonstrate that, in deftly avoiding one set of methodological failings, Gadamer proceeded to open himself up to another series of complications and compromises.

It was in this vein that Habermas objected to the arch-conservative implications of Gadamer's hermeneutics, arguing that its glorification of tradition was unacceptable, since, historically speaking, traditions concealed relations of domination that were inconsistent with the (Kantian) precepts of autonomy and self-determination. Playing Kant to Gadamer's Burke, he insisted on the ineliminable prerogatives of "reflection" (*Reflexion*); thus, the principles of democratic citizenship mandated that only those traditions were acceptable that could be explicitly and rationally agreed to by those who were subject to their dictates and decrees. In this respect, Gadamer's unabashed "prejudice in favor of prejudice" was fundamentally irreconcilable with the values of social emancipation.

In Habermas's view, Gadamer's defense of tradition (*Überlieferung*) was reminiscent of the discredited worldview of the German *Obrigkeitsstaat* (authoritarian state) that had flourished during the *Kaiserreich* or Second Empire, a mentality conducive to the cultivation of "subjects" (*Untertanen*) rather than "citizens" (*Staatsbürger*) who possessed the capacity for self-rule or autonomy. As Habermas points out, "understanding" (*Verstehen*) worthy of the name does not mean blindly surrendering to the authority of tradition, but always entails its critical appropriation. When all is said and done, Gadamer's celebration of prejudice and tradition indicated that he valued authority over reason: the preservation of the political status quo in opposition to the ideals of collective self-determination.

Thus, whether one casts one's lot with Dilthey, Gadamer, or Heidegger, it becomes apparent that the hermeneutic tradition suffers from certain *rationality deficits*. This aversion to universal reason was one of the legacies of the German *Sonderweg* (special path): Germany's self-understanding as a *Kulturnation* in opposition to the purportedly superficial practices of *Räsonieren* that predominated in the West. In this respect, the lineaments of the hermeneutic approach were *geopolitically conditioned* and betrayed what one might call an *anti-civilizational affect*—a disposition that surfaced, above all, in the aforementioned valorization of "life" over "reason." As a philosopher and public intellectual, Habermas undertook to cure German political culture of these longstanding prejudices—intellectual habits that had had such a deleterious impact on the nation's moral and political development.

With these considerations in mind, it is not surprising to find that in *Theory of Communicative Action* (1981), Habermas reconceived the theoretical framework he had originally developed in *Knowledge and Human Interests*, to all intents and purposes, eliminating the earlier, positive references to *Verstehen* and hermeneutics. Instead, in a momentous conceptual shift, he relied on the tradition of social phenomenology as developed by the late Husserl in *The Crisis* and by Schütz and Thomas Luckmann in *Structures of the Lifeworld*. In retrospect, this change in perspective seems both plausible and consistent, since Habermas's social theoretic reformulation of the "critique of instrumental reason" paralleled Husserl's indictment of science in the *Crisis*. Thus, in *Theory of Communicative Action*, Habermas reconceptualized his earlier critique of the "scientization of politics" (in *Theory and Practice* and elsewhere) by resorting to the Husserlian–Schützian construct of the "colonization of the lifeworld."

In the opinion of most commentators, Husserl's *Crisis* represented a radically new departure. As Paul Ricoeur enquired in one of the first comprehensive studies of Husserl's phenomenology, "How can a philosophy of the cogito, of the radical return to the ego as the founder of all being, become capable of a philosophy of history?" (Ricoeur 1967, 145). Conversely, in the eyes of Maurice Merleau-Ponty, the *Crisis* represented a genuine breakthrough, since, by abandoning the program of eidetic phenomenology or search for timeless essences (*Wesensschau*), Husserl succeeded in exposing phenomenology to new possibilities and horizons.

Although in the *Crisis*, one can unquestionably detect the political tumult of the 1930s—W.H. Auden's "low, dishonest decade"—hovering in the background, Husserl was only indirectly concerned with real history. Instead, his main focus concerned the *meaning* of history when viewed from an "eidetic" point of view. Accordingly, he addressed the fact that, in an "essential" sense, the West had lost its way—by which Husserl meant the *telos* that had been established during the halcyon days of the 4th-century Greek Enlightenment. The idea that *nous*, or reason, should govern the world—as opposed to myth, fate, or brute force—represented an intellectual breakthrough of the highest order that had been codified by the Socratic School. Yet, since the late 19th century, there could be no gainsaying the fact that the West's trust in reason had been irreparably tarnished. Thereafter, to quote Max Weber, a set of "warring gods" had arisen, which sought to supplant the virtues of intellection with irrational appeals to the instinctual forces of blood and race. (For example, in his 1933 Freiburg University Rectoral Address, Heidegger praised the Nazi regime for having reawakened the autochthonous "forces of earth and blood.") Under the circumstances, Husserl, who previously had paid scant attention to moral or political concerns, was compelled to undertake a metahistorical enquiry concerning reason's fate in modern times.

Yet, the real conceptual innovation offered by this rich and fascinating text concerns the idea of the "lifeworld" (*Lebenswelt*), a sphere of implicit meanings or unspoken normative assumptions that underlie more formalized domains of social interaction. As such, in Husserl's view, the lifeworld embodied the indispensable horizon and basis of what Heidegger in *Being and Time* called Being-in-the-world. As such, the lifeworld possessed an irrevocable existential primacy in light of which all other spheres of life appear as secondary elaborations or constructions. As Husserl explains, "the lifeworld (. . .) is pregiven to us, the waking, always somehow practically interested subjects, not occasionally but always and necessarily as the universal field of all actual and possible praxis, as horizon" (Husserl 1970, 142).

In *Ideas I* and *II*, Husserl had spoken of the "natural attitude" to describe our naïve, everyday, pre-critical relationship to the phenomenal world and its modalities. These self-evidences needed to be "bracketed" via the *epoché* or "eidetic reduction" in order for phenomenology to distill the "essential" dimensions of intentional experience. In certain respects, the idea of the lifeworld represented a reformulation of Husserl's earlier conception of the natural attitude. Yet, the lifeworld signifies a positive reevaluation of this earlier perspective, insofar as it embodies a sphere of potential resistance vis-à-vis the presumptions and depredations of formal reason. As Husserl explains:

> The lifeworld is the realm of original self-evidences [...] All conceivable verification leads back to these modes of self-evidence [...] lies in these intuitions themselves as that which is actually, intersubjectively experienceable and verifiable; it is not a substruction of thought; whereas such a substruction, insofar as it makes a claim to truth, can have actual truth only by being related back to such self-evidences.
> (Husserl 1970, 127f)

There are two basic attitudes we as individuals can assume toward the self-evidences of the lifeworld: a naïve attitude, or one that is reflective. It is the latter that Husserl associates with the philosophical point of view and which, for this reason, he judges to be superior. The naïve attitude, for its part, declines to go beyond the lifeworld in its immediate givenness. It remains immersed in these experiences and rests content with this immersion. Conversely, in Husserl's view, the *reflective attitude* represents what one might call the "beginning of wisdom." Rather than accepting the lifeworld as given, it systematically enquires into its "how": the lifeworld's fundamental modalities of givenness. Husserl appositely describes this approach as a *"transformation of the thematic consciousness of the world that breaks through the normality of straightforward living"* (Husserl 1970, 144). Thereafter, what was once self-evident and unproblematic ceases to be so.

The reflexive approach is the fruit of what Husserl refers to in the *Crisis* as the transcendental epoché, a standpoint that permits the phenomenologist to break with the familiarity of the natural attitude. For a philosophical analogy, one might have recourse to the celebrated "cave allegory" in Plato's *Republic*, in which one prisoner breaks free from his chains in order to perceive the shadow play that his fellow prisoners take for reality or the truth. From standpoint of Hegel's *Phenomenology of Spirit*, the reflexive attitude expresses the transition from consciousness to self-consciousness. Metaphorically speaking, it signifies the "conversion experience" that distinguishes the philosophical point of view from common sense perspective of the everyday life. The epoché affords access to what Husserl describes as the "miracle" of transcendental subjectivity: the realization that the world does not exist as a self-subsistent entity, as naïve consciousness or Hegelian "Sense Certainty" might assume.[3] Instead, its being is dependent on the constitutive function of intentional consciousness. Thus, following the precedents of Descartes and Kant, Husserl alleges that the world never appears as such. Instead, its manifestations are conditioned a priori by the transcendental and constitutive modalities of intentionality. Here, "intentionality" is pivotal insofar as it suggests epistemological limits to the third-person, observer perspective favored by both the natural sciences as well as the positivistically biased social sciences (*Geisteswissenschaften*). In other words: the world—and the socio-cultural world, in particular—cannot be objectively reduced to the "totality of (self-subsistent) facts," insofar as all such "facts" are ultimately dependent on the intentionality of consciousness.

In *Theory of Communicative Action*, the lifeworld stands as a realm of informal social meanings and unproblematic cultural assumptions that social actors are able to draw upon freely in order to arrive at shared understandings and to realize their individual and collective projects. Habermas's normative concerns parallel Husserl's, insofar as both philosophers seek to parry the risks and temptations of *scientific overreach*, an ever-escalating process whereby aspects of human social life increasingly forfeit their autonomy as well as their existential integrity at the hands of highly formalized, instrumental systems of action.

In classical sociological theory (Weber, Durkheim, and Simmel), such developments had been central *topoi*. Thus, in his path-breaking studies on the *Division of Labor* (1893) and *Suicide* (1897), Durkheim addressed them under the rubric of the transition from mechanical to organic solidarity. Weber harbored similar concerns. He concluded *The Protestant Ethic and the Spirit of Capitalism* (1904/05) by denigrating the ethos of the modern *Fachmensch*, or specialist, as a cultural setback when viewed against the backdrop of the Renaissance ideal (whose most prominent exponent had undoubtedly been Jacob Burckhardt) of the well-rounded personality. Weber's critique of the fateful one-sidedness of modern cultural development—the triumph of "objective" over "subjective" culture—impelled him to interpret Western modernity as a process of twofold "loss": a "loss of meaning" and a "loss of freedom" (*Sinnverlust* and *Freiheitsverlust*).

"Loss of meaning" derives from the process of "rationalization," whereby the mores and convictions of traditional society are increasingly subjected to the corrosive force of intellectualist criteria: for example, the misguided acceptance of scientific reason as a universal solvent. Conversely, "loss of freedom" results from the universal triumph of bureaucracy as a seemingly inescapable mode of social organization. In Weber's view, ever-fewer spheres of life are able to escape the straightjacket of formal reason. Bureaucracy's rise means that, increasingly, fewer domains of social and vocational life are left to inclination, whim, individual initiative, or choice. Instead, nearly all aspects of social life are regulated and predetermined—down to the innermost "corpuscular" level, as Michel Foucault observes with reference to the growth of modern "biopower."

Reliance on the lifeworld concept allows Habermas to analyze such developments in ways that the hermeneutic approach—with its shortsighted and limited glorification of the ineffable immediacy of "life"—did not. Consequently, he can indict the illicit instrumentalist overreach of "functionalist reason," the unwonted interferences of rational-purposive approaches to social action (*zweckrationales Handeln*), in areas of society that are rooted in the lifeworld: the family, culture, community life, and voluntary associations, whose informal modalities are, according to Habermas, increasingly subjected to the formal media of money and power. In *Theory of Communicative Action*, Habermas develops the idea of the "colonization of the lifeworld" to highlight the illegitimate and destructive violations of the lifeworld's integrity by the forces of instrumental rationality deriving from the subsystems of the economy and state administration.

Nevertheless, there are shortcomings to the lifeworld approach, as developed by social phenomenologists like Husserl and Schütz, which, in *Theory of Communicative Action*, Habermas seeks to surmount. Thus, despite the pluralistic implications of the lifeworld concept, phenomenology remains wedded to the perspective of transcendental subjectivity, which perceives the world from the standpoint of individually thinking and acting subjects.[4] These are phenomenology's well-known difficulties (see especially the "Fifth" of Husserl's *Cartesian Meditations*) when it comes to the problem of "other minds" or intersubjectivity. Habermas wishes to circumvent these obstacles by reformulating the lifeworld idea in keeping with the tenets of *communicative reason*, whose alpha and omega is human intersubjectivity. But also, viewed phenomenologically, reason and rationality remain extrinsic concerns. As such, in discussions of the lifeworld, they fall out of account, insofar as implicit meanings and unspoken background assumptions predominate.

Via his communicative reformulation of the lifeworld idea, Habermas is able to introduce a *normative dimension* that, for the most part, in phenomenological approaches—with their predominant orientation toward *description* rather than *prescription*—typically remains absent. Communicative reason suggests that the denizens of the lifeworld dispose over criteria of reasonableness and fairness that may be made explicit or publicly invoked in order to adjudicate the validity of the agreements and understandings. Thus, whereas the lifeworld, as a permanent and universal feature of human societies, is presumably transhistorical, with the transition from *Gemeinschaft* to *Gesellschaft*, or community to society, its "rationality potentials" expand—as do its potentials for justice as fairness.

One of the keys to Habermas's argument revolves around a process that he denominates the "linguistification of the sacred." Among traditional societies in which religion remains a primary mode of securing legitimation, the aura of the sacred serves to immunize social authority from discursive challenges, thereby undercutting the communicative ideal of understanding oriented toward mutual agreement. Conversely, with the advent of "secularization," these immunological barriers decline. Illegitimate claims to social authority are deprived of the aura of divinity behind which they have been traditionally able to dissemble their normative and political substance. In their place, there emerges a new potential for a non-hierarchical, consensual resolution of disputes, along with egalitarian prospects of democratic will formation. As Habermas explains in a key passage in *Theory of Communicative Action*:

> Universal discourse points to an idealized lifeworld reproduced through processes of mutual understanding that have been largely detached from normative contexts and transferred over to rationally motivated yes/no positions. This sort of growing autonomy can come to pass only to the extent that constraints of material reproduction no longer hide behind the mask of a rationally impenetrable, basic, normative consensus, that is, stand behind the authority of the sacred [. . .] A lifeworld rationalized in this sense would by no means reproduce itself in conflict-free forms. But the conflicts would appear in their own names; they would no longer be concealed by convictions immune from discursive examination.
> (Habermas 1987, 145)

By the same token, the lifeworld approach ultimately shares one of the central methodological shortcomings of its hermeneutic cousin, viz., the failing of "hermeneutic idealism." This appellation suggests that the model of intentionality and implicit meanings offers inadequate means for conceptualizing problems of power and domination. Here, what is also needed is an analysis of what Habermas terms "system integration," a dimension that would complement the phenomenological approach's well-nigh exclusive emphasis on *symbolic meanings*. Systems theory's methodological point of departure is not the intentionality of the individual social actor or actors. Instead, it adopts the functionalist perspective of the (impersonal) self-maintaining system, an orientation that it inherited from 19th-century social evolutionism. Its socio-political ideal (e.g., in the work of leading exponents such as the late Niklas Luhmann) is "homeostasis," a normative standpoint that it borrows from life sciences such as biology.

Habermas's project of a "critique of functionalist reason" aims to roll back or curtail the illicit interferences of the instrumental imperatives that derive from the self-maintaining systems of economy and power, which, he argues, are adverse to the lifeworld qua repository of informal sociality and implicit meanings. In *Theory of Communicative Action*, he describes the reifying or "de-moralizing" effects of system-induced interferences in the lifeworld as follows:

> A demoralized, positive, compulsory law [. . .] makes it possible to steer social action via delinguistified media [. . .] The transfer of action coordination from language over to steering media means an uncoupling of interaction from lifeworld contexts. Media such as money and power [. . .] encode a purposive-rational attitude toward calculable amounts of value and make it possible to exert generalized, strategic influence [. . .] while

> *bypassing* processes of consensus-oriented communication. [As a result] the lifeworld contexts in which processes of reaching understanding are always embedded are devalued in favor of media-steered interactions.
> (Habermas 1987, 183)

Thus, under the conditions of advanced capitalism, domination (*Herrschaft*) assumes the impersonal form of strategic rationality. In this way, the central significance that Marx, in *Capital* and other works, attributed to the workplace or factory has been surpassed in the direction of the ascending "functionalist reason." By virtue of its central role in processes of system maintenance, instrumental reason acquires an aura of "objectivity" and is consequently, to a great extent, immunized against claims of democratic legitimacy. The upshot of this development, the *functional* imperatives of *strategic rationality*—what Weber called rational-purposive or goal-oriented action, as opposed to social action that is oriented toward the ends of mutual understanding—trump the *discursive* claims of communicative reason as they are rooted in the lifeworld.

Habermas has also described this developmental trend as the "*technicization of the lifeworld*" (Habermas 1987, 180, 183). By substituting impersonal mechanisms of strategic action for communicative reason, the colonization of the lifeworld facilitates the *demoralization of society*, in both a literal and figurative sense. This occurs insofar as, following the Kantian tradition, we associate the capacity for "moral action" with the values of collective self-determination and individual autonomy (*Mündigkeit*). Yet, individual autonomy diminishes the more that the amoral steering media of money and power degrade the discursive fabric of the lifeworld qua fount of intersubjectivity and communicative rationality.

## CRITICAL REMARKS

One of Habermas's primary goals in *Theory of Communicative Action* is to redress the question of the absent normative foundations of the Frankfurt School. Yet, in this regard, there seems to be a fundamental ambivalence at the heart of his approach—an ambivalence that has, in certain respects, persistently haunted Critical Theory.

Bluntly put: do these normative foundations possess an immanent or transcendent status? Are they rooted in universal principles or are they, instead, socially embodied? If they are "transcendent," then they risk assuming the character of standards or precepts that have been independently derived and determined by the philosopher or theorist. If, conversely, they are sedimented in the logic of social evolution, they threaten to become overly concrete, the expression of a particular cultural tradition or a given social formation. As a result, their claim to universality diminishes correspondingly.

Habermas, for his part, has shown himself to be extremely uncomfortable with the idea of timeless, unconditional claims to validity, which he views as a lapse into foundationalism. Instead, he has on numerous occasions expressed solidarity with trends in so-called "post-metaphysical thinking." Consequently, his attitude toward the question of ultimate foundations (*letzte Begründungen*) has persistently oscillated between a transcendental and empirical orientation, as can be seen by his employment of the oxymoron "quasi-transcendental" to characterize his aims. Yet, normative claims that are purportedly quasi-transcendental seem alternately too strong and too weak, insofar as they seek the irrefragable certitude of "ultimate foundations" without the attendant metaphysical baggage.

Analogous methodological ambiguities permeate Habermas's employment of the idea of the lifeworld. In earlier studies, such as *Communication and the Evolution of Society*, Habermas invoked the notion of "universal pragmatics" in order to define the "quasi-transcendental" telos of language qua understanding (*Verständigung*) that is oriented toward mutual agreement. According to this view, all other linguistic usage—for example, the instrumental employment of language in strategic action—is parasitical vis-à-vis this basic normative criterion.

However, it is unclear exactly what role the lifeworld, as a realm of informal and taken-for-granted habitudes and meanings, is meant to play in validating the normative telos of communicative reason—viz., uncoerced reciprocal agreement or mutual understanding free from ideological constraint. After all, as a diffuse congeries of values, significations, and background conditions, there is nothing inherently "rational" about the lifeworld. Instead, one can readily imagine that the lifeworld's suitability for the ends of communicative transparency would change radically depending on the extent to which it has been institutionally "rationalized," or exposed to the mechanisms and norms of democratic publicity (*Öffentlichkeit*)—a point that Habermas generally seems willing to concede. Thus, one can readily conceive of lifeworlds that function in ways that are extremely arbitrary or repressive, lifeworlds in which the distortional effects of tradition prevent the norms of equality and reciprocity that Habermas reveres from flourishing. Ultimately, there would seem to be no getting around the fact that one must judge the fabric of a given lifeworld on the basis of its normative content, insofar as lifeworlds that are obstinately mired in custom, habit, and tradition can easily present themselves as obstacles to, rather than facilitators of, the ends of social emancipation or discursive will formation. In other words: lifeworlds can be "ethical," or cohere internally, without being "moral"—that is, without adhering to broader norms of justice or fairness.

Given such questions and doubts, one cannot help but wonder whether Habermas places more methodological weight on the lifeworld ideal than it can in point of fact bear. In view of the historical variegatedness of individual lifeworlds, how universalizable is this concept as a basis or ground for a theory of communicative reason?

Accordingly, in a subsequent clarification, Habermas seems to concede too much to the lifeworld qua "ethical life" or *Sittlichkeit*—that is, as a sphere of random, "amoral" sociality—when he claims that attempts to pose questions of "ultimate justification" with respect to the lifeworld are fundamentally misplaced. As Habermas states in the passage in question, "The *moral* intuitions of everyday life have no need of clarification by philosophers." Instead, "in this case, the *therapeutic* understanding of philosophy as developed by Wittgenstein seems appropriate" (Habermas 1992, 98). In other words: when it comes to the lifeworld, philosophy should not disturb the fragile heritage of tradition, even if that heritage should turn out to be a dead weight. Instead, following the later Wittgenstein qua theorist of "language games" and what it means to "follow a rule" (both of these concepts are keywords in *Philosophical Investigations*), philosophy's job is merely to clarify the nature of life practices and the rules that underlie them, rather than to disrupt the lifeworld's integrity, as philosophical questioning, going back to Socrates, is wont to do, by seeking to establish first principles or to legislate norms.

Yet, in the preceding characterization, the lifeworld seems to be synonymous with a *conventional* approach to life, one that assumes that the totality of inherited social facts is fundamentally unalterable. A *post-conventional* approach to life, conversely, suggests the advent of "critical consciousness," a consciousness that no longer merely assumes that the contents of tradition merit acceptance merely because they have been handed down.

Consequently, it seems that, in opposition to the conventionalist approach, one must adopt a principle akin to Jaspers's notion of the "axial age," a concept that denotes the advent of "transcendence" as a precondition for critical consciousness. As Jaspers proposes in *The Origin and Goal of History* (1949), "transcendence" signifies a capacity for *discursive reflexivity* that transcends the world as a self-referential totality of facts that are merely given. In this respect, transcendence connotes the emergence of a capacity to judge the normative failings or deficiencies of "ethical life" (*Sittlichkeit*) according to considerations of *principle*: that is, according to the *higher moral standards* of "justice." Although Habermas has invoked the idea of the axial age in his later writings on the philosophy of religion, he has, somewhat surprisingly, refrained from indicating what role it might play a role in reformulating the idea of the lifeworld he develops in *Theory of Communicative Action*.

## NOTES

1 To be sure, Husserl devoted a number of detailed analyses of the social world and intersubjectivity from as early as 1913 onwards.
2 See also Iggers 1983, 124ff.
3 See Moran 2000, 60: "For Husserl, objectivity was always a particular 'achievement of consciousness' (*Bewusstseinsleistung*) and he was fascinated by the miracle of the process."
4 Not all would agree regarding such an interpretation, however; see, e.g., Zahavi 2001.

# REFERENCES

Apel, Karl-Otto (1984). *Understanding and Explanation: A Transcendental-Pragmatic Perspective*. Transl. by G. Warnke. Cambridge, MA/London: MIT Press

Dilthey, Wilhelm (1976). "Introduction to the Human Sciences." In: *W. Dilthey: Selected Writings*. Ed. by H. Rickman. Cambridge: Cambridge University Press.

Habermas, Jürgen (1973). *Theory and Practice*. Transl. by J. Viertel. Boston: Beacon Press.

—— (1987). *Theory of Communicative Action II*. Transl. by T. McCarthy. Boston: Beacon Press.

—— (1992). *Moral Consciousness and Communicative Action*. Cambridge, MA/London: MIT Press.

Husserl, Edmund (1970). *The Crisis of the European Sciences and Transcendental Phenomenology*. Transl. by D. Carr. Evanston, IL: Northwestern University Press.

Iggers, Georg G. (1983). *The German Conception of History: The National Tradition of Historical Thought from Herder to the Present*. Middletown: Wesleyan University Press.

Jaspers, Karl (1949). *The Origin and Goal of History*. London: Routledge and Kegan Paul.

Moran, Dermot (2000). *Introduction to Phenomenology*. London/New York: Routledge.

Ricoeur, Paul (1967). *Husserl. An Introduction to his Phenomenology*. Transl. by E. Ballard and L. Embree. Evanston, IL: Northwestern University Press.

Schnädelbach, Herbert (1984). *Philosophy in Germany: 1831–1933*. Transl. by E. Matthews. Cambridge: Cambridge University Press.

von Wright, Georg Henrik (1971). *Explanation and Understanding*. Ithaca: Cornell University Press.

Zahavi, Dan (2001). *Husserl and Transcendental Intersubjectivity. A Response to the Linguistic-Pragmatic Critique*. Transl. by E. A. Behnke. Athens, OH: Ohio University Press.

# 4 Second-Person Phenomenology
*Steven Crowell*

By "second-person phenomenology," I mean phenomenological reflection on the experience of being addressed by a claim, experiencing oneself "in the accusative," as it is sometimes described. Thus, second-person phenomenology is, like all phenomenology, a reflection on first-person experience, but the kind of experience it reflects upon involves some very interesting and important features. The most important feature, as I have argued in a recent paper (Crowell 2013b), is that being addressed by a claim is a normative condition for the constitution of an objective (shared) world and for the constitution of myself as a human being. But second-person phenomenology is equally constitutive for fundamental concepts such as responsibility, accountability, self-identity, and rationality. In this chapter, then, I will first summarize the path I trace in "Why is Ethics First Philosophy?" from Husserl to Sartre to Levinas. I will then turn to issues that arise within this phenomenological framework. In his account of the second-person standpoint, for instance, Stephen Darwall (2006) claims that any second-personal address necessarily presupposes symmetrical relations between free and rational beings. Since Darwall appeals to the speech act theory in order to establish his thesis, I will contrast his account with that of Jean-François Lyotard, who draws upon the speech act theory to argue against the symmetry condition and for the priority of the feeling of obligation. Finally, I will offer some thoughts about the phenomenology of address and claim in light of Heidegger's ontological concept of the conscience as a "call."

## 1 FROM HUSSERL TO LEVINAS: THE NORMATIVE GROUND OF INTENTIONALITY

What are the phenomenological conditions for the possession of robust intentional content, that is, for experiencing something *as* something? Levinas's thesis that ethics is first philosophy is an answer to this question, where "ethics" is a technical term for an essential feature of second-person phenomenology, namely, the experience of being addressed by a normative claim. Levinas's argument for the priority of ethics over ontology amounts to the idea that this experience cannot be clarified solely in terms of categories that would hold in the absence of any second-person phenomenology. The concept of the "face" emblematizes this point. Not an object of perception—i.e., something that belongs to a common world of real things accessible to everyone—the face is rather that which grounds the possibility of norm-governed perceptual experience. Second-person phenomenology is thus not *constituted*—for instance, through empathy—but *constituting*. Here, I will briefly summarize the argument.

In the fifth *Cartesian Meditation*, Husserl recognizes both that the full intentional content of perception is not available to a solipsistic subject and that intersubjectivity brings with it the normative distinction between "real" and "not real." However, his account does not explicitly link this normative moment to the constitutive role of second-person phenomenology in our sense. Instead, he tries to move from solipsistic consciousness (the "sphere of ownness") to the point where radical alterity, another constituting subject, can become an intentional content for me. The sphere of ownness involves what he calls a "*kind* of nature"—a "unitary coherent stratum of the phenomenon world," the "correlate of continuously harmonious world experience" (1969, 96)—but this unity and coherence is of a curious kind, since it does not allow for unequivocal re-identification of particulars. In *Totality and Infinity*, Levinas describes this stratum of "separated" experience as "enjoyment" correlated with "the elemental" and "mythical" (1969, 140–2), while Sartre, in *Being and Nothingness*, points toward it in describing the for-itself's "possibles" that cannot be modalized as "probablities" (1956, 353). If such a "nature" may be thought as a space of affordances correlated to the promptings of my embodied consciousness, the question is how this "mythical" nature can be constituted as an objective one, that is, how my intentional content can come to admit of genuinely normative ordering.

For Husserl, this requires that solipsism—in which I experience myself not as "I, this man," but as unique embodied ego holding sway in an affordance space—give way to being one among others. But how can *anything* in this "unitary stratum" present itself not just as a difference within it, but as *other than me*? Even another animate organism could be experienced as part of my sphere of ownness—say, as another body of my own that behaves differently from the one in which I hold sway but is still thoroughly constituted by me and *as* me. Husserl's argument turns on the idea that experiencing the other body involves an "apperceptive transfer" or "analogizing apperception" from my own "appearance systems" to a set of appearance systems in the other that *cannot* be mine because they cannot occur in my ownness sphere simultaneously with my own appearance systems (1969, 119). But this won't work, since in this respect, they are no different than the back side of a physical thing, which also cannot be experienced by me simultaneously with the front side and yet does not establish anything "other" than what is my own. A preliminary conclusion pointing to the constitutive independence of second-person phenomenology follows from this.

It is simply not the case that what signifies the radical absence or interiority of the Other is the other's *consciousness*. The Other's consciousness is beyond the reach of my direct apprehension, but this does not suffice to establish it as "other" than some peculiarly constituted part of my own transcendental subjectivity. Rather, what is radically beyond my reach—not at all part of the intentional content, the "animate organism"—is the Other's *responsibility* for his or her own life. Responsibility, whether my own or that of the Other, cannot be understood in the Husserlian framework of acts of consciousness and their intentional meaning-correlates because it is a performative—*taking* responsibility—that presupposes a very specific sort of responsiveness to the force of normative claims.

In contrast, Levinas's second-person phenomenology recognizes that to attribute this performative responsibility to the Other by analogy with my own self-responsibility cannot be the first form of my encounter with the Other. Rather, my own *taking* responsibility implies that I have already responded to a claim made upon me. For Levinas, the Other's "exteriority" does not consist of the difference between my appearance systems and his or hers, but in the Other's ability to call "my joyous possession of the world" normatively into *question* (1969, 76). Before I can constitute the Other as performatively responsible through an analogizing apperception from my own responsibility, I must *receive* this sense of myself from the face of the Other. Thus, the Other's claim on me can derive its force neither from myself nor from any property that I share with other things. And for this reason, the claim through which the Other "invests" my freedom cannot *derive* from the Other's visage; a face is a face *because* I respond to such a claim. The face is the correlate of a feeling of obligation, an experience of being commanded that first *establishes* a "relation" between me and the Other by calling me to take responsibility for my freedom. This command, in turn, establishes speech as "welcome" or dialogue—the generosity that informs reason as the "generality of concepts," the source of "commonplaces" that put "the world in common," i.e., make the norm-governed re-identification of particulars possible (1969, 76).

Sartre's modification of Husserl's analysis provides a way to appreciate the significance of Levinas's argument. Sartre recognizes that to account phenomenologically for the experience of the Other as another subjectivity, we must begin with how I come to experience myself as an object. A solipsistic for-itself cannot accomplish this on its own, since, as with Husserl, it occupies a world of affordances correlated with the upsurge of pre-reflective consciousness, a world in which the conditions for self-identification are lacking. It is only in responding to "the look" that self-objectification becomes possible and, as with Levinas, the look is not something I perceive (not "two ocular globes"), but rather that which enables the distinction, *within* perception, between what is objective or real and what is merely "my experience."

Thus, Sartre's account recognizes the constitutive function of second-person phenomenology. Prior to the look, the for-itself can disclose the world in terms of affordances (its "possibles") that correlate to what it is doing (its "project"), but it cannot *name* either its project or its motives. The for-itself has no qualities that can be said to determine it in any objective way. When I hear footsteps, two things occur at once, marking the juncture of first- and second-person phenomenologies. First, my "possibles" become objective "probables"—i.e., the affordance-world becomes a normatively structured space in which my disclosure of it is modalized and relativized by the threat of the other who can *contest* my take on things, make me deal with the fact that the world is not mine, but ours. My hiding place is *also* the site of my eventual discovery. Second, a "self comes to haunt the for-itself." This self belongs to the for-itself—*is* it—but is not constituted by it. Sartre expresses this by noting that my original consciousness of the other as a subject—that is, my original experience of myself as an object—is shame. We shall return to the issue of shame below, but first let us draw these introductory remarks to a close.

The constitutive achievement of second-person phenomenology, in contrast to a consciousness that lacks such a phenomenology, can be expressed as follows: I can only constitute the Other *as* a subject (that is, as another "rational being" or constituting ego) if I have already experienced what it is to respond to a normative claim. Such constitution is always a *second movement* attendant upon my shame, an experience of being normatively addressed, which Sartre acknowledges by calling shame "a confession" (1956, 350). The problem with Sartre's analysis, however, is that it does not explain precisely *why* my experience of myself as an object should be an experience of shame. In his account, the normative claim of the look operates, but is not explicitly theorized. The look must from the outset be a form of normative address, a second-person phenomenon, a *judgment* on my behavior; otherwise, my shame is incomprehensible. It is here that Levinas's insistence on the normative asymmetry of the second-person standpoint must be introduced.

The asymmetry in question consists of the fact that phenomenologically, I must have always already acknowledged a normative claim on me. For Levinas, this means that I must have responded to a command. The owner of the face is not perceived, but is always a matter of subsequent negotiation, i.e., part of the very response to the command that makes me take responsibility. Thus, the Other's authority to command cannot derive from ontology—that is, from some prior ontic property that the Other and I share (nature, rationality, ability to suffer, etc.). Rather, the command comes first—*You* shall not commit murder!—and it is registered as a *feeling* of interdiction, namely, obligation. If I have no such feeling, there is no second-person phenomenology. Thus, the command is "ethical resistance" that transcends any creature that putatively issues it. For, while I can kill the one whom I suppose to be issuing the command, the death of that being does not remove the obligation. The command is the affective impossibility of the I-can, an absolute limit on my freedom, because the addresser of the command is prior to all objective identification and re-identification. Here, second-person phenomenology proves to be *constitutive*, the birth of "responsible" freedom, of a consciousness responsive to the normative regulation that makes an objective world possible. Second-person phenomenology thus uncovers what is essential to the performative enactment of *taking* responsibility for my freedom.

## 2  THE SECOND-PERSON STANDPOINT

These findings of second-person phenomenology are of philosophical importance in many areas of contemporary philosophy. Here, I shall take up one recent example. In a contribution to what we might call "social ontology," Stephen Darwall has developed a powerful account of the "second-person standpoint" (SPS), which he defines as "the perspective you and I take up when we make and acknowledge claims on one another's conduct and will" (2006, 3).[1] For Darwall, the SPS provides the basis for a broadly Kantian moral theory in which key concepts (freedom, autonomy, respect, dignity, obligation, etc.) are derived from the "normative felicity conditions" for a certain sort of communicative practice. In what follows, I examine a few key points in Darwall's wide-ranging investigation, focusing on areas where second-person phenomenology might suggest somewhat different conclusions. It is not that Darwall's account ignores phenomenology, but rather that, in focusing on the SPS as already constituted, he overlooks the *constituting* role we have found second-person phenomenology to play. Specifically, his failure to recognize the ("conceptual") priority of the feeling of being claimed leads to an overly rationalistic picture of the ground of obligation.

The fact that SPS is a form of interpersonal communication and a source of what Darwall calls "second-personal reasons" situates it within the "personalistic attitude" in Husserl's sense.[2] Indeed, for Darwall, "person is a second-person concept," a Lockean "forensick term" that is "essentially connected to imputing legal or moral responsibility" (2006, 80). Neither persons nor second-personal reasons "would exist but for the possibility of the second-personal address involved in claiming or demanding" (2006, 9). Further, Darwall, like Husserl, sees SPS as grounded in "empathy" (the "capacity to put oneself in another's shoes" [2006, 44]), since the kind of communication it is requires experiencing a "reciprocity of perspectives." But this is a distinct sort of empathy. It is not merely that I see the other seeing the same things I see; rather, it involves "reciprocal recognition," because addressing a claim to her can succeed only if "both parties are committed to various normative presuppositions" (2006, 47–48). Hence "I must be able to see the other's response to my address as more or less rational from her point of view" (2006, 44).

Though it would be possible, then, to approach Darwall's account through the second-person phenomenology found in Husserl's analysis of the personalistic attitude, I shall concentrate instead on how Darwall establishes these "normative presuppositions," asking whether he does justice to the question elided by Husserl's appeal to empathy in grounding the personalistic attitude—namely, *how* the normative claims of the other can *call* me to responsibility, how being moved by "second-personal reasons" is at all possible.

In Darwall's account, SPS is essentially holistic and practical. But it is also a "version of the first-person standpoint" (2006, 9) and so amenable to second-person phenomenological analysis in our sense. This may be seen by drawing upon Darwall's own Hume-inspired example (2006, 5–10). When someone steps on my gouty toes, the suffering I endure may induce rage and violence. Such "pathological" reactions, however, are not second-personal, but "object-directed." In contrast, I might adopt SPS and insist that the other get off my toes, address a claim against the other which, with the proper uptake, gives him a second-personal reason to act in a certain way, a *justifying* reason. That this sort of reason is not merely a matter of third-person assessment of what is objectively good or desirable—that it is accessible only from first-person experience—is illustrated by the existence of what Strawson (1962) called "reactive attitudes," the phenomenology of which plays an extraordinarily important role in Darwall's analysis of SPS. Reactive attitudes, in this account, are themselves forms of communication and address. The resentment I feel when someone steps on my toes, for example, entails not merely that the other has done me an objective harm, but that he has transgressed a norm that we each expect the other to acknowledge as valid. My feeling is itself a kind of blame or sanction that asserts my authority to demand that the other respect a norm of personal relations that trumps the sort of third-person reasons of utility or benefit that might be used to justify his act. Of course, there can be excuses—the other was pushed onto my toes by the crowd in a subway—but then the resentment disappears, or becomes unwarranted.

From this, we can also see why SPS is essentially a *practical* standpoint. My address to the other does not merely attest a matter of fact—morality requires that you not step on my toes—but is an attempt to get him to do something, provide him with a kind of *practical reason* or motivation to get off my toes. Communicating my resentment, as opposed to mere displeasure, makes a normative claim on the other's behavior and is a form of "practically directed and directive thought" (Darwall 2006, 9)—a command—in which I address the other as able to be so directed "from their own volition." Such a command presupposes that the addressee is able to be motivated by "normative reasons" and not just threats or inducements. It thereby entails a "species of practical freedom" that "lacks any analogue in the theoretical realm" (2006, 22), one that can be recognized only in SPS itself.

This brings us to the third point: a first-person reactive attitude entails that I and the other already operate within a context that involves normative success conditions for the practice of making demands. SPS is thus both holistic and "closed" in the sense that the sort of second-personal reasons it provides cannot exist outside SPS. This means that to address claims and acknowledge claims addressed to me successfully, both I and the other must possess a kind of interpersonal skill that Darwall calls "second-personal competence" (2006, 22). Second-personal competence is manifested in the agent's ability to deploy "a circle of interdefinable second-personal notions," which become available to us only if we "assume"—that is, adopt—SPS (2006, 23). That we *do* adopt that standpoint is demonstrated by reactive attitudes like resentment; that we *must* adopt it is something that Darwall argues for explicitly. But what does it mean to "assume" SPS, to enter into the practice of address and claim? The existence of reactive attitudes suggests that it is not necessarily a matter of decision, but that it requires a certain skill or competence means that it is not a matter of mere "nature" either. All this requires further phenomenological clarification.

The first thing to note is that Darwall's analysis, in contrast to Levinas, ties SPS to a very strong symmetry condition. For him, both to receive and to issue a command presupposes "mutual recognition" in roughly Hegel's (or perhaps Fichte's) sense: "[A]ny second-personal address whatsoever presupposes a common second-personal competence, responsibility, and authority that addresser and addressee share as free and rational agents" (2006, 23). To assume SPS, in this view, it is not enough that I receive a command (in the "accusative") and obey because I feel obligated by it; rather, I must be able to identify the source of the command and recognize her as a free and rational being with the same authority to command that I myself possess. Only so can the command provide me with a second-personal *reason* to obey. To be under an obligation, then, is not merely to acknowledge a command as binding on me; rather, it is to have a *valid* second-personal reason, whose validity depends on the symmetry between addresser and addressee as second-personally competent agents with the requisite second-person standing. Thus, in contrast to Levinas's second-person phenomenology of the feeling of obligation as the "end of powers" and the birth of "reason," Darwall's SPS is an already constituted practice in which reason governs from the start. The phenomenological question, then, is how Darwall manages to identify the "rules" of this game and whether, in so doing, he does justice to second-person phenomenology.

The holism of SPS means that second-personal "standing"—that is, the status of being a player—can be established "only within the circle of four interrelated ideas of claim, accountability, second-person reason, and the species of authority that is related to these" (2006, 13), together with other concepts (freedom, autonomy, person, dignity, respect) that derive from them. Further, "there is no way to break into this circle from outside it" since "propositions formulated only with normative and evaluative concepts that are not already implicitly second-personal cannot adequately ground propositions formulated with concepts within the circle" (2006, 12). How, then, does Darwall discover and ground these claims? Certainly, there must be an element of second-person phenomenology involved, since to be "within the circle" is to experience oneself and the world in a second-personal way. But Darwall does not choose to proceed (entirely) phenomenologically. Nor does he follow Korsgaard in formulating a "transcendental argument" to the effect that second-personal concepts "are transcendental presuppositions of the practical standpoint" as such, since this too would be to seek justification outside SPS (2006, 32). Instead, he seems to practice a form of descriptive metaphysics in which the necessity of certain presuppositions can be demonstrated through a combination of conceptual analysis and speech act theory.

According to Austin, upon whom Darwall draws here, the success of a speech act rests upon a set of "felicity conditions," conditions which, as Austin sees it, are *conventional*. A promise depends on the conventions of the language in which it is uttered, and so a promise made in German to one who does not speak German cannot succeed; a voice vote has illocutionary force only when uttered by one who is an authorized member of the deliberating body, and so on.[3] In this conventionalist view, then, a certain speech act may succeed at one point in time and fail at another, when the relevant conventions can no longer be obtained. In adopting Austin's framework, however, Darwall attempts to specify non-conventional, "*normative* felicity conditions*,*" namely, "what must be true for second-personal reasons actually to exist and be successfully given through second-person address" (2006, 4, 55f). Thus, while an obligation might *appear* to have validly arisen through second-personal address at some point in history— Darwall discusses slavery in this context—it might be that no such obligation arose in fact, if the normative felicity conditions were not met. This means that the conditions, or "presuppositions," of SPS have an aspect of ideality and cannot be directly read off from any putative example of an address or claim. The symmetry requirements that Darwall identifies have the character of what Habermas called "rational reconstructions"—that is, attempts to specify in categorical terms (and by means of a discourse that cannot claim for itself the status of an "ultimate justification") what is taken to be the "intuitive" content of what we are committed to in being competent participants in a certain practice (Habermas 1999, 97f).

The nature of this commitment is also, in Darwall's view, something of an idealization, for he does not claim that agents must have specific commitments in mind or be able to articulate them in order to possess second-person competence. Thus, Darwall's approach seems to be a hybrid along Habermasian lines: starting with a kind of phenomenology (of reactive attitudes, of being "within the circle"), Darwall engages in a theoretical reconstruction of normative success conditions, a reconstruction that can be contested. But if any such contest must take place, as Darwall insists, from within SPS itself, the only means other than logical consistency for calling some presupposition into question is *phenomenological*—for instance, on the basis of the claim that the given reconstruction leaves out important aspects of that very phenomenology.

78  Steven Crowell

Now, Darwall's reconstruction focuses on Kantian themes and, above all, on the question of how a command that one receives can constitute a *valid* obligation, thus giving me a genuine second-person reason to obey. How can the authority to command another be legitimate? Being responsible *for* something is second-personal because it is first of all being accountable *to* someone (2006, 68), and that someone can have the requisite authority only if she and I are on an equal footing. The concern with validity—rather than the full phenomenology of SPS—drives Darwall's argument. But while relations of mutual recognition may be felicity conditions for a certain game of moral accountability as we currently understand it (and may even be *normative* felicity conditions for morality as such), the *phenomenology* of SPS, and the competence one exhibits in the practice of legitimation, are not *exhausted* by that network of conditions. And if that is the case, the phenomenology of obligation, of normative beholdenness, may not be exhausted by the way it figures in that practice either.

We can see this by turning to Lyotard, who also draws on speech act theory. Though Lyotard defended this approach in detail in *The Differend*, here I will consider only the sketch he gives of it in *Just Gaming*.

## 3  INTERLUDE: PHENOMENOLOGY, PRAGMATICS, AND INCOMMENSURABILITY

Lyotard's text, like Darwall's, focuses on the question of justice: what is the ground for *valid* claims on another's freedom? What are my *obligations* with regard to others? And, like Darwall, he explores justice through a second-person phenomenology informed by the speech act theory. For Lyotard, however, Darwall's reconstruction of SPS is not a "pure" account of address or claim, but a hybrid that consists of fusing together two separate "games"—the prescriptive and the "constative," or descriptive. Between these two, there is no "common measure" to tie the experience of being commanded to the commitments entailed in *any* specific set of theoretical principles used to justify it (1985, 50). Lyotard distinguishes between a prescriptive ("Do X!"), which can be expressed as "You *must* do X," and a descriptive ("You *ought* to do X"), which expresses a prescriptive that has already been inscribed in a constative discourse that presumes to ground it—for instance, "Among us it is the case that doing X is obligatory" (1985, 44). Here, I will briefly examine Lyotard's argument for incommensurability and then sketch his own second-person phenomenology of the uptake of a prescription.

For Lyotard, the locus of incommensurability lies in the different *pragmatics* of the speech acts involved, the structure of their illocutionary force. Any such act has three pragmatic "poles"—that of the addressor, the addressee, and the referent—not all of which need be "marked" in the act itself. In a description like, "Water boils at 100 degrees Celsius," for example, neither the addressor nor the addressee is marked, though the referent (water) is. In contrast, the constative statement, "I think that water boils at 100 degrees Celsius," *does* mark the addressor (and the referent), but not the addressee, and thereby makes a quite different move in the constative game. The basic form of a prescription, in turn, is command—"Do not kill!"—and a command leaves the addressor pole unmarked, while the addressee position is *always* "you," whether marked ("You must not kill") or unmarked ("Do not kill!"). A command is always addressed to me (in the accusative) and, according to Lyotard, "in order to understand the game of obligation, the pole of the sender *must* be neutralized" or "left hanging" (1985, 71). Why is that?

The reason is that the point or "stakes" of the game of prescription is to get "you" to *do* something; of itself it raises no questions of justification or validity. Being the addressee of a command does not depend on my being able to *identify* the addressor. There is a "feeling of obligation," I feel myself "responsible for" acting in a certain way: I (namely, as "you") have been normatively claimed by an address. Of course, I generally assume that I know who the addressor is; in *naming* the addressor, however, I no longer occupy the pragmatic position of an addressee of a command, but that of the *addressor* in an additional (and very different) discourse, constative discourse. This involves "normative felicity conditions" different from those that govern prescription, and on their basis, I can demand a reason why I should obey: "You have no right to tell me what to do; give me one good reason." But in that case, I have changed the game. I cognitively "mark" the addressor position by situating "you" within a theory (such as Darwall's) that specifies when such commands are *legitimately* delivered. According to Lyotard, however, this move can yield only aliases for the addressor. Even in Darwall's picture, when Sam demands something of me, it is not Sam in all his glory who does so, but rather Sam as an alias for "free and rational being," a concept to which I am supposedly normatively committed and which authorizes me, in turn, to cease being the "you" who is addressed by the command and become the "I" who demands that Sam provide some legitimating reasons.

Now, Lyotard's point is not that this hybrid game cannot be played; rather, he makes the *phenomenological* point that the game will yield a *differend*—the domination of one set of rules by another, between which there is no common measure—if the theoretical discourse is taken to govern the pragmatics of prescription. Following Levinas, he holds that "Western" thought—notably the Platonic expedient of subordinating prescription to truth and the Kantian expedient of subordinating prescription to autonomy—has consistently operated in this way. But neither operation succeeds in grounding prescriptions: "Between statements that narrate and describe something and statements that prescribe something, there is always some talking to be done. There is a change of language game" (1985, 17).

Lyotard does not dismiss such talking—in Levinas's terms, the rational "dialogue" that ensues upon welcoming the command of the Other (1969,

101)—but he argues that the "normative felicity conditions" of the *legitimation process* cannot be taken to govern the prescriptive character of the command. Phenomenologically, there is a "feeling of obligation," and in deciding how I am to respond—in interpreting what the command means and what it entails about how I am to go on—I can employ only Aristotelian *phronesis* or Kantian "reflective" judgment. To do justice to the prescriptive, I cannot subordinate it to theory; instead, according to Lyotard, I am "guided by an Idea" in the Kantian sense. A concern with justice, for instance, is guided by what Lyotard calls "the faculty of the social bond" (1985, 91), a form of empathy concerned with how *my* situated and therefore creative response to the command (including its possible rejection) contributes to what ought to be the case among *us*. In this way, I put myself forward as an example—not as justified in the sense of possessing a demonstrable right, but as (fallibly) *exemplary* of what is best in regard to justice. Possession of this faculty of the social bond (empathy) is a kind of "second-person competence" that does not depend on there being a common measure between descriptive and prescriptive games.

In contrast to Platonistic approaches, in which obligations are grounded in something like the third-person truth of an objective theory of the good, it might appear that an appeal to autonomy—the idea of self-legislation that arises from the first-person practical standpoint—could provide the missing "common measure." But here too, according to Lyotard, there is a subtle change of game, since the very idea of self-*command* assumes that there can be an uncontested passage between the pragmatic positions of addressor and addressee. Prescription situates the addressee in the "accusative," and autonomy presupposes that the "you" who receives the command is *at the same time* the I (as rational being) who delivers it. But between I as the accusative addressee and the "same I" functioning as the addressor, there is "always some talking to be done," namely a *theory* by means of which alone I will be able to identify the source of the command with "I myself."

Thus, even if, with Darwall, one substitutes the "I will" for the "I think" as the practical ground of obligation—that is, even if one imagines that the question of legitimacy is a matter of what all free and rational beings can *will*—one assumes that the theoretical idea of a "free and rational being" provides a common measure between the I who commands and the you who is commanded. But in fact, this eliminates the prescriptive altogether, a game in which the pole of the addressor is *always* unmarked (or occupied by an alias): "I cannot put myself in his place [. . .] since his command cannot come from me" (Lyotard & Thébaud 1985, 39). When Sam is addressed by a command, it will be as "you," whereas when Sam *addresses* a command to someone else (including himself), or expresses his reasons, or seeks the other's justification for issuing a command, it will be as "I," a function that lacks common measure with Sam as "you." As Lyotard puts it, "there will always be a multiplicity of functions for the same proper name" (1985, 40).

Can the phenomenological account of the pre-reflective self-awareness of consciousness provide an uncontested bridge between the "I" and the (accusative) "you" here, since both functions involve the same pre-reflective self-consciousness? No, because the issue is not *whether* the I-function and the you-function belong to the same being. Indeed, since second-person phenomenology is an instance of first-person experience, there is no doubt, phenomenologically, that the same entity is involved. But the question is whether the unmarked position of the *addressor* can be occupied by that being, and here, the phenomenology of obligation cannot help us. It is not the ontology of the self, but the incommensurability of the two games, that stands in the way of the appeal to autonomy. If there is no common measure between the prescriptive and the descriptive games, the same incommensurability obtains between my second-personal positioning in the "accusative" and the claim that I, as free and rational being, am the addressor of *legitimate* demands. In making the latter claim, I play another, constative game centered on the referent, a game whose outcome is not a demonstrable *presupposition* for the uptake of a command in its own terms.

In this view, then, the normative force of a command does not presuppose the autonomy of the will. As we noted above, contesting a rational reconstruction of the presuppositions of SPS can appeal only to a better phenomenology of the first-person experience of obligation. The second-person phenomenology that one attempts to reconstruct as "autonomy" is better described as a matter of *committing* myself to a claim that I *feel* to be binding and using my judgment, imagination, and "play" in trying to find an appropriate way of responding to the claim, to live up to it. In so doing, I can (and most often will) appeal to reason, but the competence I exhibit here follows from, and does not govern, my acknowledging a command that has "called me into question." Certainly, one way to go on is to engage with others in discourse oriented toward "mutual coming to terms" (*Verständigung*), and in that process 'We' may come to agree that only laws that all can agree to on the basis of "uncoerced argumentation" will be valid. Habermas suggests this when he argues that *all* substantive moral questions are to be decided through "real discourses" between all affected parties (1999, 94). But his attempt to preserve a modicum of moral cognitivism by means of a theory of the normative transcendental-pragmatic conditions of practical argumentation fails for the same reason Darwall's does: it is a rational reconstruction of certain "intuitions" about what we are committed to when engaged in the practice, and the phenomenology of that practice does not support the reconstruction.

To conclude this interlude, Lyotard's version of second-person phenomenology does not begin with SPS in Darwall's sense, but with the feeling of being obligated, an experience in which second-person phenomenology exhibits its *constituting* role. Such feeling is the entry move into SPS, but it can also stand alone, and in that case, the pole of the addressor is "transcendent." I need not *know* who is sending the prescription, who has a "face," but I am "bound" to go on in some way (1985, 69). When the command concerns justice (what we owe one another), I will be guided by my idea of the social bond, will judge in its light how I am to act in particular circumstances. Since such reflective judgment is not governed by law, I cannot justify the way I go on by saying that it conforms to what all rational beings would choose, but I *do* put myself forward, in a certain way, as exemplary. Grounded in empathy, "the faculty of the social bond," justice is my social sense. It does not require mutual recognition (though the demand for mutual recognition may be an outcome of it) or *any* specific theoretical account of what it is about me that authorizes me to go on in this way. The faculty of the social bond requires only that I find myself in the situation of the addressee of a command that calls my "powers" normatively into question.

## 4 SHAME, GUILT, AND CONSCIENCE

Can second-person phenomenology get us any further than what appears to be a choice between a second-person standpoint that elides the constitutive achievement of second-person address and a kind of antinomy between the addressor and addressee poles that leaves the command "transcendent" to all ontology? Later, I will argue that Heidegger's account of conscience provides a way of bringing the addressor and addressee poles together without subordinating one to the other. But first, it will be useful to return briefly to Darwall—specifically, to his account of guilt and shame, which involves an instructive phenomenological distortion. For if in our view, shame is a paradigmatic second-person phenomenon, for Darwall, it is specifically *third-personal*, and his reasons for this view reflect a failure to see the constitutive role of second-person phenomenology.

Darwall's discussion of shame occurs in a section dedicated to reactive attitudes, attitudes which themselves presuppose the normative felicity conditions that characterize SPS generally. In these terms, it appears that shame fails to be a second-person phenomenon: "Like guilt, shame feels as if one is rightly regarded or seen in a certain way. But here the relevant regard is not second-personal; it is third-personal" (1985, 71). Darwall arrives at this conclusion by appealing to Sartre's example of the look: shame is the result of the other's *objectifying* gaze; the other's look does not *address* my freedom but ossifies it, encrusting me with an "outside" that is mine to acknowledge but is not "my responsibility." The shame that thus arises does acknowledge the other's authority, but in Darwall's view, such authority is not second-personal; it is "fundamentally epistemic and third-personal. One sees the other as having standing to see one in a certain way (and oneself as correctly thus seen)" (2006, 72). "To feel guilt," in contrast, "is to feel oneself authoritatively addressed as free," a view that is "incompatible with a purely 'objective' view of oneself" (2006, 72).

Thus, Darwall's argument depends on two points: first, that shame arises from the other's purely epistemic judgment, one that attributes to me features that I acknowledge possessing; and second, that this judgment does not address me in my freedom. It is not blame, a stance that makes a *normative* claim on me, to which the genuinely second-personal reactive attitude would be guilt, "an acknowledgment of one's blameworthiness that recognizes both the grounds of blame and [. . .] the authority to level it" (2006, 71).

There are, of course, differences between shame and guilt, but is it true that shame is a reaction merely to being seen by the other but not addressed by her? Is the authority granted the other in this feeling exclusively epistemic? It seems that Darwall has been misled here by the same lacuna we found in Sartre's original view: the phenomenological character of shame cannot be adequately explained merely as a consequence of being *objectified*, no matter what objective predicates are attributed to me by the other and acknowledged by me. If I feel ashamed of being naked, this is not merely because the other has seen that I am naked; rather, it is because I simultaneously feel that I *ought not to be* naked, that the other judges what he or she sees in a *normative* way. Darwall seems to admit as much in a latter passage, where he says that "shame" must be connected to "some ideal of a presentable or morally decent self" (2006, 163). The self that "haunts" the pre-reflective for-itself is me, but this "me" is simultaneously an object for the other and the recipient (you, accusative) of a normative address. Whether or not shame is a reactive attitude in Darwall's sense, then, in the phenomenological sense it is one: it acknowledges a claim on me ("You should not peek in keyholes") made by another who possesses something *like* second-personal authority, an authority which I affectively acknowledge as having normative force: "My shame is a confession" (Sartre 1956, 350).

Darwall might object that unlike guilt, in which I affectively "take responsibility" for what is claimed in the other's address, shame yields the response of "wanting to escape from view" (2006, 72). But while this may well be an aspect of shame (and perhaps also guilt), the phenomenology of shame already includes taking responsibility for the way I am judged by the other. "Confession" itself is a kind of taking-responsibility, even when it is also possible for me to try to cover up that confession by making excuses, dominating the other, and so on. If Darwall is right that shame is connected to "some ideal of a presentable or morally decent self," then it is not merely a matter of fleeing the other's gaze but, more deeply, of *desiring* the other as what establishes in me the possibility of such an ideal. As Levinas puts it: "The Other is not initially a fact, is not an obstacle, does not threaten me with death; he is *desired* in my shame" (1969, 84). Indeed, "this way of measuring oneself against the perfection of infinity"—i.e., the *ideality* of a "morally decent self"—"is not a theoretical consideration; it is accomplished *as shame*, where freedom discovers itself murderous in its very exercise" (1969, 84). For Levinas, then, the "shame that freedom feels for itself" is first a "welcoming" of the other's normative judgment (command) and only subsequently a kind of flight. This feeling oneself addressed in one's freedom, of being "called into question" and thus desirous of measure, is what Levinas calls "conscience" (1969, 86). If SPS governs our relations to one another by means of the presuppositions of symmetry that Darwall details, second-person phenomenology shows how SPS itself is *constituted* in conscience, which is not governed by the same presuppositions.

For Levinas, conscience is announced in the affect of shame, which acknowledges the Other's normative, though occult, authority. Conscience, the feeling of obligation, is thus the *original* second-personal phenomenon. For Darwall, in contrast, whose book contains no entry for "conscience" in the index, conscience is something like the internalized voice of the moral community. It is a second-personal phenomenon, but a derivative one, possible only where I and the other are already committed to the normative felicity conditions of SPS.

According to Darwall, shame differs from guilt in that the latter acknowledges normative blame. Thanks to empathy, I am "vulnerable to the other" who blames me; that is, I can see my behavior from the point of view of the other's moral (and not merely epistemic) judgment and so come to feel its justice in the form of guilt (2006, 168). Such guilt seems to be what Darwall means by conscience, which, following Mill, he characterizes as a kind of "internal sanction"—"not merely a painful feeling," but "a painful 'appearance' that we shouldn't have done what we did, that not doing it was 'in itself obligatory.' We have a putative awareness of having acted contrary to what members of the moral community (and we ourselves as such members) justifiably demand" (2006, 169).[4] Thus, empathy yields conscience by "bringing others' views inside our perspective so that they can be part of our own critical reflection and not just recorded as what others think" (2006, 170). Conscience or guilt, but not shame, is second-personal because only conscience exhibits the requisite second-personal *competence*. It is like an affective internal sanction that depends on empathetically acknowledging the claim of my moral community to have authority to establish blame-*worthiness*.

But does the idea of an internal sanction—and with it the (putative) connection between second-person authority, the moral community, and accountability in the sense of *valid* claim or command—exhaust the phenomenology of conscience? There is no doubt that conscience can involve pangs, painful feelings of having failed to do what we ought to have done (which is not quite the same thing as saying that we have transgressed a "valid" command that can be "justified" rationally). But there is more to the phenomenon of conscience than this. I can be guided by conscience—be oriented conscientiously toward a measure of the good or right—even when I don't have a "guilty" conscience, and such guidance need not be registered as fear of censure by the internalized moral community. Nor is it a matter of what Nietzsche calls "good conscience," i.e., a kind of sanctimoniousness arising from toeing the community's moral line. Further, conscience can bother me even when it is not intentionally directed toward some specific act. It can attach, in a far more diffuse way, to a concern for my being *as such*, my "not being as I ought," in a sense not reducible to the moral. Though this "existential" conscience, too, involves being oriented by a normative claim, and thus has a second-personal aspect, it is not properly described as being governed by an already established moral community whose norms I have internalized. To see this, we may turn to Heidegger's contribution to second-person phenomenology.

## 5  SECOND-PERSON PHENOMENOLOGY IN HEIDEGGER'S ACCOUNT OF CONSCIENCE

Elsewhere, I have argued that Heidegger's ontological account of the call of conscience as "guilty," when seen as part of the tripartite care-structure in breakdown, describes how I "must" take over "being-a-ground"—which I interpret to mean measuring one's facticity (in the form, say, of one's inclinations) in light of better and worse.[5] Since this gives rise to justifying (or normative) reasons, conscience is a phenomenological condition on SPS. Given Heidegger's claim that the care structure in breakdown discloses *Dasein* as *solus ipse*, however, it is fair to ask whether conscience is a second-personal phenomenon at all. To approach this issue, we may begin with a much-debated moment in Heidegger's description of the "call":

> 'It' calls, against our expectations and even against our will. On the other hand, the call undoubtedly does not come from someone else who is with me in the world. The call comes *from* me and yet *overcomes* me (*Der Ruf kommt aus mir und doch über mich*).
>
> (Heidegger 1962, 320)

To understand the implications of this description, we must first note that *Dasein* is *essentially* Being-with (*Mitsein*). The "solipsism" achieved in breakdown reveals I-myself, individuated from *das Man*, but it does not involve the absence of all relation to others (1962, 233). Thus, it has neither the structure of Levinasian "separation" nor that of a Sartrean "for-itself." But how can the address registered in the call of conscience be second-personal, since it comes "from me"? And what does it mean that it "overcomes me"?

I have argued that what is essential to the second-personal phenomenology of normative address is the feeling of obligation, an affective response to a command that for that very reason binds me. It is not necessary that the caller be identified, and Heidegger's description registers this. To say that the call "overcomes me" signals (in Levinasian terms) its "height"—that is, its *normative* character. But as affective, as feeling, what overcomes me can arise neither from my decision nor from self-legislation based on what any rational being as such could will. It is not a matter of second-person competence in Darwall's sense. Nor can it be the internalized demand of the moral community, since in a breakdown, my ties to that community have lost their grip: "the 'world' can offer nothing more, and neither can the Dasein-with of others" (1962, 232). Yet Heidegger goes on to identify the caller as *Dasein* "in its uncanniness" (1962, 321), which calls to *Dasein* as "fallen" in its character as the "one-self." Is this, then, another hybrid theory that moves from a second-personal phenomenology of obligation to a third-personal ontological *account* of the source of the call?

Closer examination reveals a more complex picture. To say that the caller is "Dasein in its uncanniness" is not to eliminate the transcendence of the call's source, but to illuminate something about the care structure that constitutes selfhood. If *Dasein* is defined as a being "for which, in its being, that very being is essentially an *issue*" for it (1962, 117), then to be (something) at all is to *try* to be it, to care about what it (normatively) means to be what I am trying to be: father, teacher, morally presentable person, and so on. In Heideggerian terms, the meaning of what I am *doing*—the abilities that I exercise "in order to" get things done—depends on that "for the sake of which" I do what I do, a certain way of trying to *be* something (1962, 116). Being for the sake of something is always socially informed; what it is to be a father or teacher is measured by social-role norms in light of which I assess my achievement. But such measuring is not equivalent to robotic conformity: I *try* to live up to what I *take* to be the meaning of fatherhood or teaching. For the most part, I do so inauthentically, that is, I operate in conformity with social norms as though I had no responsibility for the norms themselves, as though "what one does" were grounded in the social whole as an immutable fact. But in *Angst*—the affect that gets "articulated" in conscience—I come to recognize that in addition to the roles I occupy more or less successfully, my "ownmost possibility" lies in succeeding or failing at *being a self* at all. This is where to look for second-person phenomenology in Heidegger's account of the call of conscience.

The ontological fact that to be a self at all is to be at issue for oneself is brought to light phenomenologically in the breakdown of all my social roles in *Angst*. To be at issue for myself means that even when these measures of my being have lost their grip, I still "must" understand myself as oriented toward measure. The call of conscience is how I register this demand, and to "hear" the call is to recognize the stakes: my commitment ("resoluteness") is what allows specific norms to "bind" me in the manner of "freedom." I am in this sense responsible for the normative force of the norms in light of which I act. To act authentically is to act in *light* of this responsibility, in which case the command to "take over being a ground" has become "transparent" (1962, 346). *Dasein* is not the *source* of norms, but of their normative force, and in acting transparently, that very fact is integrated into my trying to be: I take a stand on what such norms mean, how to go on; I put myself forth not as justified by the given rules of the game, but as exemplary of what it means to succeed in some way of being.

Though this account of authenticity might seem to reinforce the idea that conscience is not a second-personal phenomenon, the appearance is misleading, since it has not yet taken the ontological role of *Mitsein* into consideration. Because *Dasein* is always Being-with, the call that reveals my responsibility *for* normative force also reveals my responsibility *to* others. If responsibility consists of standing toward the givens of my situation ("facticity") as toward potentially justifying reasons (i.e., doing things *because* I hold it *best* that they be done), then I am already *accountable to* others with who I am. The call of conscience involves the second-personal claim that I be *answerable* to others, "give an account" of myself. Because *Dasein* is essentially Being-with, being accountable to others is not tacked on to the call of conscience, but is a second-personal structural feature of the call itself. I owe others an account, prior to any SPS that would presuppose a distinct set of normative felicity conditions, a specific second-person competence, or any substantive notions of second-person standing.

Thus, the fact that Heidegger identifies the caller as "Dasein in its uncanniness" does not undermine the idea that the call is a second-person phenomenon, since the second-personal character of the call that overcomes me is already included in the ontology of *Dasein*. Furthermore, the *way* in which it is included preserves the essentially unmarked character of the caller: the others with whom *Dasein* is make a claim on it in a way that is not reducible to any characteristics that might be named. As Heidegger put it, the caller "is not someone else who is with me in the world" (1962, 320)—a phenomenological point that rules out identifying it with any individual, moral community, Freudian, internalized parents, or indeed, *any* entity at all.

This, finally, allows us to address Lyotard's argument that any identification of the addressor with the addressee does an injustice to the prescriptive game. Does Heidegger's apparent identification of the addressor with *Dasein* itself assume, contra Lyotard, that an uncontested passage from the addressee to the addressor is possible? Again, Heidegger's post-Cartesian ontology of care suggests the answer: in conscience, I do not give commands to myself; rather, I "hear" the call of the (unmarked) addressor—my first-person experience is as second-personal "you" (accusative)—and in responding resolutely, I do not substitute myself for the addressor; commitment is not self-legislation. Rather, I am *claimed*, undergo a feeling of obligation, and I try to live up to what that means. If I subsequently engage in discourse with others about what we ought to do—that is, if I practice grounding and legitimation (as I must, if I am to be authentically answerable)—we may decide that the *differend* between prescription and description is best negotiated through the justificatory protocols of the second-person standpoint, or we may decide that what Lyotard calls a "justice of multiplicity" (1985, 100) is the way to go. But in neither case may the identifications and aliases that get adopted in such conversations be seen as *presuppositions* for the phenomenology of the original address. This holds equally of Heidegger's own ontological account of the caller. The uncanny *Dasein* who delivers a call that overcomes me is no more I-myself than Levinas's Other is this or that other person. The transcendence of the normative—second-personal address—is as well preserved in the one case as in the other.

## NOTES

1 Many of the points taken up in this section receive more detailed analysis in Smith 2012, chap. 3.
2 The phenomenology of the personalistic attitude is extensively developed in Husserl 1989.
3 Darwall makes room for this conventionalist view in his example of the kind of obedience a private owes to his sergeant, whose authority depends on his institutional role. But for Darwall, even such institutional authority is ultimately based in the authority of a free and rational being, which belongs to the normative felicity conditions of SPS as such. Institutional authority is a derivative sub-species of second-personal authority (2006, 12f).
4 Here, the term "putative" marks the place where the *differend* appears between the "moral community"—however idealized a given theory might present it—and the "transcendence" (in Levinas's sense) of the source of the command. As we shall suggest below, Heidegger's account of conscience addresses this point.
5 The points made in this section are extensively explained and defended in Crowell (2013a). Here, I can only lay them out in schematic form.

## REFERENCES

Crowell, Steven (2012). "Sartre's Existentialism and the Nature of Consciousness." In: S. Crowell (Ed.). *The Cambridge Companion to Existentialism*. Cambridge: Cambridge University Press, 199–226.
——— (2013a). *Normativity and Phenomenology in Husserl and Heidegger*. Cambridge: Cambridge University Press.
——— (2013b). "Why Is Ethics First Philosophy? Levinas in Phenomenological Context." *European Journal of Philosophy* (Early View: doi: 10.1111/j1468-0378.2012.00550.x).
Darwall, Stephen (2006). *The Second-Person Standpoint. Morality, Respect, and Accountability*. Cambridge, MA: Harvard University Press.
Habermas, Jürgen (1999). "Discourse Ethics. Notes on a Program of Philosophical Justification." In: *Moral Consciousness and Communicative Action*. Transl. by Ch. Lenhardt, and S. W. Nicholsen. Cambridge, MA/London: MIT Press, 43–115.
Heidegger, Martin (1962). *Being and Time*. Transl. by J. Macquarrie, and E. Robinson. New York: Harper & Row.
Husserl, Edmund (1969). *Cartesian Meditations. An Introduction to Phenomenology*. Transl. by D. Cairns. The Hague: Martinus Nijhoff.
——— (1989). *Ideas Pertaining to a Pure Phenomenology and to a Phenomenological Philosophy, Second Book: Studies in the Phenomenology of Constitution*. Transl. by R. Rojcewicz and A. Schuwer. Dordrecht: Kluwer.

Levinas, Emmanuel (1969). *Totality and Infinity. An Essay on Exteriority.* Transl. by A. Lingis. Pittsburgh: Duquesne University Press.
Lyotard, Jean-François, and Thébaud, Jean-Loup (1985). *Just Gaming.* Transl. by W. Godzich. Minneapolis: University of Minnesota Press.
Sartre, Jean-Paul (1956). *Being and Nothingness. A Phenomenological Essay on Ontology.* Trans. by H. Barnes. New York: Washington Square Press.
Smith, William H. (2012). *The Phenomenology of Moral Normativity.* New York: Routledge.
Strawson, Peter F. (1962). "Freedom and Resentment." *Proceedings of the British Academy* 48, 1–25.

# Part II
# Intersubjectivity, the "We-World," and Objectivity

# 5 Concrete Interpersonal Encounters or Sharing a Common World
## Which Is More Fundamental in Phenomenological Approaches to Sociality?

*Jo-Jo Koo*

A central question along which phenomenological approaches to sociality or intersubjectivity have diverged concerns whether concrete, interpersonal encounters or sharing a common world is more fundamental in working out an adequate phenomenology of human sociality.[1] On one side, we have philosophers such as the early Sartre (1956), Martin Buber (1965, 1970), Michael Theunissen (1984), and Emmanuel Levinas (1969, 1985, 1996), all of whom emphasize, each in his own way, the priority of some mode of interpersonal encounters (broadly construed) in determining the basic character of human co-existence. To be sure, grouping these philosophers together under this particular aspect does not imply that they share other philosophical commitments: quite the contrary, in fact. On the other side, we have philosophers such as the early Heidegger (1979/1985, 1993, 1996) and Merleau-Ponty (1964, 2012), who argue that an adequate account of human sociality must begin, in the proper order of understanding and hence explanation, with how we always already exist in a shared or common world.[2] Which side is right in this debate? I will argue in this chapter that existential phenomenologists such as the early Heidegger and Merleau-Ponty provide more compelling arguments in this debate.

## 1 EARLY HEIDEGGER ON THE NECESSARY SOCIALITY OF HUMAN EXISTENCE

To begin with, Heidegger claims in *Being and Time*[3] that being-with-others (*Mitsein, Miteinandersein*) is an "existential" (44f.), i.e., a necessary constitutive condition or enabling structure of being human (*Dasein*) at all (120, 125; cf. 129f.). More precisely, his claim is that the "average everyday" or "undifferentiated" way (43; cf. 124, 232) in which the human being *primarily and mostly* (*zunächst und zumeist*) exists in the world is always already conditioned by being with others. It is crucial, however, not to understand this claim in the first instance as an empirical, statistical, or merely factual claim. Rather, Heidegger is asserting that insofar as any human being is *being-in-the-world at all*, he or she always already coexists with others (120,

123; cf. 130, 179). How does each human being qua being-in-the-world coexist primarily and mostly with others if this manner of co-existence is not exhausted by factual co-existence? What sort of co-existence is this?

Heidegger works out this idea by first drawing our attention to how we coexist with others in terms of the *world*, in his rich sense of that term as that most fundamental structure on the basis of which we typically make sense of all phenomena and act at all (see especially §§9, 12–18, 25–34, 41–44; cf. Heidegger 1979/1985, 326–334/237–243).[4] It is important to notice that co-existence is not initially defined in terms of how we factually live among other people or how we are constituents of larger social wholes. Rather, the world that engages and matters to us in our lived experience is fundamentally a *space of intelligibility* (*Verständlichkeit*), within which entities and, more generally, the phenomena through which entities show themselves, can make sense at all. This space has the following basic constituents and structure: (1) a set of holistically determined "ready-to-hand" (*zuhandene*) equipment, each of which is used for performing some specific task; (2) more encompassing short-term and medium-term goals that are accomplished by the execution of these nested tasks; and (3) the roles or self-interpretations for the sake of which (*Worum-willen*) human individuals initially project and go on mostly to actualize who they are. This they do by engaging in certain activities that accomplish certain short-term and medium-term nested goals that are bound up with some role or self-interpretation that they have either simply taken over without further ado or else deliberately assigned to (chosen for) themselves. As Heidegger shows, the world that engages and matters to us is always a pragmatically and holistically understood "referential nexus of significance" (*Verweisungszusammenhang der Bedeutsamkeit*), a structured space of intelligibility in terms of which phenomena initially and mostly make sense to us (§18). Moreover, our understanding of the world as exhibiting this underlying pragmatic-holistic structure of intelligibility, i.e., the "worldliness" (*Weltlichkeit*) of the world, often goes unnoticed by us (§16), functioning as an indispensable but largely inconspicuous context of situational meanings that must already be in place in order for us to be intentional agents and human selves at all.

When Heidegger claims that we primarily and mostly understand people, including ourselves, in terms of the world, his key point is that we typically make sense of ourselves and other people by reference to how people's self-interpretations and projections of possible actions are thoroughly intertwined with the context of the situational meanings in which they are immersed (§ 26). Now, why must the worldly background in terms of which we make sense of ourselves and others in ordinary life be *shared*?[5] Why can it not be the case that each human individual possesses and relies on his or her own referential nexus of significance from occasion to occasion (Olafson 1987, 70–74; cf. 1994, 54–63)? Heidegger argues that such an individualistic conception of the world is mistaken by failing to take into account how public norms already *permeate* the worldliness of the world in which we ordinarily live and act. That is, the everyday world that makes sense *to* and also *of* us is not only pragmatically and holistically structured; it is also *constitutively normalized* by way of our general tacit conformity to public norms as a necessary enabling condition of being human at all.[6] Heidegger's conception of the "one" or the "anyone" (*das Man* [§ 27]) captures both the constitutively normalized intelligibility of the everyday world, including how we understand ourselves and others as normalized in living our lives and thereby sharing a common world, and how there is also a standing and easy tendency on our part to *slide* from this public, undifferentiated way for ourselves and other people to exist to a specific mode of individual existence that fails to live up to its potential for self-ownership (*eigentliches Selbstsein*, *Eigentlichkeit*, often misleadingly translated into English as 'authenticity'[7] [129 and Second Division, Ch. 1–3, especially §§53, 60, 62, 64]). That is, it is important to notice, on the one hand, the frequent tendency for this sort of slippage to happen, without thinking, on the other hand, that "unownedness" (*Uneigentlichkeit*, often misleadingly translated into English as 'inauthenticity') in the broad sense qua undifferentiated, everyday existence (*Indifferenz, durchschnittliche Alltäglichkeit*) describes the same exact phenomenon as "unownedness" in the narrow sense qua a way of existing in everyday life that is *completely* lost in and conforms *totally uncritically* to the normalized intelligibility that the "anyone" prescribes (especially 128, 175f.; cf. 12, 43, 53, 129, 232, 304). In other words, a human being's undifferentiated existence in a common world (i.e., unownedness in the broad sense) does not ipso facto entail that we are "inauthentic" (i.e., unownedness in the narrow sense). Unfortunately, this is what orthodox, existentialist readings of *Being and Time* all too often conflate.[8] In any case, as far as the constitutive enabling function of the "anyone" is concerned, Heidegger's key move is to argue that any human individual qua *Dasein* cannot help but draw on the tacit, normalized intelligibility of the world that the "anyone" effects in order for such an individual to project possible concrete ways for her to be at all, regardless of whether she eventually comes to own or fail to own her way of being in the world (145, 152f., 169, 179). No particular individual can ever completely spontaneously create the totality of her possible ways of being herself, though to be sure, she can partially modify and even seriously challenge the normalization (normativity) of her inherited way of being in the world. Self-ownership can at most only be an "existentielle" (i.e., concrete and individual) modification of, never a complete detachment from, the public, normalized intelligibility in terms of which we typically understand ourselves and others as constitutive aspects of the world in its worldliness (129f., 299; cf. Keller and Weberman 1998, 373ff. and Rousse 2013, 14ff.). In short, each human being always already exists with others in a common world by drawing on the shared, public, normalized intelligibility that both enables and constrains how we primarily and mostly project possible ways for entities to be, including ourselves and other people, as aspects of the world in its worldliness (cf. Heidegger 1979/1985, 339/246).

## 2  MERLEAU-PONTY ON THE INTERSUBJECTIVE ASPECTS OF HUMAN EXPERIENCE

Although the early Heidegger shows convincingly how human beings must always already *coexist with others* (*Mitsein*) in this non-factual, constitutive sense, his position is not very informative, to say the least, when it comes to characterizing the nature of *intersubjective* experiences or interactions. Moreover, as he himself explicitly acknowledges, his critique of the demand among certain followers of Husserl's transcendental phenomenology for an account of "empathy" (*Einfühlung*) only shows how intersubjective experiences or interactions are possible *in general*, without doing full justice to the *specificity* of these modes of human co-existence (122 and 125). Thus, we may assert that while *Being and Time* provides us with penetrating insights about the fundamental nature of human sociality, it does not do nearly as well regarding the nature of intersubjectivity (cf. Schroeder 1984, 160–169). Here, we can draw for our purposes a terminological distinction between 'sociality' and 'intersubjectivity': While 'sociality' refers to the set of basic conditions that must be tacitly satisfied in order for human co-existence to be intelligible and thus possible at all, 'intersubjectivity' refers to the modes of interpersonal interaction that such co-existence both enables and constrains. In light of this distinction, the early Heidegger's account of intersubjectivity in *Being and Time* is seriously wanting by at most noting in passing that there are "mixed forms" between what even he himself describes as two extreme forms of "caring-for" (*Fürsorge*): one that either "leaps in" for another human being and thereby relieves this person's burden of existing for herself, or else "leaps ahead" of her so as to enable her to perceive and take up this burden in the right way (122). It is at this juncture in my view that Merleau-Ponty's conception of others and the human world in his *Phenomenology of Perception*[9] nicely complements and extends the early Heidegger's conception of human social existence by providing a much more developed account of *intersubjectivity*, which the early Heidegger in *Being and Time* chooses not to work out, but which in my view, he could have. Although Merleau-Ponty does not explicitly claim with the early Heidegger that sharing a common world is "transcendentally" prior to concrete interpersonal encounters, he certainly argues that living and acting in a shared world is both developmentally and philosophically prior to our individuation and interaction as relationally autonomous selves.[10]

By the time Merleau-Ponty addresses the topic of intersubjectivity in *The Phenomenology of Perception*, he has already given ample arguments for why we are deeply mistaken in accepting any putative dualism between subject and object, or mind (or consciousness) and world.[11] He argues extensively that there can be no subjectivity without the necessary embodiment of the subject, as well as how the body schema and bodily activities of the embodied subject form the locus or site where the putative dualism of mind and world either dissolves or shows itself at least to be dynamically ambiguous (especially 100–105, 139–143, 204f.). In this view, subject and object, or mind and world, are not already self-contained relata that the body "mediates" as a discrete interface, but rather, dynamic poles of *one unitary, experiential system* that permeates our being in and toward the world, to such an extent that there cannot be subject or object, or mind or world, apart from the activity of one's own body and the oriented, lived space that bodily comportment effects (especially 308–311).

Merleau-Ponty's view about the significance of human embodiment has important consequences for how we should understand the nature of intersubjectivity.[12] First, intersubjective experience involves our experience of others as embodied beings with their own perspectives on the world. We perceive other subjects (in an innocuous sense of "subjects") by non-inferentially perceiving how others' bodily and linguistic activities express their particular perspectives on the world; in this view, the expressions of subjects' perspectives are not merely "outer clothing" in relation to such perspectives, but intrinsically bound up with the latter, barring exceptional circumstances (179–205). Second, intersubjectivity, at least typically, is reciprocal or symmetrical in the sense that others can be aware of me in the same way that I am aware of them: we readily make sense of one another by and large through our perceptions of how our respective bodily activities express our different perspectives and how what we express in communication helps to partially constitute the contents of our thoughts and emotions (182–189).

According to Merleau-Ponty, when we perceive other people's bodily activities, we certainly do not perceive them like other material objects in the world that are devoid of subjectivity, but rather perceive them as expressing distinctive powers or capacities that respond skillfully to the subtle solicitations of their surrounding environments (363–372). That is, we perceive their bodily activities as responding meaningfully to the surrounding perceptual field within which such activities are carried out, a field that is itself already permeated by sense and directionality not just for the agents of the bodily activities, but for us perceivers, too. Thus, our perception and understanding of what others do and say take for granted not only that I can in principle situate myself in their place, and they in mine, but also that we would typically respond to the solicitations of our surrounding world in similar ways. Merleau-Ponty even goes so far at one point as to write that the other's body qua embodied subjectivity appears to me almost as "a miraculous extension of its own intentions, a familiar manner of handling the world. Henceforth, just as the parts of my body together form a system, the other's body and my own are a single whole, two sides of a single phenomenon [. . .]" (370). Although other people and I are obviously numerically distinct bodies, my experience of them does not privilege either perspective as far as the typical perception and understanding of others' behavior (*comportement*) are concerned. It is also in this sense that our experience of others are anonymous, i.e., not geared to any particular individual at the level of generic behavior (363f., 369).[13]

That said, Merleau-Ponty's account of intersubjectivity is nuanced because he fully acknowledges that despite this symmetry of perception and understanding, there nonetheless remains a sense in which each subject can never *actually live* the experience of the other. For it is one thing to argue that we normally have little trouble perceiving and making sense of others' behavior, but quite another to hold that we actually live (have or enjoy) their experiences (372–375). Although Merleau-Ponty describes this as a sort of "lived solipsism" (374, an expression that is rather misleading because of the philosophical associations that the term 'solipsism' carries), it is clear that his point here is simply that there is an obvious and defensible way in which one's first-personal perspective can never be eliminated or be fully capable of being experienced by others, despite how we typically have little trouble perceiving and making sense of other people's behavior in ordinary life. It may seem, then, that Merleau-Ponty contradicts himself here by emphasizing, on the one hand, that there exists by and large *symmetry* in how we perceive and make sense of others as expressed through their bodily and linguistic activities, but also noting, on the other hand, that there is *asymmetry* at play here because the first-personal or purely subjective perspective is ineliminable or incapable of being fully experienced by others. This appearance of self-contradiction, however, is mere appearance. Although Merleau-Ponty does not quite put it as follows, he in effect defuses this appearance of self-contradiction by drawing a distinction between *local* and *global* cases of solipsism. The local case of "lived solipsism," which on my construal, just means the ineliminability or impossibility of the first-personal perspective to be fully experienced by others, is philosophically innocuous, for it is clearly true that we do not know on every particular occasion what is *exactly* going through the minds of others. But Merleau-Ponty in effect argues that it is a mistake to infer from *local, lived* "solipsistic" experiences to any *global or philosophical* solipsism because it is a fallacy to move from an innocuous sort of localized "solipsism" *in practice*, from occasion to occasion, to a scenario where philosophical solipsism becomes committed to the impossibility of our knowledge of others *in principle*. That is, one cannot infer with justification from a claim about the way something is *in practice in local circumstances* to how it is or may be *in principle in all circumstances* (379). Finally, Merleau-Ponty also deploys an immanent argument against traditional solipsism, for the latter assumes that the solipsistic self can be fully transparent to itself on every single occasion. But this can never be the case simply on account of any subject's experience of inner time (362, 381, 392, 437–448), which constitutively can never be fully self-present in any case.[14] If so, philosophical solipsism collapses because there is no longer a sustainable contrast between a fully self-transparent subject and others who are not so transparent to this subject. In summary, then, Merleau-Ponty as I interpret him breaks new ground in the phenomenology of sociality (in the broad sense) by drawing our attention to some phenomenologically supported and indispensable aspects of our intersubjective experience that the early Heidegger neglects.

## 3 OBJECTIONS AND REPLIES

The early Sartre, Buber, Theunissen, and Levinas have each raised some important objections against the line of argument that at least the early Heidegger makes for the priority of sharing a common world over concrete, interpersonal encounters in adequately understanding the phenomenology of sociality. The early Sartre claims that the early Heidegger (and presumably also Merleau-Ponty) fundamentally misunderstand the experience of the Other. In his discussion of the dialectic of "the look" (*le regard*), Sartre construes intersubjective experience as fundamentally *objectifying, alienating, and confrontational* (Sartre 1956, 340–76, 534–56). Specifically, his strongest objections against Heidegger are that Heidegger's conceptions of Being-with and the "anyone" fails to explain (1) how concrete intersubjective experiences or interactions are actual and, furthermore, (2) how others can be concretely differentiated from oneself given the impersonal normalizing character of our existence in the mode of the "anyone" (Sartre 1956, 334f.). In short, the thrust of Sartre's strongest critique of Heidegger's conception of human social existence is summarized by Sartre's assertion that being-*for*-others is more basic in the order of experience than being-*with*-others (Sartre 1956, 537), given Sartre's particular conception of what it is for me to be *for* others and for others to be *for* me (Sartre 1956, 340–50).

The basic problem with Sartre's critique, however, is that it takes the *general background meaningfulness* of being-for-others in his sense for granted. For example, there is an entire referential nexus of significance that enables, as a structure that is already in place in the background, the experience of shame and thereby the objectification of oneself by the other to be meaningful and thus concretely possible. With regard to Sartre's famous example of being seen by another while I look through a keyhole at him or her (Sartre 1956, 347–9), this activity takes for granted our shared understanding of how keyholes and doors, etc., are normally used; how we are bodily situated in different rooms that at that moment are closed off from each other; what the meanings of personal privacy, jealousy, or sexual arousal are, etc. Sartre takes all of this for granted in his use of this example. In short, he errs by claiming that being-*for*-others in his sense is more basic than being-with-others in early Heidegger's (or Merleau-Ponty's) sense. Instead, it is precisely being-*with*-others that makes being-for-others in Sartre's sense meaningful and thus concretely possible at all.[15] More generally, Sartre continues to presuppose the dualism of subject and object (in Sartre's terminology, being-for-self and being-in-itself); his correct emphasis on the non-thetic or pre-reflective awareness of oneself as a subject changes nothing in this regard. But Heidegger and Merleau-Ponty have argued extensively and in my view, convincingly, that we have many compelling reasons for rejecting this dualism.[16]

By contrast, philosophers like Buber and Theunissen break with Sartre by emphasizing the positive and, indeed, normatively prescriptive way in which two or more persons can and should be for each other in a way that is the very opposite of unwanted intersubjective objectification, alienation, and confrontation. Rather, they argue that unalienated Being-with or being-for-others (unlike Sartre, they do not make a distinction between these experiences) is what actualizes a genuine I-Thou relation that is wholeheartedly open, unmediated, mutual, and responsible for one another (Buber 1965, 8–25, 30–33, 97–101 and 1970, especially the first part; Theunissen 1984, Part III, especially 271ff.). The ideal consists of interpersonal encounters that are genuinely *dialogical*, where the interlocutors really listen, speak to (not just at or about), and respond to the distinctive otherness of the Other. Against Heidegger, Buber and Theunissen object specifically that Heidegger's conception of being-with-others is too undifferentiated, anonymous, and above all, overly negative regarding the significance of being-with-others in terms of our predominant existence in the mode of the "anyone" (Buber 1965, 173–81; Theunissen 1984, 183–98). Furthermore, Theunissen objects that others for Heidegger are always *mediated* by the world (in Heidegger's sense): according to Heidegger, other people can never encounter one another in their distinctive otherness or alterity because they can only do so by way of the worldliness of the world (Theunissen 1984, 182f.).

Now, the emphasis on this idealized conception of dialogical immediacy and genuine mutuality is all well and good. But as is the case with Sartre, it is evident that Buber and Theunissen take the context of situational meanings (i.e., the worldliness of the world) for granted, to the point where it even seems that dialogical immediacy and genuine mutuality require that the dialogical encounter be as *worldless* (*weltlos*) as possible (Buber 1970, 82–85; Theunissen 1984, 323–9). But can there be any appreciation of the distinctive otherness of the Other if we abstract away, as much as possible, all background context of situational meanings from such an encounter? How can the I-Thou relation be *determinate* or *contentful* at all if the world is so abstracted away? For example, when I am engaged in a heart-to-heart conversation with a loved one or a dear friend, our dialogical immediacy and mutuality tacitly rely on, and hence precisely do *not* do away with, our ongoing ability to find *meaningfulness* in our dialogical situation, as well as in the various situations or relationships we are discussing in conversation. Thus, Theunissen's objection that the world "mediates" and thus supposedly distorts or interferes with the actualization of genuine I-Thou relations is misguided, because any mutuality absent its embeddedness in the world would actually *disable* the actualization of dialogical immediacy and genuine mutuality between interlocutors.[17] Moreover, there is a confusion on Buber's and Theunissen's parts about the way in which being-with-others in Heidegger's sense is prior in the order of understanding and explanation. In my interpretation, Heidegger's point here pertains to how phenomena, including ourselves and others, can be *intelligible* (*verstehbar*) at all. Buber and Theunissen for some reason claim that this focus precludes how other people can be personally significant for those who are in genuine I-Thou relations. But why should this conclusion follow? Understanding others as initially meaningful in a generic way, i.e., as meaningful initially in terms of certain ranges of activities that are bound up with some social roles, would only preclude or obstruct alterity if someone understood the identities of these individuals as *exhausted* by these social roles. But how often does this actually happen in human life? Right now, I understand the readers of this chapter as performing certain activities that are bound up with certain social roles that make sense within a range of situational contexts. Thus, the readers and I are making sense of one another in Heidegger's sense, in an undifferentiated but still determinate way. But our mutual ascriptions to one another of certain social roles do not hinder, but actually enable and enhance the ongoing basis on which we can further explore each other's distinctive otherness. Provided that we do not understand one another solely in terms of our social roles, making sense of one another in terms of ranges of activities that are bound up with such roles is not only innocuous, but makes the deepening of mutuality and thus the experience of distinctive otherness (alterity) really possible. While it is true that Heidegger in *Being and Time* rarely mentions the occurrence of genuine mutuality and experience of the distinctive otherness of others (but consider Heidegger 1993, §§60, 74), a more nuanced interpretation of this text reveals that his fundamental ontology can make room for it.[18]

Thus far, I have replied on behalf of the early Heidegger (and Merleau-Ponty) to these familiar objections against their claim that sharing a common world is more basic in the order of understanding and explanation than concrete, interpersonal encounters. What these replies have in common is the key argument that such encounters must always already occur against some *worldly background*, i.e., some context of situational meanings, if these encounters are supposed to be meaningful and realizable at all. But this sort of reply by recourse to necessary conditions of meaningfulness cannot convince someone like Levinas. Levinas insists that the Other is "signification without context" (Levinas 1985, 86; 1969, 23, 51f., 194; 1996, 53), i.e., signifies and matters apart from *any* holistically structured configuration of situational meanings. Thus, Levinas rejects all attempts to make sense of the Other by way of situating and understanding anything of ethical significance (very broadly construed) via any context of meanings whatsoever. Rather, the Other as such always "exceeds" our comprehension because the Other possesses an insurmountable "height" of ethical significance; the Other is always exterior to and at an infinite remove from my encounters with it (Levinas 1969, 38–52, 194–219; 1996, Essays 1 and 2). In this view, we can never fully grasp the Other's alterity, for this alterity is absolute and never relational to us (Levinas 1969, 48–51). The Other is the first principle of philosophy as such, not just of ethics, because it is the Other who effects freedom for me at all by at once giving me the opportunity, as well as issuing the demand on me, to respond to and thus be responsible for the Other (Levinas 1969, especially Sections I.A and I.C).[19]

Limitation of space prevents me from further elaborating these provocative claims of Levinas's, so I conclude this chapter by making the following queries about his position. First, it is tempting for a proponent of the early Heidegger's and Merleau-Ponty's respective conceptions of sociality and intersubjectivity to ask Levinas how our encounters with and responsibility for the Other is possible at all if such encounters must take place outside of *any* context of significance whatsoever. But this query would beg the question against Levinas, so it cannot be made in fairness to him. Nevertheless, it remains very puzzling just how the Other can *encounter* us given Levinas's philosophical commitments, for the "face" of the Other is not ultimately something perceivable, but the infinite source of moral summons or demands (Levinas 1969, 194–7; Perpich 2008, Ch. 2 and 3). Does this mean that our encounters with the Other are intuitively sensed or felt? How can we precisely encounter or be summoned (or addressed) by the Other, then, according to Levinas? Although he clearly recognizes that he must answer this important question, his attempt to do so seems wanting by either resorting to the use of metaphorical language (he speaks of the "nudity" of the face) or else question-begging through sheer assertion (Levinas 1996, 48–57). That is, unless the crucial claim that the Other is always signification without any context is just a bald, dogmatic assertion, how is this "claim" supported exactly?[20] Second, and more generally, it seems that Levinas's philosophy resists any *argumentative* approach or reconstruction of his position regarding the Other; but nor may one request phenomenological evidence for how the Other signifies, given how the Other according to Levinas is ultimately permanently elusive. Does this mean that one can never ask for or offer *arguments* for the metaphysical and thereby ethical significance of the Other, because the Other is supposedly the first principle of philosophy? For the sort of human co-existence invested with the type of peculiar and yet absolute significance that Levinas has in view cannot seemingly be argumentatively derived; the apparent argument that he gives for the primacy of the Other seems either question-begging, too weak to justify its conclusion (Levinas 1969, 83–89), or else oddly reminiscent of Habermas's discourse ethics (ibid., 96–98). If so, how does Levinas's insistence on the primacy of the Other not advance a "new dogmatism, centred now around the other rather than the self or ego" (Moran 2000, 351)?[21] Ironically, this sort of move reminds one of Fichte's absolute idealism, according to which the self-positing I can only be absolutely, never argumentatively, established (Williams 1992, 10–12 and especially 297–301). Is this the sort of move that Levinas makes regarding the status of the Other as philosophy's first principle?[22] Lastly, it also remains unclear how his insistence on the absolute asymmetry of each person's relation to the Other can contribute to our understanding of human sociality and intersubjectivity, except perhaps as a prescriptive ideal. If it is meant to make such a contribution, Levinas would need to say much more about how the absolute alterity of the Other can play some role in the phenomenology of human sociality and intersubjectivity.

In conclusion, I have argued that the early Heidegger's conception of the necessary sociality of human existence, as supplemented and extended by Merleau-Ponty's conception of intersubjectivity, provides more compelling arguments that show how sharing a common world is more fundamental than concrete, interpersonal encounters in adequately understanding the phenomenology of sociality. This does not imply that the modes of concrete, interpersonal experience or encounter that the early Sartre, Buber, Theunissen, and Levinas each emphasize are insignificant. In this spirit, I end by loosely adapting the retrospective assessment of Theunissen about the result of this debate from his perspective (Theunissen 1984, 367): we should grant primacy to the sharing of a common world as the proper point of departure for the phenomenology of sociality, but give emphasis to concrete, interpersonal encounters as far as one of the worthy goals or final destinations of such a phenomenology is concerned. The beginning of such a phenomenology should be the embodied and socially constituted self who exists in a common world. This phenomenology can then pursue, as one of its worthy goals or final destinations, the distinctive individuality of such a self as this develops through concrete, interpersonal encounters.

## ACKNOWLEDGMENTS

I thank Thomas Szanto and Søren Overgaard for their helpful comments and suggestions about this chapter.

## NOTES

1 For a very succinct and informative account of the debate generated by this question, see Zahavi (2012, 186f.).
2 In this regard, I would also include the later Wittgenstein (2009) and Gadamer (2004).
3 Until further notice, all page references in the body of this chapter are to Heidegger (1993). The English translation by Macquarrie and Robinson (Heidegger 1962) provides the German pagination in its margins.
4 For a much more extensive interpretation and defense of the conception of Being-with and *das Man* in early Heidegger's philosophy that I sketch in this section, see Koo (forthcoming).
5 It is noteworthy that Heidegger explicitly and extensively discusses how human beings share a common world in terms of how they *share the unconcealment (truth) of entities* in a lecture course given just a year and a half after the publication of *Being and Time* (Heidegger 1996, §§13–20, especially 14 and 18).
6 Dreyfus's influential interpretation (1991) of the First Division of *Being and Time* is, to my knowledge, the first to emphasize the constitutive significance of public and social norms for Heidegger's conception of being-in-the-world. For forceful critiques of this interpretation, see, e.g., Olafson (1994) and Mulhall (2013); for Dreyfus's response to Olafson's critique, see Dreyfus (1995) and also Carman (1994). Regarding this important debate, I agree very much

with Keller and Weberman's convincing assessment (1998, 375–383) that while public and social norms (*das Man*) no doubt constitute the *typical* significance of the everyday world in its worldliness, in response to which we ordinarily exist in the world and from which we can never fully detach ourselves, such significance is itself further grounded as a whole on the structure of *care (Sorge)* and ultimately on the *"ecstatic" temporality* of the care structure itself (Heidegger 1993, especially §65). It is beyond the scope of this chapter to elaborate on and defend this line of argument.

7 For convincing interpretations that reject construing Heidegger's conception of self-ownership in terms of the notion of "authenticity," see Boedeker (2001) and Carman (2005).
8 For a paradigm of the existentialist reading of Heidegger's *Being and Time*, see Sartre's *Being and Nothingness* (1956). I will briefly examine Sartre's conception of human social existence below. A vestige of such a reading remains in Mulhall (2013, 68–73 and Chap. 5).
9 Henceforth, all page references in the body of this chapter are to Merleau-Ponty (2012).
10 For his most extended argument for this conclusion, see especially Merleau-Ponty (1964); cf. Dillon (1997, Ch. 7) for a lucid interpretation of this argument.
11 For illuminating interpretations of this key move of Merleau-Ponty, see Dillon (1997, Part Two), Carman (2008, Chaps. 2–3), and Romdenh-Romluc (2011, especially Chaps. 2–4, 6–7).
12 My remarks in this paragraph are partially indebted to Romdenh-Romluc (2011, 138–143).
13 As already noted in footnote 10, Merleau-Ponty also argues that his conception of intersubjectivity is supported by empirical research in developmental psychology (Merleau-Ponty 1964). He argues on both philosophical and empirical grounds that prior to the emergence of full-fledged (adult) intersubjectivity, human beings are always already immersed in "syncretic sociability" (ibid., 119f.), i.e., the experience of a *lack* of even very basic kinds of differentiation that very young human beings undergo both toward others (their caregivers) and their immediate environment (ibid., especially 113–121).
14 Merleau-Ponty to this extent clearly appropriates Husserl's account of the phenomenology of the consciousness of inner time without much reservation; cf. Husserl (1991, especially §§11–19).
15 For a reasonable but not wholly convincing defense of Sartre's early philosophy against the explicit objections of Merleau-Ponty (and implicitly of Heidegger), see Langer (1998).
16 Although his interpretation of the early Heidegger's conception of human social existence is not in my view wholly satisfactory, Schroeder (1984, Chap. 3, especially 144–159) generally gives a very thorough, balanced, and instructive examination of the disagreements between Sartre and Heidegger about this issue.
17 In the postscript of *The Other*, Theunissen effectively concedes this point (1984, 366f.; cf. Dallmayr 1987).
18 Although his reading of *Being and Time* still takes for granted the orthodox, existentialist horizon within which this text tends to be understood, Vogel's "cosmopolitan" interpretation of Heidegger's conception of human social existence shows well how genuine mutuality and, indeed, the basis at least for a certain sort of ethics are possible within this conception (1994, Ch. 4).
19 For a very lucid and instructive interpretation of Levinas's philosophy as a whole, see Perpich (2008).
20 Steven Crowell's instructive chapter in this volume provides some important resources for answering the questions raised in this paragraph.

21 I am inclined to endorse Moran's forthright criticism of Levinas's philosophy as dogmatic (Moran 2000, 342–353). As Moran writes, "Levinas does not open a space for questioning; indeed, for him, the other presents itself as a demand, not a question" (ibid., 352).
22 For a brief but informative comparison of Levinas and Fichte in general, see Scribner (2000).

## REFERENCES

Boedeker, Edgar (2001). "Individual and Community in Early Heidegger: Situating *das Man*, the *Man*-self, and Self-ownership in Dasein's Ontological Structure." *Inquiry* 44 (1), 63–99.

Buber, Martin (1965) [1947]. *Between Man and Man*. Transl. by R. Gregor Smith. New York: Macmillan.

———— (1970) [1923]. *I and Thou*. Transl. by W. Kaufmann. New York: Charles Scribner's Sons.

Carman, Taylor (1994). "On Being Social: A Reply to Olafson." *Inquiry* 37 (2), 203–223.

———— (2005). "Authenticity." In: H. Dreyfus and M. Wrathall (Eds.). *A Companion to Heidegger*. Oxford: Blackwell, 285–296.

———— (2008). *Merleau-Ponty*. London/New York: Routledge.

Dallmayr, Fred (1987). "Dialogue and Otherness: Theunissen." In: *Critical Encounters: Between Philosophy and Politics*. Notre Dame: University of Notre Dame Press.

Dillon, M.C. (1997). *Merleau-Ponty's Ontology*, 2nd ed. Evanston: Northwestern University Press.

Dreyfus, Hubert (1991). *Being-in-the-World: A Commentary on Heidegger's* Being and Time, *Division I*. Cambridge, MA/London: MIT Press.

———— (1995). "Interpreting Heidegger on *das Man*." *Inquiry* 38 (4), 423–430.

Gadamer, Hans-Georg (2004) [1960]. *Truth and Method*. Transl. by W. Glen-Doepel. Transl. rev. by J. Weinsheimer and D. Marshall. London/New York: Continuum.

Heidegger, Martin (1962). *Being and Time*. Transl. by J. Macquarrie, & E. Robinson. San Francisco: Harper & Row.

———— (1979) [=GA 20]. *Prolegomena zur Geschichte des Zeitbegriffs*. Frankfurt am Main: Vittorio Klostermann.

———— (1985). *History of the Concept of Time: Prolegomena*. Transl. by T. Kisiel. Bloomington/Indianapolis: Indiana University Press.

———— (1993) [1927]. *Sein und Zeit*, 17th ed. Tübingen: Max Niemeyer.

———— (1996) [=GA 27]. *Einleitung in die Philosophie*. Frankfurt am Main: Vittorio Klostermann.

Husserl, Edmund (1991) [1966]. *On The Phenomenology of the Consciousness of Internal Time*. Transl. by J. Brough. Dordrecht: Kluwer.

Keller, Pierre, & Weberman, David (1998). "Heidegger and the Source(s) of Intelligibility." *Continental Philosophy Review* 31 (4), 369–386.

Koo, Jo-Jo (forthcoming). "Early Heidegger on Social Reality." In: A. Salice and H.B. Schmid (Eds.). *Social Reality: The Phenomenological Approach*. Dordrecht: Springer.

Langer, Monika (1998). "Sartre and Merleau-Ponty: A Reappraisal." In: J. Stewart (Ed.). *The Debate between Sartre and Merleau-Ponty*. Evanston: Northwestern University Press, 93–117.

Levinas, Emmanuel (1969) [1961]. *Totality and Infinity: An Essay on Exteriority*. Transl. by A. Lingis. Pittsburgh: Duquesne University Press.

―――― (1985) [1982]. *Ethics and Infinity*. Transl. by R. Cohen. Pittsburgh: Duquesne University Press.

―――― (1996). *Basic Philosophical Writings*. Ed. by A. Peperzak, S. Critchley, & R. Bernasconi. Bloomington/Indianapolis: Indiana University Press.

Merleau-Ponty, Maurice (1964) [1960]. "The Child's Relations with Others." Transl. by W. Cobb. In: J. Edie (Ed.). *The Primacy of Perception*. Evanston: Northwestern University Press, 96–155.

―――― (2012) [1945]. *The Phenomenology of Perception*. Transl. by D. Landes. London/New York: Routledge.

Moran, Dermot (2000). *Introduction to Phenomenology*. London/New York: Routledge.

Mulhall, Stephen (2013). *Heidegger's* Being and Time, 2nd ed. London/New York: Routledge.

Olafson, Frederick A. (1987). *Heidegger and the Philosophy of Mind*. New Haven/London: Yale University Press.

―――― (1994). "Heidegger *à la* Wittgenstein or 'Coping' with Professor Dreyfus." *Inquiry* 37 (1), 45–64.

Perpich, Diane (2008). *The Ethics of Emmanuel Levinas*. Stanford: Stanford University Press.

Romdenh-Romluc, Komarine (2011). *Merleau-Ponty and Phenomenology of Perception*. London/New York: Routledge.

Rousse, B. Scot (2013). "Heidegger, Sociality, and Human Agency." *European Journal of Philosophy*, DOI: 10.1111/ejop.12067.

Sartre, Jean-Paul (1956) [1943]. *Being and Nothingness*. Transl. by H. Barnes. New York: Washington Square Press.

Schroeder, William (1984). *Sartre and His Predecessors: The Self and the Other*. London: Routledge & Kegan Paul.

Scribner, F. Scott (2000). "Levinas Face to Face with Fichte." *Southwest Philosophy Review* 16 (1), 151–160.

Theunissen, Michael (1984) [1977]. *The Other: Studies in the Social Ontology of Husserl, Heidegger, Sartre, and Buber*. Transl. by C. Macann. Cambridge, MA/London: MIT Press.

Vogel, Lawrence (1994). *The Fragile "We": Ethical Implications of Heidegger's* Being and Time. Evanston: Northwestern University Press.

Williams, Robert R. (1992). *Recognition: Fichte and Hegel on the Other*. Albany: State University of New York Press.

Wittgenstein, Ludwig (2009) [1953]. *Philosophical Investigations*. Transl. by G. E. M. Anscombe. Ed. and Transl. rev. by P. Hacker, & J. Schulte. Malden, MA/Oxford: Wiley-Blackwell.

Zahavi, Dan (2001). *Husserl and Transcendental Intersubjectivity. A Response to the Linguistic-Pragmatic Critique*. Transl. by E. A. Behnke. Athens: Ohio University Press.

―――― (2012). "Intersubjectivity." In: S. Luft, & S. Overgaard (Eds.). *The Routledge Companion to Phenomenology*. London/New York: Routledge, 180–189.

# 6 *Ineinandersein* and *L'interlacs*
The Constitution of the Social World or "We-World" (*Wir-Welt*) in Edmund Husserl and Maurice Merleau-Ponty

*Dermot Moran*

"The problem of the existential modality of the social is here at one with all problems of transcendence."

(Merleau-Ponty 1945, 423 [417])[1]

"Others are implicated in me as (already) implicated in one another, and I am, in turn, implicated in them; and 'the' world is constituted in the liveliness of the egoic life implicated in me, which is (in turn) implicated in the egoic within-one-another (*Ineinander*)."

(Husserl, Hua 15, 200, my translation)

"This interiority of the *being-for-one-another* (*Füreinandersein*) as an intentional being-within-each-other (*Ineinandersein*) is the 'metaphysical' fundamental fact; it is a within-one-another (*Ineinander*) of the absolute. Each has his or her primordiality, in which is implicated the transcendental capacity of his or her 'ego,' and each is similarly in another, albeit no one can have the least really in common with the other. But each, as a primordiality of intentional experiences of his or her experiencing—his or her self 'self-sufficient'—ego implicates each other primordial intentionality."

(Husserl, Hua 15, 366, my translation)

## 1 THE PRIMACY OF THE INTERSUBJECTIVE, PERSONAL WORLD IN HUSSERL AND MERLEAU-PONTY

As these three opening epigraphs indicate, both Edmund Husserl and Maurice Merleau-Ponty were deeply interested in the kinds of intentional intertwinings that constitute the collective social and cultural life of human beings, for which both use the German term *Ineinandersein*. Overall, Merleau-Ponty was extraordinarily prescient in his interpretation of Husserl. He identified specific—and at the time, unnoticed—threads, especially in the Husserl's musings that never became prominent enough to be explicitly thematized. Merleau-Ponty thus particularly underscored and reinterpreted

Husserl's emphasis on the priority of intersubjectivity and the on the touching-touched relationship as a cipher for human being-in-the-world.

Much has been written on Merleau-Ponty's reading of Husserl, but here I want to focus explicitly on Merleau-Ponty's interpretation and adaptation of Husserl's conception of the intersubjective constitution of 'sociality' (*Sozialität*) by examining in particular the manner in which Merleau-Ponty takes up Husserl's conception on 'being-within-one-another' (*Ineinandersein*), a concept that the mature Husserl usually discusses in relation to his own conception of the intersubjective joining together of subjects, which he calls, borrowing from Leibniz, the 'community of monads' (*Gemeinschaft der Monaden*, Hua 1, 149; *Monadengemeinschaft*, Hua 1, 158) or the 'within-one-another of monads' (*Das Ineinander der Monaden*, Hua 15, 268).[2] In his mature research writings (although without ever foregrounding it thematically), Husserl invokes this intersection of human living and striving (*Leben und Streben*) in terms of *Ineinandersein* (and *Ineinanderleben*) usually in relation to the collective constitution of the experience of one world 'for all.'[3]

Since the publication of Iso Kern's three-volume Husserliana edition of Edmund Husserl's writings on intersubjectivity, *Zur Phänomenologie der Intersubjektivität* (Hua 13, 14, 15), it has no longer been credible to portray Husserl as a Cartesian methodological solipsist who sought to reduce the entire meaningful world to the activity of the *solus ipse*. Indeed, anyone who reads the *Cartesian Meditations* to the end will see that even there, where he is being most Cartesian, Husserl is stressing the ontological primordiality of intersubjectivity in his discussion of the community of monads. In fact, beginning from around 1910, the mature Husserl stresses that phenomenological explorations must recognize the concreteness of intersubjective human social and cultural life, the collective 'life of spirit' or 'spiritual life' (*Geistesleben*) as it is grasped in the 'personalistic attitude' (*die personalistische Einstellung*), as he calls it in *Ideas II*, § 49 (Hua 4), which he thinks has primordiality over the 'naturalistic attitude' (*die naturalistische Einstellung*) that saturates the modern sciences (including contemporary social sciences, especially empirical psychology). Indeed, Husserl insists, in *Ideas II* and elsewhere, that the chief error of the naturalistic outlook consists of thinking of the natural world (i.e., primarily 'the world of things,' (*Dingwelt*) which, more or less, equates to the world as studied by the physical sciences) as in some sense *prior to* and *independent of* the human cultural world (which is explicitly excluded by the methodology of the natural sciences). For Husserl, the truth is precisely the reverse: 'nature' as such—the nature that is explored in natural scientific investigation—is itself a discovery and constituted achievement of human beings, a discovery of scientific inquiry as carried out by humans adopting a very peculiar and historically specific attitude (discovered by 'Galileo'—a name that stands for a whole movement of thought), for which he has various names including, 'the physicalistic attitude,' 'the naturalistic attitude,' and so on. It is one of the ongoing consequences of modern

Galilean science that a mathematically formalized, abstract concept of nature has been prioritized over the concrete, cultural world. Thus, in a note (Beilage XIII) accompanying his 1925 *Phenomenological Psychology* lectures, Husserl writes, "natural science—abstract; personal science—concrete" (*Naturwissenschaft—abstrakt; Personalwissenschaft—konkret* (Hua 9, 418).

Taking his cue from Husserl, Merleau-Ponty always accepts the priority of the intersubjective, cultural world as his starting point. The 'world' (*le monde*) for Merleau-Ponty—as for Husserl—means first and foremost the concrete *social, historical,* and *cultural* world, the common shared world of collective human interrelationality, the world of what Husserl calls 'spirit' (*Geist*). This is a temporally unfolding 'world' that is never given all at once, since it stretches into the past and points towards the future. This temporal world of social and cultural contexts can never be surpassed; it is 'unsurpassable' (*unhintergehbar*).

We know that Merleau-Ponty's fateful encounter with Husserl, especially his 1939 visit to the newly opened Husserl Archives in Leuven, transformed his research, as already is evident in his *Phenomenology of Perception* (1945), where a meditation on Husserlian phenomenology dominates the famous preface. He read Husserl's *Ideas II*, first in typescript in Leuven in 1939 and later in the 1952 Husserliana edition of Marly Biemel (Hua 4).[4] Merleau-Ponty was deeply influenced by what he knew of Husserl's analyses of 'empathy' (*Einfühlung*) or 'experience of the other' (*Fremderfahung*), and indeed, he several times emphasizes that the problem of empathy is one with the problem of the constitution of the commonly shared world 'for all' (*für Jedermann*) (a familiar theme in Husserl, cf. Hua 13, 14, 15). As Merleau-Ponty will put it in his commemorative essay, "The Philosopher and His Shadow" (Merleau-Ponty 1959) in *Signs* (Merleau-Ponty 1960):

> It is never a matter of anything but co-perception. I see that this man over there sees, as I touch my left hand while it is touching my right. Thus the problem of *Einfühlung*, like that of my incarnation, leads into the meditation of the sensible, or, if you prefer, it is borne within it. (*Le problème de l'Einfühlung comme celui de mon incarnation débouche donc sur la méditation du sensible, ou, si l'on préfère, il s'y transporte*). (Merlau-Ponty 1960, 215 [171])[5]

In other words, the issues of embodiment and of other-experience are both instances of this sensuous intertwining and self-doubling that characterizes being-in-the-world itself. The problematic of being embodied and the problematic of experiencing others both depend on a certain kind of sensibility or sensuousness which itself is interlaced with its surrounding world. Merleau-Ponty sees the world as the outcome of the experience of intertwined perspectives. This is why in this very chapter on "Other People and the Human World," he writes, "Transcendental subjectivity is revealed subjectivity, revealed to itself and to others, and is for that reason an intersubjectivity" (PP, 361; 415).

## 2  THE CONSTITUTION OF THE ONE COMMON WORLD

In general, Husserl's discussions of embodied 'self-experience' (*Selbsterfahrung*), the 'experience of others' (*Fremderfahrung*) in 'empathy' (*Einfühlung*), and of the being-within-one-another or interpenetration (*Ineinander*) of subjects in the constitution of the common shared world-for-all, were all hugely influential on Merleau-Ponty's philosophy, a fact he underscores by often invoking these themes using Husserl's German terms as a kind of shorthand (*Einfühlung, Ineinander*). Furthermore, Merleau-Ponty also understood how these themes mutually support and reinforce each other. In fact, the term *Einfühlung* and its cognates convey for Husserl this sense of intentional interwovenness (*Verflechtung*) and mutual implication as between persons, their bodies, and their streams of conscious life, in the commonly shared world. Human existence, for both Husserl and Merleau-Ponty, is essentially embodied, egoic, conscious, and intentional, and is best understood as 'being-in-the-world.' In all human experience, there is always the backdrop of the shared horizon of the world. He writes, "To be born is both to be born of the world and to be born into the world" (PP 453; 517). Furthermore, empathy is only possible against the background of a constituted common world:

> Egotism and altruism exist against a background of belonging to the same world; and to want to construct this phenomenon beginning with a solipsist layer is to make it impossible once and for all—and perhaps to ignore the profoundest things Husserl is saying to us. (*Signs*, 175; [220f.])

Both Husserl and Merleau-Ponty are preoccupied with how the sense of a one, common, shared, always ongoing world (a world that always transcends and outruns individual subjectivities and their intentional lives) itself emerges from living, finite, intersubjective intentionalities cooperating together. How is it that this world always appears as 'always already there' (*immer schon da*)? This constitution of the world as a whole involves a necessary paradox: how can subjects who find themselves already in the 'pregiven world' (*die vorgegebene Welt*, a concept that Husserl borrowed from Richard Avenarius) and who live finite lives with fixed temporal spans within that world, at the same time be, in their transcendental dimensions, responsible for the intentional *constitution* of a world that has the *sense* of being an ongoing, enduring, unending, unified world, a world that continues across generations and is always there as the permanent horizon for all human cultural achievements? For instance, Husserl writes about this common world in his 1924 lecture, "Kant and the Idea of Transcendental Philosophy":

> If we begin with human life and its natural conscious course, then it is a communalized life of human persons (*ein vergemeinschaftetes Leben menschlicher Personen*) who immerse themselves in an endless world, i.e., viewing it, sometimes in isolation and sometimes together with one another (*Miteinander*), imagining it variously, forming judgments about it, evaluating it, actively shaping it to suit our purposes. This world is for these persons, is for us humans, continually and quite obviously there as a common world surrounding us all (*als eine uns allgemeinsame Umwelt*); obviously *there*—it is the directly tangible and visible world in entirely immediate and freely expandable experience. It embraces not merely things and living beings, among them animals and humans, but also communities, communal institutions, works of art, cultural establishments of every kind. (Hua VII, 280 [cf. Husserl 1974b])

Merleau-Ponty already stresses the inexhaustibility of this one common world in the preface to his *Phenomenology of Perception*:

> The world is not what I think, but what I live through. I am open to the world, I have no doubt that I am in communication with it, but I do not possess it; it is inexhaustible. 'There is a world,' or rather: 'There is the world'; I can never completely account for this ever-reiterated assertion in my life. This facticity of the world is what constitutes the *Weltlichkeit der Welt*, what causes the world to be the world [. . .]. (PP, xvi-xvii; xii)

And again in the same text, he writes, "[T]he world remains the same world throughout my life because it is the permanent being within which I make all corrections to my knowledge, a world which in its unity remains unaffected by those correlations" (PP, 327f. [378]). Much later, in his final working notes (1959–1961), in order to capture the character of this intentional world that outruns all our intentionalities, Merleau-Ponty recognizes that a new concept of infinity is required—not the infinity of mathematics, but "what exceeds us: the infinity of *Offenheit* and not *Unendlichkeit*—Infinity of the *Lebenswelt* and not the infinity of idealization—Negative infinity, therefore—Meaning or reason which are contingency" (VI, 169 [221]). Merleau-Ponty, therefore, follows Husserl not only in his conception of the open-ended, temporal, and horizontal character of world, but also in thinking of human subjectivity as essentially *embodied* within this world and essentially implicated with others. For both phenomenologists, the deepest form of embodied self-experience *coincides* with the equally primordial experience of others in empathy. Merleau-Ponty, accordingly, develops his account of the 'I-other' experience, for which he often uses the Husserlian term *Einfühlung* as a shorthand in relation both to the intertwined intentionalities of living subjects and with the peculiarities of embodiment. Merleau-Ponty similarly stresses intersubjectivity, language, and 'communication with other' more and more in his later works. As he writes in *The Primacy of Perception*, "My first two books sought to restore the world of perception. My works in preparation aim to show how communication with others, and thought, take up and go beyond the realm of perception which initiated us into truth" (Merleau-Ponty 1964a, 3).[6]

For Merleau-Ponty, the world that we usually experience is specifically the *human* world, the world of commerce and culture, the world invested with specifically human signification. As he writes in the chapter "Other People and the Human World" (*Autrui et le monde humaine*) in *Phenomenology of Perception*:

> Not only have I a physical world (*un monde physique*), not only do I live in the midst of earth, air and water, I have around me roads, plantations, villages, streets, churches, implements, a bell, a spoon, a pipe. Each of these objects is moulded to the human action which it serves. Each one spreads round it an atmosphere of humanity (*émet une atmosphère d'humanité*) which may be determinate in a low degree, in the case of a few footmarks in the sand, or on the other hand highly determinate, if I go into every room from top to bottom of a house recently evacuated. [. . .] The cultural world is then ambiguous, but it is already present. (PP, 347f. [399f.])

The experienced surrounding world, for Merleau-Ponty, as for Husserl, is a distinctly human *Welt* that is much more complex than the '*Umwelt*' (*milieu*) of animals (see PP, 87 [102]).[7] This is what he calls "the social world, not [. . .] an object or sum of objects, but [. . .] a permanent field or dimension of existence" (*champ permanent ou dimension d'existence*, PP, 62 [415]). The human world is a world of embedded situatedness, but also, precisely because meanings are ambiguous, a domain of freedom. For Merleau-Ponty, our relation to this social world is "deeper (*plus profund*) than any express perception or any judgment" (PP, 362 [415]).

Following Husserl, Merleau-Ponty always understands embodiment (*Leiblichkeit*) as twofold: as my experience of myself and also my experience of the other animate organism. To express the two-sidedness of the embodied situation, the mature Merleau-Ponty chooses the term 'flesh' (*la chair*)—inspired by Jean-Paul Sartre's discussions of the flesh in *Being and Nothingness* (1943) (cf. Moran 2010)—to characterize not only the *individual* living organic body (Husserl's *Leib*), but also to explicate and negotiate the physical, emotional, and symbolic mediating spaces that allow one human being to encounter another human being. This is sometimes called 'the inter-world' (*l'intermonde*) by Merleau-Ponty. But in his late work, he settles on the word 'flesh.' Flesh is what joins us together as well as what separates us, the inside and outside of the one 'skin' (*le peau*).[8] Indeed,

Merleau-Ponty not only develops his notion of 'flesh,' but also other notions such as 'chiasme,' 'intertwining,' or 'interlacing' (*l'interlacs*) to express the manner in which one's bodily awareness is unified within oneself and also 'doubled' or 'reversed' such that one can experience oneself as other, e.g., when one hand touches the other, and a double sentience is revealed. Merleau-Ponty speaks of a general 'duplicity' (*duplicité*) of the flesh and a 'reflexivity of the sensible' (*une réflexivité du sensible*; Merleau-Ponty [1964a], 168). There is an "insertion of the world between the two leaves of my body" and "the insertion of my body between the two leaves of each thing and of the world" (VI, 264 [312]). Elsewhere, I have explored the relation between this conception of reversibility and Husserl's conception of *Verflechtung* (see Moran 2013, and 2014); here, I shall explore primarily Merleau-Ponty's conception of intersecting sociality as part of his concept of embodied being-in-the-world (*être au monde*, PP, vii and 94; and see '*le corps et le véhicule de l'être au monde*,' PP, 97).

Although Merleau-Ponty affirms over and over again in *Phenomenology of Perception* that the 'world' is primarily the *human* world, in his later writings, again following some of the late Husserl's meditations, which do refer to animality, he also expands his discussions in his later writings to talk of 'nature' in a broad sense (already implicit in the *Phenomenology of Perception* when he writes, "The natural world, we said, is the schema of intersensory relations" PP, 327 [377]). The late Merleau-Ponty even invokes the notion of 'interanimality,' where humans also encounter other animals within their world. In a late working note from January 1959, for instance, Merleau-Ponty comments on the need to develop a concept of the human with both physical and spiritual sides (following from Husserl), but also on the need for a new conception of nature (to replace the Cartesian conception), and to think about the human relation with animals: "Our relation with animality, our 'kinship (*parenté*)' [Heidegger] made explicit" (*The Visible and the Invisible* 168 [220]).[9] The concept of 'world,' then, continues to become more complex, nuanced, and indeed somewhat more horizontal and symbolic in the later Merleau-Ponty, but here, we shall remain focused on the human social world.

## 3 PHENOMENOLOGY OF INTERSUBJECTIVITY AND THE INTERWEAVING OF SUBJECTS

As we have seen, Husserl regards the spiritual or cultural world as that which is most immediate and primary. Already in a meditation written in 1910, he writes:

> I am positing now other I's, other minds, and I do this, of course, through interpretative entering in (*Hineindeutung*). [. . .] In my cogitationes I myself am 'attuned' to these I's being subjects of their cogitationes, in

particular, in acts of my position-takings, of love, of pity, etc., in acts of communication, and acts made possible by (those that presuppose) communication, acts of commanding, etc. Likewise, the other I-subjects have a stock of such cogitationes attuned to their *socii* and to me as well. [...] These relations—the relations of life—which, through these acts, are brought forth between all subjects of mind, signify that each I, each 'mind' knows itself as a member of a 'spiritual' world and at the same time knows itself as a subject vis-à-vis a world of things. However, other minds confront me in a quite different manner than things. Things confront me as lifeless objects; minds are present to me as addressed or addressing me, as loved or loving me, etc. I do not live in isolation; I live with them a common, integrated life, in spite of the separation of subjectivities.

(Husserl 2006, 167f. (translation modified); Hua 13, 92)

As human subjects, we live and move and have our being in an intersubjective, cultural world, a world where we recognize each other as partner citizens, '*socii*' (a word Husserl occasionally uses in his intersubjectivity writings, see Hua 15, 52; 193; 510; 512), a world of pregiven significations, a common, shared world of cultural objects, whose character is discovered rather than invented by us. Egological phenomenology not only must be complemented by intersubjective phenomenology, but intersubjective phenomenology must finally have primacy or, as Husserl would say, absoluteness (cf. Hua 9, 321f., Husserl 1997, 229]; Hua 9, 321f.).

This phenomenology of intersubjectivity will describe how intentional subjects cooperate to co-constitute and jointly make up their experienced cultural world with its corresponding and enduring sense of a shared, common world of nature. Nature is, as it were, revealed *within* our cultural world, and especially in and through natural scientific research, which is itself a cultural activity. As Husserl would write much later in the "Vienna Lecture" (1935), (Husserl 1997) nature is drawn into the cultural realm:

Here the spirit (*Geist*) is not in or alongside nature; rather, nature is itself drawn into the spiritual sphere. Also, the ego is then no longer an isolated thing (*ein isoliertes Ding*) alongside other such things in a pregiven world; in general, the serious mutual exteriority of ego-persons (*das ernstliche Außer- und Nebeneinander der Ichpersonen*), their being alongside one another, ceases in favor of an inward being-for-one-another and mutual interpenetration (*eines innerlichen Ineinander- und Füreinanderseins*).

(*Crisis*, 298; Hua 4, 346)

What is first for Husserl is our intentional intertwining and interweaving, our *Ineinandersein*. Personalistic phenomenology studies human lives in their interwovenness, "in their ways of living and acting with one another and in-and-through one another" (*ihrer Weisen des Miteinander- und Ineinanderlebens und -wirkens*) (Hua 9, 418). Indeed, Husserl emphasizes that we can take a 'social' or an 'asocial' attitude in our personal lives—there is a 'private attitude' (*die private Einstellung*, Hua 15, 510), which is 'asocial' and a public one, which is social.

Hans-Georg Gadamer has commented that Husserl came to recognize that his earlier phenomenological reduction had overlooked two essential insights, namely, concerning the nature of intersubjectivity and the constitution of what is not explicitly intended. Gadamer further claims that Husserl's later thinking of the horizon and world were efforts to remediate his earlier egoic phenomenology. He writes:

> Husserl saw, in particular, that at least two unnoticed presuppositions were contained in this radical beginning [the discovery of the transcendental ego]. First of all, the transcendental ego contained the 'all of us' of human community, and the transcendental view of phenomenology in no way poses the question explicitly as to how the being of the thou and the we, beyond the ego's own world, is really constituted. (This is the problem of intersubjectivity). Second, he saw that the general suspension of the thesis regarding reality did not suffice, since suspension of the positing only touched the explicit object of the act of intentional meaning, but not what is cointended and the anonymous implications given along with every such act of meaning. [. . .] Thus Husserl arrived at the elaboration of his doctrine of the horizons that in the end are all integrated into the one universal world-horizon that embraces our entire intentional life.
> (Gadamer 1977, 154f.)

Gadamer astutely recognizes that Husserl does indeed seek to articulate the world's sense as a world for all. Furthermore, this 'for all' has the character of an insurmountable horizon. We cannot get past our sense of belonging to the one world—spatial, temporal, cultural—the horizon of the world outruns everything.

The composition of the unified world gradually emerged in Husserl's thoughts from around 1911 onward (he seems to have regarded the encounter with Avenarius's work as particularly significant). Husserl originally began discussing the interweaving and intersection of experiences in the unified flow of a single consciousness. His thinking on intersubjective interaction, furthermore, essentially parallels the way in which he describes the interweaving of our individual mental experience (*Erlebnisse*, such as perceiving, remembering, imagining, and so on) in the unity of a single stream of consciousness. The peculiar unity of the 'flow' of conscious experience (*Erlebnisstrom*) is unlike any object in nature. Thus, in his 1925 *Phenomenological Psychology* lectures, where he is meditating on the legacy of Wilhelm Dilthey, he writes:

> But psychology and consequently all the socio-cultural sciences refer to the one mental nexus universally given by internal experience (*durch innere Erfahrung*). Internal experience gives no mere mutual externality

(*kein bloßes Außereinander*); it knows no separation of parts consisting of self-sufficient elements. It knows only internally interwoven states (*nur innerlich verflochtene Zustände*), interwoven in the unity of one all-inclusive nexus (*verflochten in der Einheit eines universalen Zusammenhanges*), which is itself necessarily given along with them as nexus (*Zusammenhang*) in internal intuition. Whether or not we look at it and its moments becoming singly prominent—the single perceptions, recollections, feelings, willings—whether or not we direct our noticing special regard towards their intertwinings, their passing over into one another and proceeding forth from one another (*auf ihre Verflechtungen, ihr Ineinander-übergehen und Auseinander-hervorgehen*): all that and as *one* nexus, is *lived experience* (*Erlebnis*).

(Hua 9, 8; Husserl 1997, 4f.)

Indeed, Husserl had sharply criticized Brentano for retaining a naturalistic orientation that prevented him from seeing the intentional interweaving and syntheses of psychic states in the stream of consciousness (cf. Hua 9, 36f.; Husserl 1997, 26;).

Husserl is here talking about the 'intertwining and involution' (*Verflechtung* and *Ineinandersein*) of individual, conscious experiences within the unified 'nexus of consciousness' (*Bewusstseinszusammenhang*)—but he expands this to include the peculiar manner in which groups of conscious lives and other subjectivities can intersect, interweave, and contribute to the constitution of higher collectivities. Indeed, Husserl's *Encylopaedia Britannica* (Draft A2, written in 1927) explicitly talks about the necessarily interwoven layers of self-experience, intersubjective experience, and the experience of community (*die Erfahrung der Gemeinschaft*, Hua 9, 242), and in this text, Husserl further speaks, besides the Cartesian reduction to ownness, of an 'intersubjective reduction' (Hua 9, 246; Husserl 1997, 94;), which brings to light the nature of community and 'intersubjectively entwined acts' (*intersubjektiv verflochtenen Akten*) understood as communal acts (*Akten des Gemeinschaftslebens*, Hua 9, 246) that constitute the sense of a shared, common, natural world as well as the sense of a shared objective community.

Husserl sees the two kinds of interwovenness, singular and plural, as intrinsically related. Just as individual experiences (*Erlebnisse*) can be joined together, synthesized, modified, negated, crossed out, and so on, so can intersubjective experiences. Intersubjective experiences constitute a new class of experiences, *founded*, to be sure, on individual experiences, but creating new levels of higher objectivities, including the very objective sense of a common, natural world. These higher unities, as Edith Stein has insisted, are always spiritual unities.

Husserl insists that every subjective stream is not only in principle 'open-ended,' but in face implies other streams and is in turn 'implied' in every other conscious stream, leading to an 'open plurality of such egos' (*eine offene Vielheit solcher Egos*). (cf. Hua 17, 246 [239f.]).

Husserl maintains that self-consciousness and the consciousness of others in the context of an overall 'intersubjectivity' are inseparable. Thus, he writes in *Crisis of European Sciences*:

> Here we soon see, as another a priori, that self-consciousness and consciousness of others are inseparable (*untrennbar*); it is unthinkable, and not just a mere fact, that I be human in a world without being *a* man (*es ist undenkbar, und nicht etwa ein bloßes Faktum, dass ich Mensch wäre in einer Welt, ohne dass ich ein Mensch wäre*). There need be no one in my perceptual field, but fellow men are necessary as actual, as known (*Mitmenschen sind notwendig als wirkliche und bekannte*), and as an open horizon of those I might possibly meet. Factually I am within an interhuman present (*in einer mitmenschlichen Gegenwart*) and within an open horizon of mankind; I know myself to be factually within a generative framework (*generative Zusammenhang*), in the unitary flow of a historical development in which this present is mankind's present and the world of which it is conscious is a historical present with a historical past and a historical future.
> 
> (*Crisis* § 71, 253; Hua 6, 256)

Furthermore, Husserl focuses not just on current intertwinings, as in cases of contemporaneous subjectivities in communication with each other, but he also frequently speaks of the complex 'interweavings' (*Verflechtungen*) of human subjects in collective social life in history (See Moran 2014). Indeed, historical happenings have precisely this character of having-been-the-case, of having been 'on hand,' whereas in fact, history itself is possible only because of human interaction and historicity. Thus, in his late *Origin of Geometry* text, Husserl writes:

> We can now say that history (*Geschichte*) is from the start nothing other than the vital movement (*die lebendige Bewegung*) of the with-one-another (*Miteinander*) and the interweaving (*Ineinander*) of original formations (*Sinnbildung*) and sedimentations of meaning (*Sinnsedimentierung*).
>
> (*Crisis*, 371; Hua 4, 380, transl. modified)

We intertwine not just with present others, but with others in the past, and in preceding generations, and we also carry out intentional acts that are directed towards future generations (planting trees, planning urban expansion, and so on).

In his later works, more generally, especially those around 1931 when he was attempting to rewrite the *Fifth Cartesian Meditation* for publication in the German edition, Husserl describes this intentional interrelatedness between human subjects as involving 'generativity' (*Generativität*), i.e., the interrelatedness continues across generations, and allows, for instance, poets and philosophers to take up another thinker or writer from the past, to see oneself as belonging to the same tradition, exploring the same questions, and so on. Thus, in his research notes from August 1931 entitled "The pregiven world in intuitive discovery—the systematics of expansion" (Hua XV, 196–214), he recognizes that it belongs to consciousness to be able to iterate itself—to be able to see commonalities with other consciousnesses and to expand and enlarge its horizons to include not just the present now, but experiences in the past and future, and even experiences had by others, even others not directly experiencable by me at this time. This is, for Husserl, the phenomenon of intersubjective generativity (Hua 15, 199). As he writes, "In the same manner, generatively, I have my parents, I have also known the parents of my parents, but they in turn had their parents, who also had [. . .] etc.; those latter, I myself could absolutely not have known" (Hua 15, 200, my translation).

A kind of intergenerational community is founded and this is the typical kind of community for philosophers, poets, and indeed, for natural scientists. These different individuals are bound together by shared goals and shared values. As Husserl makes clear in the *Fifth Cartesian Meditation* § 56, there is a real communion between subjectivities, although each subject is, in Husserl's Leibnizian formulation, a 'monad' and thus an absolutely separately existing self, and at the same time, "[s]omething *that exists is in intentional communion with something else that exists*. It is an essentially unique connectedness, an actual community and precisely the one that makes transcendentally possible the being of a world, a world of humans and things" (CM § 56, 129; Hua 1, 157). Let us turn now to Merleau-Ponty.

## 4 THE INTERSUBJECTIVE REDUCTION AND THE LIFE-WORLD

Initially, Merleau-Ponty, in the preface to his *Phenomenology of Perception* (1945), praises phenomenology for not assuming a world that exists independently of our intersubjective involvements. He speaks of the 'intersubjective world' and he also recognizes that 'monadic and intersubjective experience' form 'one unbroken text' (PP, 54 [66]). It is through sensuous experience that I have a sense of the world as the 'familiar setting of my life' (PP, 52f. [64f.]). When we wake from sleep, we wake into the intersubjective world.

Merleau-Ponty was always aware of the limitations of Husserl's conception of the reduction. He recognized that Husserl's approach tended to be too one sided, too Cartesian. The transcendental reduction, for Merleau-Ponty, ought not to end in a monadological, transcendental subjectivity, in a Cartesian *mens sive animus*, but rather there must be—as Husserl also confirmed—an intersubjective reduction:

> The passage to intersubjectivity is contradictory only with regard to an insufficient reduction, Husserl was right to say. But a sufficient

reduction leads beyond the alleged transcendental 'immanence,' it leads to the absolute spirit understood as *Weltlichkeit,* to *Geist* as *Ineinander* of the spontaneities, itself founded on the aesthesiological *Ineinander* and on the sphere of life as sphere of *Einfühlung* and intercorporeity.
(VI, 172 [223f.])

Although it is not clear what Husserlian texts Merleau-Ponty is reflecting on here, he does recognize that for Husserl, intersubjectivity comes together to produce 'absolute spirit,' understood as *Ineinandersein*, which produces the sense of one, objective, shared, common world for all. In *Ideas II* § 62, Husserl emphasizes the ontological primacy of the personalistic world over and against the naturalistic world (*Ideas II*, 294; IV 281), and in this section, he speaks of the Janus-faced experiential body that is experienced as an 'aesthesiological body' (which seems to find echoes in Merleau-Ponty's passage (quoted above) in *The Visible and the Invisible* [1964]) and the 'body for the will.' The aesthesiological body is the substratum underlying the body for the will. In this *Ideas II* § 62, Husserl has a footnote in which he states:

> According to our presentation, the concepts I and we (*Ich-Wir*) are relative: the I requires the thou, the we and the 'other.' And, furthermore, the Ego (the Ego as person) requires a relation to a world which engages it. Therefore, I, we and world belong together (*gehören zusammen*); the world as communal environing world (*als gemeinsame Umgebungswelt*), thereby bears the stamp of subjectivity.
> (*Ideas II*, 301f.; Hua 4, 288)

Merleau-Ponty is both gauging correctly and reaffirming the Husserlian idea of the 'spiritual world' as a complex *Ineinander* of intercorporeal and intersubjective relations and interactions. In his notes on Husserl's *Origin of Geometry*, he again invokes the '*Ineinander* between present and past' (*Ineinander du présent et du passé,*) in speaking of the 'openness' of historicity (Merleau-Ponty 1998, 22 [20]). Merleau-Ponty also speaks of *Ineinander* to express the peculiarly human character of embodiment in his *Nature* lectures (Merleau-Ponty 1995, 269). We are not a mechanistic body plus spirit, but an interweaving of a physical body and an animate body. Merleau-Ponty writes of an *Ineinander* which is not that of one body inside another, but a 'lived, perceived Ineinander' (*notre Ineinander vécu, perçu, La Nature,* 270) that we experience in terms of the blending of the senses in the world, as well as the 'animality-humanity *Ineinander*' (*L'Ineinander animalité-humanité,* ibid.), that we experience in terms of our occupation of both domains of nature. This focus on *Ineinander* in its various senses requires a new ontology and an overcoming of the "philosophy of 'consciousness'" that Merleau-Ponty considered still to haunt his *Phenomenology of Perception* (VI, 183 [234]). In his *Course Notes for the Origin of Geometry*, he similarly writes of *Ineinander* in our relation to our occupation of both the corporeal and the symbolic (irreal) spheres—in this case, the token is geometry.[10]

Merleau-Ponty believes we live as human beings primarily in the realms of the imaginary and the symbolic. Merleau-Ponty is influenced not only by Cassirer's *Philosophy of Symbolic Forms* (especially *Volume Two: The Mythical World*; Cassirer 1955), but also by the writings of Lévy-Bruhl, Lévi-Strauss, and possibly also Roger Caillois. Subsequently, Jacques Lacan would criticize Merleau-Ponty for not having an adequate account of the symbolic world (Lacan 1986, and 1991), and this view has become established in the literature. I believe, however, that Merleau-Ponty wants to emphasize our finite rootedness in the social world rather than the infinite horizons that entrance into the symbolic world affords.

Already in his first book, *The Structure of Behavior* (Merleau-Ponty 1942),[11] Merleau-Ponty had distinguished environment and 'milieu' from 'world':

> Science is not therefore dealing with organisms as the completed modes of a unique world *(Welt)*, as the abstract parts of a whole in which the parts would be most perfectly contained. It has to do with a series of 'environments' and 'milieu' (*Umwelt, Merkwelt, Gegenwelt*) in which the stimuli intervene according to what they signify and what they are worth for the typical activity of the species considered.
> (SB, 129–30 [139–40])

In fact, it is into this human world that nature and the natural world intrudes. Merleau-Ponty begins this chapter on "Other People and the Human World" by asserting that we are 'thrown into a nature' that is itself discernible at the center of subjectivity (PP, 346 [398]). He asserts that "nature finds its way to the core of my personal life and becomes inextricably linked with it" (PP 347; 399). For Merleau-Ponty, as for Husserl, natural things and the natural world that is experienced external to me are *secondary* to my incarnate experience of the human and of human others in an intersubjective cultural (or "spiritual") world. What we encounter first is the body of the other person. As Merleau-Ponty writes in this section on "Other People and the Human World" (echoing a similar statement in Husserl that the other (*Leib*) is the first objective other): "The very first of all cultural objects, and the one by which all the rest exist, is the body of the other person (*le corps d'autrui*) as the vehicle of a form of behaviour (*comme porteur d'un comportement*)" (PP, 348 [401]).

For Merleau-Ponty, this 'objective spirit' (PP, 348 [400])—this 'subjectless and anonymous' cultural world (PP, 349 [401]) challenges the sense of subjectivity as always emanating from an 'I,' but it also challenges purely objectivist thought that things it can simply think about humans as objects—animals—relating to other objects in a world: "the existence of other people is a difficulty and an outrage for objective thought" (PP, 349

[401]). Merleau-Ponty had already made the social, human world to be the center of life in *The Structure of Behavior*. There, he says that the relation of soul to body has to be relativized. There are a number of layers, and each one is the soul to the lower body (cf. SB, 210 [227])

Merleau-Ponty regards the cultural, human world as precisely that which overcomes both solipsistic egoism and objectivism. Rather than enjoying a 'pure contemplation' of the world, Merleau-Ponty claims in *Sense and Nonsense* that each of us has to take up as best we can "the acts of others (*actes d'autrui*), reactivating from ambiguous signs (*à partir des signes ambigus*) an experience which is not his own, appropriating a structure [. . .] which he puts together as an experienced pianist deciphers an unknown piece of music" (*Sense and Nonsense*, 93 [109]).¹² Rather than 'positing an object,' we have 'communication with a way of being' (*Il n'y a plus ici position d'un objet, mais communication avec une manière d'être*, SNS, 93; 110). Constitution cannot be considered as meaning-making done by an isolated subject, but more like the experience of being carried along on the wave of intersubjectively constituted meanings.

Following Husserl, the experience of others is understood from my initial relation to myself. But for Merleau-Ponty, my initial relation to myself is also somehow dispersed. Just as I experience myself first in a kind of pre-personal way, so also I grasp the other in a similar way:

> The possibility of another person's being self-evident is owed to the fact that I am not transparent for myself, and that my subjectivity draws its body in its wake [. . .] the positing of the other does not reduce me to an object in his perceptual field [. . .] The other person is never quite a personal being, if I myself am totally one, and if I grasp myself as apodeictically self-evident. But if I find in myself, through reflection, along with the perceiving subject, a pre-personal subject given to itself and if my perceptions are centred outside me as sources of initiative and judgment, if the perceived world remains in a state of neutrality, being neither verified as an object nor recognized as a dream, then it is not the case that everything that appears in the world is arrayed before me, and so the behaviour of others can have its place there.
>
> (PP, 352f. [405])

Our perspectives slip into one another—they are not separate and independent (PP, 353 [405f.]).

Already in *Phenomenology of Perception* in 1945, Merleau-Ponty is explicating the manner in which we experience ourselves not in the full plenitude of self-aware subjectivity, as in the Cartesian tradition, but rather as partial and limited perspectives whose views are intertwined with those of others. I experience myself just as I experience others, and indeed objects in the world—as transcendencies that are never complete. This is the basis for Merleau-Ponty's conception of 'intertwining,' 'intercorporeality,' and '*l'intermonde*'—all concepts that receive much fuller elaboration in *The Visible and Invisible*.

## 5 THE SPLITTING OF SELF-CONSCIOUSNESS AND THE CONSTITUTION OF THE OTHER

For Merleau-Ponty, self-experience and 'primary presence' (*Urpräsenz*) are experiences already of a transcendence according to which we already are not one with ourselves. Merleau-Ponty elaborates on this self-distantiation, that we experience in our own selves in terms of a very unique concept found in Husserl's *Crisis*—the concept of 'depresentation' (*Entgegenwärtigung*), which Merleau-Ponty invokes on rare occasions but specifically in his chapter on "Other People and the Human World" (see PP, 363 [417]).[13] Husserl uses the term 'depresentation' (*Entgegenwärtigung*) just once in *Crisis*, in his discussion of 'self-temporalization' (*Crisis* § 54b, 185; Hua 6, 189), another theme that recurs throughout the *Phenomenology of Perception*. The passage in Husserl's *Crisis* reads:

> Thus the immediate 'I' performs an accomplishment through which it constitutes a variational mode of itself as existing (in the mode of having passed). Starting from this we can trace how the immediate 'I,' flowingly-statically present, constitutes itself in self-temporalization as enduring through its pasts. In the same way, the immediate 'I,' already enduring in the enduring primordial sphere, constitutes in itself another as other. Self-temporalization through depresentation (*Ent-Gegenwärtigung*), so to speak (through recollection), has its analogue in my self-alienation (*Ent-Fremdung*) (empathy as a depresentation of a higher level—depresentation of my primal presence (*Urpräsenz*) into a merely presentified (*vergegenwärtigte*) primal presence). Thus, in me, 'another I' achieves ontic validity as copresent (*kompräsent*) with his own ways of being self-evidently verified, which are obviously quite different from those of a 'sense'-perception. (*Crisis*, 185; Hua 6, 189)

Merleau-Ponty invokes this exact passage in the *Phenomenology of Perception* when he says (in the passage from which I have extracted the opening epigraph for this chapter):

> The problem of the existential modality of the social is here at one with all problems of transcendence. Whether we are concerned with my body, the natural world, the past, birth or death, the question is always how I can be open to phenomena which transcend me, and which nevertheless exist only to the extent that I take them up and live them; how the presence to myself (*Urpräsenz*) which establishes my own limits and conditions every alien presence is at the same time depresentation

(*Entgegenwärtigung*) and throws me outside myself (*et me jette hors de moi*). (PP, 363 [417])

In this sense—and this is where Merleau-Ponty takes up Heidegger's notion of *ex-stasis*—I am always thrown outside myself. It is this possibility of self-transcendence that already gives an opening to others and to the world (cf. VI, 180 [232] and *Signs*, 176f. [222]). Merleau-Ponty is obsessed with this transcendental intersubjectivity, but he is also keen to defend Husserl against solipsism. In his essay "The Philosopher and His Shadow," Merleau-Ponty correctly points out:

> For the 'solipsist' thing is not *primary* for Husserl, nor is the *solus ipse*. Solipsism is a 'thought-experiment' (*Gedankenexperiment*; Hua 4, 81); the *solus ipse* is a 'constructed subject' (Hua 4, 81). (*Signs*, 173 [219])

Following Husserl, Merleau-Ponty argues against the possibility of even conceiving aloneness without reference to others. A genuine *solus ipse* would be ignorant of itself. To posit oneself is to posit *one* self as already a self among other selves. This is a point that Merleau-Ponty already labors in the *Phenomenology of Perception*. There can never be a Robinson Crusoe (as Scheler also observes) in the pure sense of a totally isolated ego. As Heidegger, points out, even being alone is a mode of *Mitsein*.

True dialectical thinking has to recognize the spoken word, the silence out of which the word comes. It becomes dead if it focuses solely on the spoken world, *la langue parlée*, on the 'thesis,' as Merleau-Ponty says. This, Merleau-Ponty, says is the "*Ineinander* which nobody sees, and which is not a group-soul either, neither object nor subject, but their connective tissue, which *west* [becomes]" (VI, 174 [226]). In these and other fragmentary texts, Merleau-Ponty draws on his intellectual resources (Freudian, Lacanian, Saussurian, Lévi-Straussian, Marxist) to try to articulate this hidden invisible *Ineinander* that makes culture possible, that makes possible "the being society of a society, the being history of history," as he puts it in working note from February 1959 (VI, 174 [226]). Unfortunately, Merleau-Ponty did not live to complete his planned project, and it remains to us to try to piece together his mature conception of *Ineinander*, which seeks always to mine the resources bequeathed from the equally unfinished work of his master Edmund Husserl, in whose shadow he worked.

## NOTES

1 Henceforth, 'PP,' followed by the page number of Colin Smith's English translation; then, the pagination of the French edition.
2 The term '*Ineinander*' and its cognates appear 16 times in the *Krisis* (at Hua 4, 25, 52, 153, 177, and especially in § 71 at 258, 259, 260) and 262 (twice),

319, 346, 364, 380, 514, 530, 548. In *Ideas II*, the term '*Ineinander*' appears approximately seven times, especially at § 58, 281, 283 (*Ineinandergreifen* of naturalistic and personalistic attitudes), but more usually in terms of the manner in which *Erlebnisse* are unified with one another in the stream of experience; see Hua 4, 92, 122, 150, 228, 300 (the interrelation of the temporal phases). In *Formal and Transcendental* Logic, it appears at Hua 17 pages 87, 210, 261, 366, usually to refer to the mutual entanglement of ideal entities and real, of psychological and transcendental attitudes, or between words and meaning. See also Husserl, *Erste Philosophie* Hua 8, 102.

3 The term *Ineinander* is primarily associated with the late Husserl from the mid-twenties on. There are only three references to *Ineinander* in anything like a technical sense in Husserliana XIII, which covers the period from 1905 to 1920 (75, from 1913; 206 (*Ineinanderverflechtungen*) from c. 1924; and 390, from 1918); but Husserliana 14 has an important text (no. 13) from early 1922 that discusses '*Das personale Wirken, das Miteinander- und Ineinanderleben*' (Hua 14, 268). The term '*Ineinander*' appears more frequently (more than a dozen times) in Husserliana 14 (at 90, 150, 172 (the interconnected caring between I and you, *die Ineinandergeborgenheit von Ich und Du*), 174, 219 (*Ineinander* between *Außenwelt* and *Innenwelt*), 268, 269, 271, 292, 318, 348 (*Ineinanderschlingung von Apperzeptionen*), 381, and 548. Hua 15 discusses *intentional Ineinander* at pages 371, 602, and *ineinander* at 9, 90, 148, 170, and 200.

4 Hereafter, '*Ideas II*' followed by English pagination, and 'Hua 4' with the German pagination.

5 Hereafter, '*Signs*' followed by English translation page number, and then the French original. Translation modified.

6 Hereafter, '*Primacy*' and the page number of the English translation.

7 In PP, Merleau-Ponty references the *La structure du comportement* (1942).

8 For a Freudian psychoanalytical discussion of the interrelation between egoic subjectivity and skin, which in many ways represents a parallel development of Merleau-Ponty's thoughts, see Anzieu 1985.

9 Hereafter, 'VI' followed by the pagination of the English translation and then the French original.

10 "E. Husserl, '[. . .] c'est une humanité transcendantale, intérieure; c'est le ressort philosophique de toute humanité qui est découvert par moi dans l'irréalité, le vide caractéristique, la précarité de ce qui a été librement créé. C'est dans cette irréalité que nous sommes *Ineinander*. Nous sommes hommes en ce que précisément nous visons une unicité à travers l'épaisseur de nos vies, en ce que nous sommes groupés autour de cet intérieur unique où personne n'est, qui est latent, voilé et nous échappe toujours laissant entre nos mains des vérités comme traces de son absence'" (Merlau-Ponty 1998, 34 [29])).

11 Hereafter, 'SB' and the page number of the English translation; then, the page number of the French.

12 Henceforth, 'SNS' followed by the page number of the English translation; then, the page number of the French edition.

13 Merleau-Ponty, in his working notes, wants to model his inquiry for a new ontology on Husserl's *Crisis* (see VI, 183 [234]).

## REFERENCES

Anzieu, Didier (1985). *Le Moi Peau*. Paris: Dunod.

Ayouch, Thamy (2012). *Maurice Merleau-Ponty et la psychanalyse: la consonance imparfaite*. Lormont: Éditions le bord de l'eau.

Cassirer, Ernst (1955). *The Philosophy of Symbolic Forms. Volume 2: Mythical Thought.* Transl. by R. Manheim. New Haven: Yale University Press.
Gadamer, Hans-Georg (1977). "The Phenomenological Movement." In David Linge (Ed.). *Philosophical Hermeneutics.* Berkeley, CA: University of California Press.
Husserl, Edmund (1950) [=Hua 1]. *Cartesianische Meditationen und Pariser Vorträge.* Ed. S. Strasser, Husserliana 1. The Hague: Martinus Nijhoff.
―――― (1952) [=Hua 4]. *Ideen zu einer reinen Phänomenologie und phänomenologischen Philosophie.* Book 2. *Phänomenologische Untersuchungen zur Konstitution.* Ed. by M. Biemel. The Hague: Nijhoff. [Engl.: (1989). *Ideas Pertaining to a Pure Phenomenology and to a Phenomenological Philosophy. Second Book. Studies in the Phenomenology of Constitution.* Transl. by R. Rojcewicz, & A. Schuwer. Dordrecht: Kluwer.]
―――― (1954) [=Hua 6]. *Die Krisis der europäischen Wissenschaften und die transzendentale Phänomenologie: Eine Einleitung in die phänomenologische Philosophie.* Ed. by W. Biemel. The Hague: Nijhoff. [Engl.: (1970). *The Crisis of European Sciences and Transcendental Phenomenology: An Introduction to Phenomenological Philosophy.* Transl. by D. Carr. Evanston, IL: Northwestern University Press.]
―――― (1959) [=Hua 8]. *Erste Philosophie (1923/24). Zweiter Teil. Theorie der phänomenologischen Reduktion.* Ed. by R. Boehm. The Hague: Nijhoff.
―――― (1960). *Cartesian Meditations: An Introduction to Phenomenology.* Transl. by D. Cairns. The Hague: Nijhoff.
―――― (1965) [=Hua 7]. *Erste Philosophie (1923/24). Erster Teil: Kritische Ideengeschichte,* Ed. by R. Boehm. The Hague: Nijhoff.
―――― (1968) [=Hua 9]. *Phänomenologische Psychologie: Vorlesungen Sommersemester 1925.* Ed. by W. Biemel. The Hague: Nijhoff. [Engl.: (1977). *Phenomenological Psychology: Lectures, Summer Semester, 1925.* Trans. John Scanlon. The Hague: Nijhoff.]
―――― (1973a) [=Hua 13]. *Zur Phänomenologie der Intersubjektivität. Texte aus dem Nachlass.* Ed. by I. Kern. The Hague: Nijhoff.
―――― (1973b) [=Hua 14]. *Zur Phänomenologie der Intersubjektivität. Texte aus dem Nachlass.* Ed. by I. Kern. The Hague: Nijhoff.
―――― (1973c) [=Hua 15]. *Zur Phänomenologie der Intersubjektivität. Texte aus dem Nachlass.* Ed. by I. Kern. The Hague: Nijhoff.
―――― (1974a) [=Hua 17]. *Formale und transzendentale Logik.* Ed. by Paul Janssen. The Hague: Nijhoff. [Engl. (1969). *Formal and Transcendental Logic.* Transl. by D. Cairns. The Hague: Nijhoff.]
―――― (1974b). "Kant and the Idea of Transcendental Philosophy." Trans. by Ted E. Klein and William E. Pohl. *Southwestern Journal of Philosophy* 5, 9–56.
―――― (1997). *Psychological and Transcendental Phenomenology and the Confrontation with Heidegger (1927–31), The Encyclopaedia Britannica Article, The Amsterdam Lectures "Phenomenology and Anthropology" and Husserl's Marginal Note in Being and Time, and Kant on the Problem of Metaphysics.* Transl. by T. Sheehan, & R. E. Palmer, Husserl Collected Works VI, Dordrecht: Kluwer.
―――― (2006). *The Basic Problems of Phenomenology from the Lectures, Winter Semester, 1910–1911.* Transl. by I. Farin, & J. G. Hart. Husserl Collected Works XII. Dordrecht: Springer.
Leonard, Lawlor, & Bergo, Bettina (2002). *Husserl at the Limits of Phenomenology.* Evanston, IL: Northwestern University Press.
Lacan, Jacques (1986). *Séminaire VII: L'éthique de la psychanalyse.* Paris: Seuil.
―――― (1991). *The Seminar of Jacques Lacan: Book II: The Ego in Freud's Theory and in the Technique of Psychoanalysis, 1954–1955.* Ed. by J.-A. Miller. Transl. by S. Tomaselli. New York: Norton.

Merleau-Ponty, Maurice (1942). *La structure du comportement*. Paris: Presses Universitaires de France. [Engl.: (1963). *The Structure of Behavior*. Transl. By A. L. Fisher. Boston: Beacon Press.]

—— (1945) [=PP]. *Phénoménologie de la perception*. Paris: Gallimard. [Engl.: (1962). *Phenomenology of Perception*. Transl. by C. Smith. London: Routledge & Kegan Paul.]

—— (1948). *Sens et non-sens*. Paris: Nagel. [Engl.: (1964d). *Sense and Nonsense*. Transl. by H. Dreyfus & P. A. Dreyfus. Evanston, IL: Northwestern University Press.]

—— (1960). *Signes*. Paris: Gallimard. [Engl.: (1964c). *Signs*. Transl. by R. McCleary. Evanston, IL: Northwestern University Press.]

—— (1964a). *L'oeil et l'esprit*. Paris: Gallimard.

—— (1964b). *Le visible et l'invisible*. Paris: Gallimard.

—— (1995). *La Nature. Notes. Cours du Collège de France*. Établi et annoté par Dominique Séglard. Paris: Éditions du Seuil.

—— (1998). *Notes de cours sur l'origine de la géométrie de Husserl, suivi de Recherches sur la phénoménologie de Merleau-Ponty*. Sous la direction de R. Barbaras. Paris: Presses Universitaires de France. [Engl.: (2002). *Husserl at the Limits of Phenomenology*. Transl. by L. Lawlor with B. Bergo. Evanston, IL: Northwestern University Press.]

Moran, Dermot (2010). "Sartre on Embodiment, Touch, and the 'Double Sensation'," *Philosophy Today* 54 (Supplement), 135–141.

—— (2013). "'There Is No Brute World, Only an Elaborated World': Merleau-Ponty on the Intersubjective Constitution of the World", *South African Journal of Philosophy*, 32 (4), 355–371.

—— (2014). "The Phenomenology of Embodiment: Intertwining (*Verflechtung*) and Reflexivity". In: D. Moran, & R. T. Jensen (Ed.). *The Phenomenology of Embodied Subjectivity*. Dordrecht: Springer, 285–230.

# 7 Davidson and Husserl on the Social Origin of Our Concept of Objectivity

*Cathal O'Madagain*

## 1 INTRODUCTION

In his later papers, Davidson repeatedly returns to the notion that our interactions with others may have a central role to play in the development of our cognitive abilities. Specifically, Davidson argued that without interacting linguistically with others, we could not recognize that we ourselves have thoughts. And understanding that we have thoughts is essential to grasping the concept of objectivity, since grasping the latter amounts to realizing that the world might not be the way we think it is. So, he concludes, our grasp of objectivity depends on our linguistic interactions with others.

Husserl arrived at a similar conclusion, but via a different line of reasoning. Husserl argued that in order to realize that objects exist independently of our experience of them, we need to realize that there are possible perspectives on those objects that we do not have. The way we come to realize this is by interacting with others. So, again, our concept of objectivity depends on our interactions with others.

Both arguments have been subjected to scrutiny, and found unsatisfying. Nevertheless, research in developmental psychology over the last 30 years has found a remarkable correlation that supports the views of Davidson and Husserl: that only given a significant amount of socialization, particularly only upon the acquisition of the ability to construct propositional-attitude attribution sentences (sentences like, "Sally believes that . . ."), can children grasp the appearance/reality distinction, or properly understand that others might have false beliefs (see Wellman et al. 2001 for an overview). For example, until that time, a child will not understand that an object that looks like a rock might actually be a sponge (Flavell et al. 1983), or understand that another child whose toy has been moved without her seeing it moved may have a false belief about its location (Wimmer & Perner 1983). Importantly, in deaf children raised by non-signing parents, these abilities are delayed—suggesting that the acquisition of the linguistic ability is playing a causal role (de Villiers 2005).

This apparently causal relationship has remained difficult to explain, although various proposals are on offer (see de Villiers 2007 for an overview). Here, I suggest that by combining the more convincing aspects of Davidson and Husserl's approaches to this issue, an as-yet-unexplored, possible explanation emerges. I will discuss first Davidson's view, then Husserl's, and in the last section how their ideas might be combined to shed light on the empirical results we have found.

## 2  DAVIDSON'S ARGUMENT

The overall form of Davidson's argument for the dependence of our concept of objectivity on our interactions with others, distilled from several discussions,[1] seems to be the following:

> *D1:* To grasp the concept of objectivity, I must grasp the concept of thought.[2]
> *D2:* To grasp the concept of thought, I must interact linguistically with others.
> *D:* Therefore, to grasp the concept of objectivity, I must interact linguistically with others.

The first premise is defended in "Rational Animals" (1982). Davidson reasons as follows: to grasp the concept of objectivity, we need not only to have thoughts about chairs and tables and trees and the sky, but we also need to have thoughts about our thoughts about these things. To grasp the concept of objectivity, after all, is just to recognize that the way the world actually is might be different from the way we believe the world to be. If we do not understand that we have thoughts such as beliefs about the world, we cannot understand that the way the world is could be distinct from the way those beliefs represent it to be. You can't think about a relation without thinking about the relata. And so, it is necessary to grasp the concept of thought in order to grasp the concept of objectivity.

We might worry that tying the concept of objectivity to the concept of thought over-intellectualizes it. Masrour (2013, 124), for example, argues that instead, we should take a grasp of objectivity to be constituted simply by our ability to have experiences that represent the world as remaining constant even though its appearance changes. This is found in the perceptual phenomenon of 'size constancy': as we approach a tree, its image in our visual field grows, but we represent the tree as remaining the same size. A natural assessment of such cases is to take the constant size of the tree as belonging to the world, and the changing size of its appearance as belonging to our mental lives alone.

Certainly, in our assessment of such experiences, we ordinarily appeal to our concept of objectivity. But we can also assess such experiences without appealing to objectivity. I can coherently suppose that the constant size I believe the tree possesses as its image changes and the changing size of its image are both projections of my mind. Such experiences can, after all, be had in dreams—where objects may seem to us as having a size that remains the same even as their image in our dream grows or shrinks as we appear to approach them. But we do not assess our experiences in dreams as objective. Since we can undergo such experiences without applying the concept of objectivity, such experiences of ours cannot be constitutive of our grasp of objectivity. It therefore seems to me that Davidson is right to require our concept of objectivity to depend on a grasp of thought. The concept comes online not in first-order intentional states, such as experiences of size constancy, but in second-order intentional states—our thoughts about our thoughts.

Let's turn to Davidson's second premise. Davidson has two principal arguments for why grasping the concept of thought depends on linguistic interaction. After Bridges (2006), I will call these the argument from object directedness, and the argument from error.

The first argument is that if I am to grasp the concept of thought, I need to understand that my thoughts are directed at specific objects. Thoughts are individuated in part, after all, in terms of the objects they are directed at. A thought about an apple, that it is tasty, is not the same as a thought about a banana, that it is tasty. What distinguishes the two is that one is about an apple, and the other about a banana. If you don't get that, you don't understand what thoughts are. So how do we come to recognize that our thoughts are directed at particular objects?

The idea that we need to interact with others to realize that our thoughts are directed at particular objects is introduced by considering whether we could understand this object directedness without any interaction. Take Pavlov's dog. We all suppose that Pavlov's dog salivates in response to the ringing of a bell. But can we be sure that this is what he is responding to?

> [A]s psychologists have noticed, there is a problem about the stimulus. In the case of the dog, why say the stimulus is the ringing of the bell? Why couldn't it be the vibration of the air close to the ears of the dog—or even the stimulation of its nerve endings? Certainly if the air were made to vibrate, in the same way the bell makes it vibrate, it would make no difference to the behavior of the dog. And if the right nerve endings were activated in the right way, there would still be no difference.
>
> (Davidson 1992, 117)

Davidson insists that in fact there is nothing in the dog's behavior taken on its own to allow us to decide which is the right answer. Instead, what singles out the bell rather than any of the other stimuli is our response to the dog:

> What explains the fact that it seems so natural to say the dog is responding to the bell, the child to tables? It seems natural to us because it is

natural—to us. Just as the dog and the child respond in similar ways to certain stimuli, so do we. *It is we* who find it natural to group together the various salivations of the dog; and the events in the world that we effortlessly notice and group together that are causally linked to the dog's behavior are ringings of the bell. (ibid., my emphasis)

What Davidson is proposing is that because the only thing that identifies the bell ringing as the object of the dog's reaction is *us*, rather than something about the dog's behavior, then if there is a fact of the matter of what the dog is responding to, it is our interpretation that is constitutive of that fact. Generalizing this view to humans, Davidson holds that it is only in the context of interpretations by others that there is any fact about which object a thought is about—our interpretation of each others' behavior in terms of object-directed thought is constitutive of that behavior being guided by object-directed thoughts.

Unfortunately, the argument is extremely problematic. First, it's not clear why producing interpretable object-directed actions or utterances is required to have object-directed thoughts. That is, even if an interpreter is required for actions like salivating or speaking to have an object, it's not clear why object-directed thought could not take place prior to or independently of interpretable behavior. Many thoughts have no behavioral output—such as armchair ruminations on how to fix the washing machine that come to nothing. Surely, however, those thoughts have objects.

But let's grant that interpretable behavior is required for object-directed thoughts, and even that only given an observer's interpretation do those thoughts have objects. Now we need to ask how this process of interpretation could endow us with the concept of object directedness. And here we are confronted with a worrying circularity—the process seems to require the very concept that it is supposed to endow us with (Bridges 2006, 16; Pagin 2001, 8). Consider the case of two people interpreting each other's linguistic reactions to a common stimulus: each judges of the other that his linguistic output refers to some object of joint attention—a table, for example. But what does this judging amount to? It would appear to amount to each individual attributing a thought about the table to the other. But if that's true, then each individual must already know what thoughts are, and therefore what object directedness is, to engage in the 'triangulation' process in the first place. And if that's true, then the very idea of object directedness could not be conferred upon the actors by the interaction.

Next, let's consider the argument from error. Here, the strategy begins in the same way: by identifying an essential feature of thoughts, and urging that the only way we can come to understand that feature is by interacting with others. This time, the essential feature is the fallibility of propositional thought. If we are to grasp the concept of objectivity—that the world might not be as our thoughts represent it to be—we must understand that our thoughts have contents that can be true or false. We must also understand that the truth of these contents—which we call propositions—is independent of whether we believe them or not. That's just what it is for something to be true or false—not to be believed to be true or false, but to have a truth value independently of what anyone believes:

> Propositional thought is objective in the sense that it has a content that is true or false independent of the existence of the thought or the thinker.
> (Davidson 1997, 129)

If we can grasp this, we must understand what error is, or what false beliefs are. So where do we get the idea of error? For this, Davidson takes us back to triangulation:

> The triangle I have described stands for the simplest interpersonal situation. In it two (or more) creatures each correlate their own reactions to external phenomena with the reactions of the other. Once these correlations are set up, each creature is in a position to expect the external phenomenon when it perceives the associated reaction of the other. What introduces the possibility of error is the occasional failure of the expectation; the reactions do not correlate. [. . .] if this is right then thought as well as language is necessarily social.
> (Davidson 1997, 129)

Unfortunately, once again the argument is obscure. Why does seeing someone else's linguistic reactions failing to match my own introduce me to the idea of error? Two options seem available. First, if the speaker says 'gavagai' a thousand times in the presence of rabbits, I might decide that by 'gavagai,' she means *rabbit*. If she then uses the term when no rabbits are around, I might think, "Aha, she has a false belief that there is a rabbit present!" But the problem here is that this once again presupposes the concept of false belief, rather than endows us with it. If we don't already know what false beliefs are, how can we use them to explain the observed discrepancy?

Alternatively, perhaps the process is supposed to draw our attention to *our own* errors. If I earlier thought the speaker will only say 'gavagai' when rabbits are around, and now realize that this isn't true, then perhaps I can notice that I had a false belief myself. But if that's all that's required to hit on the idea of false beliefs, then why do I have to interact with someone else? I can discover my own false beliefs all by myself: I expect all red berries to taste sweet, and then discover a sour one; I expect this branch to hold my weight but it breaks when I stand on it, etc. If my expectations simply failing to be met were enough to prompt in me the idea of false beliefs, I should be able to discover this without interacting with anyone (Lepore & Ludwig 2005, 402).

The state of Davidson's discussion of the concept of objectivity seems to me, therefore, to be as follows. We have been given a good reason to think that without understanding what thoughts are, we couldn't grasp the concept of objectivity. And we have been given two important points about thought. First, we can't know what thoughts are unless we realize that thoughts are directed at objects. Second, we can't know what thoughts are unless we understand that the propositions we entertain in thought are in an important sense independent of us—they can be true or false whether we believe them or not, or even think about them. Where the trail runs cold is at the point where these claims are supposed to depend on our interactions with other speakers, linguistic or otherwise. Davidson leaves us, then, without a satisfactory answer to the question, "Why does my recognition that the propositions I entertain are independent from me depend on interaction with others?" However, Husserl has an alternative approach that may help to make the connection.

## 3  HUSSERL'S ARGUMENT

Husserl introduces an argument in the *Cartesian Meditations* (CM) that ties our concept of objectivity to our interactions with others. The overall form of Husserl's argument, I suggest, is the following:

> *H1:* To grasp the concept of objectivity, I must recognize that there are current possible perspectives on the world that I do not have.
> *H2:* To recognize that there are current possible perspectives on the world that I do not have, I must interact with others.
> *H:* To grasp the concept of objectivity, I must interact with others.

I will now try to fill out the argument, before considering in the next section how it might connect with the points Davidson has raised.

Husserl's discussion opens by introducing to us the essential puzzle raised by the concept of objectivity: how can an individual thinker come up with the idea of a world that is independent of his own experiences, when all he has available to him to construct that concept are his own experiences?[3] The answer, Husserl tells us, comes from our postulation of the experiences of others. This postulation comes about when we encounter other minds.

The key element of Husserl's account of our encounters with other minds is something he calls 'appresentation.' Appresentation is that aspect of experience whereby features of the world not currently visible to us are included in our experience of the things we encounter. For example, when we look at an apple, we experience it as having a front and rear side out of view: "An appresentation occurs even in external experience, since the strictly seen front of a physical thing always and necessarily appresents a rear aspect" (CM, § 49). When we realize that other minds inhabit our world, however, our experience includes another kind of appresentation. We imagine the world not only as it would look to us if we changed position, but as it looks from the perspective of the other mind. Husserl thinks this latter kind of appresentation differs in various ways from the first kind, and these differences are key to our acquisition of the concept of objectivity.

The first difference concerns our access to the content that is appresented. What is appresented in our experience of ordinary objects is something we can 'verify': "Appresentation of [the first] sort involves the possibility of verification by a corresponding fulfilling presentation (the back becomes the front)" (ibid.). To return to the apple, let's suppose that when I see it, the first side is presented to me, and the far side is appresented in my experience—as a side that would come into view were I to change position. I can now verify whether the rear side is as I have appresented it by walking around to the other side and taking a look.

But Husserl tells us that I cannot similarly verify what I have appresented of the perspective of another. Indeed, he says that the possibility of such verification can be 'excluded a priori.' Why is this? Husserl's discussion is a little elliptical here, but there is a straightforward reason why this might be the case, which he may have had in mind. Although we generally take it for granted that the world looks more or less the same to others as it does to us, it is always possible that it does not, as Locke's inverted spectrum argument famously illustrates (Locke 1689/1975, II, xxxii, 15). For all I know, when others see surfaces we both call 'red,' they experience the visual quality I experience when I see surfaces we call 'blue,' and vice versa. As a result, we cannot with certainty verify that the world looks to another just as we expect it to, simply by standing in their position. All that we can do is to see how the world looks to *us*, when we stand in the position of the other.

The second difference is that although the first kind of appresentation involves postulating experiences that I could myself have in the future, there is a sense in which I cannot have the experiences of someone else:

> Neither the other Ego, nor his subjective processes or his appearances themselves, nor anything else belonging to his own essence, becomes given in our experience originally. If it were, it would be merely a moment of my own essence, and ultimately he himself and I myself would be the same. (ibid.)

I think the claim here is that at least insofar as I recognize that someone else has a perspective distinct from my own, I am also recognizing that they are having a token experience I cannot have. I could have a type-identical experience in the future, of course, but I cannot have a token experience that occurs concurrently with and is distinct from my own experience, any more than I can be somewhere that I am not. Recognizing experiences in others that I do not have brings with it, then, the recognition of the existence of token experiences that I cannot have.

So how does this contribute to our acquisition of the concept of objectivity? Husserl insists the recognition of another perspective on the world (the 'other Ego') causes my experience of the world to change into an experience of an objective world:

> [It] becomes the appearance of an objective world, as the identical world for everyone, myself included [. . .] The other Ego makes constitutionally possible [. . .] an objective nature, and a whole objective world. (CM, § 49)

Why would this be the case? The answer can be seen in the contrast Husserl makes between the two kinds of appresentation. In a nutshell, my experience of the world, when it includes only the first kind of appresentation, is consistent with solipsism, but when the second kind of appresentation is introduced, I can no longer coherently be a solipsist.

Consider again the first kind. Here, we represent the world such that if we moved our bodies into different positions, it would change its appearance: if I walk around the apple, my experience will change. But this view of the world is consistent with solipsism. It is perfectly coherent for me to suppose *both* that if I move in such and such a way, my experience will change, *and* that there is nothing more to the world than my experiences. All that we need to suppose is that the projected changes in my experience are future possibilities that depend on my acting to come about (*pace* Zahavi 1997).[4] I can believe that when I move my body, my future experience will change, without also believing that the world exists independently of those experiences.

However, once my view of the world includes the posited current experience of another, it is no longer coherent for me to suppose that the world might not go beyond my own experiences. These are not posited future possible experiences that depend on my doing something to come about— they are posited current experiences that exist without my undergoing them, and that therefore cannot depend on me. And I cannot coherently believe both that a token experience of an apple exists that does not depend on me, and that the apple is reducible to my experience of it. Once I recognize that there are current perspectives on the world that I do not have, therefore, I cannot coherently be a solipsist. Until that point, however, I can, so it would seem to be necessary for me to recognize these possibilities to be *forced* to reject solipsism.

What about premise two? Husserl seems to insist that actual interactions with other persons are necessary for our recognition of the possibility of these perspectives. But why is that necessary? Certainly, other people have perspectives that I do not have. But why shouldn't it occur to me all on my own that there are current possible perspectives on the world that I do not have, for example, perspectives I could have had if I were standing somewhere else, but do not have because of where I am standing?

It is not clear from Husserl's texts what his answer to this might be. But the question invites us to consider what the difference is between my postulating an actual perspective in another observer I have encountered, and postulating a possible perspective I could have had if I were standing somewhere else right now. The salient difference is that the latter requires counterfactual reasoning—it requires me to think about how things would look were I standing somewhere I am not actually standing. But counterfactual reasoning itself already requires the concept of objectivity—understanding that the way the world is can be distinct from the way it could have been. If that's right, then we could not acquire the concept of objectivity by engaging in counterfactual reasoning, since such reasoning will require us already to have the concept. For what it's worth, empirical evidence gives fairly strong support to the claim that we do not use counterfactual reasoning to acquire the concept of objectivity, since on many accounts counterfactual reasoning only emerges well after four or five years, that is, well after the time at which we grasp the appearance/reality distinction or pass the false-belief task (Beck et al. 2013).

If recognizing the possibility of current perspectives on the world I do not have is required to grasp the concept of objectivity, then, it will only be through recognizing *actual* perspectives on the world that I do not have that I could grasp the concept of objectivity. And the only source of evidence for such actual perspectives will be in encounters with others.

With that rationale for premise two, we have a reconstruction of what may have been Husserl's thinking: to recognize that the objects we encounter go beyond our experience, we need to recognize that there are current possible perspectives on those objects that we do not have, and to recognize *that*, we must encounter others with actual perspectives that we don't have.

But has this given us the concept of objectivity? Recall Davidson's first point: what is required for the concept of objectivity is grasping the notion of thought, and the possible mismatch between how my thoughts represent the world and how it really is. But Husserl's story gets us only as far as postulating alternative *visual* perspectives on concrete objects—objects of joint visual attention, for example. This kind of visual perspective-taking is accomplished by children at around three years of age, well before they are able to pass the false-belief test or the appearance/reality tests (Moll & Meltzoff 2011). It would seem that the story Husserl tells is not sufficient, therefore, to get us the concept of objectivity. But perhaps Husserl's insights can be applied to Davidson's, as I explore next.

## 4  A HUSSERL-DAVIDSON ARGUMENT

Let's lay out the arguments as they appear so far. Davidson's persuasive claim is that in order to grasp the concept of objectivity, I must recognize that what I believe needn't be true—that whether *it's raining* is true is independent of whether I believe it's true, and that it could be true that *grass is green* even if I believe it's false. What this amounts to is realizing that the propositions I take attitudes to are in an important sense independent from me: they can be true even if I believe they are false, they can be true or false, indeed, independently of whether I think about them or not. Let's call this Davidson's Thesis:

> *DT:* In order to grasp the concept of objectivity, I must recognize that the propositions I entertain in thought are independent from me.

Husserl's discussion does not provide us with a fully satisfying account of the concept of objectivity, since he does not address the essential belief-truth contrast. Rather, the compelling aspect of Husserl's discussion is the claim that to recognize the independence of objects from my experience of them, I need to recognize the existence of possible perspectives on the those objects that I don't have, and for that I need to encounter others with actual perspectives that I don't have. This claim of Husserl's, if true, can be generalized to apply to any object whatsoever. We can call this Husserl's Thesis:

> *HT:* For any X, in order to recognize that X is independent from me, I must recognize that there are actual perspectives on X that I do not have.

We can see now that Husserl may now have provided the premise that was missing from Davidson's argument. The question Davidson left us hanging on is, "Why does my recognition that the propositions I entertain are independent from me depend on interacting with others?" And Husserl has provided us with an answer. Supposing it is the case that for any X, to recognize that X is independent of my perspective, I must recognize that there are actual perspectives on X that I do not have; then, to recognize that the propositions I entertain in thought are independent from me, I must recognize that there are actual perspectives on those propositions that I do not have.

But what is an actual perspective on a proposition that I do not have? Simply the attitude of another person to a proposition that I believe is true, that it is false, or vice versa. And just as in the case of concrete objects considered above, recognizing that others have perspectives on the propositions I entertain that I do not have will force me to recognize that these propositions are not reducible to my perspective on them, and hence are not reducible to the attitude I take to them. With that comes the possibility that these propositions have properties that go beyond what I take them to have—including being potentially true when I take them to be false, and vice versa.

That gives us a fairly abstract account of what it might take to recognize the independence from us of the propositions we entertain in thought. But we now need to ask, in practical terms, how it is that we might recognize that another has an attitude to a proposition that is distinct from our own. The mechanism by which we recognize that another has a visual perspective on an object that we do not have is known as 'joint attention,' and its role in our acquisition of the recognition of conflicting perspectives on objects around us is well studied (Tomasello 2014, 33–76). In joint attention to an object, each party attends to the object, recognizes that the other is attending to the same object, and each attends to the reactions of the other. In this way, we come to recognize that others don't always react to these objects as we expect them to (reacting with surprise to what seems like a familiar object to us, for example), and that they can have distinct perspectives on those objects that are different from our own (they can see a side of the object we can't, for example). But this, again, is at the level of visual perspective-taking. How are we supposed to engage in joint attention to a proposition? A proposition is an abstract object. We cannot see, hear, or smell a proposition. Due to their abstract nature, indeed, several theorists have suggested that in order to have thoughts about propositions, we may need language (Clark 1998; Bermúdez 2003). By thinking of a proposition as the content of a sentence, they have suggested, we are given a 'mode of presentation' for the proposition: a way of thinking about it in concrete terms that would be unavailable without language, which in turn makes it possible for us to think about the propositional contents of our thoughts. But whatever about the claim that we need language to *think* about propositions, it is surely all the more plausible to suppose that the only way that we can engage in *joint attention* to a proposition with another is via language. How else, after all, are we to evaluate other people's reactions to the very propositions that we are entertaining in thought? We need some means by which we can observe the reaction of another to a proposition. The obvious facilitator for such joint attention to propositions is language—allowing us to observe the reactions of others to the propositions we assert. Not just any language, however, but a language that contains the expressive power to represent conflicting attitudes to propositions, or, propositional-attitude attribution sentences—in which Sally can say, for example, "I believe that it's raining," while Anne can say, "Not me—I don't believe that." With these linguistic resources, we can directly evaluate each other's attitudes to the propositions we are thinking about, and come to recognize that others may have distinct attitudes to those propositions that are different from our own, that is, the very linguistic resources that have been found to correlate with the ability to pass the false-belief tests, and the appearance/reality tests.

We now have a complete 'Husserl-Davidson' argument:

> *HD1:* In order to grasp the concept of objectivity, I must recognize that the propositions I entertain in thought are independent from me.
> *HD2:* In order to recognize that the propositions I entertain are independent from me, I must recognize that there are actual attitudes to those propositions that I do not have.

*HD3:* In order to recognize that there are actual attitudes to those propositions that I do not have, I must interact with others linguistically.

*HD:* In order to grasp the concept of objectivity, I must interact with others linguistically.

Davidson has given us a rationalization for premise one. Husserl has given us a rationalization for premise two. And premise three seems highly plausible given the abstract nature of propositions and what it might take to engage in joint attention to them.

The story told here ties together the three phenomena, the apparent causal interrelation of which developmental psychology is in need of an explanation: passing the appearance/reality task, passing the false-belief task, and the mastery of propositional-attitude attribution sentences. It ties the latter two together, since on this account it is necessary to have the linguistic resources required to recognize that others have distinct attitudes to the propositions we entertain in thought in order to recognize the independence of those propositions from our attitude to them, and hence the possibility that our beliefs about them may be false. And it ties the passing of the false-belief task and the appearance/reality task together, by highlighting that it is necessary to understand that we have beliefs that can be false in order to understand that appearance and reality might be distinct. Whether or not this will turn out to be the true story of our acquisition of the concept of objectivity, it would, if true, go some way toward explaining the developmental data we have, and it may also serve to highlight the relevance of Davidson's and Husserl's thoughts on these puzzles.

## ACKNOWLEDGEMENTS

Thanks to the editors of this volume, Uriah Kriegel, John Hyman, and Michael Tomasello, and to audiences at University College Dublin and Oxford University.

## NOTES

1 Davidson (1982, 1984, 1991, 1992, 1997).
2 Davidson also defends the converse—that the concept of objectivity is required for us to have the concept of thought, as the concepts of thought and objectivity are interdependent in Davidson's view.
3 Or, in Husserl's inimitable prose, the challenge is to explain how the objective world "can occur as experience and become verified as evidence relating to an actual existent with an explicatable essence of its own, which is not *my* own essence and has no place as a constituent part thereof, though it nevertheless can acquire sense and verification only in my essence" (CM, § 48).

4 Zahavi (1997) argues that the content of these apperceptions could not be simply future expectations, since in ordinary experience, we represent objects as having both front and rear sides at the same time. This is only true, however, if 'We' are adults who already have a grasp of the concept of objectivity. It needn't be the case that infants who have not yet grasped the concept of objectivity understand that objects around them afford multiple perspectives at the same time—indeed, it must be a part of a Husserlian developmental theory that they don't.

# REFERENCES

Beck, Sarah, & Riggs, Kevin (2013). "Counterfactuals and Reality". In: M. Taylor (Ed.). *The Oxford Handbook of the Development of the Imagination*. Oxford: Oxford University Press.
Bermúdez, José Luis (2003). *Thinking Without Words*. Oxford: Oxford University Press.
Bridges, Jason (2006). "Davidson's Transcendental Externalism". *Philosophy and Phenomenological Research* 73 (2), 290–315.
Clark, Andy (1998). "Magic Words: How Language Augments Human Computation". In: P. Carruthers, & J. Boucher (Eds.). *Language and Thought: Interdisciplinary Themes*. Cambridge: Cambridge University Press, 162–183.
Davidson, Donald (1982). "Rational Animals". In: D. Davidson (2001). *Subjective Intersubjective Objective*, Oxford: Oxford University Press, 95–105.
——— (1984). "Thought and Talk". In: D. Davidson. *Inquiries into Truth and Interpretation*. Oxford: Clarendon Press.
——— (1991). "Three Varieties of Knowledge". In: P. Griffiths (Ed.). *A.J. Ayer Memorial Essays, Royal Institute of Philosophy*, Suppl. 30, 153–166.
——— (1992). "The Second Person". In: Davidson (2001). *Subjective Intersubjective Objective*. Oxford: Oxford University Press, 107–122.
——— (1997). "The Emergence of Thought". In: D. Davidson (2001). *Subjective, Intersubjective, Objective*. Oxford: Oxford University Press, 124–134.
de Villiers, Jill (2007). "The Interface of Language and Theory of Mind". *Lingua* 117 (11), 1858–1878.
de Villiers, Peter (2005). "The Role of Language in Theory of Mind Development: What Deaf Children Tell Us". In: J. Astington, & J. Baird (Eds.). *Why Language Matters for Theory of Mind*. Oxford: Oxford University Press, 266–297.
Flavell, John, Flavell, Eleanor, and Green, Frances (1983). "Development of the Appearance-Reality Distinction." *Cognitive Psychology* 15, 95–120.
Husserl, Edmund (1929). *The Paris Lectures*. Transl. by P. Koestenbaum. Dordrecht: Kluwer.
——— (1931) [=CM]. *Cartesian Meditations*. Transl. by D. Cairns. Dordrecht: Kluwer.
Lepore, Ernest, & Ludwig, Kirk (2005). *Donald Davidson: Meaning, Truth, Language and Reality*. Oxford: Oxford University Press.
Locke, John (1975 [1689]). *An Essay Concerning Human Understanding*. Oxford: Oxford University Press.
Masrour, Farid (2013). "Phenomenal Objectivity and Phenomenal Intentionality". In: U. Kriegel (Ed.). *Phenomenal Intentionality*. Oxford: Oxford University Press, 116–136.
Moll, Henrike, & Meltzoff, Andrew (2011). "Perspective-Taking and Its Foundation in Joint-Attention". In: J. Roessler, H. Lerman, & N. Eilan (Eds.). *Perception, Causation, and Objectivity*. Oxford: Oxford University Press.
Pagin, Peter (2001). "Semantic Triangulation". In: P. Kotatko, P. Pagin, & G. Segal (Eds.). *Interpreting Davidson*. Stanford: CSLI Publications.

Tomasello, Michael (2014). *A Natural History of Human Thinking*. Cambridge, MA: Harvard University Press.

Wellman, Henry, Cross, David, & Watson, Julanne (2001). "Meta-Analysis of Theory-of-Mind Development: The Truth about False Belief". *Child Development* 72 (3), 655–684.

Wimmer, Heinz, and Perner, Josef (1983). "Beliefs about Beliefs: Representation and Constraining Function of Wrong Beliefs in Young Children's Understanding of Deception". *Cognition* 13, 103–128.

Zahavi, Dan (1997). "Horizontal Intentionality and Transcendental Intersubjectivity". *Tijdschrift voor Filosofie* 59 (2), 304–321.

# Part III
# Social Cognition, Embodiment, and Social Emotions

# 8 From Types to Tokens
## Empathy and Typification
*Joona Taipale*

### INTRODUCTION: SURFACE AND DEPTH

> Others, as living beings, are constantly threatened by possible stereotyping that encloses their roles. It is possible that the other disappears and only leaves his or her role. Other people may appear to me as they really are, but they are also given as concealed. Others are only seen-through [*transparaître*]; they appear as a living sense [*sense vivant*], a sense that maintains itself or deteriorates. [. . .] *The perception of others is the perception of freedom that shines through a situation.* We cannot fail to notice how much the perception of others becomes increasingly comparable to language: indeed, language is likewise threatened by stereotypes and [even] fertile language.
>
> (Merleau-Ponty 2010, 456f.)

Merleau-Ponty famously builds an analogy between empathy and linguistic understanding, arguing that experiencing the other is like deciphering a language (ibid., 445). Despite the structural differences between these cases (see Taipale 2015a, forthcoming a), I find the comparison illuminative and fruitful in the following sense: just as our grasp of linguistic expressions may remain more or less superficial, vague, approximate, and general, so too our experiences of other people oscillate between surface and depth. I believe that this analogy can shed new light on the discussion concerning levels of empathy, and developing it a bit further serves to introduce my main claim.

What I would like to stress is that reading comprehension comes in levels. In one extreme, the meaning of an expression is grasped carefully, with "thought," while in the other extreme, it is emptily "registered" or "received." It should be emphasized that, in the latter case too, the words *make sense* to us. Just consider the case of skimming over the headlines of a newspaper or the table of contents of a book, in order to examine whether something might be worth *a closer look*—common searching strategies like this would not serve us well if already by a quick glance we couldn't build expectations concerning the contents of the articles or chapters.[1] Such expectations arise passively; they require no effort from the perceiver's part.

Rather than relying on explicit pondering, they rely on pre-established associations and sedimented meanings. I will here suggest that our perception of others involves a similar structure. Already, our fleeting impression of a stranger tacitly gives rise to vague expectations and preconceptions that are motivated not by our previous experiences of *this* particular person, but by a more impersonal and general grasp of *people like that*: people of that age, of that profession, of that gender, of that way of dressing, of that race, and so on. In short, our preconceptions arise from *typification*.

It is worth highlighting that, like in the case of perceiving headlines, also in the case of perceiving other people we may, and indeed often do, *remain content with* the vague and approximate grasp. After all, in the vast majority of cases in urban life, others whom we perceive are perfect strangers to us: we encounter them in a fleeting manner, do not know them from before, and are not even interested in getting to know them more closely and personally. It is actually a rather limited group of people whose unique and complex singularity actually interests us; the rest are more like headlines or chapter titles of texts that we are not going to read, indexes of depths that we do not follow. What I am suggesting here is, in other words, that in most cases, our perception of others structurally resembles "superficial skimming over" rather than "careful and thoughtful reading." Furthermore, I will argue that these two are not equally original possibilities: we are bound to *set off* from heavily typifying expectations, from a rough approximation as it were, while working our way into grasping the other as a unique singular. In other words, empathy comes with a *foundational order*: to grasp others in their singularity is to "see through" the supra-individual (social, occupational, etc.) typicalities that we have already ascribed to them from the outset. This "seeing through" does not imply, however, that we then experience others without typification; rather, typification, I will claim, is an indispensable feature of empathy.

To avoid misunderstandings, already at this point it should be noted that by "typification," I am not just pointing at the fact that we perceive other persons as having *properties* or *attributes* that could be equally ascribed to other people as well. To perceive someone as "a young man," for instance, does not, *in itself*, prevent me from viewing this person in his singularity; my judgment concerning the mentioned attributes—youth and masculinity—as applying to the present object can indeed be perceptually founded and thus intuitively justified. What I rather have in mind here is that features that are given intuitively and are tacitly associated—or "grouped"—with further features and attributes, which are *not* presently given in my experience of this other person (such as the expectation, for instance, that this person probably prefers football over figure skating). Typification, generally put, refers to the process whereby features that are not experientially present are smuggled into the anticipatory horizon of our present experience. That is to say, by rule, typification makes our experience of others *prejudiced*. The term "*pre*-judice" is actually particularly illuminative here because of its literal form: instead of building my "judgment" or "opinion" concerning the other solely on characteristics, properties, and ways of behaving that are presently given to me, my "judgment" or "opinion" concerning the other's characteristics, properties, and ways of behaving is *partly already made beforehand*, as it were, in the sense that I ascribe features to the other before having directly witnessed these features in *this* individual—in this sense, to typify the other is to pre-judge the other.

My claim here is that our experiences of others always *to some extent* rely on typifications. There are two central factors that largely pre-determine this "extent": prior knowledge and personal interest. The less we know of this particular other from before, and the less we are interested in him or her as a person, the more our experience of him or her will rely on supra-individual types.[2] Moreover, I will argue that interpersonal experience does not characteristically *set out* from a situation in which we already marvel at the "otherness" and freedom of the other with awe and respect; on the contrary, it sets out from a situation in which we already tacitly typify the other, subordinate the expressions and behaviors that we perceive to supra-individual types, and thus already consider the other as a more or less predictable representative of groups of people. Also, we necessarily rely on typifications even with people that we already know from before or are interested in getting to know, as I will clarify in the following, a way of viewing others in which we thematize them purely in the light of what is immediately present to us, without relying on any typifying apperceptions (i.e., without ascribing features to the other that are not directly given). This is something like a *guiding idea*—an ethical *telos* perhaps, but nonetheless a *limes* in the mathematical sense of something that is never experientially reached (cf. Taipale 2015b). In other words, in my reading, our *experience* of others is always prejudiced to some extent: by rule, we always assume more than what the other's factual appearance here and now offers.

To capture this idea of gradation in empathy, I will be speaking of "type-orientation" and "token-orientation." With the term, "orientation," I wish to highlight that our experience of others normally dwells somewhere in between the extremes of considering the other *exclusively* in the light of supra-individual types, on the one hand, and considering the other *exclusively* in the light of what is actually given in his or her presence, on the other. Moreover, I will be suggesting that empathy has something like a teleological structure to it: it necessarily sets off with strong typification, as "type-oriented," and is able to develop into a singularizing, "token-oriented" grasp of the other only subsequently. To clear a possible objection, the following note ought to be added here: even if empathy can be said to be structured 'teleologically,' *from types to tokens*, as I suggest, this obviously does not imply that our experience all the time faithfully follows this direction. In fact, occasionally even the opposite can be said to be the case: for instance, when I come to realize that someone I already esteem highly as a unique individual is, after all, just a typical, middle-aged, grumpy man, or when I realize that someone's political insights and visions that I had earlier considered unique are in fact rather typical for advocates of this or that political party. However, with such realization, my experience of the other in his or her individuality is by no means abolished: having already viewed the other in a singularizing manner keeps on figuring in my experience of him or her—to put it in Husserlian terms, my token-oriented grasp of him or her is *sedimented*. Moreover, my experience of this other person must nevertheless have *initially* been strongly type-oriented: the way in which I have initially come to value the other as a unique individual or thinker (even if, retrospectively considered, partly with illegitimate grounds) has grown from an experience where I have not yet known the other and hence have had to strongly rely on typifying apperceptions. That is to say, when we grow interest in the other in his or her singularity, we initially altogether lack the required background data that would enable us to locate the other's current expressions in their singular factual context, and already for this reason, our experience of the other is initially bound to unfold in a type-oriented manner. It is worth adding here that this holds even in cases where one is strongly *interested* in the other's person from the outset: e.g., if I have set a meeting with a sister of mine that I had not even known to exist, I would (probably) be interested in her as a singular and unique individual, and yet without knowing her from before, I would have no means of situating her expressions in her unique, factual life context, and I would have no choice but to begin to make sense of them by situating them in a typical context.

Given that the vast majority of our everyday experiences of others is comprised of fleeting encounters with strangers, whose unique personhood is of no interest to us, empathy tends to be largely type-oriented. Moreover, as the term 'token-orientation' is meant to indicate, even if we manage to "see through" the supra-individual typicalities that we have initially ascribed to the other, this does not mean that we then grasp the other as *devoid of* these supra-individual typicalities: it rather means, I will argue, that we focus on the unique manner in which this other appropriates and incorporates supra-individual typicalities. To view the other as "one of a kind" is, in this sense, to view the other as a unique "token": a unique manifestation of various typicalities that are not unique in themselves or exclusively bound to this person.

Introducing the vocabulary of "orientation" in this connection allows for addressing the question of levels of empathy in terms of typification: proceeding from type-oriented empathy to token-oriented empathy (e.g., from considering the other as *a* living being to considering the other as *this* living being) amounts to proceeding from "basic" or "minimal" empathy to more "extended" forms of empathy (on these notions, see, e.g., Stueber 2006, 20f.; Zahavi 2014, 137–141). If my hypothesis concerning the heavily typified outset of empathy is correct, the most minimal and basic forms of empathy can accordingly be interpreted in terms of strong typification.

## TYPE-ORIENTATION AND TOKEN-ORIENTATION IN EMPATHY

Questions concerning empathy and social cognition are often addressed in terms of the particular mental states of others. While this approach is undeniably justified and revealing in many ways, it also simplifies the picture remarkably, since it is only in exceptional cases that we grasp others *only* in terms of their current mental state. On the contrary, whenever things go smoothly in our social interaction, the other's fleeting expressions precisely do not stand out in isolation from the stream in which they unfold: what we primarily grasp in normal cases of empathy are not isolated "slices" of mentality, but temporally transcendent, diachronically unfolding persons (see Taipale forthcoming a).

However, considering that other persons are temporally extended beings, and considering that our experience of them is nevertheless bound to a particular (i.e., limited) temporal perspective, in what sense can we said to be grasping their "total existence"? Such worries can be dispelled with a few notes on temporality. Husserl, Merleau-Ponty, and Stein frequently compare the experience of others with the experience of a melody or rhythm (e.g., Hua 4, 241, 349; Merleau-Ponty 2002, 96, 133, 153–155, 185, 199, 217, 248). In a melody, notes come and go, and there is nothing substantial that remains identical as the melody unfolds; the identity of a melody rather resides in the *manner or style* in which notes temporally relate to one another. A melody, in other words, is a unitary way of temporal becoming—a point nicely captured in Merleau-Ponty's claim that already, "the first notes of a melody assign a certain mode of resolution to the whole" (Merleau-Ponty 1963, 87). Building on the melody analogy, Husserl and Merleau-Ponty argue that the recognizable identity of persons similarly resides in the manner in which their experiences motivate and resonate with one another (see Taipale 2014, 94–98). Both discuss personal identity in terms of the *manner or style* of temporal becoming: "The ego is a unitary *person* [. . .] if it possesses a certain *pervasive unitary style*" (Hua 4, 277), each person has his "determinately specific modes of relating to the surrounding world" (Hua 4, 326), "his style of life in affection and action with regard to the way he has of being motivated by such and such circumstances" (Hua 4, 270), and this "manner of dealing with situations" (Merleau-Ponty 2002, 382), this "rhythm" (*Rhythmus*) of experiential life, which is manifest already in the other's "unitary pulse of perception" (Hua 38, 69), throughout pervades the subject's modes of comportment and defines him as person (cf. Stein 1989, 109–112; Hua 9, 215). These notes already largely lift the aforementioned perplexity. Namely, just as while listening to music we not only experience the current note but also retain experiences of notes passed and anticipate certain melodic continuation (which can be confirmed or annulled in the further course of experience), so too when it comes to empathy, the other's perceived expression is at once experientially situated in *a* temporal context: it is organized against *a* background of motivations and as anticipating *a* range of possible continuations. In this sense, while perceiving particular expressions, we are at once faced with a way of becoming, a manner of being or unfolding (see Taipale 2015a; cf. Taipale forthcoming a). It is in this sense that we should understand Merleau-Ponty's claim, according to which the human subject is "wholly present in every one of its manifestations" (see Merleau-Ponty 2002, 192, 138).[3]

Like with melodies, however, our prior expectations concerning others can be confirmed or annulled in the further course of experience. This brings us to the topic of *generality*—a feature that I emphasized by italicizing the indefinite articles in the end of the preceding paragraph. As already said, often, the necessarily implied motivational context is in fact unknown to us, and we might not even be interested in its singular details. Just as our anticipation concerning the continuation of a melody may be more or less vague and general depending on whether we have heard it before or not, depending on our general knowledge of music, our interests, focus, etc., so too depending on the circumstances (prior knowledge and current interests, in particular), we may locate the other's perceived expressions in more or less singular and definite personal contexts. Husserl writes:

> In the sensuous-intuitive content of the [perceived other person]—facial expressions, gestures, spoken words, the intonation, and so on, *whether considered as general typicalities of bodiliness or as individual peculiarities*—is expressed the mental life of persons, their thinking, feeling, desiring, their deeds and omissions. And so is also already their individual mental character.
> (Hua 4, 235; *my emphasis*; cf. Hua 15, 183)

In other words, the other person can stand out—as Husserl specifies in the middle of the sentence—not only in the light of "individual peculiarities," but also in the light of "general typicalities." In this sense, our grasp of others comes in levels.

Let me illustrate this with an example. Escaping the pouring rain, I storm into a busy coffee shop, and while entering, someone holds a door for me, giving a friendly smile in passing. I am primarily interested in just getting myself out from the rain, and hence, I might remain altogether ignorant of this person in his or her singularity. I do register a *gesture* of holding the door, and I perceive precisely a *friendly smile* (instead of as an unqualified intentional movement or as a twisted face), and this suggests that I must already be locating the expression in *a* motivational context. Yet, insofar as I have no detailed knowledge of the motivations of this particular person, I am *unable* to locate the gesture in this other person's *unique and singular* motivational context; I have no choice but to rely on rather general assumptions. In other words, I locate the gesture not in a personal-singular context, but in a typical context; I grasp it as expressing a general, customary way of behaving in such and such situations, and my empathic experience can thus be said to be heavily type-oriented. Echoing Merleau-Ponty's formulation in the opening quote, it can be said here that I do not then properly see the other through the situation, but only grasp the other in the light of her current circumstantial "role" or "function." To repeat, it is hardly an exaggeration to say that in most of our everyday perceptions, other people do not stand out in their singularity, but in the light of their circumstantial role, occupation, function, personality type, and so on—and we build our expectations of them accordingly. Their uniqueness is, in this sense, "ignored" or "overlooked"—in terms of the reading analogy, they are like headlines of articles that we are not going to read.

Moreover, even if our experience of others can also be token-oriented, something like an "absolutely unique person" should be conceived of as a *'limit concept'*. To echo Wittgenstein's private language argument: if the other's bodily expressions would literally be absolutely unique, one of a kind, their meaning could not be conveyed to others, and they could not even be understood as expressions. It seems, therefore, that the empathically grasped other is always, to some extent, clothed in typicalities: initially, this clothing is rather dense, and even if we may lighten it subsequently, we never manage to strip the other naked, as it were. Each person is indeed a unique individual (Hua 4, 271; cf. EU 331; Hua Mat 8, 386), and it can be said that "every single person is already himself a type" (Stein 1989, 114), but this uniqueness should be understood in terms of a peculiar combination of supra-individual typicalities (Merleau-Ponty 2002, 415, 417; Hua 4, 278). For instance, each person has a peculiar unique way of moving, and impersonating someone else's idiosyncratic style of moving is hence rather difficult, but this does not rule out that this way of movement is a modification of moving with two feet, in an upright posture, in a masculine or feminine manner,[4] and so on. In other words, general typicalities do not threaten the person's uniqueness, but on the contrary, serve as its necessary presupposition: as Merleau-Ponty points out, the uniqueness of a person resides, not in altogether unprecedented and non-typical features, but in the ways in which the person takes up, appropriates, and modifies general, anonymous, and pre-personal typicalities (Merleau-Ponty 2002, 185). As Husserl and Stein put it, general types are "made peculiar" (*besondert*) in individual typicalities, and "the individual type is constituted through its 'participation' in more general types" (Husserl Ms. D 11, 3b; Stein 1989, 114f.). Heidegger, too, underlines this point: "*Authentic being-one's-self* is not based upon an exceptional state of the subject, a state detached from the 'they' [*Man*]," but it rather designates a peculiar *"modification of the 'they,' whereas the latter is an essential way of relating to the world"* (Heidegger 1996, 122).

As univocally emphasized by classical phenomenologists, personal uniqueness is not gained by way of *stripping off* the supra-individual (cultural, historical, biological, etc.) typicalities, but by way of appropriating and thus *clothing oneself* with these typicalities in a unique and hence personal manner.[5] Somewhat paradoxically, therefore, a person can be understood in his or her unique singularity only insofar as he or she is at once grasped as typical, and in this sense, empathy is bound to fluctuate between type-orientation and token-orientation: the other may be grasped as an anonymous implementer of a function, role, or occupation, whereby she is more or less "ignored" as a singular token, or she may be experienced as a singular being that realizes such-and-such supra-individual features in a peculiar manner. The latter orientation better applies to our experience of people with whom we already are, or want to become, acquainted with, whereas the former orientation better captures our fleeting experiences of strangers with whom we have no interest in interacting with on a more personal level. Initially, others are present to us as fellow citizens, as children or adults, as men or women, as clerks or police officers, as Europeans or Asians, as patients, as ice-hockey players, as rock stars, as "just that kind of person," and so on (see Stein 1989, 115f.), and their singularity is discovered and recognized—more or less extensively, *if at all*—underneath, yet in the light of, such typifications.

In this sense, when it comes to empathy, type-orientation seems to be more primary than token-orientation, which is another way of saying that even if we were interested in getting to know others and understanding them, at the outset, we are bound to ignore them as unique beings. In the picture that I am here presenting, the other's uniqueness, singularity, and alterity designate a *challenge* rather than an *experiential starting point*.[6]

## TYPIFICATION, TEMPORALITY, AND THE MODES OF IGNORANCE

We can now examine in more detail the essence of typification, and investigate its structure vis-à-vis temporality. As Husserl puts it, typification requires no activity on the perceiver's part. It is not just that we are *able to* consider things that we perceive as cars, as iPads, as books, or as trees, but we already from the very onset *perceive* them as such—regardless of whether we have previously perceived precisely *this* car, *this* iPad, *this* book, or *this* tree. Similarly, we already typify the other (as an adult, as a child, as a woman, or as a man, for instance) from the outset. Typification endows the other with a certain familiarity: we expect others to conform to the types that we tacitly impose on them, and this enables us to act as if we knew what the other will do or say next. In this sense, typification entails a modification of the other's *future and freedom*. Let me now explicate this in more detail.

Recall that in all the examples above, I have emphasized that already the first impression—be it of a text, of a melody, or of another person—serves as an indication of a direction, an index for something to be discovered in closer scrutiny—and hence, *later on*. The future aspect of typification has been emphasized by phenomenologists.[7] Stein, for instance, associates types with "pre-dispositions" and emphasizes that typification primarily modifies our *expectations* (Stein [1922/2000], 264). Husserl likewise underlines the temporal dimension in his analysis:

> An object [. . .] is always apprehended apperceptively *in advance* in such and such a way as an object of this or that type. *From the outset*, the apprehended sense implies determinations which have not yet been experienced with *this* object but which nevertheless are of a known type insofar as they refer back to earlier analogous experiences concerning other objects.
> (EU 127, *my emphasis*; cf. EU, 38, 124; Lohmar 2003, 118)

In other words, our earlier experiences are associatively smuggled into our current perceptions and provide the latter with an anticipatory horizon. This explains why an object may at the same time be experienced both as new and as familiar. Even if we have never witnessed *this* water glass breaking into pieces when falling to the floor, we nevertheless expect that *it* would break down if it falls to the ground; even if we have never seen *this* bird spreading its wings and fly, we nevertheless expect *it* to do so if we go close enough. Given that this is something that also preschool children can do, we can rule out the suggestion that such anticipations are owing to our knowledge of physics, biology, or statistical averages, and partly for the same reasons, we cannot assume that this is owing to conceptual inferences. Particular exemplars fall under the same type on the basis of their apparent similarity, associatively—and hence by drawing on one's experiential past in building expectations of the object's future. Husserl elaborates:

> The table is characterized as being *familiar* [*Wiedererkanntes*] *and yet new*. What is given as a new object of experience is *at first glance* known according to what is actually perceived [. . .]. But the typically apprehended object also has a horizon of possible experience with corresponding prefigurations of familiarity: typical features that are *not yet experienced but anticipated*. When we see a dog, we right away anticipate its further modes of behavior: its typical way of eating, playing, running, jumping, and so on. We do not actually see its teeth; but although we have never yet seen this dog, *we know in advance* how its teeth will look—not in their individual determination but *according to type*, inasmuch as we have already had previous and frequent experience of 'similar' animals [. . .] *We anticipate this, and actual experience may or may not confirm it*.
> (EU 331, *my emphasis*)

As Lohmar summarizes, "typifying apperception allows us to see as if 'in advance' what we cannot actually see yet" (Lohmar 2003, 111).

Whereas Husserl himself discusses typification rather generally, and mainly in respect to the familiarity of sensuously perceived objects, Schutz develops the question of typification vis-à-vis empathy, and he also explicitly claims that to typify other people is to conquer their future:

> When I am face to face with someone, I immediately grasp him as a spontaneous and freely acting being: *His future is as yet open and undecided, and I can only hazard a guess as to what he is going to do.* The ideal type, on the other hand, is, when rightly conceived, *without freedom*; he cannot transcend his type without ceasing to be a mere contemporary and becoming a consociate of mine in direct experience.
> (Schutz 1967, 219–20)

In my view, Schutz's description of what he calls the "face-to-face encounter" with others should be considered as something quite exceptional—as a *limit case*, as I suggested above—because it is not at all clear whether it even is possible to consider others as others without having *any* idea of what they will or won't do next.[8] By speaking of "mere contemporaries" or "the They," Schutz by contrast refers to impersonally and indirectly experienced others, to "those who I know coexists with me in time but whom I do not experience immediately," and he emphasizes that this also applies to persons with whom we are already acquainted (Schutz 1967, 181). He also adds that even the natural expectation that a temporarily absent other remains the same during the absence already exceeds the range of direct observation and reliance on types (Schutz 1967, 182). In the terms introduced above, our experience of others always oscillates between type-orientation and token-orientation; the other is never experientially reached without any typification, and in this sense, others, regardless of how well we know them, are always to some extent veiled by anonymity.

Elaborating on different degrees and forms of anonymization, Schutz further distinguishes between what he calls the "course-of-action type" and the "personal type" (Schutz 1967, 187), and he illustrates this distinction with an example of witnessing a game of poker:

> Insofar as I myself look upon the players as examples of an ideal type, to the same extent must I disregard their individuality. No concrete lived experience of *A* is ever either identical or commensurable with one of *B*. For these experiences, belonging as they do to different streams of consciousness, are unique, unrepeatable, and incapable of being juxtaposed. *The typical and only the typical is homogeneous*, and it is always so. In the typifying synthesis of recognition I perform an act of anonymization in which I abstract the lived experience from its setting within the stream of consciousness and thereby render it impersonal.
> (Schutz 1967, 186)

In this sense, typification counts as a case of abstraction—as Natanson puts it, in typifying the other "we set aside [i.e., "ignore"] the question of which exemplars [i.e., "tokens"] of the type we are actually given" (Natanson 1970, 13). On the other hand, as Schutz adds:

> The opposite process is also possible. [. . .] Thus I may say, 'Oh, he's one of those!' or 'I've seen that type before!' This is the explanation for the fact that I experience my contemporary as an individual with an ongoing conscious life, yet one whose experiences I know by inference rather than by direct confrontation. Therefore, even though I think of him as an individual, still he is for me an individual exhaustively defined by his type, an 'anonymous' individual.
> (Schutz 1967, 186)

Of the two quotations, the first one exemplifies how we can sacrifice the other's singularity for what Schutz calls a "course-of-action type," whereas the latter quote illustrates how *seeing through* the other's situational role might not necessarily portray the other as a unique singular, but as exemplifying what Schutz calls the "personal type":

> Certainly an inner relation exists between these two. [. . .] Once I am clear as to the course-of-action type, I can construct the personal ideal type, that is 'the person who performs this job.' [. . .]. The personal ideal type is therefore *derivative*, and the course-of-action type can be considered quite independently as a purely objective context of meaning.
> (Schutz 1967, 187)

That is to say, others are primarily realized in certain circumstances that associatively awaken anticipations of how "one" acts in a similar course of action, yet even when we manage to glance through the others' circumstantial, situational, or occupational roles, we might not grasp others in their singularity, but consider them as exemplifying such-and-such persons. In the latter case, as Merleau-Ponty might put it, we manage to see through the situation, and yet others "deteriorate" or remain "concealed." Like Merleau-Ponty, Schutz emphases that typification results in the other's "decreasing vividness" (Schutz 1967, 177).

Here, we need not dig deeper into the different forms of typification; for our purposes, it only suffices to note that, in both cases, the other is considered in terms of an anonymous type, and not thematized as a singular token. Typification overlooks the singularity of others, and targets them as anonymous representatives of certain types of people—of "anyone" (ibid., 244).[9]

## CONCLUSIONS

I have here argued for the central role of typification in our experiences of others. My main claim has been that empathy has a direction, a certain teleology, in the sense that it necessarily sets out as *type-oriented* and (possibly) develops into a *token-oriented* experience subsequently.[10] This is another way of saying that our initial expectations concerning other people are always more or less arranged according to general typifications, and not in the light of the past of this singular person. To put it differently, instead of marveling at the "otherness" of others from the outset, instead of automatically respecting their freedom and singularity, empathy is fundamentally characterized by typifying anticipations, whereby the singularity of others is more or less ignored. I have suggested that there are basically two ways in which our empathic experience can proceed from this initial typification: (i) we can retain the initial typifying grasp of the other, safeguard our general expectations from revisions, and thus continue to treat the other, not as a singular being, but as a (more or less) contingent exemplar of a type. In this path, our empathic experience is guided by typicalities: it remains *type-oriented*. It should not be neglected, as I have repeatedly emphasized, that it often suffices for our daily routines to contend ourselves with the initial, general, and hence in many ways prejudiced grasp of the other person. (ii) Alternatively, our experience can proceed in a *token-oriented manner*, pursuing others in their singularity. In this connection, I have emphasized two features. First of all, in both alternatives, the other's perceived expressions and actions are *initially* situated within a general, supra-individual context: in the first alternative, we remain content with this general and anonymizing grasp, whereas in the second alternative, we gradually work our way into the other as a singular being, thus relocating the perceived expressions and actions in the context of the other's unique, experiential life. Yet, secondly, I have underlined that the absolute singularity of the other remains a limiting idea: it is something to be pursued, not something to be experientially reached—should the other's expressions be absolutely unique, they could not be understood as such. The singularity of others—their perceivable "personal identity"—is discovered in the unique manners in which they appropriate general, supra-individual typicalities (e.g., situational, occupational, and communal roles, developmental typicalities, and general personality traits), and hence, even when we target others in the most "singularizing" manner, our experience remains partly veiled by types. To underline this essential "incompletion" in the teleological structure of empathy, I have been employing the vocabulary of *orientation*.

By arguing that empathy is, by rule, initially a type-oriented experience, and can develop into token-oriented experience only subsequently, I have suggested that when experiencing other people, we necessarily build on assumptions concerning supra-individual typicalities, and thus tacitly initially take others, not as singular and unique individuals, but as more or less predictable representatives of various groups of people. Exemplified groups come in plural; other persons might at once be taken as representatives of "people of that age," "of that gender," "of that culture," "of that profession," and so on. Now, if my reading is on the right track and empathy necessarily sets out as type-oriented, then even the most "basic" or "minimal" forms of empathy seem to be embedded in a social context—or, more accurately put, in a variety of social contexts. In short, while experiencing particular others, we always already implicate a multiplicity of groups whom we find represented in their expressions, actions, and manner of being.

To conclude, let us take another look at the opening quote by Merleau-Ponty in the light of what I have presented here. Others are "concealed" in the sense that we initially discover them in their situational or functional role. In their singularity, others can "disappear" altogether, in the sense that we can consider them exclusively as contingent fillers of a role: they are veiled by types. To see others "as they really are" is to see the other—not next to these social roles or independently of them—but *in and through* such roles. When others are strongly typified, and hence not properly "seen-through," they cannot "maintain" their visibility; others thus "deteriorate" under the type that we tacitly ascribe to them. Their actions are then considered not as free, but as obediently following the rules of the supra-individual types that they are tacitly taken to exemplify. In this sense, typification amounts to conquering others' freedom, their future, their transcendence; it amounts to the "anonymization" of the other. A token-oriented experience of others may accordingly be characterized as the perception of a "freedom that shines through" the situational role. Yet, this ignorance concerning the other's singularity, this failure to discern the singular other through the typicalities, serves as the phenomenological point of the departure of empathy, as its first level—and as the challenge.

## ACKNOWLEDGEMENTS

I want to express my gratitude to Dan Zahavi and the staff at the Center for Subjectivity Research (University of Copenhagen), Zach Joachim (Boston College), and Sara Heinämaa and her Subjectivity, Historicity, and Communality network (Universities of Helsinki and Jyväskylä) for valuable discussions on earlier versions of the chapter. In particular, I want to thank Søren Overgaard, who generously commented upon one of the last versions of the chapter and offered several insights that enhanced the final draft.

## NOTES

1 Husserl refers to this issue while discussing what he calls the *seduction of language*: "Consider, for example, the way in which we understand, when superficially reading the newspaper, and simply receive the 'news'; here there is a passive taking-over of ontic validity such that what is read straightway becomes our opinion" (Husserl 1954, 374). Cf. Heidegger's analysis of "chatter" (Heidegger 1996, 157ff.). As both point out, it is not possible to proceed straight to the detailed meaning without passing through the general and the quotidian. It might also be noted here that ads and commercials deliberately

employ related mechanisms: without thinking about the content of ads, our minds are tacitly fed by them, and the more implicitly (i.e., uncritically) they are received, the stronger their effect on us. A more detailed analysis of this interesting topic would exceed the limits of this chapter, however.

2 It should be noted here that *prior familiarity* and *personal interest* play different constitutive functions in empathy, and they can also occur separately; e.g., even if I "knew" the cleaner who visits my office everyday, I might view him or her exclusively in the light of his or her occupational role, as *a cleaner*, without being interested in him or her as a person. On the other hand, I might have strong personal interest toward someone in particular without prior knowledge of this person (like in the case of being just told I have a sister somewhere that I did not know to exist).

3 Also, Frege might be quoted here: "It seems absurd to us that a pain, a mood, a wish, should rove about the world without a bearer, independently. An experience is impossible without an experient. The inner world presupposes the person whose inner world it is" (Frege 1967, 27).

4 Sara Heinämaa has argued that sexuality can be seen phenomenologically as an individual modification of the masculine and feminine styles of relating to the world, to others, and to oneself (see Heinämaa 2003).

5 An interesting phenomenon vis-à-vis this idea is the so-called Capgras delusion, a psychiatric condition in which the patient experiences a particular person close to him or her (e.g., spouse) as an impostor who just looks like the person the patient knows. The Capgras delusion has been linked with a disturbance in the autonomic, unconscious level of experiencing, while the conscious, cognitive level remains intact: the other does not *feel* familiar even if he or she *looks* familiar (in patients of the reverse disturbance, prosopagnosia, the conscious recognition of faces is disturbed, while the patient still produces the expected emotional response to the other person.; here, the other may ambiguously *feel* familiar, yet he or she is not *consciously recognized* as familiar). The Capgras delusion might serve as a counter argument for the view according to which the experienced singularity of others is *ultimately* based on the other's peculiar bodily manner of being. On the other hand, in clinical literature, the Capgras delusion seems to be mainly linked with impaired *visual* recognition (recognition of faces in particular), and it has been discussed in terms of a disturbance in the recognition of the *static* outlook of others, while what I am suggesting here is something broader and dynamic. The recognition I have in mind covers not only the other sense fields as well, but it also extends to the recognition of temporal and dynamic patterns (the other's peculiar way of responding and reacting, etc.).

6 I have discussed this idea also in Taipale 2015b, 150–3. One might tend to object here that when it comes to infants, what is suggested here does not apply. After all (thus might the objection go), as babies, we start by relating precisely to particular individual caregivers, and not just to anyone; it clearly matters to the baby *who* takes care of him or her, *who* holds him or her, and so on—to say nothing of the vast empirical evidence for the fact that already newborns react differently, e.g., to the scent of their own mother's milk than to the scent of other mothers' milk. However, it is less clear whether it really matters *at the very outset* to the infant who takes care of him or her, who is it that enables the continuation of being and satisfaction; this might well be something that the infant learns, even if fairly quickly, in the course of time. That is to say: even if the infant would tend to instinctually prefer the milk of his or her biological mother (as we can observe from the outside), one might not be justified in inferring from this that the infant thus *experiences* the mother, from the outset, as a unique (and separate) individual. Along these

lines, it might be replied that also for infants, others are initially perceived in a functional manner, as fillers of a role or function—to paraphrase Kant: as means (facilitating objects), not as goals in themselves (unique subjects). I will not go into this complicated matter in more detail, as I have partly dealt with it elsewhere (Taipale forthcoming c). Yet, to be sure, admittedly it might not be that fitting to speak of the *infant's* experience of the mother in terms of a strongly "typifying" grasp; typification, after all, draws from one's experiential past, and what rather seems to be at stake in the infant's experience of its caregivers is the pre-history of typification of other people—an arche-typification, if you will.

7  For Gurwitsch's concept of typification, see Chelstrom's chapter in this volume.
8  Schutz occasionally seems to make this point himself as well: "[T]ypes are interpretive schemes for the social world in general, they become part of our stock of knowledge about that world. As a result, we are always drawing upon them in our face-to-face dealings with people. This means that ideal types serve as interpretive schemes even for the world of *direct* social experience" (Schutz 1967, 185; see also Luckmann & Schutz 2003, 107).
9  Staudigl discusses related ideas while analyzing different forms of violence (see Staudigl 2007, esp. 248–249).
10 I have examined similar experiential structures vis-à-vis normality and transcendental intersubjectivity in Taipale 2012 and Taipale 2015b.

REFERENCES

Frege, Gottlob (1967). "The Thought". In: P. Strawson (Ed.). *Philosophical Logic.* Oxford: Oxford University Press.
Heidegger, Martin (1996). *Being and Time.* Transl. by J. Stambaugh. Albany: State University of New York Press.
Heinämaa, Sara (2003). *Toward a Phenomenology of Sexual Difference: Husserl, Merleau-Ponty, Beauvoir.* Lanham: Rowman & Littlefield.
Husserl, Edmund (1952) [=Hua 4]. *Ideen zu einer reinen Phänomenologie und phänomenologische Philosophie. Zweiter Buch: Phänomenologische Untersuchungen zur Konstitution.* Ed. by M. Biemel. Haag: Martinus Nijhoff.
—— (1954 [1970]). *The Crisis of European Sciences and Transcendental Phenomenology.* Transl. by D. Carr. Evanston: Northwestern University Press.
—— (1962) [=Hua 9]. *Phänomenologische Psychologie. Vorlesungen Sommersemester 1925.* Ed. by W. Biemel. Haag: Martinus Nijhoff.
—— (1973) [=Hua 15]. *Zur Phänomenologie der Intersubjektivität. Texte aus dem Nachlass. Dritter Teil: 1929–35.* Ed. by I. Kern. Haag: Martinus Nijhoff.
—— (2004) [=Hua 38]. *Wahrnehmung und Aufmerksamkeit. Texte aus dem Nachlass (1893–1912).* Ed. by Th. Vongehr and R. Giuliani. Dordrecht: Springer.
—— (2006) [=Hua Mat 8]. *Späte Texte über Zeitkonstitution. (1929–1934). Die C-Manuskripte.* Ed. by D. Lohmar. Dordrecht: Springer.
Lohmar, Dieter (2003). "Husserl's Type and Kant's Schemata." Transl. by J. Jansen and G. Zavota. In: Welton (Ed.). *The New Husserl.* Bloomington: Indiana University Press.
Merleau-Ponty, Maurice (1963). *The Structure of Behavior.* Transl. by A. Fisher. Boston: Beacon Press.
—— (2002). *Phenomenology of Perception.* Transl. by C. Smith. London/New York: Routledge.
—— (2010). *Child Psychology and Pedagogy. The Sorbonne Lectures 1949–1952.* Transl. by T. Welsh. Evanston, IL: Northwestern University Press.

Natanson, Maurice (1970). "Phenomenology and Typification. A Study in the philosophy of Alfred Schutz". *Social Research* 37 (1), 1–22.
Schutz, Alfred (1967). *The Phenomenology of the Social World*. Transl. by G. Walsh. Evanston, IL: Northwestern University Press.
Schutz, Alfred, & Luckmann, Thomas (2003). *Strukturen der Lebenswelt*. Konstanz: UVK Verlagsgesellschaft.
Staudigl, Michael (2007). "Towards a Phenomenological Theory of Violence: Reflections Following Merleau-Ponty and Schutz". *Human Studies* 30, 233–253.
Stein, Edith (1989). *On the Problem of Empathy*. Transl. by W. Stein. Washington: ICS Publications.
—— (2000). *Philosophy of Psychology and the Humanities*. Ed. by Marianne Sawicki and Transl. by M.C. Baseheart, & M. Sawicki. Washington: ICS Publications.
Stueber, Karsten (2006). *Rediscovering Empathy. Agency, Folk Psychology, and the Human Sciences*. Cambridge, MA/London: MIT Press.
Taipale, Joona (2012). "Twofold Normality. Husserl and the Normative Relevance of Primordial Constitution." *Husserl Studies* 28 (1), 49–60.
—— (2014). *Phenomenology and Embodiment. Husserl and the Constitution of Subjectivity*. Evanston, IL: Northwestern University Press.
—— (2015a). "Beyond Cartesianism. Body-Perception and the Immediacy of Empathy". *Continental Philosophy Review*, 48 (2), 161–178.
—— (2015b). "Similarity and asymmetry. Husserl and the transcendental foundations of empathy". *Phänomenologische Forschungen*, 2014, pp. 141–154.
—— (Forthcoming a). "Empathy and the Melodic Unity of the Other". *Human Studies*.
—— (Forthcoming b). "The Anachronous Other. Empathy and Transference in Early Phenomenology and Psychoanalysis". *Studia Phaenomenologica*, XV.
—— (Forthcoming c). "Interoception and the Emergence of the Object". In Jagna Brudzińska and Dieter Lohmar (Eds.). *Phänomenologie des Menschen und die Grundlagen einer modernen Sozialtheorie. Neuere Beiträge zur Phänomenologie und Anthropologie des Sozialen*. Berlin: Springer.
Zahavi, Dan (2014). *Self and Other. Exploring Subjectivity, Empathy, and Shame*. Oxford: Oxford University Press.

# 9 An Interactionist Approach to Shared Cognition
## Some Prospects and Challenges
*Felipe León*

## 1 INTRODUCTION

The capacity to share mental states with other people is an important aspect of human life. It grounds the ability to act jointly, when individuals share an intention to do something together, but it is also at the basis of widespread phenomena that presumably are ontogenetically prior, such as joint attention and affective sharing (Moll and Meltzoff 2011; Reddy 2008). Although it has been argued that the sharing of mental states, and of intentions in particular, plays a pivotal role in the development of cooperation and the establishment of human forms of sociality (Tomasello et al. 2005; Rakoczy 2008), it is still an open question what this sharing or "We-ness" amounts to (Tomasello 2014, 152). Many theorists would agree, however, that the talk of sharing isn't merely metaphorical when applied to mentality, insofar as it shouldn't be understood, at least in some crucial cases, as an aggregation of structurally independent individual mental states.

More in detail, the idea that different theorists tend to agree on, and that in the following will be taken for granted, is that in order for two (or more) individuals to share a mental state, it is not sufficient that they each undergo individual mental states that they could also have on their own (i.e., independently of each other), supplemented by those states being relevantly similar, and by the individuals' common knowledge about this fact. To illustrate this idea, in order for John and Michael to intend to carry a log together from one place to another, it wouldn't be sufficient that they each have the intention, "I intend to carry the log," that their individual intentions are directed to the same object, and that both John and Michael are aware of this. In philosophy, contemporary debates about shared or collective intentionality have spanned about three decades, and theorists like Michael Bratman (1999, 2014), John Searle (1990, 1995, 2010), Margaret Gilbert (1989, 2014), and Philip Pettit (2003) have put forward influential proposals that, in spite of their many differences, aim to overcome what might be dubbed an aggregative or 'summative' (Gilbert) view of sharing (for reviews, see Tollefsen 2004; Schweikard & Schmid 2013).

Somewhat surprisingly, the ongoing debates about shared intentionality have rarely intersected with debates about social cognition, concerning how we go about attributing or ascribing mental states to others (or how we 'mindread') (cf. Goldman 2012; Gallagher 2012; Zahavi 2011; also see section 2 below). Of course, the idea that there is a connection between the practices of attributing and sharing mental states with other people shouldn't be, at least *prima facie*, highly controversial. One natural way of understanding the link between the two practices is to see social cognition as an enabling condition for shared intentionality. If you and I are to engage in the joint action of going for a walk together, each of us must at least presuppose that the other is a minded being, having the right disposition to take a walk, maybe being happy about it, etc. If, while walking together, I suddenly notice that you are distressed or sad, I will most probably react accordingly. My attribution to you of a state of distress or sadness will, in all likelihood, have an influence on the continuation of our joint endeavor.

One might say, along these lines, that social cognitive abilities enable and constantly feed back into concrete instances of joint action, in such a way that the latter can be adjusted and, if all goes well, carried out successfully. Paradigmatic cases of joint action (those on which philosophers have primarily focused, like painting a house together, preparing a hollandaise sauce together, going for a walk together) presuppose, from a participant's perspective, that "others are agents like yourself, that they have a similar awareness of you as an agent like themselves, and that these awarenesses coalesce into a sense of us as possible or actual collective agents" (Searle 1990, 414). Another possible route for thinking about the relationship between social cognition and shared intentionality would be to consider to what extent the latter can deliver a distinctive form of social cognition, insofar as interacting individuals may gain a kind of knowledge about each other that they could not have had independently of their interaction (Butterfill 2013).

My focus in the following will not be on whether and in what precise sense social cognition might be an enabling condition for sharing, or the other way around, but rather on exploring to what extent a recent account put forward in the field of social cognition research, interaction theory (henceforth IT; De Jaegher et al. 2010; De Jaegher & Di Paolo 2007; Gallagher 2012),[1] may offer valuable resources for thinking about the phenomenon of shared cognition, broadly construed. After outlining the main claims advanced by proponents of IT in the context of social cognition debates (section 2), I discuss one of the main strands of empirical evidence presented in support of IT, which comes from perceptual crossing experiments (section 3). I suggest that the results of those experiments can be interpreted as indicating the presence of a rudimentary form of shared cognition, which can be accurately captured using the conceptual resources offered by IT. I conclude (section 4) by recapitulating and formulating some questions for further research.

## 2 INTERACTION THEORY OF SOCIAL COGNITION

Traditional accounts of social cognition have been framed under the so-called 'Theory of Mind' (henceforth ToM) paradigm (Davies and Stone 1995; Goldman 2012). Premack and Woodruff introduced the expression 'theory of mind' for investigating primates' capacity for attributing mental states. As they write,

> In saying that an individual has a theory of mind, we mean that the individual imputes mental states to himself and to others (either to conspecifics or to other species as well). A system of inferences of this kind is properly viewed as a theory, first, because such states are not directly observable, and second, because the system can be used to make predictions, specifically about the behavior of other organisms.
> (Premack & Woodruff 1978, 515)

With this characterization of what might be involved in the possession of a theory of mind, Premack and Woodruff not only introduced a terminology that has had a long career in the literature, but also indicated two features of mental state attribution that a large number of theorists have taken as uncontroversial. The first one is the idea that mental states are not accessible to direct observation, and the second one is that the possession of a theory of mind is related to the capacity to predict the behavior of other organisms. The two most influential approaches developed under the ToM framework are theory theory (e.g., Gopnik & Wellman 1995; Baron-Cohen 1995; Carruthers 1998) and simulation theory (e.g., Gordon 1998, Goldman 1995; Gallese 2010). Roughly speaking, theory-theory approaches maintain that our ability to ascribe mental states to others relies on the possession of a relevant theory of mind—i.e., on a body of folk-psychological knowledge that allows us to infer that another person is undergoing a certain mental state. On the other hand, defenders of simulation-theory approaches hold that instead of relying on a body of theoretical knowledge and law-like generalizations, we use our own mind as a model in which we run simulation routines that have as an outcome the mental states that we attribute to others. Both theory-theory and simulation theory include each several sub-varieties, and some authors have recently put forward 'hybrid' theories that include elements from both (e.g., Goldman 2006).

In spite of its general dominance, the ToM framework has not remained unchallenged. Drawing on work in phenomenology, developmental psychology, psychopathology, and enactive and extended cognition, among other sources, a number of recent approaches to social cognition have put pressure on some traditional assumptions on which the ToM paradigm appears to be grounded (Gallagher 2001, 2008, 2012; Zahavi 2008, 2011; Reddy 2008; Di Paolo et al. 2010; Krueger 2011; León 2013). Among the challenged presuppositions, we find the features that Premack and Woodruff already linked to the notion of a 'theory of mind': the unobservability of other minds, and the idea that we primarily attribute mental features to others in order to predict their behavior. A further and not less relevant presupposition of ToM approaches that has been challenged is what is sometimes called an observational or 'spectatorial' stance, that is, the idea that "our normal everyday stance toward the other person is a third-person, observational stance. We observe their behaviors in order to explain and predict their actions, or to theorize or simulate their mental states" (Gallagher 2012, 188).

In philosophy, the third-person perspective has been often contrasted with the first-person perspective, to indicate the asymmetry in the access that someone has to another's mind and to her own mind. In the last years, however, another contrast has gained increasing attention, not only in philosophy (cf. Elian 2014), but also in psychology (Hobson 2002, 2007; Reddy 2008) and social neuroscience (Schilbach et al. 2013), namely the contrast between a third- and a second-person perspective. For instance, in the field of developmental psychology, Hobson has highlighted the centrality that emotional and interpersonal engagements have for the infant's construction of the mind, and how fruitful this approach can be for the study of autism (Hobson 2002, 2007). Along similar lines, Reddy has remarked that if one of psychology's main concerns is to investigate the dimension of the personal, it is questionable that psychologists are required in the first place to adopt an impersonal and detached stance, in order to fulfill prefixed standards of scientific rigor. What would be called for, according to Reddy, is a "second-person methodology" whose implications are "so radical as to strike many as an unimaginable method for a science" (Reddy 2008, 33).

In the cognitive sciences, some authors have developed the concept of interaction as an alternative to the classic third-personal approaches to social cognition research (De Jaegher & Di Paolo 2007; De Jaegher et al. 2010; Gallagher 2012). Curiously enough, proponents of these approaches have occasionally criticized not only ToM accounts, but also some of the alternative proposals to the ToM framework, due to their apparent lack of radicalism and their implicit reliance on basic assumptions of the ToM paradigm (De Jaegher 2009). Since the notion of interaction is not absent from the writings of ToM, this criticism demands some clarification. In fact, there is a sense in which hardly anyone would deny that interaction is important for social understanding. For instance, in their foreword to Baron-Cohen's *Mindblindness*, Tooby and Cosmides write that the author "explores how a universal, evolved language of the eyes, which is mutually intelligible to all members of our species can bring two separate minds into an aligned interpretation of their interaction. What we take for granted—the achievement of coordinated models of our mutual social interactions—he shows to be a triumph of automated modules and evolutionary cognitive engineering" (Baron-Cohen 1995, xvi). Along similar lines, Peter Carruthers writes that "theory-theorists have always emphasized that the primary use of mindreading is in interaction with others" (Carruthers 2009, 167). As it becomes clear from these citations, Tooby, Cosmides, and Carruthers are willing to recognize the role of interaction, but, significantly, the latter is characterized as something that we would merely take for granted, or as the context within which mindreading capacities (the proper *explanandum* for a theory of social cognition) would be primarily exercised.

Proponents of IT hold that interaction is not merely an epiphenomenal property of social engagements, or an extrinsic feature of the latter, to be accounted for in terms of underlying cognitive capacities, but rather a concept endowed itself with explanatory power. To clarify this, it may be useful to locate IT within the broader field of enactive approaches to cognition. From a traditional view, cognition can be understood in terms of the manipulation of internal representations that a system forms on the basis of environmental inputs that it passively registers. As an outcome of this information processing, the system displays certain behavioral outputs. The enactive approach challenges the view that cognition involves the passive registering of information, and that the patterns of action of an organism can be exhaustively explained in terms of central processing that is isolated from the environment (Di Paolo et al. 2010, 39).

From the enactive approach, meaning is not simply retrieved from the environment, but it emerges from the interactions between the organism and the latter. Accordingly, the enactive approach highlights the role of the body, claiming that the latter "is not a puppet controlled by the brain but a whole animate system with many autonomous layers of self-constitution, self-coordination, and self-organization and varying degrees of openness to the world that create its sense-making activity" (Di Paolo et al. 2010, 42). And, concurring with phenomenological approaches, this approach recognizes the centrality of the experiential dimension, thinking of it not merely as an *explanandum* or as a puzzling feature of cognition, but as "a guiding force in a dialog between phenomenology and science, resulting in an ongoing pragmatic circulation and mutual illumination between the two" (Di Paolo et al. 2010, 43).

IT can be understood as an extension of the enactive approach to the field of social cognition research (De Jaegher & Di Paolo 2007, 485). The crucial notion of social interaction is defined by proponents of IT in the following way: "A co-regulated coupling between at least two autonomous agents, where: (i) the co-regulation and coupling mutually affect each other, constituting an autonomous self-sustaining organization in the domain of relational dynamics and (ii) the autonomy of the agents involved is not destroyed" (De Jaegher et al. 2010, 443. Cf. De Jaegher & Di Paolo 2007; Gallagher 2012). There are two features of this definition that are worth retaining for the following discussion. In the first place, the definition stipulates that there is autonomy not only at the level of the individual agents, but also at the level of the coupling between the individuals. In spite of its usual linkage with agency, the idea of autonomy at the level of the interindividual coupling is not meant to suggest, of course, that the coupling would itself have agentive powers. Secondly, and in connection with the last point, social interaction involves an active co-regulation carried out by the involved individual agents, which consequently do not disappear as a result of their coupling. Since agents perform such an active role in maintaining the social interaction, the definition also rules out that, for example, the transfer of body heat at a crowded bus stop may qualify as social interaction in the specific sense of IT (De Jaegher & Di Paolo 2007, 493).

Arguably, one of most contentious claims advanced by IT theorists is that social interaction, as defined above, can be not only a contextual or enabling factor of social cognition, but also a constitutive feature of the latter (De Jaegher et al. 2010). IT theorists understand the roles of being a contextual, enabling, or constitutive factor along a spectrum of increased specificity (De Jaegher et al. 2010, 443). That social interaction is a *constitutive* factor of social cognition means that the former would not only be a feature such that variations in it would produce variations in social cognition (that would correspond to the role of a contextual condition), or such that the absence of social interaction would prevent social cognition from occurring (that would correspond to the role of an enabling condition), but rather that social interaction would be part of the processes that produce social cognition (De Jaegher et al. 2010, 443).

The support offered in favor of IT is diverse. It includes developmental studies, phenomenological and behavioral evidence, and dynamic systems modeling (cf. Gallagher 2012, 2001; De Jaegher et al. 2010). However, the claim that social interaction may be a constitutive factor of social cognition (call this claim CC) has met criticisms from different sides. Herschbach, for instance, has pointed out that there is an important ambiguity in the notion of constitution that IT proponents appeal to: they seem to vacillate between characterizing a constitutive element as part of the whole phenomenon (such that all the constitutive elements would be the phenomenon itself) or as part of the processes that *produce* the phenomenon. The latter option would lead to the risk of committing the coupling-constitution fallacy, familiar from discussions about extended cognition (Herschbach 2012, 478. Cf. Menary 2010). Along similar lines, Overgaard and Michael (2015) have argued that some of the purportedly decisive evidence presented in support of CC is insufficient. This evidence comes from perceptual crossing experiments, to which I now turn.

## 3 PERCEPTUAL CROSSING

The perceptual crossing paradigm was developed by Auvray and colleagues (Auvray et al. 2009; Lenay and Stewart 2012) and was inspired by Murray and Trevarthen's double-video experiment (Murray & Trevarthen 1985), in which a two-month old infant was presented with either a real-time video or a pre-recorded video of her mother. In the first case, the infant-mother interaction developed smoothly (the mutual contingency of their expressive movements is preserved), but in the second, the interaction broke down, as the infant became distracted or upset. This experiment suggests that the infant is responsive not merely to the expressive character of the mother's movements (which is maintained in the pre-recorded video), but to her movements being contingent upon the infant's own movements.

Perceptual crossing situations are defined as those in which "two perceptual activities of the same nature interact with each other (as in the case of mutual touch or catching one another's eye)" (Auvray et al. 2009, 33). In the phenomenological tradition, situations in which one is perceptually aware of someone who is at the same time aware of him or herself have been described as cases of iterative empathy (Walther 1922, 85; Stein 2010, 30), which would play a crucial role in the establishment of "We-experiences" (Walther 1922, 85). Psychological research indicates that perceptual crossing situations allow for an immediate reciprocal recognition of another intentional subject (Farroni et al. 2002), and that those situations are associated with feelings of intimacy and emotional value (Argyle & Cook, 1976). As noted by Auvray and colleagues, however, the recognition of these psychological features conceals disagreement on how to explain them. According to one view, along the lines of theory-theory approaches sketched above, the recognition of perceptual crossing is inferential in nature: an observer would perceive the behavior of another organism, discriminate among the behavioral patterns of the latter those that can be attributed to an intentional subject, and among the latter class of behavioral patterns, the observer would discriminate those intentional behavioral patterns that are directed to himself (Auvray et al. 2009, 34).

According to an alternative view, in order to account for perceptual crossing situations the perceptual interaction itself should be granted an explanatory role. In order to investigate whether "some of the mechanisms underlying the recognition of others are intrinsic to the shared perceptual activity itself (i.e., intrinsic to the interdependence between the two perceptual activities)" (2009, 34), Auvray and colleagues designed a minimalistic experimental setup, involving two participants, blindfolded and located in different rooms. Each participant controlled with a computer mouse a sensor that could be moved along a shared, one-dimensional virtual line. Importantly, participants did not know that a mobile lure, or 'shadow' object, was connected to their sensor at a fixed distance, in such a way that the 'shadow' copied the sensor's movements. Whenever participants encountered an object (which could be the other's sensor, the 'shadow,' or a static object) they received a tap on a finger of their free hand. The task for each participant was to click on the mouse whenever they recognized that they were in contact with the other participant.

The results of the experiment indicated that a clear majority of clicks occurred when the participants' sensors were in contact with each other. It is important to emphasize that each participant's sensor and the corresponding 'shadow' object had identical trajectories of displacement. The 'shadow' replicates the exact movements of the sensor at a fixed distance. Thus, participants were consistent in recognizing each other's presence not simply because of an individual ability to categorize the different stimuli, since the probability of clicking when encountering the 'shadow' or when encountering the other's sensor was the same (Auvray et al. 2009, 43). As Auvray and colleagues write, "[T]he high proportion of correct responses was explained by the participants' exploratory trajectories which converged toward joint strategies of mutual exploration" (2009, 43). This speaks in favor of the experimenters' principal hypothesis that "the interdependence of the two perceptual activities might be a sufficient factor to enable the participants to click more often after having met the partner's avatar than after having met the mobile lure" (Auvray et al. 2009, 35).

Let us now go back to IT, and to the claim that social interaction is constitutive of social cognition (CC). There are at least two divergent ways of interpreting the results of the perceptual crossing experiment with respect to this claim. According to proponents of IT, "participants consistently find each other's sensors in spite of their individual inability to tell the difference between sensors and shadows [. . .]. The variation in the number of clicks is attributable only to the differences in the stability of the coupling and not to individual strategies. This experiment shows that the interaction process is not only enabling but plays a constitutive role" (De Jaegher et al. 2010, 445). Michael and Overgaard, in contrast, argue that all that the experiment shows is that the perceptual interaction provides scaffolding in order for the participants to form their social judgments (to the effect that contact has been made with the other participant at a given moment). However, as they put it, "affecting the distribution of outcomes of a social cognition task is not sufficient to constitute social cognition" (Michael & Overgaard 2012, 298; cf. Herschbach 2012, 479). Criticizing CC, they also write that "the actual (sensor-sensor) interaction has no influence on, and thus certainly is no part of, the process that leads participants to form their social judgements" (Overgaard & Michael 2015, 176). In order to support this idea, they consider a possible scenario in which participants receive an electric shock whenever they move away from the other's sensor. As Overgaard and Michael point out, in such a scenario, it would be odd to suggest that, by the mere fact of influencing the participant's correct social judgments, the electric shocks would 'constitute' in any sense their social cognition.

Nonetheless, there appears to be room for another interpretation of the experimental results. *Pace* IT theorists, more would need to be said in order to substantiate the claim that the experiment shows that the interaction pattern constitutes social cognition. As Overgaard and Michael point out, the experiment clearly indicates, instead, that the interaction pattern *influences* the individual's performance of the experimental task. But, *pace* Overgaard and Michael, this interpretation does not rule out that the perceptual interaction might play a constitutive role for shared cognitive processes occurring at the level of collective dynamics. Developing this suggestion involves taking seriously the idea that the there is an autonomous level of organization at the level of relational dynamics, and that this level, although dependent upon individual strategies, is irreducible to the latter. To put it differently, although not detachable from what is happening at the individual level, this autonomous relational domain may nevertheless be distinguishable from it. And, importantly, it does not annihilate the individual agency of the participants. My basic suggestion is thus that two interrelated levels of analysis should be distinguished when assessing the experimental results: the individual level, at which subjects are performing the social cognitive task of recognizing the presence of another subject, and the collective level, at which both subjects are coordinating (and as a matter of fact, emergently cooperating) in such a way that their interaction determines a new level of organization. From this perspective, although the collective dynamics is *caused* by the individual strategies, one might well be reluctant to accept that it is "exhaustively explained" in terms of the latter (Michael & Overgaard 2012, 297). At the very least, the question of whether there is a reduction of the collective dynamics to the participants' individual strategies remains open for further investigation.

Now, introducing the distinction between the two levels of analysis, individual and collective, does not yet clarify in what sense the experiment would testify to the presence of shared cognitive processes at the collective level. Here, I will limit myself to comment on two initial worries that one could have concerning this interpretation. The first one is that, although the idea that groups can have cognitive properties is not foreign to contemporary research on shared intentionality (cf. Tollefsen 2015), current debates are often concerned with quite sophisticated forms of group cognition, involving beliefs, trust and, more recently, emotions (von Scheve & Salmela 2014). A second worry is that, given the very minimalistic experimental setup, it would be wrong to map the perceptual interaction going on in the experiment onto the I-Thou relationship and the "interlocking of experiences" that some phenomenologists consider as a distinctive feature of "We-experiences" (Schütz 1967; Cf. Walther 1922). In fact, given that the participants in the experiment did not report any social phenomenology (Froese & Di Paolo 2011, 24), and that the experiment testifies to "a dissociation between task performance and awareness of this performance with respect to the detection of reciprocity" (Schilbach et al. 2013, 399), to what extent, one might ask, could one describe the processes involved in the perceptual crossing scenario as properly shared by the involved participants?

I think that both worries can be dissipated by adopting a sufficiently broad characterization of shared cognition, one encompassing not only the sharing of beliefs, emotions, and desires, but also, for instance, the capacity of group problem solving (Theiner et al. 2010). Although the absence of social phenomenology indicates that there isn't first-personal sharing involved, it does not rule out the presence of emergent group-level properties and patterns, which, as Goldstone and colleagues write, "are rarely understood or intended by any individual" (Goldstone et al. 2008, 10. Cf. Theiner et al. 2010). The question of whether these properties should be described in terms of shared or group cognition turns out to be more terminological than substantial, as long as one recognizes the distinctiveness of the collective level of organization.

More would have to be said in order to develop and substantiate the interpretation of the perceptual crossing experiments that I have suggested, but a point that I would like to emphasize before concluding is that the plausibility of this interpretation depends partly on recognizing that there is an important difference between social cognition and shared cognition. If there is such a difference, it is likely that the *explanandum* of IT, as stated by its main proponents, turns out to be too coarse-grained: "We use social cognition as a general term to describe cognition involving others, for example, understanding others' emotions, intentions and actions and acting towards and with them in social settings" (De Jaegher et al. 2010, 442). There are a number of different ways in which others may be involved in cognition, and there appears to be a relevant difference between acting *towards* others (or understanding others, for that matter) and acting *with* others. Concededly, the experimental setup of the perceptual crossing scenario is quite far away from everyday instances of shared intentionality, like painting a house or going for a walk together, but the experiment suggests the relevance of investigating group or collective processes in the accomplishment of joint actions. When there is mutual interdependence involved, whether or not it is acknowledged by the participants, the question is not merely about how individuals understand each other (this would be a question for social cognition), but rather about how they can understand, coordinate, and accomplish tasks collectively (shared cognition).

One might still wonder, though, to what extent drawing the line between social and shared cognition is a matter of stipulation. Is there something else to be said in favor of it?[2] As suggested in the Introduction, at least phenomenological and evolutionary considerations indicate that the distinction is a useful one. There does seem to be a clear a difference between being directed to another's mentality, and sharing a mental feature with another person. At the very least, the former is not sufficient for the latter, since paradigmatic cases of shared experiences involve reciprocity, whereas social cognition can well be unilateral or one-sided (Schütz 1967; Zahavi 2015). Moreover, from an evolutionary perspective, Tomasello has argued that in spite of being capable of basic social cognitive capacities, like the attribution of intentionality to other agents, other great apes lack something specific to human cognition, namely the capacity to engage in shared intentionality: "[T]he critical difference now seems to be that humans not only understand others as intentional agents but also put their heads together with others in acts of shared intentionality, including everything from concrete acts of collaborative problem solving to complex cultural institutions" (Tomasello 2014, x). Even if we lack a full account of the human capacity of sharing, it might be advisable to operate with a sufficiently rich conceptual framework, within which one distinctive feature of human cognition with respect to other great apes can be accommodated.

## 4 CONCLUDING REMARKS

One of the leading ideas of IT theorists in the field of social cognition research has been that "the interaction involves processes that go beyond what any one individual brings to the interaction" (Gallagher 2012, 193). In this chapter, I have explored the idea that IT offers valuable resources for current discussions about sharing. In order to investigate to what extent IT sheds light on the phenomenon of shared cognition, broadly construed, I have focused on one of the strands of empirical evidence presented in support of it, which comes from perceptual crossing experiments. As far as these experiments are concerned, my suggestion has been that the prospects for developing strong claims concerning the constitutive character of interactive processes are more suitable for shared cognition than for social cognition. IT can be interpreted as targeting one very basic form of shared cognition, corresponding to a rudimentary form of emergent coordination. The latter would be basic to the extent that other and arguably more paradigmatic forms of sharing should be acknowledged, including face-to-face shared experiences, and experiences of sharing mediated by a subject's process of identification with a specific group or community. Analyzing the specific structures of these varieties of sharing, as well as the interrelations between them, remain as topics for further research.

## ACKNOWLEDGEMENTS

Thanks to Hanne de Jaegher, Shaun Gallagher, John Michael, Søren Overgaard, Thomas Szanto, and Dan Zahavi for their helpful comments on previous versions of this chapter. Special thanks to Dermot Moran and Thomas Szanto for their editorial work and for comments and suggestions that helped me to improve the text. I have also benefited from discussions with audiences in Memphis, Copenhagen, and Aegina, where first versions of this material were presented. Finally, I acknowledge the generous support from the organizers of the 2014 Spindel Conference "Alternative Models of the Mind," from the PhD School of the Faculty of Humanities, University of Copenhagen, and from the University of Copenhagen's Excellence Programme for Interdisciplinary Research.

## NOTES

1 In a recent publication, De Jaegher and Di Paolo describe their position in terms of 'enactivism' instead of 'interactionism' (De Jaegher & Di Paolo 2013). For the purposes of the present chapter, nothing crucial depends on this distinction, insofar as De Jaegher and Di Paolo endorse IT as presented in section 2.
2 Thanks to Shaun Gallagher for pressing this point.

## REFERENCES

Argyle, Michael, & Cook, Mark (1976). *Gaze and Mutual Gaze*. Cambridge: Cambridge University Press.
Auvray, Malika, Lenay, Charles, & Stewart, John. (2009). "Perceptual Interactions in a Minimalist Virtual Environment." *New Ideas in Psychology* 27 (1), 32–47.
Baron-Cohen, Simon (1995). *Mindblindness: An Essay on Autism and Theory of Mind*. Cambridge, MA/London: MIT Press.
Bratman, Michael (1999). *Faces of Intention*. Cambridge: Cambridge University Press.
——— (2014). *Shared Agency. A Planning Theory of Acting Together*. Oxford: Oxford University Press.
Butterfill, Stephen (2013). "Interacting Mindreaders." *Philosophical Studies* 165, 841–863.
Carruthers, Peter (1998). "Simulation and Self-knowledge: A Defense of Theory-Theory." In: P. Carruthers, & K. Smith (Eds.). *Theories of Theories of Mind*. Cambridge: Cambridge University Press.
——— (2009). "How We Know Our Minds: The Relationship Between Mindreading and Metacognition." *Behavioral and Brain Sciences* 32, 121–182.
Davies, Martin, & Stone, Tony (Eds.) (1995). *Folk Psychology. The Theory of Mind Debate*. Oxford: Blackwell.
De Jaegher, Hanne (2009). "Social Understanding Through Direct Perception? Yes, by Interacting." *Consciousness and Cognition* 18, 535–542.
De Jaegher, Hanne, & Di Paolo, Ezequiel (2007). "Participatory Sense-Making. An Enactive Approach to Social Cognition". *Phenomenology and the Cognitive Sciences* 6, 485–507.
——— (2013). "Enactivism Is Not Interactionism." *Frontiers in Human Neuroscience* 6 (345). DOI: 10.3389/fnhum.2012.00345.
De Jaegher, Hanne, Di Paolo, Ezequiel, & Gallagher, Shaun (2010). "Can Social Interaction Constitute Social Cognition?" *Trends in Cognitive Science* 14 (10), 441–447.
Di Paolo, Ezequiel, Rohde, M., & De Jaegher, Hanne (2010). "Horizons for the Enactive Mind: Values, Social Interactions and Play". In: J. Stewart, O. Gapenne, & E. Di Paolo (Eds.) *Enaction. Toward a New Paradigm for Cognitive Science*. Cambridge MA/London: MIT Press.
Eilan, Naomi (2014). "The You Turn." *Philosophical Explorations*. 17 (3), 265–278.
Farroni, Teresa, Csibra, Gergely, Simion, Francesca, & Johnson, Mark H. (2002). "Eye Contact Detection in Humans from Birth." *Proceedings of the National Academy of Sciences of the United States of America* 99 (14), 9602–9605.
Froese, Tom, & Di Paolo, Ezequiel (2011). "The Enactive Approach: Theoretical Sketches from Cell to Society." *Pragmatics & Cognition* 19 (1), 1–36.
Gallagher, Shaun (2001). "The Practice of Mind: Theory, Simulation, or Interaction?" *Journal of Consciousness Studies* 8, 83–107.

—— (2008). "Direct Perception in the Intersubjective Context". *Consciousness and Cognition* 17, 535–543.
—— (2012). "In Defense of Phenomenological Approaches to Social Cognition: Interacting with the Critics." *Review of Philosophy and Psychology* 3, 187–212.
Gallese, Vittorio (2010). "Embodied Simulation and Its Role in Intersubjectivity." In: T. Fuchs, H. C. Sattel, & P. Henningsen (Eds.). *The Embodied Self. Dimensions, Coherence and Disorders.* Stuttgart: Schattauer.
Gilbert, Margaret (1989). *On Social Facts.* London and New York: Routledge.
—— (2014). *Joint Commitment. How We Make the Social World.* Oxford University Press.
Goldman, Alvin (1995). "Interpretation Psychologized". In: M. Davies & T. Stone (Eds.) *Folk Psychology. The Theory of Mind Debate.* Oxford: Blackwell.
—— (2006). *Simulating Minds: The Philosophy, Psychology, and Neuroscience of Mindreading.* New York: Oxford University Press.
—— (2012). "Theory of Mind". In: E. Margolis, R. Samuels, & S. Stich (Eds.). *The Oxford Companion to Philosophy of Cognitive Science.* Oxford: Oxford University Press.
Goldstone, Robert, Roberts, Michael, & Gureckis, Todd (2008). "Emergent Processes in Group Behavior." *Current Directions in Psychological Science* 17 (1), 10–15.
Gopnik, Alison, & Wellman, Henry (1995). "Why the Child's Theory of Mind Really Is a Theory." In: M. Davies, & T. Stone (Eds.) *Folk Psychology. The Theory of Mind Debate.* Oxford: Blackwell.
Gordon, Robert (1998). "Radical Simulationism." In: P. Carruthers, & K. Smith (Eds.). *Theories of Theories of Mind.* Cambridge: Cambridge University Press.
Herschbach, Mitchell (2012). "On the Role of Interaction in Social Cognition: A Mechanistic Alternative to Enactivism." *Phenomenology and the Cognitive Sciences* 11, 467–486.
Hobson, Peter (2002). *The Cradle of Thought.* London: Macmillan.
—— (2007). "We Share, Therefore We Think." In: D. Hutto & M. Ratcliffe (Eds.). *Folk-Psychology Re-assessed.* Dordrecht: Springer.
Krueger, Joel (2011). "Seeing Mind in Action". *Phenomenology and the Cognitive Sciences* 11 (2), 149–173.
León, Felipe (2013). "Experiential Other-Directness: To What Does It Amount?" *Tidsskrift for Medier, Erkendelse og Formidling* 1 (1), 21–38.
Lenay, Charles, & Stewart, John (2012). "Minimalist Approach to Perceptual Interactions." *Frontiers in Human Neuroscience* 6, 1–18.
Menary, Richard (Ed.) (2010). *The Extended Mind.* Cambridge, MA/London: MIT Press.
Michael, John, & Overgaard, Søren (2012). "Interaction and Social Cognition: A Comment on Auvray et al.'s Perceptual Crossing Paradigm." *New Ideas in Psychology* 30, 296–299.
Moll, Henrike, & Meltzoff, Andrew (2011). "Joint Attention as the Fundamental Basis for Understanding Perspectives." In: A. Seemann (Ed.). *Joint Attention. New Developments in Psychology, Philosophy of Mind and Social Neuroscience.* Cambridge, MA: MIT Press.
Murray, Lynne, & Trevarthen, Colwyn (1985). "Emotional Regulations of Interactions Between Two-month-olds and Their Mothers." In: T. M. Field, & N. A. Fox (Eds.). *Social Perception in Infants.* Norwood: Ablex, 177–197.
Overgaard, Søren, & Michael, John (2015). "The Interactive Turn in Social Cognition Research: A Critique". *Philosophical Psychology* 28 (2), 160–183.
Pettit, Philip (2003). "Groups with Minds of Their Own." In: F. Schmitt (Ed.). *Socializing Metaphysics.* New York: Rowman & Littlefield, 167–193.

Premack, David, & Woodruff, Guy (1978). "Does the Chimpanzee Have a Theory of Mind?" *Behavioral and Brain Sciences* 4, 515–526.

Rakoczy, Hannes (2008). "Collective Intentionality and Uniquely Human Cognition." In: E. Neumann-Held, & L. Röska-Hardy (Eds.). *Learning from Animals? Examining the Nature of Human Uniqueness*. London: Psychology Press.

Reddy, Vasudevi (2008). *How Infants Know Minds*. Cambridge, MA: Harvard University Press.

Searle, John (1990). "Collective Intentions and Actions." In: P. Cohen, J. Morgan, & M. E. Pollack (Eds.). *Intentions in Communication*. Cambridge, MA/London: MIT Press.

——— (1995). *The Construction of Social Reality*. New York: The Free Press.

——— (2010). *Making the Social World. The Structure of Human Civilization*. Oxford: Oxford University Press.

Schilbach, Leonhard, Timmermans, Bert, Reddy, Vasudevi, Costall, Alan, Bente, Gary, Schlicht, Tobias, & Vogeley, Kai (2013). "Toward a Second-Person Neuroscience." *Behavioral and Brain Sciences* 36 (4), 393–414.

Schütz, Alfred (1967) [1932]. *The Phenomenology of the Social World*. Evanston, IL: Northwestern University Press.

Schweikard, David, & Schmid, Hans-Bernhard (2013). "Collective Intentionality". In E. N. Zalta (Ed.). *The Stanford Encyclopedia of Philosophy* (Summer 2013 Edition). http://plato.stanford.edu/archives/sum2013/entries/collective-intentionality/. [18.09.15]

Stein, Edith (2010) [1917]. *Zum Problem der Einfühlung*. ESGA 5. Freiburg i. B.: Herder.

Theiner, Georg, Allen, Colin, & Goldstone, Robert (2010). "Recognizing Group Cognition." *Cognitive Systems Research* 11 (4), 378–395.

Tollefsen, Deborah (2004). "Collective Intentionality". In: J. Fieser, & B. Dowden (Eds.). *Internet Encyclopedia of Philosophy*. http://www.iep.utm.edu/coll-int/ [18.09.15]

——— (2015). *Groups as Agents*. Cambridge, MA: Polity Press.

Tomasello, Michael (2014). *A Natural History of Human Thinking*. Harvard: Harvard University Press.

Tomasello, Michael, Carpenter, Malinda, Call, Joseph, Behne, Tanya, & Moll, Henrike (2005). "Understanding and Sharing Intentions: The Origins of Cultural Cognition." *Behavioral and Brain Sciences* 28, 675–735.

von Scheve, Christian, & Salmela, Mikko (Eds.) (2014). *Collective Emotions*. Oxford: Oxford University Press.

Walther, Gerda (1922). *Ein Beitrag zur Ontologie der sozialen Gemainschaften. Mit einem Anhang zur Phänomenologie der sozialen Gemeinschaften*. Halle a. d. S: Max Niemeyer.

Zahavi, Dan (2008). "Simulation, Projection and Empathy." *Consciousness and Cognition* 17, 514–522.

——— (2011). "Empathy and Direct Social Perception: A Phenomenological Proposal." *Review of Philosophy and Psychology* 2 (3), 541–558.

——— (2015). "You, Me and We: The Sharing of Emotional Experiences." *Journal of Consciousness Studies* 22 (1–2), 84–101.

# 10 "If I had to live like you, I think I'd kill myself"
## Social Dimensions of the Experience of Illness

*Havi Carel*

## 1 INTRODUCTION

The social experience of illness is complex and layered. It is made up of one's own experience of illness, the ill person's experiences of other people's experiences of her illness, and finally, the ill person's experience of her own illness in light of those intersubjective experiences. This complex web maps on to Sartre's tripartite schema in *Being and Nothingness* (2003) of the three orders of the body, accounting for the complex dynamic between the body as lived, the biological body, and the body in its social being.

In this chapter, I explore the experience of illness using this schema, aiming to uncover the complex ways in which this experience is textured by its social dimension. In particular, I attend to the ways in which one's own bodily experiences are informed, interpreted, and modulated by intersubjectivity. I claim that shared bodily experiences underpin much of our social commerce and that modifying bodily experiences such that they become alien to others, a focal feature of illness, exacts a social cost that can be formulated in terms of lost bodily empathy.

I then turn to respiratory illness to test Sartre's schema. I begin by examining the perceived and experienced differences between normal and pathological breathlessness as an expression of the widening gap between the ill person's bodily experiences and those of healthy others. Using George Canguilhem's notion of health as an individual norm, as formulated in *The Normal and the Pathological* (1991), I ask what happens when bodily norms are modified so that they no longer act as social, or shared, norms. This change can be captured by looking at how breathlessness, a major symptom of respiratory illness, modifies the ill person's ability to perform everyday tasks, curtails her independence, and reshapes 'normal living.' These, I suggest, are core features of human experience that underpin much of our social existence.

I end by looking at a specific social situation: the clinical encounter. There is strong evidence that there is little correspondence between lung function measured objectively (e.g., in spirometry) and subjective experiences of breathlessness. I suggest that this gap can be at least partly explained by appealing to the loss of shared bodily norms that characterizes the clinical encounter between the (healthy, objective) health professional and the (ill, subjectively experiencing) patient. For example, respiratory patients have described breathlessness as akin to suffocating, drowning, and a near-death experience. These subjective, qualitative ways of describing breathlessness do not have objective, measurable correlates. I suggest that this asymmetry can be explained by the loss of shared bodily norms. However, the strong juxtaposition between the patient and health professional as contrasting objectivity and subjectivity, normality and pathology, health and illness, must be understood in a more nuanced way, as interlacing and overlapping in rich ways.

## 2 THE OBJECTIVE BODY, THE LIVED BODY, AND THE SOCIAL BODY

In order to provide an account of the social dimension of the experience of illness, we need to begin with the distinction between the objective body and the body as lived. This distinction, formulated by Husserl and further developed by Merleau-Ponty, accounts for the dual nature of the body that comes to the fore in the experience of illness. This account distinguishes between the objective body (which Husserl called *Körper* and Merleau-Ponty called *le corps objectif*) and the body as lived (*Leib* and *corps proper*, respectively) (Husserl 1989; Merleau-Ponty 2012). The objective body is the physical body, the object of medicine: it is what becomes diseased. Sartre (2003) calls this body the 'body of Others' (*le corps d'autrui*): it is the body as viewed by others, not as experienced by me. The body as lived is the first-person experience of this objective body, the body as experienced by the person whose body it is. And it is on this level that illness, as opposed to disease, appears.[1]

This distinction is fundamental to the experience of illness: the ill person is only and ever the one who experiences the illness from within, although others do have an experience of someone else's illness. Only the ill person can say if she feels pain or fatigue, or what a medical procedure or a particular symptom *feels like*. Thus, the experience of illness contains a measure of idiosyncratic and privileged experience that may hamper a shared understanding of it, and hence, to an extent, defy sociality (Carel 2013; Carel & Kidd 2014). Sartre puts it more strongly, by claiming that "the existed body is ineffable" (Sartre 2003, 377). Even if not ineffable, having extreme or unusual bodily experiences will make articulating such experiences at least more onerous, and some experiences may only be communicated partially or with great difficulty (e.g., the experience of childbirth).

Disease, on the other hand, is a process in the objective body that may be observed by any other person and may yield information that is not available through first-person reports. For example, one may have elevated cholesterol levels or an early stage of renal disease while having no experience of these. Often, objective knowledge comes from medical tests that yield objective facts with no experiential correlate. For example, hypertension may not *feel like* anything. Only once it is revealed via a blood pressure test does it begin to feature in the diseased person's experience.

However, the relationship between illness and disease is not simple: the two aspects do not simply mirror one another. Illness may precede one's knowledge of one's disease: disease is commonly diagnosed following the appearance of symptoms. These symptoms are part of the ill person's illness experience and are lived by the patient. Disease may appear without illness (as in the example above). Or more usually, we encounter illness and disease, but the two do not cohere.

Evidence shows that severe disease or disability may give rise to an illness experience that is entirely at odds with our external expectations. Thus, disability activist Harriet Johnson, who suffered from a spinal deformity, recounts how strangers on the street turned to her to say, "If I had to live like you, I think I'd kill myself" (Johnson 2003). The lack of correlation between disease severity and the arising illness experience can be explained by ill people's ability to adapt to their situation (Carel 2007, 2009; Haidt 2006), but also by a documented general limited ability to imagine or remember what such an experience is like (Gilbert 2006; Carel 2013). So although a disease may be classed as severe on some clinical scale, the arising illness experience may not be correspondingly negative, counter to expectations (Gilbert 2006; Angner et al. 2009).

For example, a study of renal patients undergoing hemodialysis compared their well-being with that of healthy controls (Riis et al. 2005). We would expect the renal patients tethered to a dialysis machine three times a week, unable to travel and often incapacitated, to be markedly less happy then the healthy controls. But both groups report a similar level of well-being (ibid., 6). Both the dialysis patients and the healthy controls overestimated the impact of hemodialysis on their well-being, and both focused too much on dialysis as affecting patients' well-being more strongly than it actually did. The lack of correlation between disease severity and illness experience instantiates the gap between the objective body and the lived subjective body.[2]

## 3 INTERSUBJECTIVITY IN THE CLINIC

The distinction between the objective and the lived body is useful in several respects: it makes clear the fundamental difference between the two perspectives on the body. The physician's (or others') perspective means that he or she can only perceive the illness through attentiveness to the ill person's experience. The illness experience in its first-person form is not directly accessible to the physician, by definition, other than via the patient's account or behavior (although the disease is, of course). Only the patient has direct access to the subjective experience of illness, and only she experiences it first hand. Taking an objective stance may lead the physician to seek to treat the disease, sometimes with an inadequate understanding of the illness, or to have little understanding of the impact of the illness on a patient's life as a whole.

The patient, on the other hand, can observe the objective indicators of disease (e.g., blood test results), but also has unique access to the lived experience of the disease, namely, to the illness experience. In this sense, the patient may have, at least in principle, an epistemic advantage over others because of this access to her own illness experience *and* to the objective knowledge about the disease. This epistemic advantage often goes unacknowledged and the patient's experience may be subsumed under the medical (objective) point of view, or it may be dismissed because the patient has no formal medical training and is therefore barred from contributing to the epistemic work of diagnosis or creating a treatment plan (Carel & Kidd 2014).

The patient's unique ability to oscillate between the two perspectives gives her a deeper understanding of the illness experience, and potentially of the dual nature of the body, but this may also cause confusion and miscommunication, as the patient oscillates between the two perspectives.[3] Although it is crucial to clinical practice, this point remains underappreciated and underutilized in the clinic. As Toombs (1987) notes, the physician's focus on disease may clash with the patient's primary interest in her illness, so although they may seem to speak of the same entity, they in fact refer to different entities and therefore encounter a communicative gap.

Seeing the physician as occupying an objective position, while the patient occupies a subjective one, sheds light on communication problems in the clinic. However, it is important to acknowledge that the physician's suggested objectivity is in fact a more complex position. The complexity stems from the fact that both the body of the physician and the body of the patient exist under both the objective (material, physical) and the subjective (experienced, first-person) order, and moreover, that both are revealed to each other as belonging to both orders.

This gives rise to a third order in which the body partakes: the order of intersubjectivity, or my body as I experience it *as* reflected in the experience of it by others. "I exist for myself as a body known by the other," writes Sartre (2003, 375). He gives the example of feeling shy or self-conscious about one's body. This is only possible, he claims, because of this third order. The shy person is "vividly and constantly conscious of his body not as it is for him but as it is *for the Other*" (ibid., 376). The uneasiness the shy person feels is "the horrified metaphysical apprehension of the existence of my body for the Others" (ibid.). Only my body as it is for another person can embarrass me, not my body as I exist it.

When a patient feels self-conscious, it is as a body experienced in this third order: the body experienced as socially perceived. Sartre points to alienation, embarrassment, and social unease, claiming that in these situations, I experience my body *as it is experienced by another*, not in the pre-reflective way I normally experience it. This process continues: I may then begin to treat my body—or indeed to experience it—not as my pre-reflective opening to the world, but as an object that can be worked on, changed, and assessed in modes suited to objective bodies.

An example of this third order is the attitude of plastic surgeons to their patients' bodies, which reflects this objectifying mode of self-regard: the person seeking plastic surgery is happy for the surgeon to draw on her body with a pen, marking out 'excess' flesh or skin that needs to be removed like excess clay on a sculpture. The patient does not experience that flesh as part of 'my body as I exist it,' but as inert matter that occludes 'my real figure.' But that 'real' figure is, in fact, merely a projection of a social ideal—how I think I *should* look, according to prevalent social norms. The 'real me' is an internalized social norm experienced as a personal preference. Plastic surgeons trade on this masquerade when they uncritically accept their patients' projections of fantasies of acceptance and omniscience onto the carving of their own flesh.

But it is not only the patient's, but also the physician's body that falls under the duality captured by the disease/illness distinction, as well as by the third order of the social body articulated by Sartre. The physician may experience herself as a subject examining an object (the patient's physical body), but because of this duality, the object can 'touch back.' When the physician's examining hand is 'touched back' by a body responding to its touch with a quiver or a tensing of muscles, we no longer have a subject touching an object, but a subject that is also an object touching an object that is also a subject (Carel & Macnaughton 2012). Following Sartre (2003), we can see that this seemingly simple situation contains within it a complex nexus of metaphysical relations, which in turn give rise to the complex phenomenon of human sociality.

The recognition of myself as a subject for myself and an object for others is elaborated in the next step in the dance of reciprocity: the recognition of the other as an object for myself and as a subject for her. I meet the other *both* in her object-making subjectivity *and* as an object (ibid., 377). These positions are not fixed and constrained by some a priori stipulation. On the contrary: the oscillation between perceiving myself as a subject that has been objectified (the patient) and is then re-subjectified in the act of touching back continues as long as the intersubjective interaction continues. Subjectivity is forever challenged and then reclaimed, only to be challenged again.

Similarly for the physician: to take an objective stance, only to have it punctured by sensations, emotions, and biases that subjectify it, and yet need to be checked, is also an ongoing process. But there is one important difference. The objectified patient does not experience her body as an object; instead, she experiences it as "the flight of the body which I exist" (ibid., 378).[4] The sense of discomfort, self-consciousness, and alienation does not arise from my being objectified qua the diseased body of a patient, and thus becoming an object for myself, but from the escape, or draining away, of my being qua subject, dissipated by the objectifying medical gaze. This experience is not mirrored by the physician's experience because she actively sets out to adopt an objective stance. The complexity of both positions and the ensuing social interaction arises from the body's unique metaphysical position: it is "a non-thingly living flesh" that is neither purely an object nor pure consciousness (Moran 2010, 42).

There is another possibility of a mode of interaction between physician and patient, one that is deeply intersubjective in ways that exceed the dialectic described above. This is the second-person perspective. The mother of a child with chicken pox does not have direct access to her itching and pain, but as someone witnessing the suffering of a loved one, she does not occupy the objective observer's position. Although she has no direct access to her child's pain, she is still able to empathize with it through memory, imagination, or authentic witnessing and to transcend the objective position in order to come closer and share in her pain. The demand to recognize the other's humanity (and animality), their capacity for suffering, and our shared mortality is present in the second-person position: the I-Thou relationship, or the face-to-face encounter, and their ensuing ethical demands stem from the recognition of the uniqueness and irreducibility of each person (Levinas 1969; Buber 2010).

The simplistic picture of the physician as subject who objectifies the patient is far more complex because of the oscillation of roles arising from the fact that we each partake in the three orders of the body. Moreover, the acceptance of objectivity as the ideal stance of the medical practitioner should be tempered by the additional possibility of the second-person perspective available to the physician: "By recognising each other's subjectivity both physician and patient stand to gain. The physician gains a more natural mode of expression, and the patient has a feeling of being listened to by a fellow human being who neither purports to stand in her shoes, nor to be completely objective" (Carel & Macnaughton 2012, 2335).

## 4  EMPATHY AND ITS BREAKDOWN IN ILLNESS

The intersubjective dimension of one's experience of oneself and of the other, as well as the other's experience of me and of herself, relies fundamentally on empathy. Husserl and Merleau-Ponty agree that intersubjectivity depends on empathy, which in turn depends on intercorporeality. And intercorporeality itself arises from my experience of my own body as partaking in the two different orders, as shown in Husserl's analysis of 'double sensations' (Moran 2010, 41; Bernet 2013). Empathy depends on intercorporeality because fundamentally, I perceive others as bodies that are similar to mine in that they, too, sense, perceive, etc., and I am perceived by others as a body that is similar to theirs. I am there for others, and this being-there "is precisely the body," writes Sartre (2003, 375). However, the ways in which my body exceeds the first two orders and enters the third, social order, are the ways in which "my body escapes me on all sides" and returns to me as gazed upon by others (ibid.).

My body is my point of view, but it is also a point of view on which other points of view are brought to bear, including points of view I could never take (ibid.). In other words, the body as lived encompasses not only one's experience, but also the social aspect of one's experience of their and others' bodies, as well as how others' experiences of one's own body might impact on their own experience of their body. The experience of empathy is fundamental to this exchange and requires careful examination to see whether a radically different lived body experience may modify or curtail empathy with others or even self-empathy.

What happens in illness, I suggest, is that empathy breaks down, or is reconfigured, in light of a growing distance between the embodied being-in-the-world of the ill person and that of her healthy counterparts. Such a distance may increase or become more salient if the social norms admit less variability. For example, the shared meaning of terms like 'difficult' and 'far,' the ability to partake in taken-for-granted social activities like walking to the pub, the spontaneity with which we engage with others, and the ability to reciprocate social gestures are lost or modified in illness.

Bodily empathy itself is damaged when bodily social norms and shared meanings cease to capture the ill person's experience, accentuating and exacerbating her sense of social isolation and exclusion. Instead of serving as social glue, such norms serve as a sad reminder of the shared meaning that has been lost through illness. The tool that was once ready to hand, and understood as such, is now a present at hand thing that obstructs the action it once facilitated and as such serves as a sad reminder of lost shared abilities that endowed it with meaning in the first place. As S.K. Toombs writes:

> The bookcase outside my bedroom was once intended by my body as a 'repository for books'; then as 'that which is to be grasped for support on the way to the bathroom,' and is now intended as 'an obstacle to get around with my wheelchair' (1995, 16).

Illness can give rise to a loss of social meaning, related to the loss of the ability to perceive things as useful tools, and experiencing the breakdown of bodily empathy and the contingency and irretrievability of meaning. Somatic illness may cause a sudden and often disturbing sense of the contingency of the meanings and uses we assign to things: "The bookcase holds books. Of course it does! What else might it do? It might obstruct, impede, sadly remind . . ." There is also a sense of the irretrievability of certain social meanings: "[T]he bookcase will always be an obstacle and will only cease to be so once I cease to be so."

The sense of inhabiting a space of shared meanings and possibilities is replaced by a sense of this space becoming delimited and static. Illness can expose not only the limits of human existence, but also how the sharedness of that existence can be disrupted. The ill person no longer experiences embodied interactions in a socially shared way; the radical difference between her embodied being and that of others undermines the foundational power of empathy and will require deliberate and forceful effort to overcome.

## 5 RESPIRATORY ILLNESS: MEDICAL AND SOCIAL NORMS

The social experience of illness can be accounted for by the growing distance between the ill person's bodily experiences and those of her healthy counterparts. In illness, bodily norms are modified and as a result, they no longer act as social or shared norms. Let us now turn to the case of respiratory illness to examine the framework proposed thus far. Respiratory illness is a good test case for several reasons. First, breathing is automatic, but also has voluntary override. In this respect, it has an 'objective,' unexperienced dimension, but it can be made conscious and, moreover, the object of attentional focus (e.g., in practices such as meditation and *pranayama*). It is also useful here because of the perceived and experienced differences between normal and pathological breathlessness, which I suggest are an expression of the widening gap between the ill person's bodily experiences and those of healthy others. Finally, breathlessness is a common symptom of a wide range of respiratory and cardiac diseases as well as other disorders, such as panic attacks and disorders of the chest muscles. As such, it affects a huge number of patients around the world. Indeed, chronic obstructive pulmonary disease, which is characterized by progressive and debilitating breathlessness, is estimated to become the third leading cause of death globally by 2020 (Barnes and Kleinert 2014).

Breathlessness seems like a simple bodily sensation. In fact, it is multifaceted and incorporates several sources of input, such as oxygen saturation level, respiratory effort, chest muscles work, and blood pH levels. In severe desaturation, feelings akin to suffocation, dizziness, sense of loss of control, and incontinence can be present. Overall, the sensation is one of extreme unpleasantness and distress, but not of pain as we normally understand it. However, recent work in the neurophysiology of breathlessness shows that the same brain pathways are activated in breathlessness as in pain, hunger, and thirst (Herigstad et al. 2011). Herigstad and colleagues reviewed a series of papers that revealed at least nine areas involved in the voluntary control of breathing, including corticolimbic structures that also subserve sensations such as thirst, hunger, and pain, and the amygdala (also part of the limbic system), which deals with memory and emotions (ibid., 813). Such neuroimaging studies have the potential to help delineate sensory from affective components of breathlessness and improve the understanding of how emotional and cognitive processes affect not only the perception but also the pathophysiology of breathlessness.

Breathlessness is not only common; it is also unique. Unlike many other medical symptoms, breathlessness (and breathing more generally) has a psychological, cultural, and spiritual dimension. We 'take a deep breath' to calm ourselves; we 'inhale deeply' the fresh air of the countryside; a remarkable artwork 'takes our breath away.' Breathing is deeply and intimately connected to, and reflective of, our state of mind, feelings, mood, and sense of well-being. That is why breathing is central to many spiritual practices, such as *pranayama*, meditation, and some religious practices in which breath is identified with the Holy Spirit. When one is anxious or frightened, her breathing becomes fast and shallow. Panic attacks are often accompanied by a deadening fear of being unable to breathe, and the fear of suffocation that follows exacerbates the attack. In short, both normal and pathological breathing are complex phenomena, with many levels of expression and a multifactorial physiological, psychological, spiritual, and cultural underpinning.[5]

Phenomenologically speaking, breathlessness is remarkable in two intertwined ways: it is an overpowering sensation, which we are deeply sensitive to, but it is also behaviorally subtle, and so often invisible to others. However, even we ourselves are not always aware of when we start to become breathless and why. Techniques like meditation and mindfulness training help practitioners become more aware of their breathing, but this is hard to do when one is immersed in an activity and her attention is turned away from herself. This phenomenon has led Gysels and Higginson (2008) to coin the term 'invisible disability.' The Janus-faced duality of breathlessness—the fact that it is so real and overwhelming to the person experiencing it and yet so invisible to those around her, in particular to health professionals—make respiratory illness a particular challenge to medicine. I suggest that a phenomenological analysis may reveal facets of this symptom that have hitherto been unrecognized or have been obscured by a purely physiological analysis.

I have described the experience of respiratory illness elsewhere (Carel 2008), so in this section, I would like to focus on its social aspect. The respiratory patient's ability to perform everyday tasks, her independence, and the terms of 'normal living,' which are core to one's social existence, are radically modified by respiratory illness. Such illness poses a challenge not only through the practical and psychological demands it places on the patient and her family, but also through distancing the patient from shared norms and being a social obstacle. This distancing is intertwined with the practical and psychological demands, of course. If a respiratory patient faces significant practical barriers in mobility, energy levels, and the carrying out of routine tasks, her social world will necessarily be impacted by these barriers. If she suffers distress as a result of a dramatic diagnosis or a poor prognosis, that will also affect her social being.

The change can take place in one of three interlinked ways: it could affect her social being, shared norms can be undermined, and the sense of normality that characterizes wellness can be modified. Let us take each of these in turn. First, the ill person's social being can be affected in several ways. She may be less able to participate or reciprocate socially. She may feel more self-conscious, or the illness may hamper social interactions. Respiratory illness disrupts everyday activities. It therefore also interrupts social activities. The respiratory patient may no longer be able to dance, play sports, or go for a walk. She may feel that she impedes social events and may consequently remove herself from them. She may experience more acutely the lack of empathy and understanding in the way in which health professionals address her illness. And she may come to dread clinical encounters that accentuate her health deficits. She may come to think of meeting new people as an awkward affair, in which the illness needs to be explained and limitations justified (cf. Goffman 1963). The respiratory patient may become dependent on others for her daily care, so that these relationships become characterized by asymmetry.

Second, shared norms are truncated by such bodily changes. The concepts underpinning many of our social exchanges are modified in illness. For example, short distances may now seem long and exhausting, small inclines may become insurmountable mountains, and simple tasks may seem superhuman feats. As a result, the use of concepts such as 'near' or 'short walk' becomes detached from the shared meanings these concepts once had. In addition, the structure of the ill person's experience of space and time may change, especially in cases of poor prognosis or reduced mobility. In these changes not only the respiratory patient's relationship to the environment changes, but also her relationship to the shared norms that underpin our understanding of that environment will have changed. The ways in which we understand and use ready-to-hand tools, such as the bookcase described above by Toombs, changes in illness. This changes our relationship to the tools, but also undermines the shared meaning that makes up the common background of our understanding (cf. Dreyfus 1991).

Third, the social and other norms that make up the norms of health are also modified in illness. Canguilhem writes, "[A]n organism's norm of life is furnished by the organism itself, contained in its existence. And it is true that no doctor dreams of promising his patients anything more than a return to the state of vital satisfaction from which illness hurled them down" (1991, 258). In his view, the norms of health are individual and express the relationship of an organism to its environment. So health is not a set of norms, but a *normativity*, a deep sense of successfully relating to a given environment in a way unique to the organism. Thus, illness is not a deviation from a healthy statistical 'norm' (as Boorse (1977) conceives of it), but the emergence of a new individual norm—a new way of relating to the environment, or a new way of being. This is echoed in Merleau-Ponty's (2012, 110) statement that illness is a "complete form of existence." Illness is an inferior norm, but only because the sick person's possibilities within a given environment are narrowed compared to a healthy person. While normality is a statistical concept, normativity means that the organism's ability to tolerate an environmental change has been reduced (Gayon 1998, 313).

Canguilhem's view seems to capture the emphasis on first-person experience in respiratory (and other) illness. In this view, the illness experience matters, indeed motivates, clinical medicine. As Canguilhem says, "medicine always exists [. . .] because there are men who feel sick, not because

"If I had to live like you, I think I'd kill myself" 183

there are doctors to tell men of their illnesses" (1991, 93). However, the individual norm of health interacts with and is affected by social norms and one's social being more generally. Once these norms cease to include the ill person's lived experience, that person's social being will necessarily be further removed from the social norms. In that sense, the individual norm of health must be placed within the broader context of its relation to other (non-medical) norms in the three senses discussed above. In illness, our individual norm is modified, or replaced by a new, less flexible norm. But this putative neutrality of description must be tempered by locating the norm as now farther away from social and shared norms, which serves to distance the ill person from others in important respects, as discussed above. In this respect, Canguilhem's emphasis on individuality fails to consider that the flexibility and openness of an individual norm will always be affected by its position vis-à-vis social norms.

## 6 THE GAP BETWEEN SUBJECTIVE AND OBJECTIVE IN RESPIRATORY ILLNESS

Let us now turn to respiratory illness in the clinic. There is strong evidence that there is little correspondence between lung function measured objectively (e.g., in spirometry) and subjective experiences of breathlessness. Jones states that "some patients may have very poor health despite mild spirometric impairment," while there are patients with severe airway obstruction "who appear to have little disturbance to their daily lives, despite severe airflow limitation" (2001, 883). This gap poses a significant challenge in clinical work and research, to the extent that objective lung function measurements such as the $FEV_1$ are no longer taken as an endpoint for a clinical trial, unless combined with a (subjective) quality of life measurement (ibid.).

I suggest that this gap can be at least partly explained by the phenomenological insights discussed above. First, the rift between the objective body and the body as lived is a fundamental way of accounting for this gap. Measuring the objective function of the biological body simply does not correlate with the subjective experience of the lived body (cf. Merleau-Ponty's (2012, 81–82) discussion of blindness). Second, the loss of shared bodily norms, which also affects the clinical encounter between the (healthy, objective) health professional and the (ill, subjectively experiencing) patient can also explain the gap. Respiratory patients have described breathlessness as akin to suffocating, drowning, being unable to get air in, unable to exhale, chest tightening, and a near-death experience. These subjective, qualitative ways of describing breathlessness do not have objective, measurable correlates and are therefore poorly understood by health professionals. The misunderstanding is further compounded by the gap between normal and pathological breathlessness. The medical descriptions of both types of breathlessness use the same terms (e.g., 'breathless,' 'panting'), thus masking the deep difference between the two. Pathological breathlessness is often described as 'unpleasant' by health professionals, which stands in stark contrast with the extreme metaphors (e.g., drowning, suffocating) used by patients. This breakdown in understanding reflects the loss of shared bodily norms discussed above.

However, the strong juxtaposition between the patient and health professional as contrasting objectivity and subjectivity, normality and pathology, health and illness, must be understood in a more nuanced way, as interlacing and overlapping in rich ways. As was discussed in section III, the relationship between the patient and physician in the clinic is not one of subject vs. object, but a rich dialectic process of gaining, losing, demanding, and regaining subjectivity, both from oneself and from the other. Similarly, the objective aspect of one's body also continuously comes to the fore or recedes to the background through continuous shifts in thematization. Neither health professional nor patient is purely object (or purely objective) or purely subject. Both patient and health professional are in a constant oscillation between subjectivity and objectivity.

The clinic is a locus of important social interaction around illness. Dramatic milestones such as diagnosis and prognosis take place in the clinic, and it is also there that the ill person's understanding of herself as ill is often shaped. Lessons from phenomenology for the clinic have been proposed by S.K. Toombs (1987) and others (e.g., Carel 2008). Jenny Slatman proposes to emphasize the social dimension of phenomenology in clinical work (2014). However, the full force of a phenomenological analysis of the clinical encounter as a social encounter par excellence has not yet been fully articulated. What I hope this chapter has illuminated is not only the important contribution of phenomenology to concrete and pragmatic clinical issues, but also the centrality of the social dimension of the experience of illness.

## ACKNOWLEDGEMENTS

This chapter was written while I was a senior investigator working on the Life of Breath project (www.lifeofbreath.org), funded by the Wellcome Trust (grant number 103340/Z/13/Z). I am grateful to the Trust for funding the project and enabling this research to take place.

## NOTES

1 Some authors (e.g., Hofmann 2002) suggest a third category, sickness, to denote the social dimension of human ailment.
2 Merleau-Ponty (2012) helpfully terms the latter the 'body-subject' to indicate the inseparability of the body from the subject under this mode.
3 Illness can be seen, from this epistemic point of view, as a process of edification and as having a distinctly *philosophical* value. The split between the

two perspectives reveals the duality of the body and as such is metaphysically important. See Kidd (2012) on the edifying role of illness and Carel & Kidd (2014) for a discussion of the philosophical role of illness.
4  The health professional may also be objectified, of course, but it is the patient's objective body that is the object of medicine.
5  A current Wellcome Trust-funded project, the Life of Breath, which I am leading with Professor Jane Macnaughton from Durham University, is looking at breathlessness from a multidisciplinary perspective, trying to bring the clinical and cultural perspectives into dialogue. See www.lifeofbreath.org.

## REFERENCES

Angner, Erik, Midge N. Ray, Kenneth G. Saag, & Jeroan J. Allison (2009). "Health and Happiness among Older Adults." *Journal of Health Psychology* 14 (4), 503–512.
Barnes, Peter J., & Sabine Kleinert (2014). "COPD—A Neglected Disease." *The Lancet* 364, 564–565.
Bernet, Rudolf (2013). "The Body as a 'Legitimate Naturalization of Consciousness'". *Philosophy* 72, 43–65.
Boorse, Christopher (1977). "Health as a Theoretical Concept." *Philosophy of Science* 44 (4), 542–573.
Buber, Martin (2010) [1923]. *I and thou*. Eastford, CT: Martino Publishing.
Canguilhem, Georges. (1991). *The Normal and the Pathological*. New York: Zone Books.
Carel, Havi (2007). "Can I Be Ill and Happy?" *Philosophia* 35 (2), 95–110.
——— (2008). *Illness*. Durham: Acumen.
——— (2009). "'I Am Well, Apart from the Fact that I Have Cancer': Explaining Wellbeing within Illness." In: Lisa Bortolotti (Ed.). *Philosophy and Happiness*, Basingstoke: Palgrave, 82–99.
——— (2013). "Illness, Phenomenology, and Philosophical Method". *Theoretical Medicine and Bioethics* 34 (4), 345–357.
Carel, Havi, & Macnaughton, Jane (2012). "'How Do You Feel?': Oscillating Perspectives in the Clinic". *Lancet* 379 (9834), 2334–2335.
Carel, Havi, & Kidd, Ian James (2014). "Epistemic Injustice in Healthcare: A Philosophical Analysis." *Medicine, Healthcare and Philosophy*. DOI: 10.1007/s11019-014-9560-2.
Dreyfus, Hubert (1991). *Being-in-the-World. A Commentary on Heidegger's* Being and Time, *Division I*. Cambridge MA/London: MIT Press.
Gayon, Jean (1998). "The Concept of Individuality in Canguilhem's Philosophy of Biology." *Journal of the History of Biology* 31, 305–325.
Gilbert, Daniel (2006). *Stumbling on Happiness*. London: Harper Press.Goffman, Erving (1963). *Stigma: Notes on the Management of Spoiled Identity*. New York: Simon & Schuster.
Gysels, Marjolein, & Higginson, Irene J. (2008). "Access to Services for Patients with Chronic Obstructive Pulmonary Disease: The Invisibility of Breathlessness." *Journal of Pain and Symptom Management* 36 (5), 451–460.
Haidt, Jonathan (2006). *The Happiness Hypothesis*. London: Heinemann.
Hofmann, Bjørn (2002). "On the Triad Disease, Illness and Sickness." *Journal of Medicine and Philosophy* 27 (6), 651–673.
Husserl, Edmund (1989) [1952]. *Ideas Pertaining to a Pure Phenomenology and to a Phenomenological Philosophy. Second book*. Dordrecht: Kluwer.

Herigstad, Mari, Hayen, Anja A., Wiech, Katja, & Pattinson, Kyle T.S. (2011). "Dyspnoea and the Brain." *Respiratory Medicine* 105 (6), 809–817.

Johnson, Harriet M. (2003). "Unspeakable Conversations." *The New York Times*. February 16, 2003.

Jones, Paul W. (2001). "Health Status Measurement in Chronic Obstructive Pulmonary Disease." *Thorax* 56, 880–887.

Kidd, Ian James (2012). "Can Illness Be Edifying?" *Inquiry* 55 (5), 496–520.

Levinas, Emmanuel (1969) [1961]. *Totality and Infinity: An Essay on Exteriority*. Pittsburgh, PA: Duquesne University Press.

Merleau-Ponty, Maurice (2012) [1945]. *Phenomenology of Perception*. London/New York: Routledge.

Moran, Dermot (2010). "Husserl, Sartre and Merleau-Ponty on Embodiment, Touch, and the 'Double Sensation'". In: K. Morris (Ed.), *Sartre on the Body*. London: Palgrave Macmillan, 41–66.

Riis, Jason J., Baron, Jonathan, Loewenstein, George, & Jepson, Christopher (2005). "Ignorance of Hedonic Adaptation to Haemodialysis: A Study Using Ecological Momentary Assessment." *Journal of Experimental Psychology: General* 134 (1), 3–9.

Sartre, Jean-Paul (2003) [1943]. *Being and Nothingness*. London/New York: Routledge.

Slatman, Jenny (2014). "Multiple Dimensions of Embodiment in Medical Practices." *Medicine, Health Care and Philosophy*. DOI: 10.1007/s11019-014-9544-2.

Toombs, Kay S. (1987). "The Meaning of Illness: A Phenomenological Approach to the Patient–Physician Relationship." *Journal of Medicine and Philosophy* 12, 219–240.

# 11 Shame as a Fellow Feeling

*Christian Skirke*

## 1 INTRODUCTION

A central theme in the phenomenology of intersubjectivity is how we experience others. Essential for how we experience others is that we experience others as subjects who are distinct from us. Yet describing experiences of distinct others is notoriously difficult. Our troubles start when we try to understand what it is to experience intentionality that is distinct from our own. For this seems to require of us that we live through intentional experiences we cannot live through because they are not ours.[1] Further difficulties arise when we try to determine the right mode of experience to achieve this. Intuitive candidates are fellow feelings such as empathy.[2] My contribution develops and defends a somewhat less intuitive view. I propose that shame, on a certain phenomenological understanding of it, can be just as relevant to the experience of distinct others as empathy is usually taken to be.

The conception of shame I have in mind stems from Sartre's *Being and Nothingness*. It is crucial for my proposal that I arrive at a reconstruction of his conception of shame in terms of an intentional experience of intentional experiences that are present to the subject of shame but not lived through by the subject of shame. To strengthen the envisaged connection between shame and fellow feelings, I will draw on Stein's and Husserl's respective treatments of empathy. They treat empathy as an intentional experience of intentional experiences that are present but not lived through. My aim is to show that there is a distinctive parallelism between the intentional experiences of shame and of empathy. Finally, I will lend further credit to my proposal on shame by responding to several objections to my argument.

## 2 FELLOW FEELINGS, EMPATHY, AND SHAME

Fellow feelings give us an emotive rapport with others by making us feel something of others or as of others. Empathy stands out among fellow feelings in that it gives us a characteristic sense of what things are like for someone else. If I empathize with your boredom, I have a sense of what it is like for you to be bored without being bored myself. If I empathize with your success, I have a sense of your elation without myself feeling good on your behalf. That I have a sense of what it is like for you to be bored without being bored myself distinguishes empathy from emotional contagion. That I have a sense of your elation without myself feeling good on your behalf distinguishes empathy from sympathy. Empathy is peculiar in that it is not a specific feeling or state or experience that I undergo or live through together with you.³ Empathy is a general feeling or state or experience with respect to feelings or states or experiences that I cannot undergo or that I cannot live through.

Shame is often described as a feeling of vulnerability or nakedness in the presence of others. Gabriele Taylor introduces this emotion in her classic study by stating that "feeling shame is connected with the thought that eyes are upon one" (Taylor 1985, 53). Bernard Williams associates shame with "being at a disadvantage" or a "loss of power" (Williams 1993, 220). And it is obvious that we cannot conceive of shame as a fellow feeling if we accept anthropological or psychological accounts of shame along these lines. Although anthropological or psychological accounts often involve the presence of others in their portrayal of shame, there is no question of feeling anything of others or as of others when ashamed. Taylor specifies:

> To speak of an audience is of course to speak metaphorically. What has been described as seen from different audience points of view is the content of some of the agent's explanatory beliefs. So on the occasion of an occurrence of shame the person believes that she is defective and degraded. This is her identificatory belief.
> (Taylor 1985, 66)

All mental states and all experiences relevant to shame are undergone by oneself. Some deny, on these grounds, that the presence of others is necessary for shame.⁴ Some go even further and conclude that shame counteracts and undermines empathic attitudes.⁵

Psychological and anthropological accounts of shame focus on behavior and the motives behind it. Phenomenological accounts of shame, by contrast, treat shame as a paradigmatic intentional experience. This is sometimes reflected by terminological choices like Sartre's distinction between anthropological or psychological shame, *pudeur*, and existential shame, *honte* (Sartre BN, e312/f336).⁶ Phenomenological accounts usually portray subjects who live through shame as subjects who experience themselves in an objectified state. Despite this common tendency, phenomenological conceptions of shame can be rather diverse. Scheler's and Sartre's respective accounts of shame illustrate how far apart these conceptions can be. Scheler thinks of shame as a strictly individual experience of objectified animal nature without any specific social context. He sees shame under the perspective of "a return of the individual to itself and the feeling of a need for self-protection against all aspects of the sphere of generality" (Scheler 1957, 90). Sartre thinks of shame as the objectifying experience of being looked at. According to him, shame is an experience of oneself by virtue of which the presence of others becomes conspicuous. He writes that "it is in relation to myself as subject that I am concerned about myself, and yet this concern (for-myself) reveals me as a being which is *my* being without being for me" (Sartre BN, e245/f265, original emphasis). Sartre's shame contrasts with Scheler's shame, as Sartre's shame requires a rudimentary interpersonal setting. The objectifying experience has bite, as it were, because it is not my own experience, that is, because I cannot live through this experience.[7] Yet, I experience the experience that I cannot live through as something that impinges on my subjectivity.

## 3 SARTRE ON SHAME

In a well-known passage from *Being and Nothingness*, Sartre describes one's shock at being found out when spying through a keyhole (Sartre BN e282–3/f305). The initial situation is simple. It contains a solitary subject who spies through a keyhole. Intentionality is unidirectional. It radiates out from the subject into the scene behind the keyhole. The subject finds itself at the point of origin of all the intentional experiences that come to consciousness. In Sartre's words, "I am my acts and they carry in themselves their whole justification" (BN e283/f305). Things change dramatically, however, with the sudden appearance of another subject. I find myself, not at the point of origin of all the intentional experiences that come to consciousness, but "at the end of that look" (BN e284–5/f307). My act of spying through a keyhole becomes conspicuous precisely in the presence of another subject. Sartre characterizes this experience as shameful self-recognition, an experience in which "I recognize that I am as the Other sees me" (BN e246/f266). This is not to say that I participate in the content of the other's experiences of myself. Rather, shameful self-recognition makes me experience myself as presented from a point of view that is not my own. As Sartre emphasizes, it strikes me immediately in shame that I, who am a subject, live through an intentional experience of myself as the intentional object of an experience that I cannot live through.

Both structural elements of shame, its immediacy and the objective self-presence of the subject, merit a closer look. Sartre duly notes that shameful self-recognition possesses a specific immediacy so that shame cannot be understood as the product of reflection. However, the way he puts this point is very peculiar:

> This role which devolved only on the reflective consciousness—the making-present of the self (*la présentification du moi*)—belongs now to the unreflective consciousness (*la conscience irréfléchie*). Only the

reflective consciousness (*la conscience reflexive*) has the self directly for its object. The unreflective consciousness does not apprehend the *person* directly or as its object; the person is present to consciousness (*est présente à la conscience*) in so far as the person is an object for the Other.

(BN e284/f306, translation modified)

What is striking about this dense passage is that Sartre does not simply oppose shame to reflection as "not reflected" (*irréfléchie*). In spelling out what he takes the specific immediacy of shameful self-recognition to be, he also states what shame and reflection have in common. He describes both as instances of "presentification" (*présentification*). "Presentification" translates Husserl's term of art, *Vergegenwärtigung* (also "representation" or "re-presentation"). This term of art refers to all kinds of intentional experiences of intentional experiences. According to the passage from *Being and Nothingness* above, both reflection and shame have the role of making present, or the role of presentifying, one's self (*la présentification du moi*). It is in this respect that both reflection and shame differ from plain, straightforward, intentional experiences. Of course, plain, intentional experiences have a subject. Yet this subject is not present in them, strictly speaking. The subject simply lives through the act of experiencing. Although Sartre's subject is always self-conscious, self-awareness in plain, intentional acts is merely implicit (BN e8–10/f18–20). Reflection and shame, by contrast, make the subject of intentional acts present, and thus constitute explicit forms of self-conscious experience. Therefore, I submit, neither reflection nor shame can be plain, straightforward, intentional experiences.

I am aware that my interpretation of Sartre's shame is somewhat unusual. Indeed, there are many passages in *Being and Nothingness* that stress the immediate, visceral force of shame. For instance, Sartre describes shame as "an immediate shudder which runs through me from head to foot without any discursive preparation" (BN e246/f266). And he writes that shame brings about an "irruption of the self" (BN e284/f206) and that shame "makes me *live*, not *know*, the situation of being looked at" (BN e285/f307, original emphasis). Quotes like these make it difficult to accept the view that shame is not a plain, straightforward, intentional experience, but is composite in some sense. Yet, some defining characteristics of shame simply cannot be accommodated in plain, intentional experiences. These characteristics include the phenomenon that, in shame, subjects experience themselves as presented from a point of view that is not their own. In other words, subjects can become intentional objects of their own experiences because they can be the intentional objects of experiences that they cannot live through. This phenomenon implies that shame consists of more than one intentional experience. Sartre registers this phenomenon in passages like the one quoted in the previous paragraph. And he also registers it in other remarks where he contrasts plain, intentional experiences with intentional experiences that "point to a radically different type of ontological structure" (BN e245/ f265). Shame is Sartre's main example for intentional experiences of this kind. Although it is natural to associate unreflective, intentional experiences with plain, intentional experiences, I maintain that unreflective, intentional experiences like shame are—indeed must be—intentional experiences of intentional experiences.

This brings me to the objective self-presence that subjects experience in shame. We said that shameful self-recognition means living through the intentional experience of an intentional experience I cannot live through. And we added that being faced with experiences I cannot live through impinges on my subjectivity. What impinges on my subjectivity is the fact that I, who am a subject, experience myself directly as the intentional object of my own experience. This configuration arises on account of the presence of experiences I cannot live through, i.e., on account of my givenness to another subject. If all subjectivity were my own, I could only ever appear to myself as the intentional object of higher-order reflections on my own intentional experiences. However, if I experience the presence of more subjectivity than my own, as it were, I can be given to myself like I am given to the other, namely directly as the intentional object of plain, first-order, intentional experiences.[8] If I experience the presence of the other in an overarching presentification, the intentional object of my own plain experience can be given to me by the plain experience the other has of me (see also below, section 5). Shameful self-recognition actualizes this possibility.

## 4  STEIN AND HUSSERL ON EMPATHY

To put this line of thought into a wider phenomenological context, I suggest that we leave Sartre for the moment and turn to a more comprehensive idea of intentional experiences of intentional experiences. This idea is prominent in Husserl's various discussions of presentification (*Vergegenwärtigung*), especially in *Ideas I* and in his writings on time-consciousness. And Stein's discussion of empathy provides us with a focused and sustained account of intentional experiences of intentional experiences one cannot live through (Stein 1964).

Memory is one of Husserl's main examples for presentification. Experiences of memory reproduce our past intentional experiences. According to Husserl, this is not because the original experiences occur at some prior point on time's arrow. This is because subjects have the capacity for presentifying these experiences and their objects in various ways. Husserl writes:

> Presentifying [. . .] is something free, a free running through: We can carry out the presentification 'more quickly' or 'more slowly,' more distinctly and explicitly or more confusedly, in a single lightning-like stroke or in articulated steps, and so on.
>
> (Hua 10, 406)

Plain, intentional experiences simply present their intentional objects as given transcendent items, entities that lie outside the intentional act. Presentifications modify the manner in which these transcendent items are given. Image-consciousness, for instance, presentifies original experiences and their original objects as pictorial or symbolic placeholders. Fantasy presentifies original experiences and their original objects as figments. Memory presentifies original experiences and their original objects as past.

In an unpublished manuscript from 1932, Husserl tries to conceive of empathy in terms closely analogous to his treatment of memory:

> When I live through empathy itself, empathy proper, a motivation occurs in me in which—it is difficult to find the correct words for it—I remember, as it were, not my earlier experiences, feelings or actions, do not remember 'myself' at all, but 'remember' 'his,' the other's experiences, feelings or volitions, or remember him in his life of which I am conscious as simultaneously present with my life.
>
> (Hua 15, 514)

Husserl analogizes between empathy and memory, as both of them modify an original experience into something it originally is not. Like memory, which converts present intentional experiences into past ones, empathy converts the experiences of others into my experiences. This is not to say that I experience firsthand what the other experiences, for this would turn the other's experiences into my own. But I experience something firsthand; and this is the presence of an experience I cannot live through. Husserl's analogy between memory and empathy thus gives us empathy as the presentification of distinct others. Empathy is an intentional experience of intentional experiences. It has the distinctive feature that I cannot live through the experiences which are present to me in my experiences.

In her pioneering study *On the Problem of Empathy*, Edith Stein anticipates these thoughts. She calls the experience of empathy "an act which is primordial as present experience though non-primordial in content" (Stein 1964, 10), and continues:

> This other subject is primordial although I do not experience its primordiality; his joy is primordial although I do not experience it as primordial. In my non-primordial experience I feel, as it were, led by a primordial one not experienced by me but still there, manifesting itself in my non-primordial experience. Thus empathy is a kind of act of perceiving sui generis.
>
> (Stein 1964, 10)

Evidently, Stein understands my experience of distinct others as an experience of experiences I cannot live through. What complicates matters, however, is Stein's connection between empathy and perception. This connection seems in conflict with the idea that empathy is a presentification.

Both Stein and Husserl argue at prominent places that experiencing others comes down to having firsthand perceptions of someone else's living body (e.g., Hua 1, 113). According to a familiar phenomenological idea, perceptual objects are presented in perspective so that their co-present aspects—their backsides or insides, their general location—are featured in accompanying perceptual horizons. And these co-present aspects can be disclosed, in principle, by further acts of perception. Firsthand perceptions of someone else's living body, by contrast, cannot reach into co-present horizons in quite the same way. Stein calls empathy a sui generis kind of perception because we are perceptually aware of someone else's living body as a perceptual item with co-present intentionality. But co-present intentionality is always, and of necessity, "non-primordial" and thus closed to perception. According to Husserl,

> if what belongs to the other's own essence were directly accessible, it would be merely a moment of my own essence, and ultimately he himself and I myself would be the same. The situation would be similar as regards his animate organism, if the latter were nothing else but the "body" that is a unity constituted purely in my actual and possible experiences, a unity belonging—as a product of *my* "sensuousness" exclusively—in my primordial sphere.
>
> (Hua 1, 139)

That is, I experience co-present intentionality in someone else's living body directly by encountering a limit beyond which nothing can be perceived any longer. What remains is apperception in Husserl's sense, that is, an accompaniment to perception that gives us a sense of aspects which are not present in the primary perception. As the apperceived aspects of living bodies other than my own never are present in primary perception, apperception cannot make the other present to me.

I believe that we can address this problem by reformulating the experience so that the presentification aspect of empathy becomes visible again. Someone else's firsthand experiences have a certain presence in our intentional experience if we allow that I experience someone else's firsthand experiences as experiences I can't live through. The presence of experiences through which I can't live leaves the possibility that I am an intentional object for others. Empathy is direct because I can experience myself immediately as this intentional object. I can experience myself as an object for others, given by intentional experiences through which I can't live, provided that both, the experience through which I live and the experience through which I can't live, are aligned with each other as components of a presentification.

## 5  EMPATHY AND SHAME AS PRESENTIFICATIONS

This brings me to my main point, the parallelism of shame and empathy. My reconstruction of empathy in Stein and Husserl has yielded a structure of presentification that is strikingly similar to the structure of presentification yielded by my reconstruction of Sartre's shame. Let me highlight the most important points of coincidence.

To begin with, we are unable to give a full account of empathy in terms of direct perception. What we need for a full account is a presentification structure in which my own intentional experiences are combined with the intentional experiences of others, experiences that I cannot live through. This structure allows us to say that I can experience the presence of others, the presence of intentionality that exceeds my own, because it is possible for me to experience myself directly as an intentional object in relation to intentional experiences that I cannot live through.

Empathy is isomorphic with Sartre's shame, as reconstructed in section 3. To make perspicuous why shame strikes me immediately, we had to account for the phenomenon that I become the direct intentional object of my intentional experience. We have seen that this direct experience is not available to me if all experiences are just my own. In this case, self-objectification requires higher-order reflection. But I become a direct intentional object to myself if I can be the direct intentional object of experiences that issue from others.[9] This, however, is something I can experience only if there is scope in my intentional experience for the experience that some intentional experiences are experiences that I cannot live through. The direct experiences that strike me in shame are furnished by the component acts of a presentification that connects me to others.[10]

Shame and empathy require that more intentionality than my own is present in my experience. Others are present to myself in both cases because (a.) I have an indirect experience of more intentionality than my own, (b.) I have a direct experience of something in relation to (a.), and (c.) the other is in a position to have me as the intentional object of a plain experience.[11] It is by virtue of (c.) that I experience myself under (b.) as something with respect to (a.), namely as myself vis-à-vis a distinct other.

## 6 OBJECTIONS

I have argued for a parallelism between shame and empathy because I want to propose the view that we experience distinct others in shame. Defending this parallelism means meeting a number of objections. Let me begin with a general concern, which returns to the theme of directness. The worry here is that experiences of shame are essentially self-directed, and, for this reason, constitute merely indirect experiences of others after all. Especially if we conceive of empathy along these lines, we should be worried about distorting the nature of our empathic relations with others.

This worry rests on two assumptions about empathy. The first assumption is that empathy must allow us to experience others without the detour through self-objectification that seems necessary in the case of shame. The second assumption is that empathy specifically picks out individual others, while shame picks out a self vis-à-vis anonymous others. I will address the general worry by way of addressing these assumptions.

In response to the first assumption, let me expand on the discussion above. The discussion above suggests that empathy involves self-objectification just as shame does. According to Sartre, what strikes me in shame is that I am given to myself directly as an intentional object. As we have seen in section 3, I am given to myself in this way by virtue of an experience that I cannot live through, yet an experience that has the same intentional object as my own experience, the experience that I do live through. To experience myself in this direct way is thus indistinguishable from experiencing the presence of others who are distinct from me. Empathy also involves experiences of the presence of others in the sense of my experiences of experiences that I cannot live through. Yet, as we have seen in section 4, neither co-present experiences nor experiences we cannot live through possess self-evidence just in virtue of themselves. That is, I cannot have self-evident experiences of the presence of others who are distinct from me unless I experience myself as the intentional object of experiences that I cannot live through. I experience myself in this way when I experience myself as an intentional object that possibly coincides with intentional objects of experiences that I cannot live through. We do not have to give this experience the negative connotations that pervade Sartre's discussion of shame. All we have to do is to acknowledge that, to me, empathizing with someone is a self-evident experience of distinct others only if the experience includes the possibility that I am an intentional object to these distinct others.

The concern with identification is more difficult. Generally, it seems to me that empathy resembles shame in that it cannot pick out others without further structural support and refinement. Sartre characterizes the basic mode of shame as a "spontaneous and prenumerical" experience of distinct others (Sartre BN, e308/f331). This means that I experience others anonymously in shame, yet what I experience vis-à-vis anonymous others is that I am a discrete locus of intentionality from which all others are excluded and vice versa.[12] If we look at empathy in terms of presentification, our experience is isomorphic with what we experience in shame. In experiencing experiences that we cannot live through, we have general experiences of anonymous others that point us to our own exclusive subjectivity (cf. Hua 1, 127). Whether we look at shame or empathy, we cannot distinguish my experiences of my exclusive subjectivity from my experiences of the anonymous presence of more intentionality than my own. For us to move on to the identification of individual others, or to experiences of discrete loci of intentionality vis-à-vis myself, we have to conjoin experiences of experiences that I cannot live through with presentations of individual entities. Ultimately, this seems to be what Stein and Husserl have in mind when they conjoin experiences of experiences that we cannot live through with direct perceptions of individual entities with co-present experiences that we cannot live through with individual living bodies. Sartre does not envisage embodiment along these lines in his discussion of shame. Nothing about his discussion suggests, however, that shame cannot be joined to a similar identifying presentation. So, both shame and empathy relate me to individual others only insofar as my experiences of experiences that I cannot live through is conjoined with a concurrent, straightforward experience of individual entities with co-present intentionality.

## 7 MORE OBJECTIONS

The previous section addressed difficulties that we face when we model empathy on shame. The worry was that our resulting idea of empathy is impoverished. The current section addresses difficulties that we face when we model shame on empathy. The concern now might be that we make shame too rich of a phenomenon. I want to discuss three further objections to my proposal. These are: first, that we need empathy to make shame intelligible as a fellow feeling so that shame is not a self-sufficient intentional experience of others; second, that shame gives us a distorted picture of relations to others because it capitalizes on self-objectification; and third, that, compared with empathy, shame has little explanatory utility with respect to closely related psychological issues.

### 7.1 Empathy First

In light of the discussion so far, let's grant that experiencing others in terms of experiencing oneself makes sense. The question remains, however, whether experiencing others in terms of experiencing oneself, a paradigm case of shame, makes sense without prior experiences of others simply in terms of experiencing others, a putative case of empathy. The question is whether intentionality other than our own has to be self-evident to us before we experience ourselves as excluded from, or opposed to, intentionality other than our own. Note that this objection does not take us back to a point before the discussion of the previous section. In the previous section, we were concerned about the indirectness and anonymity of shame towards others and about the adequacy of transferring these features onto empathy. The present objection accepts that empathy is more complex than direct perception, that it needs direct perception merely to spot individual others, and that it involves self-objectification. But it raises a problem for the notion that shame can make us experience the presence of others without presupposing an empathic relation to them.

The central issue here is how to experience others with self-evidence despite the fact that distinct others are mutually exclusive loci of intentionality. As I have argued throughout, it is decisive for this kind of experience that someone else's experiences are experiences that I cannot live through. We have seen that the presence of mutually exclusive loci of intentionality cannot become self-evident for me unless their presence becomes tangible in how I experience myself vis-à-vis distinct others. Of course, experiences of others that precede experiences of myself are possible. These are intersubjective experiences where others have a presence for me because we share our experiences directly. Merleau-Ponty speaks of a whole, formed by my subjectivity and other subjectivity, so that I literally can live through the experiences of others (Merleau-Ponty 2010, 370). Evidently, such experiences are not experiences in which the self and the other are mutually exclusive. As far as others in this pregnant sense are concerned, direct experiences of others go hand in hand with direct experiences of myself.

## 7.2 Sophisticated Self-Objectification

Even if we concede that shame presentifies others just like empathy presentifies, it may still be considered problematic that our account of others involves the ego or self as an intentional object. Merleau-Ponty famously complained that if intentional relations involve distinct subjects and objects, tension is unavoidable: "In order to conceive of him (the Other) as a genuine I, I would have to consider myself as a mere object for him, which I am prevented from doing by the knowledge that I have of myself" (Merleau-Ponty 2010, 368). His antidote against this sophisticated kind of self-objectification is his suggestion that basic intentional relations are relations between bodies that may be objects but can also be embodied subjects. Therefore, he claims, straightforward, intentional relations are sufficient for experiences of others. We are familiar with each other because we have plain, straightforward, intentional experiences of distinct bodies that can be subjects without any intervening objectification or self-objectification.

I insist against this sophisticated self-objectification charge, that plain, intentional experiences do not allow us to have self-evident experiences of mutually exclusive loci of experience. Plain, intentional experiences allow us to experience with self-evidence that the individual bodies showing up in our experience differ from us. Yet to experience bodies as different from us means that they could be different simply in a local or temporal sense. To experience bodies as mutually exclusive loci of experience, as the "other" opposite the "self," we have to have intentional experiences of experiences that we cannot live through. Embodied subjects, too, must be presentified so that we can experience them as others who constitute mutually exclusive loci of experience.

## 7.3 Explanatory Utility

Phenomenological interventions in current debates often point out that a given psychological phenomenon is best understood by paying attention to underlying intentional structures. This is why judging phenomenological insights by their explanatory utility for psychological debates is of some importance. Take the example of joint attention, the phenomenon that two subjects experience the same item while they are individually conscious at the same time that they experience this item together with someone else (e.g., Pacherie 2012). Each subject is conscious of the triadic relation between object, self, and other. Phenomenologists argue that the best explanation for joint attention is that we experience shared objects as items placed in a world that we share with others (Gallagher 2008).

The explanatory utility charge against the account I propose says that, its structural congruence with empathy notwithstanding, shame tells us especially little about psychological phenomena such as joint attention. Shame primarily concerns oneself in the presence of others; it does not concern objects in a shared world. Consequently, the explanatory utility of shame is much inferior to that of empathy.

I do not think shame fares quite as badly. We have seen that shame draws attention to others in such a way that I experience myself as an intentional object for others. If we look at shame with joint attention in mind, shame exemplifies joint attention to a very special object, namely to my ego or self.[13] In this interpretation, shame shows the self-oriented and object-oriented facets of joint attention in an as-yet undivided state. That joint attention to an external object follows on from what I have just called, somewhat loosely, joint attention to my ego or self, does not seem far-fetched to me. It follows on from it once the object of joint attention is separated from the ego or self. Separating this object from the ego or self is not a big step. In the understanding of shame developed here, the ego or self is already part of the world. It is an intentional object that is given by virtue of experiences that the corresponding subject cannot live through.

These reflections carry over to empathy. Empathy explains joint attention by telling us how we experience a shared object in terms of concurrent experiences that we cannot live through. It seems obvious to me that we arrive at the same considerations that we have just mounted with respect to shame. Empathy explains the triadic relation that constitutes joint attention, the relation between object, self, and other, by way of a dyadic relation between self and other. It explains how the two of us relate to a common object by coordinating experiences that I live through with experiences that I cannot live through. The model for this coordination is the presentification of others. The dyadic relation between self and other says something about the triadic relation between object, self, and other only because the dyadic relation implies the third item, the object of joint attention. This third item is integrated in the presentification of others as my ego or self. But this is just where shame and empathy converge. Whichever explanatory utility with respect to joint attention we attribute to empathy is an explanatory utility that we can also attribute to shame.

## 8 CONCLUSION

I have argued that Sartre, Stein, and Husserl share the claim that the presence of others is self-evident only if another subject is being presentified. The reason for this is, in the last instance, that straightforward, intentional experiences do not allow us to experience something as "other" as opposed to "self." Something is other in this sense if it is a discrete locus of intentional experience from which all other loci of intentionality are excluded. Unless I experience that I am not part of some co-present experiences, that is, unless I experience experiences that I cannot live through, the presence of such a mutually exclusive locus of experience is not self-evident. As its presence is self-evident, however, experiences of distinct others must involve living through experiences of experiences that I cannot live through.

Like empathy, shame is an experience of experiences that are present but not lived through. Both empathy and shame consist of an outbound, intentional experience, issuing from myself, which meets an inbound experience, issuing from the other. Their meeting point is a joint intentional object, my self or ego. Whether we call this intentional structure shame or empathy seems to be a matter of emphasis. If we call this experience empathy, we put the accent at the far end of the structure, where the other is located. If we call this experience shame, we put the accent on the middle of the structure, where the self is located. Experiences of others who are distinct from me make sense only by virtue of the whole structure, regardless of the chosen emphasis. So we can conclude that shame and empathy are structurally isomorphic and therefore equiprimordial as intentional experiences of others.

## ACKNOWLEDGEMENTS

I would like to thank Sidra Shahid for her countless helpful suggestions on this chapter.

## NOTES

1 My formulation follows Wittgenstein's famous remark on this problem: "If one has to imagine someone else's pain on the model of one's own, this is none too easy a thing to do: for I have to imagine pain which I do not feel on the model of the pain which I do feel" (Wittgenstein 1958, § 302).
2 I use "fellow feeling" as an umbrella term for all kinds of other-directed intentional experiences, in particular emotional contagion, sympathy, empathy, and, arguably, shame. See section 2 for some relevant distinctions and note 3 for an alternative terminology.
3 Compare the Scheler-inspired distinctions in Zahavi (2008, 516–17). I agree with Zahavi that empathy differs significantly from sympathy and emotional contagion. This is because the latter are feelings-with, while empathy captures how we feel ourselves "into" others. However, my account differs from Zahavi

in that he uses "fellow feeling" in a much narrower sense than I do. He uses the term only for feelings-with, not for empathy.
4 For an overview with references to empirical research, see Tangney (1996, 742f).
5 Compare Deonna, Rodogno, and Teroni (2011, 50): "Since shame is essentially a form of distress regarding how we personally fare, episodic shame makes us oblivious to what others might concomitantly feel."
6 The page number with the prefix "e" refers to the English translation (Sartre 2003), and the page number with the prefix "f" refers to the original French text (Sartre 1976).
7 Whether shame has any bite without a dedicated second-personal component to it is controversial. Compare Crowell (this volume). As my chapter is not concerned with normative issues around shame, I remain neutral on this question.
8 See Rinofner-Kreidl (2009, 162–4). Rinofner-Kreidl describes experiences of shame as experiences that are caught up in a peculiar, enlarged presence.
9 Compare Zahavi (2012, 320): "[I]n the company of others the experience of shame can occur pre-reflectively, since the alien perspective is co-present."
10 See point 4 on the list of presuppositions of moral shame in Rinofner-Kreidl (2013, 168). She points out that I cannot be morally ashamed unless the experience that others experience me is part of my intentional experience.
11 Here is an attempt, with obvious limits, at illustrating the various combinations of intentional experiences discussed so far. Arrows stand for intentional acts.
    first-order experience         I → object
    higher-order reflection        I → (self → object)
    shame and empathy              [I → {self}] → subject}
In the case of higher-order reflection, the round brackets mark the objectified experience of mine that is presented in reflection. In the case of shame and empathy, the square brackets mark the component experience of the whole experience that I live through, while the curly brackets mark the component experience of the whole experience that I cannot live through.
12 Mark Sacks points out that anonymity is an essential part of Sartre's phenomenology of shame: "[H]e is talking about the presence or absence of human beings, it is the fundamental presence of *all men* that is unshaken by the fact that I might be wrong about the concrete presence of one man or another" (Sacks 2005, 293, original emphasis).
13 Compare Reddy (2008, 100). She argues for a connection, in child development, between developmentally earlier experiences of the attention of others to oneself and joint attention to things in the world.

## REFERENCES

Crowell, Steven (in this volume). "Second-person Phenomenology."
Deonna, Julien, Rodogno, Raffaele, & Teroni, Fabrice (2011). *In Defence of Shame: The Faces of an Emotion*. Oxford: Oxford University Press.
Gallagher, Shaun (2008). "Intersubjectivity in Perception." *Continental Philosophy Review* 41, 163–178.
Husserl, Edmund (1977) [=Hua 1]. *Cartesian Meditations: An Introduction to Phenomenology*. Transl. by D. Cairns. The Hague: Martinus Nijhoff.
―――― (1998) [=Hua 3]. *Ideas Pertaining to a Pure Phenomenology and to a Phenomenological Philosophy: First Book: General Introduction to a Pure Phenomenology*. Transl. by F. Kersten. Dordrecht: Kluwer.
―――― (1991) [=Hua 10]. On the Phenomenology of the Consciousness of Internal Time (1983–1917). Transl. by J. Brough. Dordrecht: Kluwer.

―――― (1972) [=Hua 15]. *Zur Phänomenologie der Intersubjektivität: Texte aus dem Nachlass: Dritter Teil: 1929–1935.* Ed. by I. Kern. The Hague: Martinus Nijhoff.
Merleau-Ponty, Maurice (2010). *Phenomenology of Perception.* Transl. by D. Landes. London: Routledge.
Pacherie, Elisabeth (2012). "The Phenomenology of Joint Action: Self-Agency vs. Joint-Agency." In: A. Seeman (Ed.). *Joint Attention: New Developments.* Cambridge, MA/London: MIT Press, 343–389.
Reddy, Vasudevi (2008). *How Infants Know Minds.* Cambridge, MA: Harvard University Press.
Rinofner-Kreidl, Sonja (2009). "Scham und Schuld: Zur Phänomenologie selbstbezüglicher Gefühle." *Phänomenologische Forschungen*, 165–201.
―――― (2013). "Scham und Autonomie." *Phänomenologische Forschungen*, 164–191.
Sacks, Mark (2005). "Sartre, Strawson, and Others." *Inquiry* 48, 275–299.
Sartre, Jean-Paul (1976). *L'être et le néant: essay d'ontologie phénoménologique.* Paris: Gallimard.
―――― (2003) [=BN]. *Being and Nothingness: An Essay on Phenomenological Ontology.* Transl. by H. E. Barnes. London: Routledge.
Scheler, Max (1957). "Über Scham und Schamgefühl." In: *Schriften aus dem Nachlass: Vol. 1: Zur Ethik und Erkenntnistheorie* [=GW 10]. Ed. by M. Frings. Bonn: Bouvier, 65–154.
Stein, Edith (1964). *On the Problem of Empathy.* Transl. by W. Stein. The Hague: Martinus Nijhoff.
Tangney, June Price (1996). "Conceptual and Methodological Issues in the Assessment of Shame and Guilt." *Behaviour Research and Therapy* 34, 741–754.
Taylor, Gabriele (1985). *Pride, Shame and Guilt: Emotions of Self-Assessment.* Oxford: Oxford University Press.
Williams, Bernard (1993). *Shame and Necessity.* Los Angeles: University of California Press.
Wittgenstein, Ludwig (1958). *Philosophical Investigations.* Ed. and Transl. by G. E. M. Anscombe. Oxford: Blackwell.
Zahavi, Dan (2008). "Simulation, Projection and Empathy." *Consciousness and Cognition* 17, 514–522.
―――― (2012). "Self, Consciousness, and Shame." In: D. Zahavi (Ed.). *The Oxford Handbook of Contemporary Phenomenology.* Oxford: Oxford University Press, 304–323.

# 12 Relating to the Dead
## Social Cognition and the Phenomenology of Grief

*Matthew Ratcliffe*

## 1 GRIEF AND SOCIAL COGNITION

Philosophical work on interpersonal and social cognition tends to address only our relations with the living. In this chapter, I turn to our relations with the dead and, more specifically, to experiences of grief. Many philosophers assume that social cognition centrally involves attributing beliefs and desires to other people, in order to predict and explain their behavior. The focus of discussion is on whether we do this by 'simulating' another person's situation and/or mental processes, using a 'theory of mind,' or relying on some combination of the two (e.g., Davies & Stone 1995a; 1995b). Given this, our relations with the dead do not seem to pose any special problems. When thinking about what a person, S, would have said or done were S still alive, we use the same simulation mechanism or theory that we would have used were S alive but absent from a situation. And, if one further maintains that S continues to have beliefs and desires after death, one is relying on these same abilities, but in a way that is decoupled from behavioral evidence. So, how we understand and relate to the dead might be regarded as—at most—a peripheral issue for social cognition research.

However, others have challenged the emphasis on belief-desire psychology by drawing on themes in phenomenology, developmental psychology, and elsewhere (e.g., Gallagher 2005; De Jaegher & DiPaolo 2007; Ratcliffe 2007; Hutto 2008; Colombetti & Torrance 2009). It has been argued that not all social interaction depends upon belief-desire psychology and that, even when belief-desire psychology is at work, it is just one aspect of social cognition, which should not be ascribed undue importance. Furthermore, we make sense of others' activities against the backdrop of a shared social world, where artifacts have established functions, people have prescribed roles, and behavior is regulated by shared norms. Immersion in this world makes a substantial contribution to our ability to interpret, anticipate, and explain others' behavior, a contribution that is neither reducible to nor somehow secondary to belief-desire psychology. Another criticism is that we understand others *through* our relations and interactions with them. Much of the literature on belief-desire psychology assumes that, when we address and interact with someone as a 'you,' we rely on the same cognitive mechanisms that facilitate a detached, third-person understanding of a 'she,' 'he,' or 'it.' But it is arguable that 'second-person experience'—of a kind that involves sustained interactions and feelings of connection—differs in important respects from the disengaged, third-person attribution of mental states. For instance, when relating to someone as a 'you,' it matters *who* she is, not just what kind of thing she is and what mental states she has. Hence, second-person experience is essentially a way of relating to someone as *this particular person*, something that is not captured by the attribution of mental states to one or another token of the type 'possessor of mental states' (Ratcliffe 2015, chap. 8).

It is debatable whether and to what extent such approaches pose a challenge to orthodox accounts of 'folk' or 'common-sense' psychology. To some extent, the difference may be one of emphasis, and my aim here is not to arbitrate.[1] Rather, I seek to show how three of the principal themes emphasized by critics of belief-desire psychology are also central to an understanding of the phenomenology of grief: the shared social world, interpersonal relations and interactions, and second-person experience. Furthermore, it is not just a matter of applying what we might say about our relations with the living to our relations with the dead. Grief can involve 'finding oneself in the social world' in a way that is profoundly different, along with distinctive ways of experiencing and relating to other people, both the living and the dead. So, when the emphasis is moved away from belief-desire psychology and towards a wider-ranging account of social cognition, the importance of grief as a topic for enquiry becomes clearer. In what follows, I thus adopt a broad conception of social cognition, which encompasses all of the ways in which we experience, think about, and interact with other people (alive or dead) and the social environment.

It might be objected that grief is not a pervasive aspect of social experience, but an occasional disruption that should not be overemphasized: one suffers a loss, experiences grief for a finite period, and (usually) moves on. However, such a view is simplistic and inaccurate. First of all, grief is not an emotional 'state' that is endured for however long, but a process that varies in its character and duration (Klass et al. 1996; Parkes 1996; Goldie 2011).[2] Second, the view that grief involves ultimately resigning one's attachment to the deceased is, despite its popularity in some cultures, misleading. A growing literature on 'continuing bonds' suggests that grief processes have no clear endpoint, and that relationships with the deceased are renegotiated and sustained rather than abandoned (e.g., Klass et al. 1996). These 'continuing bonds' are said to be healthy and ubiquitous, rather than occasional and pathological (e.g., Silverman/Klass 1996, 3). We should be wary of making generalizations about what grief processes involve, as there is considerable variation. Differences are attributable to a range of factors, including the circumstances of the death, the nature of the bereavement (e.g., a spouse, sibling, or child), one's inherited and acquired dispositions and vulnerabilities, the effect upon one's financial situation, and the availability of social support. There are also important cultural differences.[3] Even so, it is plausible to maintain that grief, in general, is not an emotional *state* of varying intensity and duration, but a multifaceted process, one that does not conclude with simply 'letting go.' For those who have experienced multiple bereavements, relations with the dead can be a salient aspect of daily life, perhaps more salient for some than relations with the living.

In what follows, I describe some features that are common to many experiences of intense grief. In so doing, I draw upon several published autobiographical accounts. That approach is not without its problems. The accounts I consider are all written by professional authors, who may be more inclined than others to express and interpret their experiences through narrative, and to go about this in particular ways: "Writing is what I have, and it's how I make sense of experience" (Humphreys 2013, 24). So they may not be representative of grief experiences more generally. To complicate matters, it may not be possible to separate an experience of grief from the narratives that convey it, as it is arguable that grieving processes are partly *constituted* by changing narratives that shape and re-shape experience (Goldie 2011). I concede that grief is expressed—and most likely experienced—in many different ways. Furthermore, it is often remarked that grief is hard to express in words and hard for others to comprehend. Hence, the relevant phenomenology cannot simply be 'read off' first-person descriptions; we have to interpret them. Consequently, what I say here is both tentative and partial, a preliminary attempt to open up an area of philosophical enquiry. Even so, the level of description I adopt here is fairly abstract and therefore accommodates considerable variety.

I first consider why the world as a whole often seems profoundly different following bereavement. I interpret this in terms of the effect upon habitual routines, projects, pastimes, and commitments, the intelligibility of which depended upon the deceased. The bereaved person often alternates between retention and loss of habitual ways of experiencing the shared world. There are also more localized experiences of presence (including experiences of relating to and interacting with the deceased) and of absence.[4] I conclude by turning to another aspect of grief, which we might call a 'second-person experience of death.' If my characterization of this is right, it involves a distinctive and seldom recognized kind of second-person relation.

## 2 PRESENCE AND ABSENCE

Simple descriptions and definitions of grief are easy to come by. For example, Wilkinson (2000, 290) states that "someone is grieving only if the emotional response to a real or perceived loss (usually, though not necessarily, of another person) involves some degree of distress or suffering." This might suggest that grief *follows* recognition of loss, whereas one could instead maintain (as I will) that grief is partly *constitutive* of that recognition. Whichever the case, grief looks like an intentional state directed at something specific—one grieves over 'the death of S' in a way that is analogous to regretting that $p$ or feeling happy about $q$. However, it is important to acknowledge that grief also involves a non-localized way of experiencing and relating to the social world, something that is inextricable from the more localized appreciation that a particular individual has died. There is an all-enveloping shift in how the world is experienced and how one relates to it. Whybrow offers this account:

> When it strikes, the raw intensity of the feeling comes as a surprise. Life is rolled on its head, and we find ourselves off balance. Routine patterns and familiar assumptions are called into question. Social attachments of love and friendship that gave life meaning and purpose are fundamentally changed. Inevitably we are confronted with the challenge of finding for ourselves a new fit with the world, for that which was once a stable and accustomed part of one's life routine has been irretrievably lost. The external world has changed and with it the inner world of personal meaning.
>
> (Whybrow 1997, 2)

Why would the 'external world' appear changed? This aspect of grief can be understood in terms of an effect upon projects, pastimes, commitments, habitual activities, and expectations that explicitly or implicitly implicate the deceased in some way. In any situation, what strikes us as practically meaningful and salient, 'to be done,' 'to be avoided,' 'worth doing,' 'exciting,' or 'disappointing,' reflects projects and wider concerns that are—to varying degrees—idiosyncratic.[5] How something *matters* to us surely shapes how we experience it (regardless of whether or not 'ways of mattering' are admitted as contents of more specifically *perceptual* experience). A hammer *looks* different, depending on whether one has been searching for it in the context of a DIY project or one is being chased by a hammer-wielding attacker. And, if nothing mattered in quite the same way, the world as a whole would look different.

How things matter to us is dependent upon our relations with other people, often specific individuals. For instance, when one acts purposively in relation to a goal-directed project, a particular person, such as a spouse, might be implicated in a range of ways: "I do it because you asked me to"; "I do it for you"; "I am doing it because you care"; "We do it together to achieve something that matters to us both"; "I am helping you to do something"; "You are there to fall back on if I fail." Even when a project does not concern the other person in such ways, there may remain a sense that "I will come home to you when it is finished" and "I will be able to tell you about it." Indeed, the telling can be anticipated as an end in itself, and thus serve to motivate one's activities: "As for doing what I liked: for me, this usually meant doing things with her. Insofar as I liked doing things by myself, it was partly for the pleasure of telling her about them afterwards" (Barnes 2013, 80f).

Bereavement thus undermines, to varying degrees, a previously taken-for-granted sense of what matters and how it matters. Joyce Carol Oates describes this in terms of coming to inhabit a world of "things," where "these *things* retain but the faintest glimmer of their original identity and meaning as in a dead and desiccated husk of something once organic there might be discerned a glimmer or its original identity and meaning" (2011, 63). The world ceases to offer what it once did and, as what things offer is integral to how they look, the world as a whole is somehow different, lacking. C. S. Lewis (1961, 12) describes this sense of absence as follows: "It is not local at all. [. . .] The act of living is different through and through. Her absence is like the sky, spread over everything." As Julian Barnes (2013, 81) writes, "I miss her in every action, and in every inaction."[6]

Hence, the deceased is not just a person *within* the experienced world, but also an intelligibility condition *for* a world that one once took as given. It follows that a singular experience of 'loss' is both specifically focused and—at the same time—all-enveloping. The world as a whole lacks an elaborate system of practical meanings that were previously experienced as integral to it. The bereaved person therefore feels disconnected from it, somehow dislodged: "There is a sort of invisible blanket between the world and me" (Lewis 1961, 5). This is why many people say that part of them has died too. The sense of being rooted in a meaningful world depends not just upon an isolated self and its projects, but also upon relations with particular others:

> Death feels a bit like a vanished city, like wandering through a landscape I used to recognize but that has now been radically altered. It was a mistake to think that life was solid ground under my feet, and that every day I would be able to step back down onto the same earth. To have you gone—you, who went clear to the bottom of my world—has thrown everything off balance, has left me wandering like a ghost in my own life.
>
> (Humphreys 2013, 58)

However, it is not simply that one comes to believe that S is dead, at which point all activities instantaneously lose their meaning. Certain activities may be relatively well insulated from the bereavement. Oates (2011, 172) describes how she was able to retreat into her professional duties and temporarily re-immerse herself in the world through her teaching, an aspect of her life that had always been set apart from her relationship with her husband. And, where activities are not insulated, there can be an ongoing alternation between retention and loss of practical meaning. It is commonplace to 'know that *p*' in a propositional way while continually 'forgetting that *p*' when habitually engaging with the world. For example, one might reorganize one's office, know where everything is, and yet continue to look for things in their former locations. Something like this occurs in grief, but the experience is much wider ranging. The interplay between habitual expectations and the realization that the world no longer offers any possibility of their being fulfilled amounts to an experience of negation, of continually confronting situations from which something is 'missing.'

One form that retention of practical meaning can take is what Joan Didion calls 'magical thinking.' Although one might explicitly assent to the belief that S has died, one continues to think and act in ways that conflict with it. One conceives of the loss as temporary and reversible, preserving—on some occasions and to some extent—the world from a collapse of practical meaning: "Bringing him back' had been through those months my hidden focus, a magic trick"; "I realized that since the last morning of 2003, the morning after he died, I had been trying to reverse time, to run the film backward" (Didion 2005, 44, 183f.). So it is an over-simplification to maintain that one either 'believes that S has died' or 'believes that S has not died.' To fully comprehend that someone has died is not merely a matter of explicitly acknowledging the irreversible absence of a particular entity from one's world, given that a sense of the person's being there is partly constituted by a wider context of experience, thought, and activity. Where part of a system of practical meanings endures consistently or sporadically, despite its dependence upon the deceased, one might be said to not quite 'believe' it. It doesn't seem 'real'; the world endures, and yet it cannot endure. It would be equally wrong, however, to say that one does not believe it. As Parkes (1996, 65ff.) notes, remarks such as "I can't believe it's true" are commonplace amongst the bereaved, but disbelief is "seldom complete." Hence, in using the term 'belief' to refer to the different degrees and kinds of comprehension at play here, we cannot think of it as a simple propositional attitude of the form 'R believes that *p*', where *p* is 'S has died'.

Goldie (2011, 131) suggests that grief has a narrative structure that resembles free indirect speech, a literary device exploiting the difference between internal and external perspectives on a situation: "In grief, you might well remember the last time you saw the person you loved, not knowing, as you do now, that it was to be the last time. And this knowledge will infect the way you remember it." Hence, the external perspective serves to re-shape the internal perspective. In the light of this view, slipping in and out of a world that presupposes the deceased can be construed in terms of a gradual process of revision and reconciliation of perspectives. This need not involve coming to fully inhabit a world that is no longer shaped in any way by S. Things may continue to be experienced as mattering in the ways they do in the light of how one once related to S and, indeed, how one continues to think about and relate to S (Klass et al. 1996).

The changed world of grief is also a different way of relating to the living, which can involve varying degrees of estrangement from particular individuals and from people in general. A sense of estrangement might be mitigated or exacerbated by how they respond. For example, Aleksandar Hemon (2013, 202) states that "one of the most common platitudes we heard was that 'words failed,'" but adds that "[i]t was not true that there was no way of describing our experience." What failed, he says, were platitudes and clichés that had little bearing on the situation. Sometimes, grief involves an all-encompassing loss of 'trust' in the personal and impersonal world. A sense of safety and continuity that once shaped all of one's experiences and activities is gone; one inhabits a world where the incomprehensible is possible, contingency reigns, and other people offer no possibility of support or consolation (Stolorow 2011). Whether and how this develops depends not just on the nature of the bereavement and one's reaction to it, but on subsequent relations with others. More generally, whether others share in one's grief, understand it, fail to understand it, listen, pretend to listen, offer what is perceived as genuine support, retain an emotional distance, or withdraw altogether further contributes to how the social world appears. The world not only seems different because S has gone, but because others seem different too, and they do indeed act differently.

Along with non-localized changes in one's world, there are more localized and concrete experiences of presence and absence. A system of habitual, practical expectations that implicate S, one that is to some extent retained, includes the expectation of encountering S in specific situations or locations, such as when one enters a certain room or engages in an activity that used to involve S. When these expectations are negated by the absence of S, the experience is comparable in certain respects to Sartre's (1943/1989) well-known description of waiting to meet Pierre in a café when Pierre fails to arrive. Pierre's absence is experienced in a localized way, when someone else enters and is encountered as 'not Pierre.' It is experienced in a more diffuse way too—how the café appears is shaped by the expectation of meeting Pierre; it is a background to an absent foreground. And, when that background endures, Pierre's absence is present, as when one sees a picture frame without a picture. A grieving process likewise includes frequent realizations that 'S is not here' and, occasionally, 'this is not S.' Some of these may be fleeting, and others more enduring, but they are not restricted to any one place or time. And, as one cannot simply go and sit somewhere else, incessant experiences of absence become an inescapable rather than contingent aspect of one's world.

The sense of absence is often associated with searching behaviors (Parkes 1996, chap. 4). One needs and seeks the deceased, in a way that is again to be construed in terms of habitual, practical anticipation more so than propositional attitudes of the form 'I desire to see S' and 'I believe there to be some probability that S will appear': "I could not count the times during the average day when something would come up that I needed to tell him. This impulse did not end with his death. What ended was the possibility of response" (Didion 2005, 194). However, not all localized experienced of the deceased—whether or not they are preceded by searching—involve absence. Many bereaved people also report experiences of continuing presence. 'Sensed presence' experiences are most frequent; one feels that S is actually here, now, in a way that is not attributable to perception in a particular sensory modality. But more specific auditory, visual, tactual, and olfactory experiences are not uncommon. For example, Rees (1971) conducted a study involving 227 widows and 66 widowers in Wales, where around half admitted having 'hallucinations' or 'illusions' of the deceased spouse. Of the participants, 39 percent reported a sense of presence, 14 percent visual experiences, 13.3 percent voices, and 2.7 percent tactual experiences. In some cases, these had occurred for many years, and the majority of participants (but not all) found them comforting and helpful. These findings are consistent with subsequent studies (e.g., Bennett & Bennett 2000). That such experiences persist indefinitely are often welcomed, and can constitute a feeling of continuing to relate to the deceased that lends further support to the view that grief need not and often does not culminate in loss of attachment.[7]

We should be wary of using the term 'hallucination' here. The content of these experiences is not wholly clear and could vary considerably. Some may not conform to established definitions of 'hallucination,' according to which a hallucination resembles a veridical perception but arises in the absence of an appropriate stimulus.[8] The term 'hallucination' also conflicts with many people's self-interpretations. It can be added that self-interpretation has a potential role to play a role in shaping, re-shaping, and even eliciting the relevant experiences. Furthermore, there is a fine line to be drawn between perceptual or quasi-perceptual experiences of presence and other ways in which one might experience or think of S as enduring or even as 'here, now.' S might be construed as continuing to reside in the past, or in some other realm. Also, as well as feeling that 'part of me has gone,' many have a sense that S 'endures as part of me' in the guise of commitments that are taken on, values that are adopted, ways of acting, and what one finds salient and significant.

Hence, grief involves a dynamic and evolving interplay between experiences of localized and non-localized presence and absence, rather than the simple recognition that S was present but became absent at time $t$: "The paradox of grief: if I have survived what is now four years of her absence, it is because I have had four years of her presence" (Barnes 2013, 100, 103). The sense of 'loss' is to be understood in terms of this interplay; it is integral to the grieving process rather than a form of recognition that precedes and elicits grief.

## 3 SECOND-PERSON EXPERIENCE OF DEATH

One might think that the possibility of maintaining a second-person relationship with S is only preserved when one continues to experience or think of him as present in some way, and that full acknowledgement of S's absence implies the impossibility of relating to him. But, interestingly, some narratives of grief suggest otherwise. In her book, *Time Lived, Without Its Flow*, Denise Riley describes a profound transformation of her world that persisted for three years after the death of her adult son. She focuses on an experience of time as bereft of 'flow.' It is not that 'time for everyone' stopped flowing. What Riley describes is a sense of having been removed from the time of others, from a place where time still flows: it is a "sensation of having been lifted clean out of habitual time"; the "sensation of living outside time" (2012, 10, 45). This can be interpreted (in part, at least) in terms of something I described earlier: nothing matters anymore, and so one no longer experiences significant transitions from one moment to the next. Things still change, but nothing meaningful happens. Barnes (2013, 84) offers the complementary remark, writing, "Grief reconfigures time, its length, its texture, its function: one day means no more than the next, so why have they been picked out and given separate names?"

The experience could be construed as one of recognizing S to be gone, and—in the process—recognizing the loss of all those practical meanings that implicated S. But, although this has a role to play, it is not what Riley seeks to convey. She does not say that things ceased to matter due to loss of a second-person bond with the deceased. Rather, she attributes her disconnection from the social world and from shared time to an enduring second-person relation with her son, of a kind that acknowledges his no longer being part of the world. This relation also amounts to a comprehensive disengagement from the world of the living, a kind of participation in death: "I tried always to be there for him, solidly. And I shall continue to be. (The logic of this conviction: in order to be there, I too have died)" (Riley 2012, 21).

Sustained concern for someone who is still alive can equally constitute a sense of dislodgement from the social world. For example, Hemon describes the experience of driving to the hospital to visit his terminally ill baby daughter:

> It took me about fifteen minutes to get to the hospital, through traffic that existed in an entirely different space-time, where people did not rush crossing the streets and no infant life was in danger, where everything turned away quite leisurely from the disaster [. . .] I had an intensely physical sensation of being inside an aquarium: I could see outside, the people outside could see me inside (if they somehow chose to pay attention), but we lived and breathed in entirely different environments. Isabel's illness and our experience had little connection to, and even less impact on, the world outside. (2013, 190, 201ff.)

However, what Riley describes also includes something else: a sense of relating to someone *as dead*. The second-person connection endures after the death, in a way that does not depend upon a sense of continuing presence. The combination of recognizing her son's irrevocable absence from the social world, combined with retention of a second-person connection, amounts to a sense of her own separation from that world: "My new ability to live in the present is a joining-in of that timelessness of being dead. [. . .] You already share the 'timeless time' of the dead child. As if you'd died too, or had lost the greater part of your own life" (Riley 2012, 23, 38).

We might construe this as a 'second-person experience of death.' I am thinking here of an approach to empathy adopted by Edith Stein (1917/1989) and others, according to which we are able *experience* the mental lives of others. There is, Stein admits, a substantial difference between 'second-person' and 'first-person' experience. But this is not to imply that the former is a poor approximation of the latter. Instead, they are two qualitatively different ways of accessing experience.[9] We experience the mental lives of others in their observed behavior and, when we do so, we also have a more general sense of encountering a distinct locus of experience (Ratcliffe 2015, chap. 8). I suggest—somewhat tentatively—that we can extend such an approach to at least some grief experiences. One not only recognizes the absence of a person from one's world; one also experiences, in a second-person way, the loss of intelligibility of *that person's* world. Indeed, unless we acknowledge something like this, we risk construing grief as more self-absorbed than it often is, as a matter of what is lost from *my* world. What is needed is an account of its other-directedness, of its being concerned with what has happened *to her*, as well as what has happened *to me* and to a relationship that was valuable *to me*. The recognition that grief involves a continuing second-person relationship with the deceased, one that incorporates recognition of her death, gives us that.

Other accounts also convey this aspect of experience, although not quite so explicitly. For example, Helen Humphreys's *True Story: On the Life and Death of My Brother* addresses him in the second-person throughout, sometimes referring to the time 'after you died.' She relates to him, reaches out to him, while at the same time acknowledging his death. The distinction between retaining a second-person relation and recognizing its impossibility is not always clear. Consider the following passage:

> I know that I can no longer reach her.
> I know that, should I try to reach her—should I take her hand as if she were again sitting next to me in the upstairs cabin on the evening Pan Am from Honolulu to LAX, should I lull her to sleep against my shoulder, should I sing her the song about Daddy gone to get the rabbit skin to wrap his baby bunny in—she will fade from my touch.
> (Didion 2011, 187f.)

Even so, I think this is plausibly interpreted in terms of a kind of second-person experience that recognizes absence (and with it the impossibility of reciprocity), rather than in terms of an absence of second-person experience. And let us reflect further on this 'fading from one's touch.' Interestingly, Riley's account draws on the more specific theme of touch and reversibility in Merleau-Ponty's writings (e.g., Merleau-Ponty 1945/1962, 1968). In brief, when one of your hands touches the other, the touching hand is the subject of perception, the perceiver, and the touched hand an object of perception. However, the relationship is reversible, a point that also applies to the interpersonal case. As one takes the hand of another person, one's own hand is the perceiver, and hers the perceived. Yet, as in the intrapersonal case, the relationship switches, and one acquires a sense of the other hand—and the other person—as a distinct locus of experience.[10] Riley suggests that something like this can arise when relating to the dead:

> Whatever's the name for this transfer of affect? It's rather like that blurring of physical edges that happens between lovers: you become the other one, you can feel as if through their skin. [. . .] You're fused with the dead, as if to animate them. They draw you across to their side, while you incorporate them on your side. (Riley 2012, 39f.)

Dubose (1997) similarly applies Merleau-Ponty's discussion of reversibility to the phenomenology of grief: "The chiasmic structure of self and other is drowned in the reversibility of *dis*-appearance. In numbness and shock, one's lived body has died *with* the lost loved one. *A reversibility occurs between the dis-appearance of the other and the dis-appearance of myself*" (373). So, what we have here is a more specific—although admittedly contentious—account of what a second-person experience of death involves. And, even if the account is rejected, narratives of grief at least suggest that an enduring second-person connection is not exclusively reliant upon experiencing or thinking of the other person as still present or as residing elsewhere.[11] Riley states that the absence of 'flow' she describes is specific to parental grief, and far from unusual among bereaved parents. However, less pronounced or qualitatively different second-person experiences of absence may well characterize grief more generally. Hence, remarks such as 'I died with her' and 'part of me has died' can be used to refer to importantly different aspects of grief: a second-person experience of death that dislodges one from the world, and a diminishment of one's world due to someone's absence from it.

## 4 CONCLUSION

I have briefly described how the phenomenology of grief involves alternation between localized and non-localized experiences of presence and absence. Grief is a variable and changeable way of relating to the dead, the living, and the social world.[12] I have also proposed, more tentatively, that there is such a thing as a second-person experience of death. Relations with the dead therefore constitute an important aspect of interpersonal and social experience, and any philosophical account of social cognition that seeks to be comprehensive should accommodate them. This is not so evident when we concern ourselves exclusively with belief-desire psychology. But it becomes apparent once a more inclusive approach to social cognition is adopted, one that is attentive to the roles of the shared social world, interpersonal relations and interactions, and the nature of second-person experience.

## ACKNOWLEDGEMENTS

Thanks to Thomas Szanto, Dermot Moran, Pat Waugh, and an audience at University College Dublin for their helpful comments. This research was supported by a Wellcome Trust Strategic Award (WT098455MA).

## NOTES

1. However, see Ratcliffe (2007) for a detailed critique of the view that belief-desire psychology is central to interpersonal understanding.
2. One might therefore wonder how we are to distinguish 'grief' from 'mourning.' The distinction is no doubt untidy. However, in the case of mourning, there is greater emphasis on rituals and on other culturally established public displays.
3. See, for example, Parkes et al. (1997) for discussions of cultural differences in expressions and experiences of grief.
4. I do not address the role of 'feeling' in grief here, but see Ratcliffe (2015) for a more generally applicable account of how world experience and a sense of relating to other people are inextricable from bodily feeling.
5. This is not to imply the significance things have for us is *wholly* symptomatic of personal-level concerns. For instance, many of the social norms and roles that regulate activity apply to people in general: 'one' walks on the pavement rather than the road, and 'one' pays the cashier in a shop, rather than the security guard, regardless of who 'one' is. These shared norms and roles also contribute to the sense of how a situation is significant.
6. Carse (1981, 5) describes acute grief as a "cosmic crisis," remarking on how the meaningfulness of the world depends upon relations with specific others; when someone dies, "we live in a universe that makes no sense."
7. It has also been suggested that there is cultural variation, with rates of experienced presence amongst bereaved spouses being as high as 90 percent in some cultures (Keen/Murray/Payne 2013).
8. As Frith (1992, 68) puts it, "hallucinations are usually defined as perceptions that occur in the absence of any appropriate stimulus."
9. See also Zahavi (2007) for a recent defense of this kind of approach. Zahavi draws on the work of Husserl, Scheler, and Wittgenstein, amongst others.
10. See, for example, Stawarska (2006) for a discussion of Merleau-Ponty on reversibility and intersubjectivity.
11. An interesting issue for further enquiry is that of whether and to what extent explicit beliefs about life after death serve to insulate a person from or otherwise shape such experiences.

12 One might wonder whether and to what extent my various remarks are specific to grief. For example, there are ongoing issues regarding whether and how grief is to be distinguished from depression (e.g., Lamb/Pies/Zisook 2010; Wakefield/First 2012). Although experiences of depression and grief are both heterogeneous and no doubt overlap in many cases, a key difference is that all forms of depression involve a sense of being cut off from second-person connection, whereas grief involves its retention (Pies 2008, 2013; Lamb & Pies & Zisook 2010). Even where grief and depression might seem very similar, it is important to distinguish between an estrangement from the world attributable to a lack of second-person connection and one that stems from maintaining a kind of second-person connection. Grief involves the retention—and, in 'uncomplicated grief' at least, the renegotiation—of interpersonal relationships. See Ratcliffe (2015) for further discussion.

## REFERENCES

Barnes, Julian (2013). *Levels of Life*. London: Jonathan Cape.
Bennett, Gillian, & Bennett, Kate Mary (2000). "The Presence of the Dead: An Empirical Study." *Mortality* 5, 139–157.
Carse, James (1981). "Grief as a Cosmic Crisis." In: O. S. Margolis, H. C. Raether, A. H. Kutscher, J. B. Powers, I. B. Seeland, R. DeBillis, & D. J. Cherico (Eds.). *Acute Grief: Counseling the Bereaved*. New York: Columbia University Press.
Colombetti, Giovanna, & Torrance, Steve (2009). "Emotion and Ethics: An Inter(en)active Approach." *Phenomenology and the Cognitive Sciences* 8, 505–526.
Davies, Martin, & Stone, Tony (Eds.) (1995a). *Folk Psychology: The Theory of Mind Debate*. Oxford: Blackwell.
——— (1995b). *Mental Simulation: Evaluations and Applications*. Oxford: Blackwell.
De Jaegher, Hanne, & Di Paolo, Ezequiel (2007). "Participatory Sense-Making: An Enactive Approach to Social Cognition." *Phenomenology and the Cognitive Sciences* 6, 485–507.
Didion, Joan (2005). *The Year of Magical Thinking*. London: Harper Perennial.
——— (2011). *Blue Nights*. London: Fourth Estate.
Dubose, J. Todd (1997). "The Phenomenology of Bereavement, Grief, and Mourning." *Journal of Religion and Health* 36, 367–374.
Frith, Chris (1992). *The Cognitive Neuropsychology of Schizophrenia*. Hove: Psychology Press.
Gallagher, Shaun (2005). *How the Body Shapes the Mind*. Oxford: Oxford University Press.
Goldie, Peter (2011). "Grief: A Narrative Account." *Ratio* XXIV: 119–137.
Hemon, Aleksandar (2013). *The Book of My Lives*. London: Picador.
Humphreys, Helen (2013). *True Story: The Life and Death of My Brother*. London: Serpent's Tail.
Hutto, Daniel (2008). *Folk Psychological Narratives: The Sociocultural Basis of Understanding Reasons*. Cambridge, MA/London: MIT Press.
Keen, Catherine, Murray, Craig, & Payne, Sheila (2013). "Sensing the Presence of the Deceased: A Narrative Review." *Mental Health, Religion & Culture* 16, 384–402.
Klass, Dennis, Silverman, Phyllis, & Nickman, Steven (Eds.) (1996). *Continuing Bonds: New Understandings of Grief*. London/New York: Routledge.
Lamb, Kirsty, Pies, Ronald, & Zisook, Sidney (2010). "The Bereavement Exclusion for the Diagnosis of Major Depression: To Be, Or Not to Be." *Psychiatry* 7 (7), 19–25.

Lewis, C. S. (1961). *A Grief Observed*. London: Faber & Faber.
Merleau-Ponty, Maurice (1945/1962). *Phenomenology of Perception* Transl. by C. Smith. London: Routledge.
——— (1968). *The Visible and the Invisible*. Transl. by A. Lingis. Evanston: Northwestern University Press.
Oates, Joyce Carol (2011). *A Widow's Story*. London: Fourth Estate.
Parkes, Colin Murray (1996). *Bereavement: Studies of Grief in Adult Life*. London: Penguin Books.
Parkes, Colin Murray, Laungani, Pittu, & Young, Bill (Eds.) (1997). *Grief and Bereavement across Cultures*. London/New York: Routledge.
Pies, Ronald (2008). "The Anatomy of Sorrow: A Spiritual, Phenomenological, and Neurological Perspective." *Philosophy, Ethics, and Humanities in Medicine* 3 (17), 1–8.
——— (2013). "From Context to Phenomenology in Grief and Depression." *Psychiatric Annals* 43, 286–290.
Ratcliffe, Matthew (2007). *Rethinking Commonsense Psychology: A Critique of Folk Psychology, Theory of Mind and Simulation*. Basingstoke: Palgrave Macmillan.
——— (2015). *Experiences of Depression: A Study in Phenomenology*. Oxford: Oxford University Press.
Rees, W. Dewi (1971). "The Hallucinations of Widowhood." *British Medical Journal* 4, 37–41.
Riley, Denise (2012). *Time Lived, Without Its Flow*. London: Capsule Editions.
Sartre, Jean-Paul (1943/1989). *Being and Nothingness*. Transl. by H. E. Barnes. London/New York: Routledge.
Silverman, Phyllis & Klass, Dennis (1996). "Introduction: What's the Problem?" In: D. Klass, P. Silverman, & S. Nickman (Eds.). *Continuing Bonds: New Understandings of Grief*. London/New York: Routledge, 3–27.
Stawarska, Beata (2006). "Mutual Gaze and Social Cognition." *Phenomenology and the Cognitive Sciences* 5, 17–30.
Stein, Edith (1917/1989). *On the Problem of Empathy*. Transl. by W. Stein. Washington, DC: ICS Publications.
Stolorow, Robert (2011). *World, Affectivity, Trauma: Heidegger and Post-Cartesian Psychoanalysis*. New York: Routledge.
Wakefield, Jerome, & First, Michael (2012). "Validity of the Bereavement Exclusion to Major Depression: Does the Empirical Evidence Support the Proposal to Eliminate the Exclusion in DSM-5?" *World Psychiatry* 11, 3–10.
Whybrow, Peter (1997). *A Mood Apart*. London: Picador.
Wilkinson, Stephen (2000). "Is 'Normal Grief' a Mental Disorder?" *Philosophical Quarterly* 50, 289–304.
Zahavi, Dan (2007). "Expression and Empathy." In: D. Hutto, & M. Ratcliffe (Eds.). *Folk Psychology Re-assessed*. Dordrecht: Springer, 25–40.

# Part IV
# Collective Intentionality and Affectivity

# 13 Affective Intentionality
## Early Phenomenological Contributions to a New Phenomenological Sociology

Íngrid Vendrell Ferran

## 1 THE DIALOGUE BETWEEN PHENOMENOLOGY AND THE SOCIAL SCIENCES

Phenomenology has often been accused of offering a solipsistic and subject-centered view of the human being, and of ignoring the social aspects of human life. It is widely thought that the first phenomenological contributions focus mainly on the study of intentional consciousness, ignoring its intersubjective dimensions, and that it was only with Alfred Schütz, in his phenomenological sociology, that Husserl's methodology was first applied to a systematic study of the social world. As I will show in this chapter, this is a biased view: early phenomenologists were not only very interested in social phenomena, but also provided central elements for the development of a phenomenological sociology.

It was, no doubt, Schütz himself who contributed to this biased perception. In Schütz's view, Husserl "was not conversant with the concrete problems of the social sciences," and the work of his students was naïve or incoherent (Schütz 1972, 140). In his opinion, despite Husserl's interest in the problems of intersubjectivity, of empathy, and of the status of society and community as subjectivities of a higher order, he refrained from publishing his investigations in the second volume of *Ideen* because he was unsatisfied with his solution to the problem of the constitution of intersubjectivity (in fact, it was not until the *Fifth Cartesian Meditation* and the *Krisis* that he thought he had solved the problem) (1972, 118 and 140). Husserl's relevance is, according to Schütz, without question, but a really fruitful application of the phenomenological method to the social sciences has to go beyond Husserl and in the direction of a social anthropology (1972, 119 and 140). Schütz's evaluation of the contributions of Edith Stein, Gerda Walther, Max Scheler, Merleau-Ponty, and Ortega y Gasset takes a clearly negative and sometimes even outright hostile tone. This critical view seems to be motivated by a general skepticism about the 'eidetic reduction' approach to unclarified notions of the social sciences. Stein and Walther's analyses of social relations, empathy, community, and the state are, according to Schütz, ingenuous or naïve applications of phenomenology, and he accuses both of having "contributed toward discrediting phenomenology among social scientists" (1972, 140–1). His criticism of Scheler is grounded in the same "unfortunate approach" that Scheler himself employs in his *Formalismus* to analyze the different forms of sociality—especially the concept of the collective person (*Gesamtperson*). Despite recognizing Scheler's later merits in developing an anthropological philosophy, Schütz considers his work "inconsistent" (1972, 155). Ortega y Gasset and his work *El hombre y la gente* are the objects of less severe criticism, however, since Schütz believes that Ortega deviated from Husserl's view.

Despite recent efforts to revive the work of the early phenomenologists on the problem of other minds, intersubjectivity, social cognition, social ontology, and the emotions, this biased view about the contribution of the movement to the social sciences remains uncontested in two senses: 1) until the present day, early phenomenology does not come into consideration when we examine traditional lines of *dialogue* between phenomenology and the social sciences, and 2) an account that reactivates all the valuable insights of their research program and develops the key *elements* for a new phenomenological sociology is still largely missing.[1] Before I turn to this second point, let me consider the three main forms of *dialogue* between both disciplines that have traditionally been taken into consideration (Belvedere 2007). The first form of dialogue is based on those of Husserl's works, such as the *Krisis*, in which he explains the philosophical foundations of the social sciences and establishes a relation between both disciplines. The second is based on the work of Merleau-Ponty and Schütz, where they made explicit the connection between both disciplines and question the possibility of a transcendental reduction. The third historical line of dialogue was inaugurated by Levinas and Michel Henry, under the influence of Heidegger. But despite this rough-and-ready overview about different possible 'marriages' between phenomenology and the social sciences, work dedicated to the early phenomenologists is still largely missing. Such authors have fallen into oblivion or received scarce reception, especially if we compare their destiny with the destiny of other 'heirs' of the phenomenological movement, such as Heidegger.

Which authors belong to this group? What are the elements of this 'alternative' phenomenological sociology? Early phenomenologists developed, at the beginning of the last century under the auspices of Husserl and Pfänder, and strongly inspired by Scheler, original accounts about reality, the emotions, and the social aspects of the human being. Rather than a 'school' offering common accepted theses, early phenomenology is more of a 'constellation' of authors and thoughts that can only be understood as a whole in terms of personal and intellectual influences and interrelations.[2] The main contributions important for the development of a phenomenological sociology are Reinach's analysis of the foundations of the civil law, Husserl's work on intentional sociology and intersubjectivity, Pfänder's theory of the sentiments and his psychology of the human being, Scheler's work on feelings, sympathy, social acts, the collective person, and the sociology of knowledge, Stein's books on empathy, the community, and the state, Walther's study of the social communities, von Hildebrand's ontology of communities, and Ortega y Gasset's work on the mass and the people. An analysis of these topics, ideas, claims, and arguments offers us the basic elements to develop a phenomenological sociology of a different guise than the one developed by Schütz, and shows that the dialogue with the social sciences is a characteristic mark of the phenomenological movement.

The *elements* that can be found in the works of these authors for the development of a sociological phenomenology are a theory of personality, feelings, social acts, groups, and values.[3] Since analyzing each of these elements is clearly beyond the scope of this chapter, my strategy will be to show the relevance of early phenomenology for the understanding of sociality by focusing on one concrete element of pivotal importance, in which all these elements converge: the phenomenological idea that affective phenomena are intentionally directed towards the world and others, and reveals what matters to us and what motivates us to action. This phenomenological idea of intentional feelings towards the world is amalgamated in the newly coined concept of 'affective intentionality.'[4] Long before analytic philosophy developed its accounts of the emotions as intentional, cognitive, and social phenomena, the early phenomenologists offered very detailed accounts on the intentionality of feelings and emotions. Affective intentionality is, in my view, one of the key elements of this 'alternative' phenomenological sociology.

In this chapter, I will focus on three aspects of this concept: (i) the fact that our emotional intentional directedness towards the world and the others is socially embedded, (ii) that it is socially shaped, and (iii) that it can assume shared forms. The thread that runs through this article is the idea that the analysis of affectivity is decisive for explaining and offering new perspectives on the interconnection between the individual and the social. I will develop this idea by focusing on the phenomena of feelings and sentiments analyzed respectively by Scheler and Pfänder. The result of this analysis lends further support to the idea of a relational concept of intentionality in early phenomenology, and gives key insight into the early phenomenological contribution to the social sciences.

## 2 AFFECTIVE INTENTIONALITY, SHARED FEELINGS, AND SOCIAL UNITS IN SCHELER

The early phenomenologists were very prolific in their study of affectivity. Aside from several analyses of concrete emotional phenomena such as resentment, love, inauthentic feelings, etc., they provided two broad, systematic theories of affectivity: Scheler's account of feelings, and Pfänder's psychology of sentiments. In this section, I expound Scheler's theory of affective intentionality and its relevance from a sociological point of view.

In particular, I am interested in how feelings, values, and social units, for Scheler, are interrelated.

One of Scheler's most fascinating discoveries, broadly accepted within phenomenological circles, concerns the thesis of a stratification of emotional life. Feelings can be classified according to their level of 'depth,' i.e., in virtue of the differences in the degree of their subjection to the will. Those phenomena that we can easily manipulate belong to 'peripheral' strata, whereas those that can less readily be controlled occupy a more central position in our personalities (Scheler 1973a, 330). A further aspect of this theory is that in each of these emotional strata we experience a value complex, so that the depth of feeling is symmetrical to the hierarchical rank of values (from the lower to the highest): 1) pleasure and utility, 2) vitality, 3) values of culture, and 4) spiritual values of holiness.

According to Scheler, there are four different layers of feelings: sense-feelings, vital feelings, psychological feelings, and feelings of personality. 1) The first stratum of 'sense-feelings,' to which bodily pleasure and pain belong, is actually not a feeling at all, but a sensation (here, Scheler follows Stumpf (1928, 55). Sense-feelings are localized in a specific part of the body; they are not intentionally directed towards the world, or an object, and they are not directed towards values. 2) The second level is constituted by 'vital feelings,' such as tiredness, freshness, or illness. These feelings cannot be localized in a specific part of the body. We feel fresh or tired or ill in our entire body. These non-localized feelings are intentional in the sense that they are directed towards the vital values of the noble and the mean, and it is in virtue of them that we experience the climax and decadence of life. 3) The third level corresponds to 'psychological feelings,' such as joy and sadness. Psychological feelings are bodily felt, even though they cannot be localized either. They are intentional, directed towards objects, and related to the couples of values: 'beautiful' and 'ugly,' 'fair' and 'unfair,' and 'true' and 'false.' 4) The fourth stratum is 'spiritual feelings' or 'feelings of the personality,' such as bliss or desperation, which are related to the values of the sacred and the profane. According to this theory, feelings belonging to different layers can co-exist and influence each other without blending into a unique general feeling. Similar claims about the 'depth' of the emotional life can be found in current research on the emotions (Mulligan 1998; Pugmire 2005).

Despite the fact that in each one of these strata we experience a value and its rank, values are not grasped by these feelings. Scheler works with a distinction between the *act of grasping a value* in an 'intentional feeling' (*Fühlen*) and the *emotional reaction* to it (*Gefühl*). Vital, psychological, and spiritual feelings are emotional responses to felt values; these values, however, are grasped in an 'intentional feeling' (following Scheler: Mulligan 2009). As responses, they can be right or wrong according to the value to which they react, but they cannot grasp the value. One of the advantages of this model is that it explains how it is possible to grasp a value and yet not respond to it with an emotional reaction, as happens in a case when I see an injustice but when I do not necessarily respond by being outraged. In contrast, those who construe emotions as intentional feelings of values have difficulties explaining this phenomenon (Stein 1989, and in the current debate, Tappolet 2000 and Johnston 2001). As axiological properties existing in an 'objective' realm, values are only accessible in virtue of our intentional feelings, just as we can grasp sounds only through our capacity to hear, and colors only due to our visual capabilities. In tune with the current analytic theories of the emotions, Scheler claims that reason is blind to values and only in virtue of our capacity to feel, which is intentional and cognitive, can we grasp them. Scheler regards intentional feelings as a kind of 'organ' for comprehending values, and he speaks of an '*original* emotive intentionality,' underscoring that the intentional 'feeling of something' is responsible for grasping values (Scheler 1973a, 256).

This original emotive intentionality, which is essential for understanding Scheler's account of affective intentionality, can come in two forms: 'intentional functions of feelings' and 'emotional act experiences.' The first, intentional *functions*, are responsible for grasping values and therefore play a cognitive role. The second, intentional *acts*, are responsible for discovering the rank and the existence of values. Accordingly, this category can be divided into two categories: a) *preferring and placing after (Nachsetzen)*, which are responsible for the apprehension of the rank in which values are organized; and 2) *love and hate*, as the highest level of affective life (Scheler 1973a, 261). They designate an attitude of openness (in love) or closedness (in hatred). Only after an intentional function of feeling or an intentional emotive act discovers and grasps a value and its hierarchical position, may an emotional response in the sense of a vital, psychological, or spiritual feeling arise.

The order of value given to individuals or collectives in acts of love and hate and preferring and placing after is labeled by Scheler with the Augustinian term 'ordo amoris,' in an essay that bears the same title: "The heart is itself a *structured counter-image* of the cosmos of all possible things worthy of love; to this extent it is a *microcosm of the world of values*" (Scheler 1973b, 116). The complex of preferences, interests, and order of discovery of what matters to us, which Scheler calls the 'heart,' reveals the world of values and is a counter-image of it. It is a matter of fact, however, that there are, among individuals and collectives, huge differences in terms of what matters and what is preferable. Should we embrace relativism? Scheler is clear on this point: the objectivity of values and their hierarchy is undoubtable; they are, however, not grasped by all of us in the same way because each one of us and each social group has its own and peculiar 'logic of the heart' that is responsible for grasping and preferring some values over others. Whereas an individual will prefer the values of the agreeable over the values of the noble, and be attentive to those features of the world that are bearers of such values, another individual with a different 'logic of the heart' will be interested in values of the beautiful. Given that not only individuals but also collectives have their own 'logic of the heart,' it is possible in the same sense that a cultural group could be interested in the values of the noble over the agreeable, while another group will focus on the useful.[5] Scheler calls these specific ways of being directed towards the world, which reveal our preferences, interests, and orders of discovery, 'ethos.' Each human being has her own 'logic of the heart' that is, in turn, embedded in the larger 'logics of the heart' of the social unities to which she belongs. The domains of the individual and the social, however, are not independent of each other, so these larger social unities shape and influence the logic of the heart of the individual.

Two consequences of this conception of affective intentionality should be highlighted. First, affective intentionality is not restricted to individuals. Social groups, epochs, cultural units, etc. show a specific 'logic of the heart' and are characterized by an 'ethos.' Second, the individual is never an isolated subject, but a subject embedded in a broad social background and a net of interrelations with others that influence, shape, and form her preferences, interests, and the way in which the world is presented to her.

Building upon these theses, Scheler elaborates an insightful account about different forms of being with one another. In *The Nature of Sympathy*, he analyzes two affective phenomena—fellow feeling (*Mit-fühlen*) and love, which is not a form of shared feeling—and distinguishes between four kinds of shared feelings: 1) in the 'immediate community of feeling,' two individuals share the object and the type of feeling. Two parents standing beside the dead body of the beloved child feel the 'same' sorrow and the 'same' anguish. This feeling can take place at a sub-personal level; it is a form of shared affective intentionality in the sense that two interrelated individuals share the same object and type of feeling. 2) A 'fellow feeling about something' or 'sympathy' is a form of shared affective intentionality that involves an intentional reference to the feelings of the other. The feeling is given to us through a feeling and it is mediated by a judgment or perception (Scheler 2008, 13). We are directed towards the other person, towards the content of her emotion, and we react to it. Scheler makes an important distinction here between this kind of shared feeling and a 'vicarious feeling of the other.' Vicarious feelings consist of grasping the feeling of the other in a distant way, without participating in it or feeling for the other. It is an emotional form of being related towards another person that cannot be reduced to judgment or imitation, but because there is no genuine sharing of a feeling, we cannot speak in this case of a shared form of affective intentionality. 3) Another form of feeling with others is given in 'emotional contagion'—the experience of losing ourselves unconsciously in the affective state of an individual or group. We cannot speak here of a genuine form of shared affective intentionality because this is a mere being infected by the emotions of others. 4) A special case of emotional contagion takes place in 'feeling one with the other,' where we identify completely with the other so that we can feel the same feelings as her. In this case, we cannot speak of a genuine shared affective intentionality either. Thus, only 'community of feeling' and 'fellow feeling' can be considered shared forms of affective intentionality.[6]

Now, these ideas have been further developed in the *Formalismus*—a book in which Scheler conceives the individual person as given always as a member of a social unit, i.e., as a "person acting with others" or a "man with others" (Scheler 1973a, 520). We are members of social units and would experience ourselves as such even if we lived on a desert island: "An imaginary Robinson Crusoe endowed with cognitive-theoretical faculties would also co-experience his *being a member of a social unit* in his experiencing the *lack* of fulfillment of acts of act-types constituting a person in general" (1973a, 521). This essentially social dimension of the individual becomes clear, according to Scheler (here inspired by Reinach) in 'social acts' such as commanding, obeying, promising, etc., which are in essence reciprocal because they can only be fulfilled with reference to another; i.e., their fulfilment is only possible in a community, and this is especially so for 'true kinds of love,' which also require fulfilment. In a next step, Scheler analyzes the forms of social units to which an individual may belong (in fact, we belong to more than one of these units simultaneously). This analysis, conceived as part of a 'philosophical sociology' and built upon the thesis of the stratification of the personality and the different types of shared feelings, reveals four different forms of 'being with one another' (Scheler 1973a, 525).

1) The 'herd or mass' is constituted by emotional contagion and imitation, and is devoid of any understanding of the other. Members of this social unit do not show self-consciousness, and the boundaries with the other are essentially blurred. The behavior of the mass is without ethos or responsibility. Regarding the exposition above about feelings, values, and shared forms of being with each other, this form of social unit, based on emotional contagion and identification, runs at the level of sensations, and it is not related to values, and hence cannot exhibit any genuine form of shared affective intentionality.

2) The 'life-community' is constituted in co-experiencing (*Miteinander-Erleben*) and reliving (*Nachleben*). In the immediate experience of the life-community, there is no division between the experience of the self and that of the other: the content of this co-experiencing is identical. The self has an understanding of others, itself, and of the mutual belonging to a community. The community is a supra-singular social unit and not a mere aggregate of its individual members. Its members share an attitude of trust vis-à-vis one another, and they are responsible not only for themselves, but also for the whole unit. Thus, this social unit is characterized by a kind of 'representable solidarity' in the sense that each one of the members can represent the whole. The values that the community experience and the values

of which the unit is the bearer are the values of well-being and the noble. Considering Scheler's claims on affective intentionality, we might say that this social unit is related to vital values, the stratum of the vital feelings of the personality, and its members are bonded to each other via community of feeling and forms of vicarious feelings. This is a form of affective collective intentionality in the sense that there is a dimension of shared feeling and there is a collective form of being directed towards the world.

3) The 'society' is an artificial unity of individuals in which relations among its members are established by specific conscious acts. In contrast with the community, in the society, there is no original living with one another, but just a mere addition of its members. It is, however, a self-conscious and mature unity based on conventions, instrumental behavior, and contracts between its members, established by mutual promises. The basic attitude in the society is distrust, and if there is any common will, it only arises by force or fiction. As a personal form of unity, this unit is related to personal values, and the value modalities that are taken into consideration are those of the agreeable and the useful. Community and society are interrelated in the sense that there cannot be a society without life-community: individuals who enter into a society must have gone through a union in a community (this does not imply that the same group of individuals of a society must also form a community, but only that these individuals at some time must have belonged to a community). Scheler works here with Tönnies's well-established distinction between community and society, and characterizes the latter in a negative way: in society, there is no real sharing with the others and the values experienced are the lowest rank of personal values.

4) The highest form of social unity is the 'collective person'—a unity of independent, spiritual, and individual persons in an independent, spiritual, and individual collective person. In this level, each person is self-aware of being an individual and of being a member of a collective person. Members of the collective person are responsible for themselves, but also for all the other individual persons belonging to the unit. There is an 'unrepresentable solidarity' (*unvertretbare Solidarität*) at this level, because each member is, as such, unique. The values experienced in the collective person are the spiritual values of the holy, and this form of social unity is related to the person of persons: God. Scheler distinguishes between different sub-types of collective persons according to different extents of responsibility: the state, the people, and the church. From the perspective of affective intentionality, this form of social unity experiences spiritual values that occupy the highest rank in the hierarchy, and its members are related to each other through true acts of love.[7]

This typology of social unities is strongly related to key aspects of Scheler's notion of affective intentionality exposed above. The taxonomy shows that in the same sense that feelings are related towards values, social units, in which members relate to each other through complex forms of shared feelings, also experience values. Scheler's philosophical sociology cannot therefore be understood independently from his ethics. Values—and this is one of the interesting consequences of this view—are not only experienced at the individual level, but also at the social level. Shared forms of affective intentionality are therefore possible.

To recapitulate, the aspects of affective intentionality that contribute to a phenomenological sociology are the following: 1) the individual person experiences herself always against the background of a community, i.e., she is always encompassed by a social background that influences and forms her (Scheler 1973a, 519). 2) There are different ways in which individuals can be 'with one another,' emotionally bonded, share feelings, and constitute social units. 3) Values can be experienced at an individual level and at a social level, so that it is possible to speak about shared forms of affective intentionality. Hence, we have to reject the idea that early phenomenologists were employing a solipsistic concept of intentionality. 4) Scheler's phenomenological sociology is embedded in a larger ethical project inaugurated by Brentano, which consists of attributing the cognitive function of grasping values and of providing reasons for action to affective acts.[8]

## 3  SENTIMENTS, THE SELF, AND THE SOCIAL IN PFÄNDER

This section is devoted to the role of sentiments in the understanding of sociality, and it focuses on Pfänder's theory developed in *Zur Psychologie der Gesinnungen* (1913/16). Pfänder's account offers valuable insights into the mechanisms of affective intentionality and the social nature of the human self, and it was very influential among his students. Its importance for the development of a phenomenological sociology, however, has been largely overlooked. Here, I will mainly focus on how his theory of personality and intentionality and his taxonomy of sentiments can offer new insights concerning the importance of affective intentionality for sociology.

According to Pfänder, the psychical subject is divided into a 'voluminous self' and the kernel of the self, which he calls the 'I-Center.' In this model, the I-Center has the role of a spectator, with limited power and influence over feelings and other emotions that arise in the different parts of the 'self': it can perceive them, but it cannot fully control them. All the acts of the 'I-Center,' hence, are embedded in a broader structure of the self that functions as a background. Some phenomenologists—such as Stein and Walther (Walther 1923, 60; Stein 1989, 101)—establish a parallelism between this model and the analogous Schelerian idea of a stratification of the psychic life in the central and peripheral layers of the personality. In addition to his theory of the self, we find in Pfänder a theory of intentionality. He distinguishes two main tendencies of the psychic life: a 'centrifugal' tendency, which consists of being directed towards the world; and a 'centripetal' tendency, namely, when we feel affected by something in the world. According to this distinction, intentionality, as a tendency that characterizes the direction from a subject to an object, is centrifugal. The objects of centrifugal acts are not only persons, but also animals, inanimate objects, or cultural phenomena, and they must be given in a perception, judgment, or fantasy (1913, 340).[9] Sentiments, then, are based on cognitions: loving, hating, or being hostile or friendly requires that the object towards which we are directed has been perceived, judged, or fantasized. In accordance with other authors in this circle, but also with recent developments in analytic philosophy of the emotions, Pfänder is defending here a broad form of cognitivism (Goldie 2002).

Sentiments, feelings, and moods are 'warm psychic acts,' in contrast to cold psychic acts such as perception, thought, attention, fantasy, or volitions (1913, 362). Despite their sharing this psychic feature with feelings, sentiments should, on the basis of their 'centrifugality,' i.e., of their intentional relation to objects, be strictly distinguished from feelings. The couples love and hate, friendship and hostility, and benevolence and malevolence are paradigmatic cases of sentiments and form a class different from the feelings of sadness, joy, disgust, or envy. Sentiments are essentially connected to their objects: they stream from the subject to the object and bridge the gap between both poles. Feelings, on the contrary, are mere states with no essential connection to their objects. A further difference consists of the fact that, whereas feelings oscillate between the poles of pleasure and pain, the polarity exhibited by sentiments is not explainable in terms of hedonic valence. The sentiment of love can be painful, for example, when it is not reciprocated, and hatred can be experienced as pleasure; a disagreeable feeling of happiness, however, is a contradictio in adjecto. Sentiments resemble attitudes and are not necessarily 'bodily felt,' while feelings as episodic and temporal states are bodily bound. We could, as Stein, for example, does, also interpret sentiments as belonging to deeper levels of the self than mere feelings (Stein 1989, 101).

Pfänder elaborates a taxonomy of sentiments according to their polar structure, their relation to the object, the mode in which they are given, and the different forms they can adopt. According to their polarity, sentiments can be positive or negative: 1) by virtue of their 'intrinsic quality,' positive sentiments are 'supporting' and 'warming,' while negative sentiments are characterized by a 'destructive' and 'corrosive' intentional relation to their object. Pfänder has in mind some kind of 'psychic feeling,' or qualia, and not mere hedonic valence. Our being intentionally direct towards the world is, thus, characterized by a specific psychological quality and not by mere sensations (cf. also Goldie 2002, 58). 2) On the basis of an 'act of position taking' towards the intentional object, the subject of a sentiment can join with it (*Einigung*), or avoid contact in the case of separation (*Entzweiung*). Love is a paradigmatic case of joining with the object towards which one is directed, while hatred is one of separation. Joining and separating are conceived in this account of affective intentionality as two possible intentional relations between subject and object. Pfänder's student Gerda Walther will build upon this thesis for her own account of social communities. 3) Sentiments are accompanied by an 'attitude' of approval or disapproval, which is not a judgment but rather an affirmation of, or disconformity with, the existence of the object. Love affirms and approves the existence of its object, while hatred negates it.

The given relation between subject and object provides a further way to classify sentiments as superordinate, as being at the same level, or subordinated to their object. For example, Pfänder claims that the love of the mother for the child is superordinate, the love of the child for its mother is subordinate, and love among mates is at the same level. A further way to classify sentiments concerns their mode of existence as actual, virtual, or habitual (1913, 331). Actual sentiments are accompanied by awareness; virtual sentiments are potential sentiments of which we may still be aware (Schwankl 1975, 76), while habitual sentiments form part of our psychic life—they can be felt regularly, but we are not necessarily aware of them. Pfänder considers all three modes to be important for the explanation of affective intentionality, but focuses on actual sentiments to develop his theory. The notion of 'habitual sentiment' was eventually made the object of an original analysis by Walther in her classification of sentiments as actual, unconscious, potential, and habitual (Walther 1923, 48).

Among the manifold forms that sentiments may assume, the one that concerns their inauthenticity is of special relevance to explaining both the role of social interrelations in shaping the self, and how they become an essential part of the self. Pfänder's use of the term 'inauthentic' has nothing to do with deception, delusion, or intentional fraud. Far from having a negative sense, Pfänder uses this concept as a terminus technicus to describe those sentiments that arise in jokes, make-believe, pretending, and acting as if we are moved by a sentiment. In order to understand its relevance, I will structure my exposition around three features of 'inauthenticity.' First of all, and in line with a popular thesis of the Graz School defended by Meinong and his students, Pfänder claims that all psychic phenomena can present themselves in two forms: as authentic or inauthentic. A conviction is inauthentic when it is inherited from the culture in which I am socialized, an inauthentic thought is one adopted from the testimony of others, and a love relation is inauthentic when it is motivated by the requirements of my cultural environment. Take the two-year-old child's love for his newborn sister. The first weeks after the baby's birth, the child is negatively attuned towards the baby, because he has lost some of his parent's attention. The love of the child may have been originally prompted by the demands of his parents, and this may not be in tune with his other feelings, desires, and thoughts. In this case, this love is inauthentic because it has its origins 'outside' the self, in the social world, and it is prompted by the demands of significant others.

A second feature of inauthentic psychic acts concerns their capacity to transform into authentic ones. Thus, the originally inauthentic love of the child can change into authentic love when he changes his general attitude towards his sister and that love, which was not in tune with the rest of his psychic life, is now felt as spontaneously originating from central parts of his self. This points to a possible and desirable cultivation of the sentiments, a kind of 'education sentimentale.' In this case, inauthentic sentiments lay the ground for authentic affectivity. But, in my opinion, more important than this, this possibility of conversion highlights the social structure of affective intentionality, as individuals can internalize forms of being related to others, and this 'internalization' may change the structure of the self and the way in which we are intentionally directed towards others. Inauthentic sentiments of social origin may transform into authentic ones according to the measure in which they mold and shape our psychic lives, and as we change central aspects of our selves accordingly. The intrinsic nature of the self becomes clear when we realise that some of our most intimate assumptions, expectations, judgments, feelings, and sentiments are socially constituted. The third feature of inauthentic feelings concerns their felt quality. Pfänder speaks about them having "the character of schematic imitations" of authentic feelings, and describes them as "schematic, hollow, thin, coreless or light" (1913, 383).

According to these claims, there are two conditions for inauthenticity. 1) Inauthentic sentiments have their origins in the social world of our interpersonal relations, and hence are socially constituted, even though they may become an essential part of our self. This point was developed further by Else Voigtländer (Voigtländer 1910). 2) Inauthentic sentiments, as we experience them, are not in harmony with the general tune of our psychic lives, i.e., they are not supported by other thoughts, convictions, ideas, feelings, or sentiments. This point was developed by Willy Haas in terms of feelings (Haas 1910). In the light of this second condition, it is not surprising that the terminology Pfänder uses to describe them resembles that used by Hume and the German aestheticists of the 19th century for those emotions aroused by fictions, e.g., pity for the destiny of a fictional character. In addition, these emotions are not in consonance with the rest of our psychic life, for example because, in the case of the fictional character, we judge the character as inexistent, and consequently know that he does not suffer, and that, in fact, we went to the theater just to enjoy an entertaining evening.

Pfänder's thesis on inauthentic sentiments gives us a further argument for the claim that affective intentionality in early phenomenology has a clear social dimension. Pfänder shows how the self is embedded in a net of affective interactions with others, how it participates emotionally in the social world, and how internalizing this way of relating to others shapes essential aspects of it. The arguably unfortunate choice of the term 'inauthentic' to describe feelings embedded in this process may be one of the reasons why this view has received so little attention so far, even though it can well serve to explain the social background of the self.

Pfänder's descriptive psychology of sentiments, which highlights the social aspects of the self, should be considered a crucial aspect of affective intentionality, and important for the development of a sociological phenomenology. His theory is, like Scheler's account, in consonance with a more general ethical project inherited from Brentano, according to which affective phenomena are essential for explaining what matters to us and how we should act.[10]

## 4  CONCLUDING REMARKS

To summarize, feeling and sentiments are crucial concepts for developing a phenomenological sociology based on the accounts of the early representatives of this movement. As I have argued, a phenomenological analysis of the notion of affective intentionality shows that this specific form of being directed towards the world and others is always embedded in a social context, that this context shapes us in different ways according to the way we interact with others, and that it may assume shared forms. The analysis also shows that a phenomenological sociology cannot be developed independently of value ethics.[11] Ultimately, then, from a phenomenological point of view sociology—just like ethics—requires a descriptive analysis of affective intentionality.

## NOTES

1 To be sure, some steps in this direction have been taken recently (Mulligan 1999 and Vendrell Ferran 2008). Husserl's intentional sociology has also been an object of study (Caminada 2011; Chelstrom 2013; Szanto forthcoming a). Within the current discussion of collective intentionality or social ontology, the early phenomenological accounts of Walther, Scheler, Stein, von Hildebrand, and Reinach have been discussed (Schmid 2005; de Vecchi 2012; Salice 2013; Caminada 2014; Szanto & Moran (ed.) (forthcoming); Szanto forthcoming b, and the contributions of Caminada, Salice, and Szanto in this volume). In research on 'social cognition' and 'intersubjectivity,' Husserl, Scheler, and Stein have also been objects of study (e.g., Zahavi 2001).
2 I employ this term in the sense of Dieter Heinrich 'constellation research' (Heinrich 1992).
3 In similar sense: Walther (1923, 17).
4 Exemplarily illustrated in Goldie's concept of 'feeling towards' (Goldie 2002).
5 For a detailed account on the different meanings of the notion of 'ordo amoris' in Scheler, see Sander (2003).
6 Cf. for a detailed account, Mulligan (2002), Schlossberger (2005), and Songhorian (2012).
7 Cf. Szanto (in this volume).
8 Even though my focus in this section has been on Scheler's concept of feeling and its relevance for sociological investigations, other phenomenologists have developed accounts that similarly investigate the role of feelings in the social. Amongst these, we should mention Stein's work on empathy, the community, and the state, Walter's ontology of social communities, and von Hildebrand's

metaphysics of communities. Each of these authors employs and broadly discusses Scheler's theory of feelings.

9 This view contrasts with other views that claim that only persons can be objects of sentiments (Stein 1989, 101).

10 One of Pfänder's students, Gerda Walther, used his theory of the sentiments and his model of the mind to analyze the structure of social communities and collective intentionality in *Zur Ontologie der Sozialen Gemeinschaften*. Her key concept—'habitual joining'—built upon Pfänder's idea that sentiments can exist in a habitual form and that acts of joining with others are constitutive of our selves, and, explains the possibility of communal experiences and collective intentionality.

11 Mulligan also stresses the strong link between both disciplines (Mulligan 1999). On the contrary, Caminada shows that Husserl develops his intentional sociology independently of ethics (Caminada 2011, 58).

## REFERENCES

Belvedere, Carlos (2007). "Phenomenology and the Social Sciences: A Story with No Beginning." *Sociedad* 2, 1–12.

Caminada, Emanuele (2011). "Husserls intentionale Soziologie." In: V. Mayer, C. Erhard, & M. Scherini (Eds.). *Die Aktualität Husserls*. Freiburg: Alber, 57–86.

Caminada, Emanuele (2014). "Joining the Background: Habitual Sentiments Behind We-Intentionality." In: A. Konzelmann-Ziv & H.-B. Schmid (Eds.). *Institutions, Emotions, and Group Agents*. Dordrecht: Springer, 195–212.

Chelstrom, Erik (2013). *Social Phenomenology: Husserl, Intersubjectivity, and Collective Intentionality*. Lanham: Lexington.

de Sousa, Ronald (1987). *The Rationality of Emotion*. Cambridge, MA/London: MIT Press.

De Vecchi, Francesca (Ed.) (2012) *Eidetica del diritto e ontologia sociale. Il realismo di Adolf Reinach*. Milano: Mimesis.

Goldie, Peter (2002). *The Emotions. A Philosophical Exploration*. Oxford: Oxford University Press.

Johnston, Mark (2001). "The Authority of Affect." *Philosophy and Phenomenological Research* 63 (1), 181–214.

Haas, Willy (1910). *Über Echtheit und Unechtheit von Gefühlen*. Nürnberg: Benedikt Hilz.

Henrich, Dieter (1992). *Konstellationen. Probleme und Debatten am Ursprung der idealistischen Philosophie (1789–1795)*. Stuttgart: Klett-Cotta.

Mulligan, Kevin (1998). "The Spectre of inverted Emotions and the Space of Emotions." *Acta Analytica*, 89–105.

Mulligan, Kevin (1999). "Etica y Sociología en la Fenomenología realista". Talk, University of Barcelona (27.10.1999).

Mulligan, Kevin (2002). "Actes socials i objectes socials." *Comprendre* IV (2), 71–82.

Mulligan, Kevin (2009). "On Being Struck by Value." In: B. Merker (Ed.). *Leben mit Gefühlen*. Paderborn: Mentis, 141–161.

Pfänder, Alexander (1913/16). "Zur Psychologie der Gesinnungen." In: *Jahrbuch für Philosophie und phänomenologische Forschung I*, 325–404 and *III*, 1–125. Tübingen: Max Niemeyer.

Pugmire, David (2005). *Sound Sentiments: Integrity in the Emotions*. Oxford: Oxford University Press.

Salice, Alessandro (2013). "Social Ontology as Embedded in the Tradition of Phenomenological Realism." In: M. Schmitz, B. Kobow, & H. B. Schmid (Eds.). *The Background of Social Reality*. Dordrecht: Springer, 217–232.
—— (in this volume). "Love and Other Social Stances in Early Phenomenology."
Sander, Angelika (2003). "Normative und deskriptive Bedeutung des *ordo amoris*." In: C. Bermes, W. Henckmann, & H. Leonardy (Eds.). *Vernunft und Gefühl. Schelers Phänomenologie des emotionalen Lebens*. Würzburg: Königshausen & Neumann, 63–80.
Scheler, Max (1973a). *Formalism in Ethics and Non-formal Ethics of Values*. Evanston: Northwestern University Press.
—— (1973b). "Ordo amoris." In:Max Scheler (Ed.). *Selected Philosophical Essays*. Evanston: Northwestern University Press, 98–135.
—— (2008). *The Nature of Sympathy*. New Jersey: Transaction Publishers.
Schlossberger, Matthias (2005). *Die Erfahrung des Anderen*. Berlin: Akademie.
Schmid, Hans Bernhard (2005). *Wir-Intentionalität*. Freiburg: Alber.
Schütz, Alfred (1972). *Collected Papers I, The Problem of Social Reality*. Dordrecht: Springer.
Schwankl, Peter (1975). "Alexander Pfänders Nachlass-Texte über das virtuelle Psychische." In: E. Avé-Lallemant, R. Gladiator, & H. Kuhn (Eds.). *Die Münchener Phänomenologie*. The Hague: Martinus Nijhoff, 75–77.
Songhorian, Sarah (2012). "Is Affective Intentionality Necessarily Irrelevant in Social Cognition?" *Phenomenology and Mind* 2, 108–117.
Stein, Edith (1989). *On the Problem of Empathy: The Collected Works of Edith Stein*. Washington: ICS Publications.
Stumpf, Carl (1928). *Gefühl und Gefühlsempfindung*. Leipzig: Johann Ambrosius Barth.
Szanto, Thomas (forthcoming a): "Husserl on Collective Intentionality." In: A. Salice, & H. B. Schmid (Eds.). *Social Reality: The Phenomenological Approach*. Dordrecht: Springer.
—— (forthcoming b): "Collective Emotions, Normativity, and Empathy: A Steinian Account." *Human Studies*. DOI 10.1007/s10746-015-9350-8.
—— (in this volume): "Collectivizing Persons and Personifying Collectives: Reassessing Scheler on Group Personhood." In: T. Szanto, & D. Moran (Eds.). *The Phenomenology of Sociality: Discovering the 'We'*. London/New York: Routledge.
Szanto, Thomas, & Moran, Dermot (Eds.) (forthcoming). *Empathy and Collective Intentionality: Edith Stein's Social Philosophy*. Special Issue of *Human Studies*.
Tappolet, Christine (2000). *Émotions et Valeurs*. Paris: Presses Universitaires de France.
Vendrell Ferran, Íngrid (2008). "Simpatía, empatía y otros actos sociales: los orígenes olvidados de la sociología fenomenológica." *Espacio Abierto. Cuaderno Venezolano de Sociología* 17 (2), 303–315.
Voigtländer, Else (1910). *Vom Selbstgefühl*. Leipzig: Voigtländers.
Walther, Gerda (1923). "Zur Ontologie der sozialen Gemeinsachten." In: *Jahrbuch für Philosophie und phänomenologische Forschung* VI. Halle: Niemeyer, 1–158.
Zahavi, Dan (2001). "Beyond Empathy. Phenomenological Approaches to Intersubjectivity." *Journal of Consciousness Studies* 8 (5–7), 151–167.

# 14 Love and Other Social Stances in Early Phenomenology

*Alessandro Salice*

## INTRODUCTION

Suppose there is someone with whom you wish to share an important part of your life. You go to bed and wake up with this person in mind. You desire that the other person feels the same way about you and (unless you know that he or she simply doesn't care about you) you are happy when you see him or her and sad when you do not. One could continue this phenomenological exercise, but I venture to surmise that a certain degree of familiarity with the phenomenon of romantic love can be taken for granted here.

However, it seems that, when it comes to describing what romantic love is, one element frequently goes unnoticed: if one loves someone, it matters to one whether the beloved, in turn, "knows" that he or she is loved (in a sense which has yet to be clarified, cf. section 3). To be more specific, it could be argued that, if one feels this kind of emotion, then one usually also intends to let the beloved understand how one feels. It is tempting to see the romantic lover's intention to disclose his or her feelings of love to the beloved as being closely linked to his or her desire that the beloved, in turn, reciprocates such love (cf. Nozick 1989). Although it is questionable whether these considerations apply to love in general (for love, it has been argued, does not necessarily imply desire; cf. Velleman 1999), they remain tempting in the case of romantic love because, if the lover wishes for his or her feeling to be reciprocated, then the fulfillment of such a desire appears to require that the beloved understands that he or she is the target of the lover's emotion. Only in this case can the beloved, in turn, emotionally respond to, and hence genuinely reciprocate, the love of which he or she is the target. Of course, unrequited love exists, so reciprocation does not need to occur, but luckily, it *can* occur—contingently upon the fact that the addressee knows about the lover's emotion. If these observations are so far on the right track, one could say that certain emotions (e.g., romantic love) demand that their uptake be secured by their addressees. Such a condition, insofar as it can be taken to speak for the *sociality* of certain emotions, distinguishes these "social" emotions from those that allegedly do not share the same condition (the emotion of envy, e.g., can be expressed to the envied person, but obviously does not need to be).

## Love and Other Social Stances in Early Phenomenology  235

The idea that some kinds of intentional attitudes are intrinsically social is one of the most interesting insights of early phenomenology: long before John L. Austin's work on the speech act theory (1962), in his "The A Priori Foundations of the Civil Law" (1913), Adolf Reinach describes a class of intentional acts, including promises, orders, questions, etc., that are claimed to be social because they are successfully issued if they are "heard" (*vernommen*) (Reinach 1913a: 19) by their addressees and because they are able to generate social entities (e.g., commitments in the case of promises). However, the idea that some *emotions* are social in this very same sense is alien to Reinach and has to be credited to Dietrich von Hildebrand,[1] who, in his *The Metaphysics of Community* (1930), develops Reinach's insights further and applies them to his theory of emotions—which by that period he already consistently developed against the background of realist phenomenology (cf. Hildebrand 1916, 1922; Vendrell Ferran 2008 as well as her contribution in this volume). Not only does Hildebrand stress the fact that, insofar as it has thus been illustrated, romantic love needs to secure uptake, but he also points out that, if reciprocation takes place, this emotion is able to generate a social entity or, more precisely, a social *group*. In tune with some positions within recent debates about love (Nozick 1989, Helm 2008), but also in social ontology (cf. Helm 2008), Hildebrand claims that love establishes a relation or bond between two individuals, precisely if the addressee *does* reciprocate the emotion. In this case, the mental states of the two lovers generate a bond that is itself not a mental state and that could be described as a social relation binding both individuals and making them a community of a given kind (cf. Salice 2015).

To fully appreciate Hildebrand's original contribution to social ontology, it is hence advisable to discuss his theory in the context of Reinach's view about social acts.[2] Accordingly, the present chapter is organized as follows: after illustrating some of Reinach's main ideas about social acts in the first section, in the second section, I shall tackle Hildebrand's theory of social stances and its relevance for social ontology. In the last section, a challenge for Hildebrand's position will be discussed. This challenge mainly concerns the kind of "communication" that has to be presupposed in order for the addressee to empathically apprehend the social emotion or stance that is addressed to him or her; in the conclusion, two possible strategies to solve this problem are discussed (and one of them will be favored).

## 1  ADOLF REINACH ON SOCIAL ACTS

In his 1913 monograph, Reinach approaches the notion of a social act primarily by means of investigating the act of promising. Most likely, this is due to his interest in the theory of law and to the crucial role that the notion of promise plays for the contract (the latter to be defined in terms of the previous notion). In what follows, I shall concentrate only on those properties that promises share with other social acts and that are most relevant for the comparison with Hildebrand.

What are promises? First, they are intentional acts, i.e., they are mental states directed towards an intentional correlate. For instance, if one promises *p*, *p* is the promise's correlate. Note that, if one promises something, one cannot but promise *that* such and such. This linguistic feature signals that the correlate of a promise is always a *state of affairs* (the entity referred to by the that-clause) and can never be a mere thing, quality, or object. Moreover, the promise is always about something that the *promisor* is committing oneself to bring about. That is, the promise is necessarily about the promisor and about some of the promisor's actions. In other words, Reinach maintains that the very essence of a promise does not allow for actions of persons other than the promisor to be promised—*except* in the case in which it is the promisor who will make the other person perform the promised action. This last consideration sheds light on a further issue about the content of promises: although, as stated above, the content of a promise generally comprises the promisor's very actions, such content can also be comprised of the actions' *results* (so that these remain actions performed by the promisor, cf. 1913a, 151).

For the purpose of this chapter, it is important to highlight, though, that obviously, not all social acts are directed to the subject's future actions; for instance, one can inform someone else *that* the weather in Copenhagen tomorrow will be cloudy. And still, just like promises, many social acts seem to be propositional in the sense that they point to states of affairs as their correlates.

In addition to the first intention towards a state of affairs, promises, according to Reinach, have a second intentional direction. Indeed, promises are not only promises *of* something (and hence are directed towards a correlate), but they also seem to be addressed towards someone in a peculiar way. If one promises *p*, one always promises it *to* a promisee. This person—and this is the crucial point here—has to be different from the promisor himself and is explicitly and directly addressed by the act. (To be sure, Reinach does not exclude the possibility that one can "promise [or: order] something to oneself," but he maintains that there is something artificial about these social acts—for the subject would have to represent himself as another person in order to eventually issue these acts, cf. 1913a, 159 fn. 1.) This feature is shared by promises with many other experiences that, analogously, cannot be addressed to the very subject of the mental state itself, but always have to directly point at someone else. For instance, mental states, such as giving orders, being forgiving, or experiencing envy, cannot but point at an external person. Reinach qualifies all these acts as hetero-directed (*fremdpersonal*) and never misses an occasion to repeat that the hetero-directedness of acts does *not* coincide with their sociality. That is, there are hetero-directed acts that are not social and, vice versa, social acts that are not hetero-directed (1913a, 159). For instance, the aforementioned acts of envying or forgiving are hetero-directed experiences and can never be self-directed, but do not need to be expressed (or to be apprehended by an addressee) in any way.[3] By contrast, acts such as waiving a claim or enacting a law are instances of non-hetero-directed but yet social acts; they are social insofar as they are successfully accomplished only if they are "heard" by an addressee, but the addressee is not explicitly tracked by the act (as it is in the case of hetero-directed social acts). Laws are not enacted "to or towards" someone and, similarly, claims are not waived "to or towards" someone (cf. 1913a, 173f., 242).

What is the difference between social and mere hetero-directed, i.e., non-social, kinds of experiences? If one promises something, one cannot help but express or utter the promise. Otherwise, the promisee would never have the possibility of being aware of the promise addressed to her. So the utterance of the promise towards the promisee is not a mere option, but a necessary condition for the successful realization of the act. This is a property that, Reinach contends, all social acts have due to their essence—including the social, but non-hetero-directed acts: enacting a law is successfully issued if the addressees secured its uptake, although the addressees are not explicitly targeted by the act (and in some cases, can coincide with, or involve, the very subject of the act). By contrast, inner acts (including hetero-directed acts that are not social) do not have to be uttered, for they do not have to secure their uptake. One can envy someone but, in order for the act to be successful here, there is no need to express it to someone. To put this point differently, one might say that social acts, but not inner experiences, are in need-of-being-heard (*vernehmungsbedürftig*), i.e., social experiences are successful only if their addressees "hear them" (1913a, 159).

This insight gives us the possibility to ascertain certain conditions that characterize social acts in a fairly general way. To paraphrase John Searle's terminology (1969), call these the "preparatory," the "sincerity," and the "essential" conditions.

(i.) *The preparatory condition*: the English locution "need-of-being-heard," used to render Reinach's *terminus technicus* of *Vernehmungsbedürftigkeit*, expresses a complex notion, which relates to both semantic and pragmatic competences. Reinach points out that a social act is heard when three conditions are fulfilled. These conditions can be qualified as "preparatory" in Searle's sense, for a *misunderstanding* occurs if they are not aptly fulfilled. The conditions are: first, the linguistic utterance needs to be acoustically or visually perceived (to be sure, Reinach admits that gestures and bodily clues can also express social acts, but this insight plays a minor role in his theory, cf. 1913a, 160); second, the addressee must understand the semantic content of the utterance; and, finally, the addressee must understand the type, mode, or quality of the act (1913a, 161), i.e., she must understand whether a given utterance is a promise, an order, etc.

As we saw already, although Reinach argues that such conditions can also be fulfilled by means of non-verbal communication, it is the linguistic dimension that characterizes social acts most perspicuously. Indeed, all these acts share what could be called a *locutionary* component (in Austin's sense, cf. 1962, 94ff); i.e., in performing a social act, the subject also performs a so-called "act of meaning something." Reinach describes this act as consisting of verbally uttering words that belong to the vocabulary of a language and that are related to each other syntactically, and of referring to entities and predicating something of them (1911, 102ff., 127ff.). The locutionary component is an essential part of every social act, as Reinach says, constitutes what could be called the "body" of the act (1913a, 160).

(ii.) *The sincerity condition*: in addition to a body, social acts also have a "soul." Indeed, social acts are founded (*fundiert*) by a further mental state that represents what could be labeled as their "sincerity condition." Social acts are always founded by an inner experience, i.e., by an experience that is not in-need-of-being-heard, and that points at the same correlate as the meaning act (1913a, 162). For instance, the act of informing someone could be described in mereological terms as a mental complexion that contains an act of meaning and a concomitant conviction. Analogously, a promise would be a whole founded upon an act of will and, again, an act of meaning. That is, if one promises $p$, then one linguistically points at $p$, and one also wants or intends $p$. If the social act only *pretends* to be founded by an inner act of a given type, while in reality it is not, it experiences a sort of "modification," i.e., the act is insincere. (And this justifies speaking of a "sincerity condition" here.) For instance, an act pretending to inform someone about something, but lacking the concomitant belief in what is being communicated, is not an informing act, but a lie, for the speaker asserts $p$, whereas she believes non-$p$; analogously, a promise that lacks the will to act accordingly is not a promise at all, but the deceptive modification of a promise (1913a, 162).

(iii.) *The essential condition*: in addition to the preparatory and the sincerity conditions, social acts are also asked to fulfill an "essential condition." It is essential for social acts to generate effects of a peculiar sort. What are these effects? Take again promises as an example: if my act of promising you something is successful, then I have the commitment to keep my promise and you have the claim that I do so. Now, what are claims and commitments? Obviously, they are not material objects, but they are not psychic objects either, as they exist even if the bearer sleeps or is unconscious. Furthermore, they are not abstract objects, since such objects—like numbers, propositions, etc.—are atemporal, whereas the effects of a social act, being generated by this very act, come into existence at a given time $t$ and disappear after a given time $t'$ (1913a, 148f). An attentive reading of Reinach's text may show that he considers claims and obligations to be social relations (Salice 2008). And, since within his ontology relations are states of affairs (1911, 121), one has good reason to conclude that claims and obligations are, thus, particular kinds of states of affairs. To be sure, not all social acts generate social *relations*, but all social acts do generate states of affairs. For instance, if a judge declares that a given contract is null and void, then he produces the state of affairs *that* this contract is null and void (1913a, 246f).

## 2 DIETRICH VON HILDEBRAND ON SOCIAL STANCES

In his book *The Metaphysics of Community*, Hildebrand approvingly refers to Reinach's theory of social acts (1975a, 23) but, at the same time, he rejects what he believes to be an unmotivated limitation of sociality to these kinds of experiences. In particular, he points out that there are a number of experiences that are not social *acts*, but that share, together with these acts, the essential property of being in need-of-being-heard. Hildebrand labels these attitudes *verlautbarte Stellungnahmen*, i.e., uttered position-takings, or stances (1975a, 24). Given the fact that Hildebrand considers *Vernehmungsbedürftigkeit* to be an essential property of uttered stances, in the following, we will refer to this kind of a stance also with the expression of "social stance." So, what are stances in general, and what are social stances in particular?

Volitional and emotional stances are described as responses to values and are held to be both spontaneous and intentionally directed towards an object. They are spontaneous in the sense that the subject *responds* to values and that such a response is not exacted by the value itself. That is, the subject engages in an active experience when it takes a given position towards a value. This insight seems to be demonstrated by the fact that one could grasp the beauty of an artwork or the moral value of an action and, nonetheless, remain indifferent towards the beauty or unmoved vis-à-vis the moral value of the action (note that this amounts to saying that stances are necessarily founded on cognitive acts directed towards values, which Hildebrand labels "acts of feeling" (*Fühlen*); cf. Mulligan 2010).

Stances track values: if one loves someone, enjoys something, or decides to perform a given action, the loved person, the enjoyed object, or the action to be performed have to be perceived by the subject as valuable in some sense or another, i.e., some values are "phenomenally given" in these stances. As far as these "phenomenally given" values are concerned, "the value response [. . .] can only be the correct one" (cf. von Hildebrand 1916: 40). This is because "every value has its ideally befitting response" (1916: 39) in the sense that, if one perceives (or believes to perceive, see below) a given value, the response one generates, if any, is always the "correct" one. And yet this "correctness" has to be taken *cum grano salis*: for stances can also be *objectively incorrect* given the fact that "phenomenally given" values, Hildebrand contends, can correspond *or not* to objectively existing values (cf. 1916: 40). Stances are objectively correct only if the phenomenally given values coincide with the objectively existing ones; otherwise, they should be considered as incorrect.

Within the general class of stances, one can identify a subclass whose intentional object is—and can only be—a *person*. To refer to the example at the beginning of this chapter, romantic or erotic love (but certain forms of hate, too) can be directed only towards a person and not towards things, propositions, qualities, events, etc. You love or hate someone in virtue of the values or "dis-values" that he or she exemplifies.[4] Now, such stances can again be differentiated into two kinds, according to Hildebrand: one can love, hate, or admire someone for years and hold these stances in one's "silent and solitary life" (*im stillen Seelenleben*), as Husserl would say. *Or*, these experiences demand to be expressed to their addressees in the sense that they have to be heard in order to be successfully realized (1975a: 27). Hildebrand qualifies the latter kind of stances as "uttered" (*verlautbart*) or "social"; this is a terminology that should be understood in the strict Reinachian sense as describing experiences that are in-need-of-being-heard and that generate social entities.

The way by means of which Hildebrand distils this class of emotions relies on an unprecedented investigation into the phenomenology of emotion (see also Vendrell Ferran's chapter in this volume). He claims that social emotions radically differ from solitary stances and silent acts, as well as from combinations of both. To begin with, social stances are not silent stances (*stille Stellungnahmen*) that are expressed somehow by fortuity. First, *all* stances (not only the social ones) show a natural tendency towards expression (if one is disappointed, one tends to frown). This tendency, however, is spontaneous merely in the sense that it is not conscious or planned. This is why in some cases (e.g., when required by social etiquette), we have to force ourselves to repress our emotional expressions, Hildebrand argues (1975a, 26). Of course, such a tendency may become conscious. But, even in this case, Hildebrand observes, the expression is not intentionally *addressed* to anyone. By contrast, the expression of a social stance does have an addressee (who is at the same time the intentional object of the stance) and requires that the intended addressee apprehend the expression in question—making the expression of the emotion an important part of the entire picture (see section 3).

In addition, social stances are not, properly speaking, social acts, for, as we saw, the intentional correlates of such acts are always states of affairs *that* such-and-such, whereas the object of the social stance is a person (1975a, 25). Nor are they acts in which the subject *communicates* that he or she feels a certain stance. In the latter case, the stance is something that the subject reflectively grasps, conceptualizes, and eventually expresses, whereas social stances are realized and experienced *in the very occurrence* of their expression (1975a, 25). Moreover, such acts of communication can be addressed to anybody, while social stances can only exclusively be addressed to the person to whom they "apply," as it were: of course, I can tell everybody that I love my daughter, but this love can be addressed only to my daughter.

A further salient difference between social stances and social acts concerns the roles their addressees play. As we saw in the case of social acts, the addressee is expected to hear the expressed act and understand its content and type. Things are more complex in the case of social stances, for here the addressee is in a position to produce a gradual response. Hildebrand describes four such kinds of responses (1975a, 28ff., 119ff.). The first is actually not a response at all, for here the stance is simply ignored by the addressee, e.g., because the addressee does not hear, perceive, or understand the uttered stance (this would then be a case of "misunderstanding" in the sense spelled out above, cf. section 1). In a second step, the addressee merely apprehends the stance, i.e., she takes the utterance to be something like a simple act of communication and merely takes note that someone loves or hates her. In principle, nothing differentiates this case from the one in which the addressee apprehends that the subject loves a third person. In the third stage, the addressee is affected by what could be called the "specific quality" (1975a, 29) of the stance, i.e., she is "touched" (*berührt*) by the expressed love or hate in a sense that needs yet to be clarified (cf. the next section). Finally, in the fourth stage, she can also respond to the social stance, i.e., she can reciprocate the love or hate of which she is the target.

By climbing this intersubjective ladder, as it were, the addressor and addressee come gradually closer to each other. In particular, an uttered stance, when it reaches the third level, generates a "rapport" (*Verhältnis*) between the two persons and a "relationship" (*Beziehung*) at the fourth level. For instance, a stance of social *hate*—which reaches the third intersubjective level—substantiates what Hildebrand calls a "rapport" of enmity. Enmity is a social relation in the very sense discussed by Reinach (cf. section 1), for it outlives the act and is an "interpersonal reality" of its own kind (1975a: 109ff.). Still, in contrast to a rapport, a true relationship is a genuine bond or a connection. Such a bond cannot be found in those stances that, in analogy to hate, track a detachment, or disjunction, between persons. Only when love and cognate stances attain the fourth level of reciprocation are they able to produce not only a mere rapport, but a true "relationship" between the two persons involved. In this case, Hildebrand argues, an I-Thou community arises. I-Thou communities are only one of the many different kinds of groups that are described in *Metaphysics of Community* (cf. Salice 2015, for a comparison between I-Thou and other kinds of groups, especially "We-communities").

Moreover, Hildebrand sketches a further distinction between relations of the formal and of the material kind, which overlaps the distinction drawn between rapports and relationships (1975a, 117). Relations of the material kind are all those relations that are generated by social stances in which both addressor and addressee are mutually conceived of as subjects with a personal identity. Reinachian social acts, by contrast, are able to substantiate only *formal* relations, i.e., relations into which only persons qua legal persons enter. It is worth noting that one and the same I-Thou community can instantiate *both* formal and material relations: two lovers, e.g., instantiate a material relationship insofar as they reciprocate one another's love, but they may also instantiate a formal relation if they decide to give formal or legal shape to their relationship by means of a legally relevant social act of marriage.

## 3 TWO APPROACHES TO SOCIAL STANCES

As elegant and insightful as Hildebrand's theory is, it is nevertheless open to certain objections. Hildebrand does not say much about what Reinach metaphorically called the "body" of a social stance. In other words, how should a social stance be externalized in order for it to be apprehended by its addressee? To better understand why this is an important challenge for Hildebrand, it might be helpful to refer to two points mentioned above.

First, the objective correlates of social stances are not states of affairs, but persons. This might generate a potential problem if one takes the body of social stances to be linguistic in nature. Not many possibilities are available if one wants to point at an individual person by means of linguistic expressions. Pronouns, proper names, or definite descriptions almost exhaust the syntactic options provided by natural languages. However, it seems obvious, that—whatever form social stances can assume in order to be apprehended by their addresses—this cannot be a mere list of pronouns, proper names, or definite descriptions. There must be something more than that.

This problem is made even more virulent by a further problem in Hildebrand's theory. What a social stance aims at is not simply to make the addressee aware of the fact that he or she is the target of a particular intentional attitude of the subject, nor is it to simply inform the addressee about the kind of attitude she is the target of (i.e., inform her about the fact that she, e.g., is loved). Rather, its aim is to reach at least the third stage in the interaction illustrated above and hence to let the addressee *feel* the qualitative shape of the stance itself. It is not entirely clear what Hildebrand means by that, but one possibility is to interpret his idea by introducing the notion of empathy, as this was much discussed by phenomenologists at that time. Of the many phenomenological accounts (cf. Zahavi 2010), Scheler's conception of "vicarious feeling" (*Nachfühlen*) seems to play an important role here (on Scheler, cf. also Szanto's chapter in this volume).

According to Scheler, there are many ways in which one can come to know the mental state of others: in addition to understanding (*Verstehen*), which he seems to conceive of as understanding linguistic acts of communication (1973, 220; 1955, 280), he points out that a subject also has the possibility to activate *Nachfühlen* in order to grasp the other's mental state. Nowhere does he adequately describe what he means by vicarious feeling, but, in one passage (cf. Scheler 1973, 20), he recurs to an analogy that is quite illuminating (and particularly relevant because it partially converges with the few observations that Reinach makes about empathy): there, Scheler aligns *Nachfühlen* to cases of presentifications or *Vergegenwärtigungen* (Reinach seems to agree that the other's mental state can be grasped by means of presentification, although he also argues for the "symbolic self-givenness" (*symbolische Selbsterscheinung*) of the other's mental state, cf. 1913b, 390f—and similarly so, Scheler 1973, 254). If, for instance, one once saw a landscape and now one is making it present to one's consciousness, then, in a certain sense, one has the landscape intuitively in front of oneself—although one is neither *perceiving* nor *remembering* it in the proper sense of the term (as insofar perception concerns the self-given thing and remembering concerns the state of affairs *that* the landscape was seen). Similarly, one can vicariously feel what someone else is feeling by presentifying it—however, this does not yet mean that one is feeling what the other is feeling, but only that one is making it *intuitively* and *directly* present to one's mind.

Scheler's idea of *Nachfühlen* seems to be compatible with the account of social stances proposed by Hildebrand: accordingly, when we address someone via our social stances, we want to "touch" the addressee in the sense that we intend to provoke, in him or her, an act of vicarious feeling, which, in turn, is directed towards our own stance. In other words, we want the addressee to come to "hear" our stance. But, again, how is that possible? How can we externalize an emotion so as to induce an empathic act in our addressee, and to the effect that the addressee feels touched by our own emotion?

By way of conclusion, I shall advance two suggestions. The first maintains that the body of such social stances is linguistic in nature, whereas the second denies that. I take the first option to be viable, but restricted to a limited number of cases. The latter option, I assume, tracks a more fundamental phenomenon, but is not uncontroversial.

The first option would be to recur to Gricean "implicatures." Remember that Hildebrand explicitly states that social stances are *not* social acts of communication, for these are about states of affairs (and, specifically, about the state of affairs *that* the subject feels a certain stance towards the addressee). But are there other linguistic means that enable the subject to inform the addressee about the stance without explicitly mentioning *that* he or she is feeling that stance? Suppose that, in order to express my love to you, I resort to cheap talk, or a cliché like, "You are my sun." Taken literally, this sentence is blatantly false. However, there can be no doubt that what I want to express by means of such a sentence is not a mere falsity. Indeed, I, the speaker, am implying that I love you. Of course, this has not been said literally and yet, thanks to the fact that one of the many other aspects of communication can be described as a form of collective and cooperative endeavor that is governed by a set of rational rules (cf. Grice 1989), the speaker can, based on these rules, assume that the hearer takes the sentence to be a contribution to the conversation—and this despite the sentence's manifest falsity. In this way, the hearer might grasp the feeling the speaker intends to express by means of an inference and, eventually, be touched by the expressed stance.

It seems to me that two problems are related to this option: first, in line with Hildebrand, one could still object that what the speaker is doing is to call the hearer's attention to a state of affairs (to the one, namely, that the speaker feels a certain emotion), not to an emotion. The second problem, to put it bluntly, is that not everyone is a poet, let alone a good poet. More precisely, this option requires that the two speakers possess a fairly developed pragmatic competence to communicate. This might be the case in some speech situations, but not in all communicative contexts. Because it is so demanding in terms of linguistic and social expertise, this first approach to the problem of how social stances can be expressed in order to aptly "touch" the addressee appears to be viable, but limited in its scope.

According to the second option, there are some non-linguistic actions that are intrinsically social, that is, actions that *intrinsically* express a stance that strives to be apprehended by its addressee. What might these actions be? Some good candidates include: to caress someone, to smile at someone, to kiss someone, to slap someone across the cheek, to violate someone,[5] to look at someone in one of the thousand different ways we do, etc. Since, I would surmise, these actions are intrinsically social, introducing such kinds of social actions could prove to be a more promising solution to Hildebrand's problem.

However, there is a possible objection to this second approach: imagine someone sees you smiling and comes to believe that you are smiling at him. Accordingly, he may believe you want to express some emotion you feel towards him. In reality, however, you are not at all smiling at him, but you are smiling simply because you are thinking of something pleasant. Obviously, from an external point of view, there is nothing here that enables one to discriminate the "social" smile from the non-social one, and this observation could easily be employed to jeopardize the very idea of non-linguistic, but yet intrinsically social, actions. This notwithstanding, the claim that these actions (although indistinguishable from an external perspective) belong to two completely different types still has credibility, or so I contend.

But how can this claim be squared with the above objection? Compare the scenario just discussed with the one in which one takes whales to be fishes or slow worms to be snakes. At first glance, whales look like fishes and slow worms like snakes. Similarly, the expression of a non-social stance can be equated with the expression of a social stance. Still, if one takes the time to observe whales or slow worms more closely, then one shall be able to recognize that whales are mammals, and hence not fishes, and that slow worms are lizards, and hence not snakes. This, I would suggest, is also what happens in the social world (note that this idea makes my proposal committed to a form of disjunctivism in relation to behavior: although two behaviors might be indistinguishable from an external perspective, they are expressions of two distinct kinds of mental states (cf. Overgaard 2012)). In order to discriminate between different kinds of stances and their expressions, the addressee has to rely on relevant knowledge about the addressor. But, how much knowledge has to be presupposed? Well, it depends. In some cases, one might need years to ascertain the true intention of the addressor, but, in others, simple eye contact might well suffice—as some lovers will surely confirm.[6]

## NOTES

1. In the following, I leave out the German aristocratic 'von' prefixed to his name, which Hildebrand did not employ when referring to himself (cf. Schuhmann 1992 n. 1).
2. Besides the reasons of a more systematic nature to be addressed in the present chapter, there are also cogent historical reasons to proceed in this way: Hildebrand always referred to Reinach as his only teacher in Göttingen (Reinach was "mein einziger Lehrer," cf. Hildebrand 1975b: 78). For other aspects that these two phenomenologists have in common, see Salice (2015) and Salice (forthcoming).
3. But what about self-forgiveness? Reinach does not address this issue, but one could perhaps try to defend his claim about the hetero-directedness of this experience by arguing that, in these cases, the self that is forgiven is a past self—and hence not identical with the forgiving self. At the cost of introducing an, at least to a certain extent, artificial distinction, one might be able to preserve hetero-directedness. To illustrate the peculiarity of this scenario, however, just note its difference from cases of narcissistic self-love, in which lover and loved can strictly coincide (without artificiality of any sort).
4. There can be no doubt, I believe, about the Platonic inspiration that informs certain insights of early phenomenology, and the value realism advocated by Hildebrand is a domain where the presence of Platonism is particularly appreciable. However, if that is the case, then Hildebrand's theory about romantic love would have to be confronted with the same objection that Plato was charged with (cf. Vlastos 1973: 28ff.): if love is a value-tracking attitude in the sense that it responds to the values of a person, then the genuine correlate of love (the entity that is authentically loved) is the value itself, and the individual person is considered in the attitude's intentional horizon only in virtue of the fact that one of her properties is the tracked value. Hildebrand, however, finds suitable ammunition to counter this objection in Husserl's theory of predication. According to Husserl, properties are *not* genuine parts of the object that exemplifies them; what rather inheres in the object is a *moment*, i.e., an individualized property (cf. Hua 18, A 129/B 129). Analogously, in the case of values, the good is a property and, as such, it is fully detached from (viz., is not a part of) good things. What makes a thing good, rather, is the particular nuance of good that only that individual thing can have. As a consequence, romantic love can be seen as directed towards an individual person qua bearer of a certain (set of) value(s): the person is loved in virtue of the fact that she can exemplify such a (set of) value(s) in that particular, fully individual, and non-replicable way.
5. For a phenomenological account of acts of violence that stresses their social, intersubjective dimension, cf. Salice 2014.
6. The author's work on this chapter has been supported by a fellowship of the Fritz Thyssen Foundation (Az. 10.13.1.015).

## REFERENCES

Austin, John L. (1962). *How To Do Things With Words. The William James Lectures Delivered at Harvard in 1955*. Ed. by J.O. Urmson. Oxford: Oxford University Press.

Grice, Paul (1989). *Studies in the Way of Words*. Cambridge: Harvard University Press.

Helm, Bennett W. (2008). "Plural Agents." *Noûs* 42 (1), 17–49.
—— (2009). "Love, Identification, and the Emotions." *American Philosophical Quarterly* 46 (1), 39–59.
Husserl, Edmund (1975) [=Hua 18]. *Logische Untersuchungen. Erster Band. Prolegomena zur reinen Logik* (1900, 1913). Ed. by E. Holenstein. The Hague: Nijhoff.
—— (1984) [=Hua 19/1, 2]. *Logische Untersuchungen. Zweiter Band. Untersuchungen zur Phänomenologie und Theorie der Erkenntnis* (1901, 1913/1921). Ed. by U. Panzer. The Hague: Nijhoff.
Mulligan, Kevin (2010). "Husserls Herz." In: M. Frank, N. Weidtmann (Eds.). *Husserl und die Philosophie des Geistes*. Frankfurt a.M.: Suhrkamp, 209–238.
Nozick, Robert (1989). *The Examined Life*. New York: Simon & Schuster.
Overgaard, Søren (2012). "Other Minds." In: D. Zahavi (Ed.). *The Oxford Handbook of Contemporary Phenomenology*. Oxford: Oxford University Press.
Reinach, Adolf (1989a) [1911]. "Zur Theorie des negativen Urteils." In: K. Schuhmann & B. Smith (Eds.). *Sämtliche Werke. Textkritische Ausgabe*. 2 Vols. Munich: Philosophia Verlag, 95–140.
—— (1989b) [1913]. "Die apriorischen Grundlagen des bürgerlichen Rechtes." In: K. Schuhmann, & B. Smith (Eds.). *Sämtliche Werke. Textkritische Ausgabe*. 2 Vols. Munich: Philosophia Verlag, 141–278. [Engl. trans. by J. Crosby (1983). "The a priori Foundations of the Civil Law." *Aletheia. An International Journal of Philosophy* III, 2–142.]
—— (1989c) [1913]. "Einleitung in die Philosophie." In: K. Schuhmann, and B. Smith (Eds.) (1989). *Sämtliche Werke. Textkritische Ausgabe*. 2 Vols. Munich: Philosophia Verlag, 369–514.
Salice, Alessandro (2008). "Obbligazione e Pretesa: Due Relazioni Sociali." *Rivista di Estetica* 39 (3), 225–240.
—— (2014). "Violence as a Social Fact." *Phenomenology and the Cognitive Sciences* 13, 161–177.
—— (2015). "Communities and Values. Dietrich von Hildebrand's Social Ontology." In: A. Salice, & H. B. Schmid (Eds.). *Social Reality: The Phenomenological Approach*. Dordrecht: Springer.
—— (Forthcoming). "Actions, Values and States of Affairs." *Studia Phaenomenologica*.
Scheler, Max (1955). "Die Idole der Selbsterkenntnis [1915]." In: M. Scheler (Ed.). *Vom Umsturz der Werte. Max Scheler Gesammelte Werke*, Vol. 3. Bern: Francke, 213–292.
—— (1973). "Wesen und Formen der Sympathie [1912]." In: M. S. Frings (Ed.). *Max Scheler Gesammelte Werke*, vol. 7. Bern: Francke.
Schuhmann, Karl (1992). "Husserl und Hildebrand." *Aletheia* V, 6–33.
Searle, John (1969). *Speech Acts. An Essay in the Philosophy of Language*. Cambridge: Cambridge University Press.
Szanto, Thomas (in this volume). "Collectivizing Persons and Personifying Collectives: Reassessing Scheler on Group Personhood." In: T. Szanto, & D. Moran (Eds.). *The Phenomenology of Sociality: Discovering the 'We'*. London/New York: Routledge.
Velleman, David (1999). "Love as a Moral Emotion." *Ethics* 109, 338–74.
Vendrell Ferran, Ingrid (2008). *Die Emotionen. Gefühle in der realistischen Phänomenologie*. Berlin: Akademie Verlag.
Vlastos, Gregory (1973). *Platonic Studies*. Princeton: Princeton University Press.
von Hildebrand, Dietrich (1916). "Die Idee der sittlichen Handlung." *Jahrbuch für Philosophie und Phänomenologische Forschung* 3, 126–252.
—— (1922). "Sittlichkeit und ethische Werterkenntnis." *Jahrbuch für Philosophie und Phänomenologische Forschung* 5, 426–602.

―― (1975a). "Metaphysik der Gemeinschaft, Untersuchungen über Wesen und Wert der Gemeinschaft [1930]." In: Dietrich von Hildebrand Gesellschaft (Ed.). *Dietrich von Hildebrand Gesammelte Werke*. Vol. IV. Stuttgart: Kohlhammer.

―― (1975b). "Dietrich von Hildebrand." In: L. Pongratz (Ed.). *Philosophie in Selbstdarstellungen*. Hamburg: Meiner, 77–127.

Zahavi, Dan (2010). "Empathy, Embodiment and Interpersonal Understanding: From Lipps to Schutz." *Inquiry* 53 (3), 285–306.

# 15 Gurwitsch and the Role of Emotion in Collective Intentionality

*Eric Chelstrom*

> "Ces grandes et éclatantes actions qui éblouissent les yeux sont représentées par les politiques comme les effets des grands desseins; au lieu que ce sont d'ordinaire les effets de l'humeur et des passions."
>
> (La Rochefoucauld, *Maximes* V:7)

## INTRODUCTION

Recently, a number of authors have voiced concerns about the absence of emotions in the dominant collective intentionality literature. For example, reviews of Michael Bratman's (2014) and Margaret Gilbert's (2014a) recent publications on collective intentionality expressed shared concerns about their respective works. Raimo Tuomela (2014) finds the absence of emotion in Bratman's view problematic. Seumas Miller (2014) argues the same is a problem for Gilbert's view. Since Bratman and Gilbert are two of the major voices in contemporary collective intentionality debates, this represents a broader concern with the current state of those debates. Aron Gurwitsch's contributions to social theory in the early 20th century offer important insights into emotion's place in collective intentions. The primary focus of this chapter will be affect's role in collective intentions. While most of the discussion centers around emotion in particular, other forms of affect should be considered by extension, e.g., mood, temperament, sensations of pain or pleasure. Gurwitsch holds that affect plays a constitutive role in at least some forms of collective intentions. Arguments supporting Gurwitsch's stance have implications indicative of the stronger conclusion that affect always plays a constitutive role in collective intentions. This is in stark contrast to the limited, essentially reactionary role that emotions and affect play in the works of Bratman and Gilbert.[1]

This chapter first summarizes Gurwitsch's view, beginning with the three forms of sociality found in Gurwitsch's early statement of his view in *Human Encounters in the Social World* (Gurwitsch 1979). Next, the chapter examines Gurwitsch's later amendment to his view, arguing that Gurwitsch makes important changes to his position. Following this, the chapter explores the broader implications of Gurwitsch's work. It will also be shown that Gurwitsch's view is supported by trends in contemporary interdisciplinary research.

Call the type of position found in Bratman and Gilbert intellectualism about collective intentions. The exclusion or relegation of emotion to a reactive, as opposed to a constitutive, function in forming social bonds is what I shall call the intellectualist bias. By social bond, I refer to that which enables the togetherness of a 'We' moment in experience. Collective action is dependent on social bonds, but does not exhaust the domain of experiences where social bonds are manifested. By contrast with intellectualism, early phenomenologists understood affect's constitutive role in social life (cf. Vendrell Ferran and Salice in this volume). For instance, Max Scheler, who influenced Gurwitsch, argued that there are no perceptions prior to valuations and that all valuations involve affective responses to the objects, events, and states of affairs one experiences. Scheler called this valuception (*Wertnehmen*). Martin Heidegger's inclusion of affect, especially moods, in how a subject finds herself in the world and how her experience is constituted represents another key influence on Gurwitsch.

## 1 GURWITSCH

In *Human Encounters*, Gurwitsch identifies three modes of Being-with: partnership, membership, and fusion. Partnerships are where one shares a situation with another and, by virtue of that situation, one embodies a role determined through how that situation is shaped, principally by the purpose(s) operative within it. Memberships are where one's background contexts and ways of orienting oneself and ascribing value is shared with others, communities also ground shared forms of affect or sentiment; the community(ies) of one's birth on some level(s) are instances of memberships. Fusion is where individuals come together "as one" with others, where a deep sense of identification permeates the relation. These are not just common situations or common sentiments acting as unifiers between subjects, but where one's very sense of self and world understanding "fuses" with another's.

Partnerships consist of being together in a common situation. Gurwitsch's example is that of two workers cobbling a street together: one laying stones, the other knocking them into place (Gurwitsch 1979, 104). The other worker in a situation of this sort is part of what makes this situation what it is: they play a constitutive role in our cobbling the street together. Gurwitsch states, "[T]he other also belongs to the situation in which I stand; his presence also contributes to the constituting of the situation and to making it what it is *in concreto*" (104). Our cobbling the street together not only gives meaning to and informs what we are doing; it also serves to give meaning to each individual's role in virtue of the situational context. My laying stones as part of cobbling the street is informed by your knocking them into place. I cannot simply start laying bricks however I please; I must do so in a manner informed by your actions and vice versa. The orientation adopted in partnerships, wherein one orients oneself according to how one anticipates the other will act, is only present in cases of partnership and not in memberships or fusion (105).

Partnerships are also present where we work contrary to one another within the framework of a shared end, for example, competing in a game. I select my move in chess based on how I believe my opponent will respond, and so too in their cases. In partnerships, our relations to one another are *founded* in that relation and involve prescriptions of *roles* to be filled by individuals in relation to the prescriptive nature of our situational context (109). Partnerships presuppose the essential asymmetry of different streams of consciousness. Even though partnerships are mediated by socially determined roles, the question of the other's aptitude as a role player determines one's actions. For instance, a new trainee as a barista partner during the morning rush requires a different set of responses from the veteran barista than would a more seasoned partner. It's not enough that we each intend a situation or larger action in common; we must also be responsive to one another's actions within the structure of the situation we find ourselves in. Partnership involves having some purpose(s) in common that informs and contributes to the constitution of the plurality and through which individual roles can be determined.

Individuals form partnerships. And it is the individual who is primary in this form of sociality (118). If one partner refuses to accept a role or situation, then there is no partnership. There is no 'We' in partnerships unless each of us acts as if there is a 'We'. Partnerships are also temporally limited, having definite beginnings and endings. One's responsiveness to our actions within our collective activity does not persist indefinitely. Per Gurwitsch, the *role* of the coworker begins and ends with the workday (116f.). One might argue that the coworker role can extend beyond the confines of the workplace. One can work from home, go to work retreats, or socialize *as* coworkers. Of course, the role of coworker determines the norms of our socializations, norms that may not apply in socializing with non-coworkers.[2]

Gurwitsch distinguishes between two different ways of being together: society and community. Being in society with others refers to cool, distanced, loose forms of being-together. By community, Gurwitsch understands a societal relation grounded in "a more comprehensive life context," whose basis rests in *"communal possession"*—principally a shared sense of place, though also involving a shared sense of history (122–123, 126–127). Memberships are predicated on community, while partnerships only require society. Gurwtisch rejects Gerda Walther's (Walther 1923) position that community with others involves an intimacy of connection, founded upon some shared positive sentiment, requiring a sense of "inner unity" or "inner inseparability," which is not necessary for being in society with others (120). Instead, "feeling is grounded in the community" (133), it is determined by one's shared concrete situation, the common orientation towards life. Hence communities are not necessarily dissolved solely on the basis of conflicts and rivalries within them (122). Further, they are not easily formed or dissolved, given that they are grounded in shared significations of place and history. Communities are not merely instrumental or material alignments of interests, but rather exhibit motivational structures of shared relevance in need of "implicit or explicit agreement" (119). Since memberships are grounded in "a comprehensive life-context" (121) they are not as easily formed or dissolved as partnerships.[3]

While one can freely enter into and dissolve partnerships, this is not so with memberships. "*In advance, a human being is not solus ipse; insofar as he is communalized and historicalized, he always already belongs to other human beings [. . .]*" (127). As social beings, humans always find themselves in an intersubjectively constituted world of meanings. One is enculturated to a worldview, a set of norms, a linguistic dialect, etc. In this sense, the community has a certain priority over the individuals, as it offers means by which one navigates the world one finds oneself in. Community establishes and informs how *we* experience and interpret the world. Thus, being in community with others is not a mere "*being together of individuals as individuals*," as with partnerships (130). Co-members of a community do not need to be aware of all other specific *individuals* with whom they stand in this relation. Community forms a *common ground* or *common basis* in reference to which our lives take shape. Where partnerships are established in relation to our respective roles together, memberships determine our basic way(s) of orienting ourselves in the world. Partnerships dictate *what* we do relative to a situation; memberships dictate *how* we orient ourselves in the world. Where partnerships are purpose oriented, memberships are context determinative or context structuring.

This isn't to say that all aspects of one's life are under the control of a community, as Gurwitsch's language might seem to suggest. Individuality is still preserved:

> [. . .] there remains to the member of the community a private sphere, i.e., a realm of life and action with respect to which the member does not grow older with others and for which, as a consequence, no regulations based on the life of the community even exist. . . . in this realm he is free from the community. (131)

As such, there is no problem in there being divisions within a community. One can say that communities offer symmetry in comportment, without interfering with the essential asymmetry of individuals' conscious lives. I am never you, regardless of how we share a way(s) of finding ourselves in the world. Consistent with Scheler, the integrity of the individual person is preserved, even where one is a member of a *Gesamtperson* or *Lebensgemeinschaft* (cf. Szanto in this volume).

The final form of being with that Gurwitsch discusses is fusion. With fusion, unlike for memberships, individual differences are "cancelled out" (131). Fusion involves a state in which emotional bonds or feelings bear a constitutive meaning, "[. . .] *feeling as 'one' and identification*" (139). Further, "[f]eelings of being united as 'one' have a meaning for the constitution of groups as well as for the actual being together of the members of the group" (141). And "the feeling united as 'one' with the 'spirit' is constitutive for being together in the group by which one is united as 'one' with another" (142). Gurwitsch gives the example that churches function as communities, whereas cults—like in the Jonestown massacre—operate as groups in the specific sense in which he uses the term here. Fusion is not just meaning bestowing, as memberships are, it is "world-making," transformative, and revolutionary (150).

Fusion is not necessarily pejorative. It identifies also romantic marriages and Aristotle's genuine friendships.[4] Fusion involves an intimacy between subjects, a symmetry between their lives far greater than that found in memberships or partnerships. For instance, regarding marriage, Gilbert writes, "The term 'fusion' may be an apt label for certain problematic forms of marital relationships. At the same time, many people have obviously thought that something aptly referred to as 'fusion' has the capacity to strongly enhance a marriage" (Gilbert 1996, 216).[5] Both marriages of this sort and friendships of the Aristotelian form involve unity of individuals through mutually reciprocated good will, which is itself an affective state; one that unifies individuals together with a strong bond, enhancing the individual's lives without effacing their individuality. The intimacy of fusion, at best, forms a deep symmetry between two individuals without effacing individuality, whereas the problematic forms undermine one's autonomy and individuality by exploiting the intimacy of one's relation.

In his later work, following *Human Encounters*, Gurwitsch did not engage in discussions of collective intentionality. Some of this may have been deferential to Schütz, with whom he corresponded on these and other matters (Schütz & Gurwitsch 1989). Interestingly, when he returns to collective intentionality, he appears to have modified his position. In "The Common Sense World as Social Reality and the Theory of Social Science," citing Schütz, Gurwitsch only acknowledges two forms of sociality. Gurwitsch argues that what he now terms "consociate" relationships[6] are fundamentally distinct from other forms of relationships. Consociate relations are face-to-face relationships. They are unique in that each individual-to-individual relation involves two individuals and their respective biographical situations, and that subjects "share a 'vivid present'" with one another (Gurwitsch 1974, 125). All other forms of relationships with others are mediated by socially realized typifications—expectations, anticipations, prescriptions, etc. Typifications are not formed solely subjectively, but are shaped in and through a subject's interactions with the world and others. Roles, as those present in partnerships, are instances of intersubjectively constituted typifications.

Gurwitsch argues that experiences with others mediated through intersubjectively constituted typifications are always to some degree "anonymous." He offers the following helpful example: "When I write a letter to my absent friend and submit a proposal to him, I must typify what I know about him and form some idea of his likely reaction, in order to formulate my proposal in terms acceptable to him. These typifications admit of varying degrees of anonymity" (125). When anonymity is complete, individuals in typified interactions become "interchangeable" (125). For instance, if one orders something on Amazon, one expects that the workers—whoever they might be—associated with and responsible for handling my order will do so in good faith. One's interaction is not with a particular person, nor does one intend any particular person while ordering through Amazon. Nonetheless, one has expectations about how the exchange will be conducted and that people at Amazon will play their parts in fulfilling one's order.

There are two factors in Gurwitsch's essay that suggest that a significant modification of Gurwitsch's view happened since *Human Encounters*. First, Gurwitsch argues that disinterested interactions are fundamentally non-social (126). This could be read as contrary to how one could interpret some partnerships and memberships in *Human Encounters*, e.g., the partnership relations of coworkers in a large institutional setting. Gurwitsch argues that the type of understanding that is necessary for social action is not one of disinterestedness, but rather, "the form of understanding prevailing in the actual practice of social life, without which no cooperation or social interaction would be possible" (126). I act in relation to others with an "in-order-to motive" that aims to become the other's "because motive." As Gurwitsch writes:

> All social interaction is based on the unformulated assumption that I stand a chance of attaining my objectives provided I act in a typical and socially approved way—as assumption implying the equally unformulated expectancy that my more or less anonymous partners will also conduct themselves in accordance with the requirements of the roles assigned to them.
>
> (Gurwitsch 1974, 126)

This is not to claim that all social interactions are self-interested. It is only to claim that we are engaged in the actions, as Gurwitsch is clear to stress this state of engagement is distinguished from that of the disinterested observer or social theorist (120). The nature of one's engagement is dependent on one's biographical situation, through which one's "*subjektiver*" or "*gemeinter Sinn*" is formulated (122). Since others are other than oneself, they do not necessarily share my interpretations or meanings. As such, a condition for success in achieving one's purpose in interaction with others requires acting towards establishing common meanings.

Second, Gurwitsch emphasizes the necessity of empathy in social interactions. Empathy is necessary because one must form some idea about what *my* objective means to the other in order to garner her cooperation or other form of response (127). In order to have any success in coordinating our actions together, each of us must project what the other has in mind, and how they not only understand one's objective, but also as to how they feel about it. I cannot get your cooperation on something simply by having you understand what I propose. In order to garner your cooperation, I must also appeal to your sentiments. Consider, first, that if I attempt to garner your cooperation by being a jerk, no matter the understanding you have of my meaning, I'm not likely to get you to cooperate unless I have some power over you that otherwise compels you. But then it is that power dynamic that is compelling you, not your understanding of my meaning.[7] Second, if I appeal to your sentiments and offer no understanding, you are also unlikely to cooperate. You may be sympathetic with what you can understand about my meaning, but unable to interpret it clearly enough to warrant action. Or, alternatively, there are cases where one feels a desire to cooperate, but understands that doing so would be inappropriate. Consider, thirdly, the well-documented awkwardness of those with an empathy deficit, as presented in those on the autism spectrum. The deficit there is not a lack of sentiment nor understanding, but a breakdown in their recognition of socially normative types.[8] Given empathy's role, reciprocity is necessary in all social interactions (Gurwitsch 1974, 127). We must agree on our respective meanings in order to be functioning together. The asymmetry inherent in our respective streams of consciousness must be brought to some agreement, in order to cooperate. That agreement requires some symmetry between our projections, at least as to the general nature of our shared endeavor. The specific nature of our shared projections depends on a multitude of factors, of which one's affective states, emotions included, are part.

## 2  IMPLICATIONS FOR CONTEMPORARY DEBATES

One could reasonably challenge how any of this differs from Bratman's or Gilbert's views on collective intentionality. Both are aware of the need for individuals to be in relations like that which Gurwitsch argues for. One may respond that while the general structure of a collective intention is more or less the same, Bratman and Gilbert are missing recognition of the affective component of this structure. Empathy, typically, is not dispassionate. The constitution of the other in experience is permeated with emotion and affect (Stein 1989, especially Ch. IV, §3).

The view that emotion is inherently something reactive, even if having some intuitive draw, is mistaken. Such a claim assumes that emotions result only from stimuli that provoke them. The intellectualist believes that emotions simply happen to us, perhaps even in spite of us. Against this, Evan Thompson argues, "Emotion is not a function in the input-output sense, but rather a feature of the action-perception cycle—namely, the endogenous initiation and direction of behavior outward in the world" (2007, 365). Emotion is a whole-organism event (363). Neurologically speaking, emotions are part of the feedback loops inherent in neural architecture:

> Cognition and emotion are not separate systems, for two reasons. First, there is a large amount of anatomical overlap between the neural systems mediating cognition and emotion processes, and these systems interact with each other in a reciprocal and circular fashion, up and down the neuraxis. Second, the emergent global states to which these interactions give rise are 'appraisal-emotion amalgams,' in which appraisal elements and emotion elements modify each other continuously.
> (Thompson 2007, 371)

Phenomenologically, this tracks with Husserl's descriptions of affect. Thompson reminds us that Husserl:

> describes experience as subject to 'affective force.' Affective force manifests as a rapid, dynamic transformation of experience, mobilizing one's entire lived body. The transformation is one in the 'vivacity of consciousness' or the 'varying vivacity of a lived-experience.'
> (Thompson 2007, 377)[9]

As such, one would better understand emotion to be an ever-present feature of experience. Intellectualism assumes either that an emotion-free state is one's default or that it is one's normatively preferable state. However, such a state is not even physically possible. Moreover, Thompson argues that our ability to have projects at all is dependent on emotion. "Emotion is integral to protention, for protention always involves motivation, and affective tone, and an action tendency or readiness for action" (361).

But why would this mean that emotion plays a constitutive role in forming social bonds? And why think it must be part of all social bonds? As to the first question, one should begin by referring to empathy. Again, Gurwitsch argues that empathy is necessary for all collective intentions, insofar as success in fulfilling one's collective intention requires understanding how the other takes one's meaning and modifying one's projection of meaning to be appreciable to the other. Empathy involves an emotionally constituted judgment. If empathy is itself constituted with affect, then collective intentional judgments would necessitate affect as well.

Another way to appreciate this is to examine the nature of trust. Without trust, there are no collectively pursued actions, i.e., no successful collective intentions for action.[10] The other's intentions are only ever known indicatively, through their words, actions, gestures, etc. One can never have apodictic evidence in the case of the other's thoughts, only adequate evidence (cf. Hua 1, §§ 50–54, Jacob 2011). Because we are separate subjects, because our conscious lives are essentially asymmetrical, trust is something that is built up and modified through experience. Typification is one way in which we institutionalize trust in certain actions being done in certain ways. I trust you since you are in a barista's apron, further trusting that you will make my espresso. I need not know you personally, I need only recognize what signifies your role, and that persons in your role are reliable in fulfilling the actions expected in that role. As Carolyn McLeod (2011) notes, trust also appears to have many of the hallmarks of an emotion, especially insofar as it affects our attention. Karen Jones (1998) has also argued that trust is a "distinctive, and affectively loaded, way of seeing the one trusted" (4). Perhaps Jones's most telling reasons are that distrust, trust's contrary, is clearly constituted with emotive content, and that trust in oneself refers to something similar, to having confidence and optimism about one's self and one's abilities in a given context (7f.). Further, she offers a discussion of why trust and distrust are not primarily beliefs (22ff.). Where Jones argues that trust's affective component is supplemented by an expectation structure (8), the present account argues that expectation is itself constituted in relation to affect and that it is not a feature unique to trust. If I do not feel that a given type is trustworthy, I will overlook that possibility in experience. If I have regularly received poor service or poor-quality drinks at a given coffee shop, my feeling of distrust about their abilities will lead me to discount them as a possibility for where to procure coffee. If a coffee shop is regularly too distracting, I will not feel it is a place conducive to getting work done. It is my affect—my feeling of confidence in the abilities or competence of others or a given environment—that affects the choices I attend to in experience.

Must all social bonds be constituted with emotional content? It is not unreasonable that one might answer in the negative. That is because there is something that appears to be correct in the analyses of Bratman, Gilbert, and others. They capture well partnerships, the type of relation that is most common to our everyday world of instrumental concerns. One need not feel anything in particular about one's coworkers. However, social relations are not limited to partnerships. For instance, it seems entirely wrong to conceive of a friendship as something based on a contractual model or as a series of cognitive judgments about our mutual interests, meshing subplans (Bratman 2014), or joint commitments (Gilbert 2014a). While those might be present in friendships, a friendship requires also some shared, positive emotional content. Shared, positive emotional content is the basis for friendships. For Aristotle, that would mean mutually reciprocated goodwill, and one observes, more generally, that there must be symmetry in the type of affection the two friends have for one another. Friendships require trust. And if trust is an emotionally constituted judgment, then friendships cannot be accounted for on the basis of an intellectualist position insofar as the intellectualist holds that emotions are only ever reactive and not constitutive of social bonds. Friendships are a counterexample, since emotion serves a constitutive role in said bond. Nor can parent-child relations, or any other relationship that is based on love.[11] Love is the ground for some

## Gurwitsch and the Role of Emotion in Collective Intentionality   257

relationships, not something incidental to them, nor the shared project, end, or result (cf. Salice in this volume). Unfortunately, mutual hatred or dislike can also serve as a basis for social bonds, as in the case of hate groups. Affect is required for constituting the experiential ground of a common situation, a basic bond of togetherness in experience that is also necessary for collective actions (cf. Schmid 2013).

Let us return to Gurwitsch to explore how a problem with his earlier view may have motivated his shift between *Human Encounters* and "The Common Sense World." This will add further clarity in contrasting Gurwitsch with Bratman and Gilbert. In his descriptions of fusion, Gurwitsch is explicit about emotion's constitutive function. In fusion, that foundation of a strong emotional bond, the feeling of oneness with the other, is a necessary condition. In membership, Gurwitsch asserts a foundational role of positive affect or positive sentiment. However, in *Human Encounters*, in the case of partnerships, affect seems not to constitute the relation. This is not to claim that there is no affect in partnerships, only that affect does not contribute to constituting a partnership. One need not feel any particular way or have any emotion at all towards some role players in one's life, as encounters with bureaucracies can remind us.

A problem arises for Gurwitsch's early account of partnerships if one examines one of his own examples more closely. Roles themselves, those products of typification that guide the majority of our interactions with others, have affective contents, expectations, etc. (e.g., the expectation that interactions will generally be civil or friendly, that one will not be treated with indifference). Affective contents themselves are not necessarily a problem. If roles are typified according to shared affective commitments, that would force a reconsideration of his early view. Consider how individuals in a xenophobic society will experience fear or disgust as part of the experience of any stranger and will do so on the basis of affective commitments. Us-vs.-them- based formulations of role prescriptions and social norms seem to be mostly, if not entirely, constituted by affective stances. Early on, Gurwitsch held that this is a byproduct of one's membership relations, part of one's community's way of life. If the affect is constitutive in establishing the role itself, that suggests affect's capacity to play some role in constituting partnerships more generally. It is reasonable to think that Gurwitsch may have concluded that all social interactions are "interested," i.e., have emotionally or affectively constituted contents.

While reading Bratman as relegating emotion to a reactive, not a constitutive, role, is not particularly controversial, one might object that Gilbert's view is more nuanced. Gilbert offers an analysis of collective guilt and advocates the possibility of collective emotions (Gilbert 2014a, chap. 10, 2014b). However, her concern is only with emotions expressed by or had by collectives, and even then, they are treated as having a reactionary role. Gilbert's contention in those arguments is only that one can reasonably refer to an emotion as that of a collective, e.g., German guilt over the Holocaust. Yet, when it comes to collective intentions themselves, she is perhaps the most direct: "A joint commitment is not a matter of feeling or emotion, and its positive effects are by no means limited to emotional ones—important as these are" (Gilbert 1996, 18f.). And since joint commitments are the foundations of the social world for Gilbert, that implies that emotions are not foundational to the social world for her view.

A strong interpretation of Gilbert's claim would assert that emotions play no role whatsoever in collective intentions, reading the second clause of her claim as limiting emotions to effects of joint commitments. Such a view is consistent with being a cognitivist about emotions, where one believes emotions are judgments formed in response to worldly events. In such a view, emotions cannot play a role in constituting collective intentions. At best, emotions may only be formed in response to collective endeavors (cf. Gilbert 2000, 139, fn. 5). Contrary to the strong interpretation, one need only show that emotions can play a role in decisions, collective decisions included. In this vein, Jesse Prinz argues, "Emotions contribute to our reasoning, action, and the election of ends. They are triggered by judgments and amenable to cultural influence. They are central to our comprehension of morality and other lofty domains" (Prinz 2004, viii). For example, our fear plays an important role in motivating not only the fact of our flight from something threatening, but also the means according to which we respond.

A weak interpretation of Gilbert's claim would allow that emotions do play some role; however, joint commitments themselves are not so constituted.[12] This is more plausible, and is also consistent with Bratman's view. In this view, emotion may play a motivating role, but the collective intention itself has no emotional content. Instead, one would have emotion bracketed in cases where the actual decisions about collective actions arise. Do we have reason to believe even this weaker claim? I think not. The claim depends on the modern assumption that emotions are inherently irrational and merely reactive in nature.

Antonio Damasio and others (e.g., Solomon 1984; de Sousa 1987; Slote 2014) challenge the intellectualist bias. Damasio's work has shown that the modern assumption that emotions interfere with reason is mistaken, arguing also that there is good reason to think that emotions are constitutive of reason (Damasio 1994, 1999). Similar empirical observations have been made by social scientists working in other disciplines (Haidt & Joseph 2004; De Waal 2009; Haidt 2012; Greene 2013). For the present purposes, this serves as strong evidence that emotions are not merely reactionary or extra-rational, but are partially constitutive of rational processes. In other words, reason is infused with emotion, not bereft of it, as the intellectualist bias would have it.

If emotion or affect actually plays a constitutive role in reasoning, it's implausible to maintain the position that it is merely reactionary in nature. Recall Thompson arguing that emotion is integral to protention, that one's anticipations about what is to be are emotionally shaped. This squares well with how Gurwitsch describes the role of empathy in social interactions. Collective intentions require anticipating the other's reaction, and what one anticipates is dependent on the emotional commitments one has about the other and about the actions or roles to be undertaken. This points to a more general concern; affectivity is required for experiences in the world. Donn Welton argues that it is because of affect that objects soliciting action responses are constituted in experience. Our engagements with objects transform those objects according to the action possibilities selected through our engagements.

> Things matter not just because they intrude and not just because they fit into a practical project or problem that requires their use and invests them with relevance. Things in situations also matter because they give us pleasure or cause us pain, provide gratification or drive us to frustration, capture our heart or tear it to shreds.
> (Welton 2012, 183f.)

Welton maintains that experiences always include affective content. Without affect, one would not act, nor have a purpose in one's action (191f). The claim is not just that there is no decision without *pathos*, but that there is no experience without *pathos*. In terms of collective intentionality, the import should be clear. One's intentions are dependent on one's cognition of a state of affairs and of the other(s) with whom one intends to engage in joint actions. Affect plays a constitutive role in what it is that one experiences and how one experiences it. Insofar as affect contributes to reasoning, action, and the selection of ends, affect plays a constitutive role in collective intentions. Hence, our acting together cannot be made sense of unless there is affective content constituting our engagement.[13]

## CONCLUSION

To conclude, one of the clear strengths of Gurwitsch's view is that his account captures a plurality of social formations from the outset. Instead of focusing on one type of relation and treating it as the model for all other social relations, Gurwitsch allows variation. Most importantly, this variation involves respective variations in the manner of emotional comportment. In partnerships, one need not have any particular emotional comportment towards the other. However, Gurwitsch argues that even the act of trusting an anonymous other is an emotionally constituted judgment. Memberships involve a similar affective way of being-in-the-world, and fusion involves a strongly reciprocated emotional connection between those parties. Each are ways of experiencing oneself as part of a 'we.'

This points to the more general problem, and offers an opening to argue that emotions play constitutive roles in all collective intentions. In Gilbert's case, one may ask what it means to be *committed* sans emotional content. More generally, one can note that trust is an essential condition for any functioning relationship, especially those based on agreements, shared plans, or joint commitments. One's being upset at the violation of a collective intention is not just a reaction to the violation of an explicit or implicit rational agreement. Rather, it is grounded in the very violation of trust, or generally, of an emotional relation.

## NOTES

1  John Searle's theory of collective intentionality is also implicated, though I will not directly engage with Searle's view here; see for this Chelstrom (2013).
2  Thank you to David Cerbone for suggesting this helpful amendment to Gurwitsch's view.
3  My gratitude to Dan Zahavi and Alessandro Salice for calling my attention to an error I had made in earlier versions of this chapter, in which I did not adequately appreciate or represent how Gurwitsch's position differed from Walther's.
4  See also Chelstrom (2013).
5  See also discussion in Chelstrom (2012).
6  Part III of *Human Encounters* (Gurwitsch 1979), where the three forms of sociality are established, is titled "Consociate Being Together." It's clear that there's a shift in how Gurwitsch understands consociate relations. For instance, there's nothing barring partnerships from not occurring face-to-face in *Human Encounters*. However, in the later essay (Gurwitsch 1974), he restricts consociate being together to face-to-face relations only. Where, in *Human Encounters*, partnerships counted as types of consociate being together, they are now understood to be typification-mediated relations and are no longer essentially consociate relations.
7  Gurwitsch was likely influenced by Hannah Arendt and others contemporaries who explored these concerns.
8  An alternative theory suggests these may not be deficits, but coping responses to overstimulation. See Markram/Rinaldi/Markram (2007) and Velázquez/Galán (2013).
9  Thompson refers us to Hua 11, § 35, 214–221, and 166–172.
10  This is an ancient point: cooperation requires trustworthiness and recognition thereof between those parties to the degree necessary for the given collective action (Plato 1997, 351c–352d; cf. Jones 1998). Consider, by way of example, role-playing games. A classic role-playing game, like *Dungeons & Dragons*, is a game that is fundamentally about organizing, shaping, and negotiating collective experiences and game actions. The players require trust in one another and in their dungeon master. As such, "there's an intimacy to role-playing games that's impossible to convey until you try it" (Bohn 2014).
11  True, Gilbert has an account of marriage as fusion. However, Gilbert's remark that this is marriage as romantics conceive it is distressing. Charitably, calling it romantic is not necessarily disparaging. Granted, there isn't a necessity that marriage be conceptualized as necessarily a romantic relationship—as is amply evidenced in history. See discussion in Chelstrom (2012, 138–40).
12  Gilbert's more recent contribution on collective emotions is not helpful in relation to my concern. Gilbert (2014b) argues that we can form joint

commitments to have certain emotions. That, again, reduces emotions to reactionary roles, specifically the reactions of groups, not necessarily all of the individuals who participate in those groups. It may be plausible to argue that we can choose to commit to having certain attitudes, or at least to foster dispositions to have those attitudes about some things. But it could equally be the case that collective emotions function in the fashion of a contagion; something spreads throughout a group because other group members present a certain attitude, not because we are so jointly committed. However, these worries are beside the point. My worry is not that there can be collective emotions, but that emotion is required to even form joint commitments in the first place. I don't understand what it means to be committed, especially to some action, absent affect.

13 Welton further argues that there are cases where intention arises through one's action, and that it is not always the case that intentions precipitate actions (2012, 180–3). Those cases are clear cases where affect is necessary both for action and intention. Such cases are certainly possible in collective actions, not just individual ones.

# REFERENCES

Bohn, Dieter (2014). "Slaying the Demons of 'Dungeons & Dragons'." *The Verge*. http://www.theverge.com/2014/8/18/6027647/slaying-the-demons-of-dungeons-dragons [08. 14. 2014].
Bratman, Michael (2014). *Shared Agency*. Oxford: Oxford University Press.
Chelstrom, Eric (2012). *Social Phenomenology*. Lanham: Lexington Press.
────── (2013). "Horizon Intentions and Aristotelian Friendship." In: K. Hermberg, & P. Gyllehammer (Eds.), *Phenomenology and Virtue Ethics*. New York: Bloomsbury, 60–77.
Damasio, Antonio (1994). *Descartes' Error*. New York: Penguin.
────── (1999). *The Feeling of What Happens*. New York: Harcourt.
De Sousa, Ronald (1987). *The Rationality of Emotion*. Cambridge, MA/London: MIT Press.
De Waal, Frans (2009). *The Age of Empathy*. New York: Harmony.
Gilbert, Margaret (1996). *Living Together*. Lanham: Rowman & Littlefield.
────── (2000). *Sociality and Responsibility*. Lanham: Rowman & Littlefield.
────── (2014a). *Joint Commitment: How We Make the Social World*. Oxford: Oxford University Press.
────── (2014b). "How We Feel: Understanding Everyday Collective Emotion Ascription." In C. von Scheve, & M. Salmela (Eds.), *Collective Emotions*. Oxford: Oxford University Press, 17–31.
Greene, Joshua (2013). *Moral Tribes*. New York: Penguin.
Gurwitsch, Aron (1974). "The Common-Sense World as Social Reality and the Theory of Social Science." In: L. Embree (Ed.), *Phenomenology and the Theory of Science*. Evanston: Northwestern University Press, 113–131.
────── (1979). *Human Encounters in the Social World*. Transl. by F. Kersten. Pittsburgh: Duquesne University Press.
Haidt, Jonathan (2012). *The Righteous Mind*. New York: Pantheon Books.
Haidt, Jonathan, & Joseph, Craig (2004). "Intuitive Ethics: How Innately Prepared Intuitions Generate Culturally Variable Virtues." *Daedalus* 133 (4), 55–66.
Husserl, Edmund (1999/1963) [=Hua 1]. *Cartesian Meditations*. Transl. Dorion Cairns. Dordrecht: Kluwer. *Cartesianische Meditationen und Pariser Vorträge*, 2nd ed., Ed. by Stephen Strasser. The Hague: Nijhoff.

―――― (2001/1966) [=Hua 11]. *Analyses Concerning Active and Passive Synthesis.* Dordrecht: Kluwer. *Analysen zur passive Synthesis: Aus Vorlesungs- und Forschungsmanuskripten 1918–1926*, Ed. by Margot Fleischer. The Hague: Martinus Nijhoff.

Jacob, Pierre (2011). "The Direct-Perception Model of Empathy: a Critique." *Review of Philosophy and Psychology* 2 (3), 519–540.

Jones, Karen (1998). "Trust as an Affective Attitude." *Ethics* 107 (1), 4–25.

Markram, Henry, Rinaldi, Tania, & Markram, Kamila (2007). "The Intense World Syndrome: An Alternative Hypothesis for Autism." *Frontiers in Neuroscience* 1 (1), 77–96.

McLeod, Carolyn (2011). "Trust." *The Stanford Encyclopedia of Philosophy* (Spring 2011 Edition). Ed. E. N. Zalta. http://plato.stanford.edu/archives/spr2011/entries/trust/

Miller, Seumas (2014). "Review of *Joint Commitment*, by Margaret Gilbert." *Notre Dame Philosophical Reviews*. https://ndpr.nd.edu/news/49746-joint-commitment-how-we-make-the-social-world/ [08. 14. 2014].

Plato (1997). *Republic*. Transl. by G. M. A. Grube, Transl. Rev. by C. D. C. Reeve. In: J. M. Cooper (Ed.). *Plato: Complete Works*. Indianapolis: Hackett Publishing, 971–1223.

Prinz, Jesse (2004). *Gut Reactions: A Perceptual Theory of Emotion*. Oxford: Oxford University Press.

Schmid, Hans Bernhard (2013). "Trying to Act Together." In: M. Schmitz, B. Kobow, & H. B. Schmid (Eds.). *The Background of Social Reality*. Dordrecht: Springer, 37–56.

Schütz, Alfred, & Gurwitsch, Aron (1989). *Philosophers in Exile: The Correspondences of Alfred Schütz and Aron Gurwitsch, 1939–1959*. Ed. by R. Grathoff. Transl. by J. C. Evans. Bloomington: Indiana University Press.

Slote, Michael (2014). *A Sentimentalist Theory of the Mind*. Oxford: Oxford University Press.

Solomon, Robert (1984). *The Passions: The Myth and Nature of Human Emotions*. New York: Doubleday.

Stein, Edith (1989). *On the Problem of Empathy*. Transl. by W. Stein. Washington, DC: ICS Publications.

Szanto, Thomas (in this volume). "Collectivizing Persons and Personifying Collectives: Reassessing Scheler on Group Personhood." In: T. Szanto, & D. Moran (Eds.). *The Phenomenology of Sociality: Discovering the 'We'*. London/New York: Routledge.

Thompson, Evan (2007). *Mind in Life*. Cambridge, MA: Belknap Press.

Tuomela, Raimo (2014). "Review of *Shared Agency*, by Michael Bratman." *Notre Dame Philosophical Reviews*. https://ndpr.nd.edu/news/49830-shared-agency-a-planning-theory-of-acting-together/ [08. 20. 2014].

Velázquez, José Pérez, & Galán, Roberto (2013). "Information Gain in the Brain's Resting State: A New Perspective on Autism." *Frontiers in Neuroinformatics* 7, 1–10.

Walther, Gerda (1923). "Zur Ontologie der sozialen Gemeinsachten." *Jahrbuch für Philosophie und phänomenologische* Forschung VI. Halle: Niemeyer, 1–158.

Welton, Donn (2012). "Bodily Intentionality, Affectivity, and Basic Affects." In: D. Zahavi (Ed.). *The Oxford Handbook of Contemporary Phenomenology*. Oxford: Oxford University Press, 177–197.

# 16 The Affective 'We'
## Self-Regulation and Shared Emotions
*Joel Krueger*

## 1 INTRODUCTION

Discussions of joint action and collective intentionality have mainly focused on the ways in which subjects share intentions and beliefs. Little attention has been paid to shared emotions.[1] But this is an unfortunate omission. Emotions are a crucial part of the formation and maintenance of episodes of collective intentionality. When we commit with our partner to raising a child, make plans with a group of friends to meet up later that evening, assume our place at the back of a taxi line, or dance with a stranger at a club, we are mutually coordinating our actions, intentions, and beliefs toward a common goal. Yet, instances of collective intentionality such as these are not affectively neutral episodes. They are permeated with feelings and emotions. And very often we don't just feel *for* others. We feel *with* them.

Just as we share intentions and beliefs, so too do we sometimes share emotions. But what does it mean to say that an emotion can be shared? I consider this question, focusing in particular on the relation between the phenomenology of emotion experience and self-regulation. I explore a strong sense of shared emotions: the idea that a numerically single emotion can be given to more than one subject (I term this a "collective emotion"). This idea has not only been defended by developmental and social psychologists (e.g., Tronick et al. 1998; Smith et al. 2007), as well as sociologists (Collins 2004; Rimé 2007; von Scheve and Ismer 2013), but also by a number of phenomenologists (e.g., Scheler 1954; Merleau-Ponty 1964; Schmid 2009; see also the contributions of Chelstrom and Vendrell Ferran in this volume). While I have elsewhere argued that shared emotions may occur in early infancy (Krueger 2013b), I have been skeptical that this strong sense of shared emotions continues into adulthood (Krueger 2014b). Nevertheless, I now want to consider some positive arguments in its favor, as well as briefly indicate why this strong sense of shared emotions may be of broader interest to debates in both philosophy of mind and emotion science.

## 2 REGULATING EMOTIONS

First, consider emotion regulation. It is not uncommon in emotion science literature to characterize emotions as brief neurophysiological responses beyond our conscious control (see, e.g., Izard 1974; Panksepp 1992; LeDoux 1996). But this passive characterization overlooks the extent to which we shape emotional dynamics like latency, rise time, persistence, range, and intensity (Thompson 1994). One way to highlight this enactive character of emotions is to focus on the relation between emotion experience and *self-regulation*: the processes and strategies by which individuals influence which emotions they have, when they have them, and how they are experienced and expressed.

James Gross (1998, 1999) helpfully distinguishes five forms of self-regulation: *attentional deployment* focuses on specific features of a situation in order to alter its emotional impact. *Cognitive change* involves selecting among various emotional meanings that may be attached to a given situation. *Response modulation* involves influencing behavioral response tendencies once they have been initiated. *Situation selection* involves choosing a situation for its emotional impact. Finally, *situation modification* involves manipulating specific features of that situation in order to further its emotional impact.

For simplicity, I will subsume Gross's taxonomy beneath two more general forms of self-regulation: first, *embodied* forms of self-regulation, which involve subject-centered manipulations such as attentional deployment, cognitive change, and response modulation; second, *distributed* forms of self-regulation, which involve the manipulation of environmental features extending beyond the subject and thus include situation selection and situation modification. The latter will be of special interest. I now consider these two forms of self-regulation in turn.

### 2.1 Embodied Self-Regulation

Emotions are complex phenomena comprised of multiple dimensions (Parkinson 1995). Looking at these dimensions helps clarify the role that regulative processes play in shaping their character and development. For example, emotions tend to have an *appraisal* dimension. When I am angry, it is because I evaluate features of a situation—e.g., overhearing a colleague making a crude remark about my partner—as negative, relative to my interests. Emotions also tend to have an *agentive* dimension: they put us in a state of action readiness determined by the character of the appraisal. This agentive dimension is informed by patterns of bodily arousal—in the case of anger, increased heart rate, blood pressure, respiration, tensed muscles, flushed skin, etc.—a *physiological activation* dimension. Emotions also often involve an *expressive* dimension (e.g., furrowed brow, sneer, clenched fists, etc.). Finally, emotions feel like something as we live through them.

They are individuated by their *phenomenological* dimension. My interest is primarily in this phenomenological dimension, and especially the way it is modulated by embodied and distributed processes of emotion regulation. Very often, the way an emotion *feels* reflects the manner by which it is *regulated*.

When I overhear a colleague's crude remark about my partner, for example, I have a number of options. I can embrace my anger—I can self-consciously enact a range of taut, brisk movements, shake my fists, and confront my colleague while speaking loudly and pointing a finger in his face. In this case, I am up-regulating my anger such that I deliberately enhance it. Alternatively, I can down-regulate my anger by adopting various strategies to at least partially diffuse it: closing my eyes, turning away and taking a deep breath, relaxing my posture, redirecting my attention to more pleasant matters, etc. To a certain extent, then, I can both enhance and inhibit (or at least *dampen*) my emotional phenomenology.

Since these regulative strategies draw upon subject-centered features of our embodiment, such as agency, expression, and attention, I refer to this as *embodied* self-regulation. Our capacity for embodied self-regulation is empirically well documented. For example, Paula Niedenthal's work suggests that manipulating facial expressions, posture, and gestures directly modulates the phenomenology of emotional experience (Niedenthal 2007; Niedenthal & Maringer 2009). Simply adopting a smile can bring about the feeling of happiness; similarly, a frown—even one in response to walking into the sun (Marzoli et al. 2013)—can induce the feeling of anger or aggressiveness. An exaggerated grimace can enhance pain experience (Salomons et al. 2008). And inhibiting these expressions appears to have a dampening effect. Embodied self-regulation strategies seem to modulate not only the kinds of emotions we have (e.g., smiles generate happiness, frowns generate anger), but also their qualitative character and intensity (Duclos & Laird 2001). And the latter co-varies with the different regulative tools we employ to modulate that character (e.g., facial expressions vs. whole-body gestures vs. vocal strategies vs. attentional deployment, etc.) (Ekman 1965; Levenson et al. 1990).

In order to appreciate the extent to which we enact the character of many emotions, we should note further that, in addition to shaping emotional phenomenology, embodied self-regulation also reaches down into both the *appraisal* and *physiological activation* dimensions. Manipulating facial expressions, for instance, can influence how an individual processes the same stimulus, such as the funniness of a cartoon or the friendliness of individuals (Strack et al. 1988; Ohira & Kurono 1993). And merely producing emotion-specific facial expressions produces autonomic nervous system activity associated with that emotion (Levenson et al. 1990). Taken together, this evidence suggests that we often enact various dimensions of emotion experience by employing resources made available via embodied self-regulation.

## 2.2 Distributed Self-Regulation

In addition to embodied resources, our regulatory strategies often involve resources that lie beyond the individual—cases where we use environmental tools to modulate our emotional phenomenology. As Gross (1998) notes, not only do we select different situations based upon their emotional impact, such as seeking out the comfort of a trusted friend for a good cry or going out of our way to avoid walking past the office of an irritating coworker, we also manipulate specific *features* of situations. After a long day at work, I may engage in situation selection by retreating to the solitude of my home. But by playing peaceful music, closing the blinds, lowering the lights and lighting candles, etc., I further manipulate the situation (and my emotional response to it) by creating a specific atmosphere *within* that situation; I have, in effect, called a new situation into being (Gross 1998, 283).

I want to take this idea further, however, and discuss an aspect of situation modification Gross does not consider: namely, cases where we allow features of the environment to take over and govern the regulative process *in an ongoing way*. Most of the examples Gross discusses are short-lived interactions or, alternatively, cases where we anticipate situations and avoid them altogether. Yet our emotion-specific environmental transactions often consist of more focused and sustained engagements—ongoing manipulations of environmental features that, as we engage with them, loop back onto us in complex ways and shape what we feel and how we feel it. These engagements are (or at least can be) cases of "emotional off-loading": instances where we allow features of the environment to do some of the emotional work on our behalf, and in so doing, grant access to kinds of experiences we couldn't otherwise have without their regulatory input. Considering this sort of environmentally distributed interaction will then take us into a more focused consideration of shared emotions.

## 3 EMOTIONAL OFF-LOADING: THE CASE OF MUSIC

Across cultures, one of the main reasons we listen to music is to regulate our actions and emotions (Juslin & Laukka 2004). We often use it to intentionally craft a specific atmosphere that modulates our emotional state. This is an example of using music as a tool for situation modification. Music functions particularly well this way, since it both fills and creates acoustic space (Krueger 2009, 2011); it modifies a situation by establishing a sonic landscape within the space of an apartment, restaurant, or place of worship that effectively brings a new situation-within-a-situation into being.

But we often engage with music as a self-regulatory tool in a more intimate way. Tia DeNora observes that music is often used for "venting," by which she means that music is not simply a tool for expressing pre-packaged emotions, but is rather part of the vehicle by which certain emotions are developed and experienced. DeNora argues that music can function as an "aesthetic technology" by which we actively work through emotions and moods (DeNora 2000, 56). She argues further that musical dynamics become "part of the reflexive constitution of that state; [music] is a resource for the identification work of 'knowing how one feels'—a building material of 'subjectivity [. . .] music is both an instigator and a container of feeling'" (DeNora 2000, 57). We off-load some of the regulatory work onto the music and, in so doing, allow it to open up new experiences for us.

One woman DeNora interviewed describes using music to both help induce and structure her bouts of sadness, which she claims is like "looking at yourself in a mirror being sad"; the music functions as a regulative tool for working the listener into a qualitatively deepened emotional state and then gradually leading her out of it (DeNora 2000, 57). Another woman reports using specific musical pieces (e.g., Verdi's *Messa da Requiem*) to work through and articulate felt dimensions of her grief following the loss of her child (DeNora 2000, 58). As DeNora summarizes, these kinds of reports suggest that we allow music to "define the temporal and qualitative structure of that emotion, to play it out in real time and then move on" (DeNora 2000, 58).

So how does music take over emotion-specific, regulative functions? I have considered this question in detail elsewhere (see Krueger 2014a). For brevity, I simply note that the key mechanism—also pertinent to our consideration of shared emotions—appears to be *entrainment*. "Entrainment" refers to instances where two or more independent processes become synchronized with each other, gradually adjusting toward, and eventually locking into, a common phase and/or periodicity (Will & Turow 2011). Entrainment occurs in many domains and at multiple time-scales: two pendulums slowly coming into phase synchrony (Bennett et al. 2002); Asian fireflies flashing in synchrony (Buck and Buck 1968); human interactants synchronizing gestures, facial expressions, speech patterns (Chartrand & Bargh 1999); and groups transitioning from random to synchronized clapping, etc. (Neda et al. 2000).

When we engage with music, we respond to its melodic and rhythmic properties with an array of entrainment behavior, both voluntary and involuntary, from subtle movements like tapping our fingers or feet, nodding our head, or slowly swaying back and forth, to more elaborate sequences of dance steps. Music—because it unfolds dynamically over time—invites this sort of ongoing engagement. We gear into various structural features of music (e.g., metrical and melodic patterning) by responding with movements that "fit" the dynamics of these musical cues.

To illustrate this idea, consider how movements appropriate for one style are wholly inappropriate for others. While the triple meter of the waltz, say, is not experienced as something that invites marching, a duple meter at the correct tempo establishes a different sort of entrainment context, one in which marching responses *do* feel more appropriate in that they naturally lock into, and thus are guided by, the relevant musical dynamics (Windsor & Bézenac 2012, 113). The acoustic structure of the music as we experience it thus plays a significant role in determining the kinesthetics of our entrainment responses. Again, we don't simply move in response to music. We are *guided* by it; we take pleasure in getting into the "groove" with the music and letting it guide our actions and emotions (Janata et al. 2012).

Beyond gross bodily movements, however, music elicits and regulates more fine-grained modes of spontaneous motor entrainment, including facial expressions that induce the felt experience of emotions (recall Niedenthal 2007; Niedenthal & Maringer 2009). There is evidence that listening to music—including expressive, non-vocal music—elicits spontaneous facial mimicry mirroring the affective tone of the music (i.e., happy music elicits happy expressions, sad music sad expressions) (Lundqvist et al. 2009; Chan et al. 2013). Even preterm infants will entrain respiratory patterns, sucking, tongue and mouth protrusions, eye opening and closing, and vocalizations with the up and down movements of a melodic contour (Standley 2002; Krueger 2013a). As a consequence, within a musical context, they exhibit heightened equilibrium between endogenous and exogenous processes and increased stabilization of affect (DeNora 2000, 79). And by continuing to provide ongoing feedback, music serves as a real-time emotion regulator: the temporal structure and periodic modulations of the music (its melody, rhythm, volume, and intensity) as it unfolds regulate the form that our entrainment responses takes, and the emotional responses they generate (Windsor & de Bézenac 2012).[2]

The point of this survey is to indicate how, by manipulating our behavioral responses via entrainment, music manipulates our emotions by taking over what are normally subject-centered, endogenous processes of self-regulation. We "off-load" some of the work of regulating emotions onto musical dynamics, which in turn modulate and shape the phenomenology of our emotional responsiveness in an ongoing way. Can we speak of a similar emotional off-loading process occurring in instances of collective intentionality? And if so, how does this off-loading process lead to shared emotions? These are the questions I consider next.

## 4 EMOTIONAL OFF-LOADING: OTHER PEOPLE

The discussion above considered the possibility that some emotions—and the regulatory processes that are part of them—are distributed across both embodied as well as environmental processes. As a result, these environmental processes open up kinds of emotion experiences that might otherwise be inaccessible. For example, as the discussion in the previous section indicated, there may be certain emotions only accessible within a musical context. If emotion-regulative and emotion-generative processes are inextricable (Tomkins 1984; Frijda 1986), the *kind* of regulation employed will have a direct impact on shaping the *phenomenology* of the regulated emotion experience.

If a similar off-loading process happens during instances of collective intentionality, however—that is, occasions where multiple subjects coordinate actions, intentions, and beliefs toward a common goal, and in so doing, open themselves up to the possibility of shared feelings and emotions—there will be an important difference. Environmental resources like music are not conscious subjects. But instances of collective intentionality do involve other subjects—centers of agency with their own first-person perspectives. Thus, if emotional off-loading occurs in some instances of collective intentionality, this suggests that we can share emotions with others in a way not possible in other instances of distributed self-regulation.

## 4.1 Shared Emotions

Some initial distinctions will be helpful. There are several ways an emotion might be shared. First, an emotion can be shared *expressively* via facial expressions, gestures, or verbal reports. When I wrinkle my nose, retch, and stick out my tongue after tasting some old milk, I share my disgust with my wife via these overt physical expressions. Second, emotions can be shared *contagiously*: they can "infect" multiple subjects, transferring from one to the next. If my disgust response is especially florid, my wife may respond in kind with similar facial expressions, wrinkling her nose and covering her mouth while developing her own rising feeling of stomach-churning nausea. Note that in both cases, however, the emotion remains tied to a single subject. The disgust I share via my wrinkled nose and retching is mine alone; my wife perceives it as such. She may subsequently "catch" my disgust response and develop her own disgust. But at that moment, while we have similar *types* of emotions, they remain numerically distinct *token* episodes.

There is a third sense of sharing, however, which connects back to the discussion in the previous sections. This sense refers to the way one and the same token of an emotion can be simultaneously shared by more than one subject. Call this a "collective emotion." In cases of collective emotions, a token emotion extends across multiple subjects; here, one emotion is collectively realized by multiple participants. The possibility of collective emotions is philosophically intriguing because it challenges the common intuition that the ontology of emotions is such that they can only be realized by individuals.

While the idea of collective emotions faces some difficulties (Schmid 2009, 70; see also Salmela 2012), it is not wholly implausible. There are, for example, ontogenetic arguments one might give to support its occurrence in early infancy (Krueger 2013b; see also Feldman 2007; Tronick et al. 1998). But what about shared emotions in adulthood, when individuals develop the endogenous and self-regulatory capacities that infants clearly lack? Can we still speak of a token emotion being simultaneously shared by multiple subjects? The phenomenologist Max Scheler thinks so, and he provides us with a case study: the shared grief felt by the parents of a recently deceased child.

## 4.2  Shared Emotions: Scheler on Grief

Here is how Scheler describes a shared emotion:

> Two parents stand beside the dead body of a beloved child. They feel in common the 'same' sorrow, the 'same' anguish. It is not that A feels this sorrow and B feels it also, and moreover that they both know that they are feeling it. No, it is a *feeling-in-common*. A's sorrow is in no way an 'external' matter for B here, as it is e.g. for their friend, C, who joins them and commiserates 'with them' or 'upon their sorrow.' On the contrary, they feel it together, in the sense that they feel and experience in common, not only the same value-situation, but also the same keenness of emotion in regard to it. The sorrow, as value content, and the grief, as characterizing the functional relation thereto, are here *one and identical*.
>
> (Scheler 1954, 12f.)

Instead of claiming that each parent experiences a unique token episode of sorrow, Scheler suggests here a particularly acute instance of a collective emotion, an "[i]mmediate community of feeling, e.g., of one and the same sorrow, 'with someone'" (Scheler 1954, 12). Unfortunately, Scheler does not give a detailed argument for this view.[3] I want to continue the previous discussion and attempt to make the case for Scheler's claim here by appealing to the notions of distributed self-regulation, emotional off-loading, and entrainment. This case is interesting because, unlike the music listening case, there are multiple temporal dimensions (both synchronic and diachronic) at work in the off-loading and entrainment shaping this collective emotion.

Consider how Scheler sets up this case.[4] First, we are told that there is a synchronic *bodily and spatial intimacy* between the parents and their dead child. One can easily imagine the parents clinging to each other in a state of desperation, exchanging glances, caresses, whispers, and sobs, closely monitoring and responding to the other's reactions—all while standing immediately next to their child's corpse. Additionally, the child—as the object of their shared grief—is said to have been "beloved." Along with the immediate (synchronic) bodily and spatial intimacy of this situation, we can plausibly assume both parents share what we might term a diachronic *narrative intimacy*—that is, the distinctive sort of familial intimacy that emerges over time from "pre-existing relations of marital love and marital life between the sharers of the feeling, as well as the relations of biological maternity, of care giving and of parental love to the object of the shared feeling" (Konzelmann Ziv 2009, 102). This narrative intimacy is comprised of an indefinite number of shared experiences, memories, and associations that define the internal history unique to every family. When gazing at the corpse of their beloved child, both parents draw upon this common stock of family knowledge; since they share this narrative intimacy, the child will, as an object of their mutual grief, be experientially given in a similar way, that is, via a similar network of memories and associations (e.g., his first birthday, learning how to ride a bicycle, playing with his first pet, etc.). By standing in these privileged relations of (synchronic) bodily and (diachronic) narrative intimacy, then, the child's parents—as they gaze down upon their beloved child—are affectively bound up with one another, *integrated*, on multiple levels and time-scales.

At the synchronic level, both parents experience ongoing sequences of physical feedback from the other in the form of clenched muscles, held hands, the feel of the other's body wracked with quiet heaving, the sound of their weeping, etc. Each partner can thus directly feel the grief of the other embodied within their responses; they have direct perceptual and tactile access to this grief as it plays out across their partner's bodily expressions (Krueger 2012). These grief responses will, in turn, feed back onto, permeate, and modulate that partner's own responses and feeling states. In other words, the parent's respective expressions of grief will become deeply *entrained* with one another.

There is ample empirical support for this idea. It is widely documented that social interaction rests on layers of behavioral entrainment, processes by which individuals spontaneously and involuntarily synchronize bodily movements, facial expressions, postures, gestures, instrumental behaviors, gaze patterns, and vocalizations with those whom they are interacting (Bernieri & Rosenthal 1991; Hatfield et al. 1994). One of the important psychosocial functions of interpersonal entrainment is to promote social cohesion, as well as deepened feelings of connectedness, rapport, and cooperation during joint tasks (Hove & Risen 2009; Valdesolo et al. 2010). Much like spontaneously entraining with music, entering into entrainment relations with other people seems to be something we are born poised and ready to do (Trevarthen 1979; Bernieri et al. 1988). Entrainment is thus said to be a key mechanism, the "social glue" facilitating interpersonal relations (Chartrand & Bargh 1999). The tactile dimension of entrainment (what I termed "bodily and spatial intimacy") is especially important. Chatel-Goldman et al. (2014) found that touch alone is sufficient to facilitate physiological coupling—somatovisceral resonance (i.e., aligning of skin conductance responses, pulse, respiration, etc.)—between romantic partners.

What is crucial for this argument is that these forms of behavioral and physiological entrainment support the convergence of emotions and affect between interactants, which in turn intensifies their respective feelings of mutual understanding and connectedness (Lakin & Chartrand 2003). Moreover, while many—perhaps most—of our entrainment processes are involuntary, we can nevertheless exert some top-down control over our entrainment responses, which in turn allows us to modulate the extent we "use" entrainment, so to speak, to share feelings and connect more or less deeply with others (Brass et al. 2005). For example, there is evidence that we selectively mimic others' facial expressions depending upon the social context. We more readily mimic someone who is an in-group member (e.g., they share our political views) than an out-group member (Hess & Bourgeois & 2010; McHugo et al. 1991), and we are more likely to imitate the facial expressions and gestures of someone with a higher social status than we have, since that will likely increase their affection toward us (Cheng & Chartrand 2003).

To return to Scheler's case: what I propose, then, is that given the high degree of synchronic and diachronic intimacy between the parents—their immediate bodily and spatial proximity (and subsequent entrainment responses), as well as their narrative history, including a wealth of similar memories suddenly welling up and framing how the child is given, experientially, as an object of their grief—both partners are poised to off-load part of their emotion-specific regulatory process onto the other in a way they wouldn't with strangers or perhaps even other close family members (siblings, grandparents, cousins). This is surely part of what we mean when we speak of "leaning on" a partner during times of crisis, of making ourselves open and vulnerable to them and their responses. We can assume that each partner is especially vulnerable to interpersonally distributed regulation at this moment. Due to their all-consuming grief, their inhibitory resources will have been dramatically weakened to the point that they are, in a sense, reduced to a kind of infant-like state, highly vulnerable and responsive to environmental perturbations. Consider how easily someone in the midst of tremendous grief can be plunged even further into their suffering by a seemingly innocuous environmental trigger. In this case, each partner is perhaps even more open and vulnerable to being environmentally manipulated by the other—that is, led through their grief and its various expressions—than during other periods of their life together.

Although this is rather cold language, given the details of this case, we might nevertheless characterize the synchronic and diachronic integration of both partners as a two-way relation of "continuous reciprocal causation" (Clark 1997, p. 165). In this context, both partners will be highly attuned and responsive to the other: the mother's grief expression will trigger a similar response in the father (via mimicry of facial expressions, gestures, postures, etc.), which will in turn modulate the mother's further responses, which will redound back onto the father's, etc. Their respective entrainment responses will thus bind both parents to one another in a kind of ongoing, mutually modulatory relation. The regulatory processes generating the collective grief are, in this context, distributed across both partners. Of course, each partner will offer their own idiosyncratic expressions of grief: one might be more overt, vocal, and florid; one more reserved. Each will nevertheless shape the expressions of the other, however; and this ongoing exchange will in turn collectively lead both parents to articulate and experience a kind of grief profoundly informed and permeated by the presence of the other's grief—a *shared* grief whose character articulates the specific regulatory input of both partners.

To return to an earlier point, if we grant that the *kind* of regulation employed will have a direct impact on generating and shaping the *phenomenology* of the regulated emotion experience, it follows that this episode will have a specific phenomenal character reflecting the mutual regulatory input of both parents. In other words, the phenomenology of this grief will be jointly constructed—that is, shared—in that it reflects the synchronic and diachronic entrainment of both parents, jointly standing in relation to a common emotional object (i.e., their child). It is thus a kind of shared or collective grief that can be generated only when specific sorts of relations are obtained: namely, the deep integration, supported by (synchronic) bodily and (diachronic) narrative entrainment, that is uniquely possible within this unusually intense context.

## 5  FINAL THOUGHTS

These observations alone are not sufficient to make the case for collective emotions, of course, but they do render the idea more plausible than might initially appear. Moreover, the possibility of collectively constructed emotions is potentially of interest to other debates.[5] Not only does it reinforce the idea that affectivity and emotions ought to play a prominent role in ongoing discussions of collective intentionality, it challenges the individualism informing most approaches to emotions, according to which emotions are, in principle, the sort of things given to or entertained by single subjects. It motivates a move away from thinking of emotions as discrete intracranial *states* toward a situated, multidimensional, and relational account of emotions as (potentially distributed) *processes*. This is a view with significant phenomenological and ontological implications, one which also seems to affirm the extent to which we are bound up with, and rely upon, one another when it comes to realizing central features of our emotional lives.

## NOTES

1 Although this is starting to change: see, for example, the essays in von Scheve and Salmela (2014).
2 Our musically regulated emotions are also supported by the entrainment of sensorimotor processes at the neural level (Nozaradan et al. forthcoming; Overy & Molnar-Szakacs 2009).
3 But see the chapters in this volume by Vendrell Ferran and Szanto, respectively, for further attempts to clarify Scheler on collective personhood and affectivity.

4 While developing this reading of Scheler, I belatedly discovered Anita Konzelmann Ziv's (2009) discussion, which brings out a number of very similar points. I incorporated several of her insights into this discussion.
5 See Krueger (2014a) for further discussion.

## REFERENCES

Bennett, Matthew, Schatz, Matthew F., Rockwood, Heidi, & Wiesenfeld, Kurt (2002). "Huygens's Clocks." *Proceedings of the Royal Society of London. Series A: Mathematical, Physical and Engineering Sciences* 458 (2019), 563–79.

Bernieri, Frank J., & Rosenthal, Robert (1991). "Interpersonal Coordination: Behavior Matching and Interactional Synchrony." In: R. S. Feldman, & B. Rime (Eds.). *Fundamentals of Nonverbal Behavior*. Cambridge: Cambridge University Press, 401–432.

Bernieri, Frank J., Reznick, J. Steven, & Rosenthal, Robert (1988). "Synchrony, Pseudosynchrony, and Dissynchrony: Measuring the Entrainment Process in Mother-Infant Interactions." *Journal of Personality and Social Psychology* 54 (2), 243–253.

Bourgeois, Patrick, & Hess, Ursula (2008). "The Impact of Social Context on Mimicry." *Biological Psychology* 77 (3), 343–352.

Brass, Marcel, Derrfuss, Jan, & Von Cramon, Yves D. (2005). "The Inhibition of Imitative and Overlearned Responses: A Functional Double Dissociation." *Neuropsychologia* 43 (1), 89–98.

Buck, John, & Buck, Elisabeth (1968). "Mechanism of Rhythmic Synchronous Flashing of Fireflies. Fireflies of Southeast Asia May Use Anticipatory Time-Measuring in Synchronizing Their Flashing." *Science (New York, N.Y.)* 159 (3821), 1319–1327.

Chan, Lisa P., Livingstone, Steven R., & Russo, Frank A. (2013). "Facial Mimicry in Response to Song." *Music Perception: An Interdisciplinary Journal* 30 (4), 361–367.

Chartrand, Tanya, & Bargh, John A. (1999). "The Chameleon Effect: The Perception-Behavior Link and Social Interaction." *Journal of Personality and Social Psychology* 76 (6), 893–910.

Chatel-Goldman, Jonas, Congedo, Marco, Jutten, Christian, & Schwartz, Jean-Luc (2014). "Touch Increases Autonomic Coupling Between Romantic Partners." *Frontiers in Behavioral Neuroscience* 8 (95), 1–12.

Cheng, Clara Michelle, & Chartrand, Tanya L. (2003). "Self-Monitoring Without Awareness: Using Mimicry as a Nonconscious Affiliation Strategy." *Journal of Personality and Social Psychology* 85 (6), 1170–1179.

Clark, Andy (1997). *Being There: Putting Brain, Body and World Together Again*. Cambridge, MA/London: MIT Press.

Collins, Randall (2004). *Interaction Ritual Chains*. Princeton, NJ: Princeton University Press.

DeNora, Tia (2000). *Music in Everyday Life*. Cambridge: Cambridge University Press.

Duclos, Sandra E., & Laird, James D. (2001). "The Deliberate Control of Emotional Experience through Control of Expressions." *Cognition & Emotion* 15 (1), 27–56.

Ekman, Paul (1965). "Differential Communication of Affect by Head and Body Cues." *Journal of Personality and Social Psychology* 2 (5), 726–35.

Feldman, Ruth (2007). "On the Origins of Background Emotions: From Affect Synchrony to Symbolic Expression." *Emotion* 7 (3), 601–11.

Frijda, Nico H. (1986). *The Emotions*. Cambridge: Cambridge University Press.
Gross, James J. (1998). "The Emerging Field of Emotion Regulation: An Integrative Review." *Review of General Psychology* 2 (3), 271–99.
——— (1999). "Emotion Regulation: Past, Present, Future." *Cognition & Emotion* 13 (5), 551–573.
Hatfield, Elaine, Cacioppo, John T., & Rapson, Richard L. (1994). *Emotional Contagion*. Cambridge: Cambridge University Press.
Hess, Ursula, & Bourgeois, Patrick (2010). "You smile–I smile: Emotion expression in social interaction." *Biological psychology* 84 (3), 514–520.
Hove, Michael J., & Risen, Jane L. (2009). "It's All in the Timing: Interpersonal Synchrony Increases Affiliation." *Social Cognition* 27 (6), 949–960.
Izard, Carroll E. (1974). "Emotions, Human." *Encyclopedia Britannica, Vol. 18*, 248–256.
Janata, Petr, Tomic, Stefan T., & Haberman, Jason M. (2012). "Sensorimotor Coupling in Music and the Psychology of the Groove." *Journal of Experimental Psychology: General* 141 (1), 54–75.
Juslin, Patrik N., & Laukka, Petri (2004). "Expression, Perception, and Induction of Musical Emotions: A Review and a Questionnaire Study of Everyday Listening." *Journal of New Music Research* 33 (3), 217–238.
Konzelmann Ziv, Anita (2009). "The Semantics of Shared Emotion." *Universitas Philosophica* 59, 81–106.
Krueger, Joel (2009). "Enacting Musical Experience." *Journal of Consciousness Studies* 16 (2–3), 98–123.
——— (2011). "Enacting Musical Content." In: R. Manzotti (Ed.). *Situated Aesthetics: Art Beyond the Skin*. Exeter: Imprint Academic, 63–85.
——— (2012). "Seeing Mind in Action." *Phenomenology and the Cognitive Sciences* 11 (2), 149–173.
——— (2013a). "Empathy, Enaction, and Shared Musical Experience: Evidence from Infant Cognition." In T. Cochrane, B. Fantini, & K. Scherer (Eds.). *The Emotional Power of Music: Multidisciplinary Perspectives on Musical Expression, Arousal, and Social Control*. Oxford: Oxford University Press, 177–196.
——— (2013b). "Merleau-Ponty on Shared Emotions and the Joint Ownership Thesis." *Continental Philosophy Review* 46 (4), 509–531.
——— (2014a). "Affordances and the Musically Extended Mind." *Frontiers in Psychology* 4 (1003), 1–13.
——— (2014b). "Varieties of Extended Emotions." *Phenomenology and the Cognitive Sciences* 13 (4), 533–555.
Lakin, Jessica L., & Chartrand, Tanya L. (2003). "Using Nonconscious Behavioral Mimicry to Create Affiliation and Rapport." *Psychological Science* 14 (4), 334–339.
LeDoux, Joseph E. (1996). *The Emotional Brain*. New York: Simon and Shuster.
Levenson, Robert, Ekman, Paul, & Friesen, Wallace V. (1990). "Voluntary Facial Action Generates Emotion-Specific Autonomic Nervous System Activity." *Psychophysiology* 27 (4), 363–84.
Lundqvist, Lars-Olov, Carlsson, Fredrik, Hilmersson, Per, & Juslin, Patrik N. (2009). "Emotional Responses to Music: Experience, Expression, and Physiology." *Psychology of Music* 37 (1), 61–90.
Marzoli, Daniele, Custodero, Mariagrazia, Pagliara, Alessandra, & Tommasi, Luca (2013). "Sun-Induced Frowning Fosters Aggressive Feelings." *Cognition & Emotion* 27 (8), 1513–1521.
McHugo, Gregory J., Lanzetta, John T., & Bush, Lauren K. (1991). "The Effect of Attitudes on Emotional Reactions to Expressive Displays of Political Leaders." *Journal of Nonverbal Behavior* 15, 19–41.

Merleau-Ponty, Maurice (1964). "The Child's Relations with Others." In J. Edie (Ed.). *The Primacy of Perception*. Evanston: Northwestern University Press, 96–155.

Néda, Z., Ravasz, E., Brechet, Y., Vicsek, T., & Barabási. A.-L. (2000). "Self-Organizing Processes: The Sound of Many Hands Clapping." *Nature* 403 (6772), 849–850.

Niedenthal, Paula M. (2007). "Embodying Emotion." *Science* 316 (5827), 1002–1005.

Niedenthal, Paula M., & Maringer, Marcus (2009). "Embodied Emotion Considered." *Emotion Review* 1 (2), 122–128.

Nozaradan, Sylvie, Zerouali, Younes, Peretz, Isabelle, & Mouraux, Andre (forthcoming). "Capturing with EEG the Neural Entrainment and Coupling Underlying Sensorimotor Synchronization to the Beat." *Cerebral Cortex*.

Ohira, Hideki, & Kurono, Kiyomi (1993). "Facial Feedback Effects on Impression Formation." *Perceptual and Motor Skills* 77, 1251–1258.

Overy, Katie, & Molnar-Szakacs, Istvan (2009). "Being Together in Time: Musical Experience and the Mirror Neuron System." *Music Perception: An Interdisciplinary Journal* 26 (5), 489–504.

Panksepp, Jaak (1992). *Affective Neurology*. Oxford: Oxford University Press.

Parkinson, Brian (1995). *Ideas and Realities of Emotion*. London/New York: Routledge.

Rimé, Bernard (2007). "The Social Sharing of Emotion as an Interface Between Individual and Collective Processes in the Construction of Emotional Climates." *Journal of Social Issues* 63 (2), 307–322.

Salmela, Mikko (2012). "Shared Emotions." *Philosophical Explorations* 15 (1), 33–46.

Salomons, Tim V., Coan, James A., Hunt, Matthew, Backonja, Misha-Miroslav, & Davidson, Richard J. (2008). "Voluntary Facial Displays of Pain Increase Suffering in Response to Nociceptive Stimulation." *The Journal of Pain* 9 (5), 443–448.

Scheler, Max (1954). *The Nature of Sympathy*. Transl. by P. Heath. London: Routledge and Kegan Paul.

Schmid, Hans Bernhard (2009). *Plural Action: Essays in Philosophy and Social Science*. Dordrecht: Springer.

Smith, Eliot R., Seger, Charles R., & Mackie, Diane M. (2007). "Can Emotions Be Truly Group Level? Evidence Regarding Four Conceptual Criteria." *Journal of Personality and Social Psychology* 93 (3), 431–46.

Standley, Jayne M. (2002). "A Meta-Analysis of the Efficacy of Music Therapy for Premature Infants." *Journal of Pediatric Nursing* 17 (2), 107–113.

Strack, Fritz, Martin, Leonard L., & Stepper, Sabine (1988). "Inhibiting and Facilitating Conditions of the Human Smile: A Nonobtrusive Test of the Facial Feedback Hypothesis." *Journal of Personality and Social Psychology* 54 (5), 768–777.

Szanto, Thomas (in this volume). "Collectivizing Persons and Personifying Collectives: Reassessing Scheler on Group Personhood." In: T. Szanto, & D. Moran (Eds.). *The Phenomenology of Sociality: Discovering the 'We'*. London/New York: Routledge.

Thompson, Ross A. (1994). "Emotion Regulation: A Theme in Search of Definition." *Monographs of the Society for Research in Child Development* 59 (2–3), 25–52.

Tomkins, Silvan S. (1984). "Affect Theory." In: P. Ekman (Ed.). *Emotion in the Human Face*. Cambridge: Cambridge University Press, 353–395.

Trevarthen, Colwyn (1979). "Communication and Cooperation in Early Infancy: A Description of Primary Intersubjectivity." In M. Bullowa (Ed.). *Before Speech: The Beginning of Interpersonal Communication*. Cambridge: Cambridge University Press, 321–347.

Tronick, Edward Z., Bruschweiler-Stern, Nadia, Harrison, Alexandra M., Lyons-Ruth, Karlen, Morgan, Alexander C., Nahum, Jeremy P., Sander, Louis, & Stern, Daniel N. (1998). "Dyadically Expanded States of Consciousness and the Process of Therapeutic Change." *Infant Mental Health Journal* 19 (3), 290–299.

Valdesolo, Piercarlo, Ouyang, Jennifer, & DeSteno, David. (2010). "The Rhythm of Joint Action: Synchrony Promotes Cooperative Ability." *Journal of Experimental Social Psychology* 46 (4), 693–695.

Vendrell Ferran, Íngrid (in this volume). "Affective Intentionality: Early Phenomenological Contributions to a New Phenomenological Sociology". In: T. Szanto, & D. Moran (Eds.). *The Phenomenology of Sociality: Discovering the 'We'*. London/New York: Routledge.

von Scheve, Christian, & Ismer, Sven (2013). "Towards a Theory of Collective Emotions." *Emotion Review* 5 (4), 406–413.

von Scheve, Christian, & Salmela, Mikko (2014). *Collective Emotions*. Oxford: Oxford University Press.

Will, Udo, & Turrow, Gabe (2011). "Introduction to Entrainment and Cognitive Ethnomusicology." In: J. Berger, & P. G. Turrow (Eds.). *Music, Science, and the Rhythmic Brain: Cultural and Clinical Implications*. London/New York: Routledge, 3–30.

Windsor, W. Luke, & de Bézenac, Christophe (2012). "Music and Affordances." *Musicae Scientiae* 16 (1), 102–120.

# Part V
# Collective Agency and Group Personhood

# 17 Husserl on Groupings
## Social Ontology and the Phenomenology of We-Intentionality
*Emanuele Caminada*

Husserl's phenomenology of the lifeworld influenced post-war American sociology through the works of Schütz (1932), Luckmann and Berger (1966), as well as Garfinkel (1967). This tradition of phenomenological sociology based its methodology on rich descriptions and concepts such as the lifeworld, type, and habituation. However, phenomenological sociology relies more on anthropological or pragmatist approaches (Srubar 1988) than on the methods of phenomenological reduction. As a result of Schütz's skepticism (1957), both the transcendental account of Husserl and the social-ontological framework of early phenomenology were abandoned. Schütz understands the human mind as necessarily intersubjective, but remains faithful to Weber's methodological individualism. Accordingly, he rejects Husserl's non-reductionist social-ontological accounts of groupings and refuses to analyze in detail either Husserl's concepts of the "common mind" (*Gemeingeist*)[1] and "personality of higher order" (*Personalität höherer Ordnung*) or similar accounts in Scheler, Hildebrand, Stein, and Walther (Schütz 1975, 80; cf. Szanto, Salice, and Vendrell Ferran in this volume, and Szanto/Moran 2015).

While Schütz's phenomenological theory of action faces Weber's question of how social reality can emerge out of individual meanings (*subjektiv gemeinter Sinn*) and interactions, in the last two decades, analytical theories of action have discussed intensely the ontological nature of social groups and their specific *collective intentionality*. Early phenomenological accounts found unexpected resonance in this discussion thanks to a new generation of scholars able to bridge the divide between continental and analytic traditions. Initially, only realistic phenomenologists and their ontological approaches were discussed. However, in recent years, another picture of Husserl has come to the fore (Welton 2000), and his own phenomenology of sociality has been rediscovered (cf. Perreau 2013). In this contribution, I would like to sketch Husserl's own account of groupings, both as a social ontology and as a methodological challenge—namely the challenge of outlining the specific phenomenological reduction that would uncover the structure of "We-intentionality."

## 1 HUSSERL'S SOCIAL ONTOLOGY

While the debate on collective actions questioned individualistic accounts of intentionality, within phenomenology, the alleged solipsism of the "standard Husserl" was called into question. Up until recently, Husserl's social philosophy was seen to be confined to the realm of his ethics or else viewed as a peripheral adoption of positions from the tradition of German idealism. Therefore, his phenomenology has been interpreted as both Cartesian individualism and Hegelian collectivism (Schmid 2000, 18).

From a phenomenological standpoint, the analytical understanding of "intentionality" as "mental state with representative function" is quite ambiguous. Firstly, both the givenness of the object and the directedness of the subject are described phenomenologically as the accomplishment of *motivated acts* and not as the succession of mental states. Further, according to Husserl, not every intentional act is a form of representation. He describes perception as a kind of (*ap-*)*presentation* and rejects any image theory of consciousness, according to which the mind is an internal image of the outer world (Hua 19, 436–440).

Despite these striking differences, phenomenology and analytic theories of intentionality agree in distinguishing three main classes of intentional acts: 1. through *cognitive* acts, we discover the properties of objects, 2. through *affective* acts, we feel their values, and thus 3. we can intend and endorse goals and actions in *volitive* acts.

*Collective* intentionality, in particular, can be defined according 1. to the *subject* of intentional acts, 2. to the *mode* of their accomplishment, or 3. to their *content* (Schmid/Schweikard 2009, 46ff.). In the following, I shall situate Husserl's account according to these distinctions.

Though Husserl's account is usually characterized as based on an individualistic methodology, he believed that the contemporary philosophy of the mind, due to its naturalistic and individualistic approach, is blind to the fact that each subject is intentionally socialized with others (Hua 6, 241). Husserl claims that intentional acts can (at least partially) converge in one collective whole and form super-individual mental unities. Husserl subsumes these unities under the general concept of the common mind (*Gemeingeist*) and proposes a differentiated taxonomy (cf. Szanto 2015). These unities manifest their own intentional properties, such as beliefs, decisions, actions, and sentiments (Hua 14, 192). Husserl claims that his method of phenomenological reduction, which allows insights into the deep structure of intentionality, i.e., into the correlation of constituting subject and constituted objects (Hua 6, 169), can profitably be applied to clarify the socially intertwined intentionality of what he calls the common mind. While, bracketing the natural attitude, each object can be investigated so as to discover the subjective operations that lead to its apprehension or constitution, in investigating the constitution of cultural objects, the intentional association (*Verbindung*) of constituting subjectivities, comes to the fore. Husserl addresses therefore the subjective, *noetic* side of this socialized or communalized constitution. This social association relies on personal connections (*Zusammenhang*) which, in their simplest case, are enacted through the unity of a belief, judgement, evaluation, or intention (Hua 14, 194). Therefore, Husserl considers the basic unit of what nowadays is called collective intentionality as the unity of an enduring *common* opinion or belief (*gemeinsame bleibende Meinung*). The content of this belief is fixed by acts of position-taking (*Stellungnahme*) and has to be endorsed by the subject (Hua 4, 111; Hua 14, 195). These endorsements are accomplished on the basis of motives and become habitual possessions of the subject (as convictions, resolutions, or sentiments). As long as they are not questioned by new motives, they are not given up and can always be re-actualized or otherwise simply fade or fall into oblivion. In Husserl's account, habitual position-taking is at the core of personality. To be a person is to endorse enduring convictions, evaluations, and decisions acquired in one's own struggle for evidence (Hua 14, 196). Through her enduring statements, a person develops as "a pole of multiple, actual decisions, pole of a habitual system of irradiation of actualisable potencies for positive and negative position-takings" (Hua 11, 360). Every position-taking sediments itself in passive life, and therefore can contribute to reforming its underlying drive system in a habitual fashion (Hua 4, 377). Personality thus becomes the expression of the intentional life of both affects and activities.

Correspondingly, the intentional association of two or more persons can be viewed as a personal connection, that is, if they are grouped both in their passivity as well as in their activity. For instance, socio-communicative connections are realized through social and communicative acts. Following Reinach (1913, 707), Husserl (Hua 14, 166) defines *social acts* as those acts that are spontaneous and *in need of uptake* (*vernehmungsbedürftig*). Some of these social acts require a practical position-taking from the addressed person (i.e., orders or requests), from the addressing person (promises), or from both of them and *mutually* (agreements). Thanks to these acts, individuals can group together through understanding (*Einverständnis*). For instance, a community of will can only be grouped through a super-individual, unifying, and enduring position-taking that emerges from the agreement of the "enacting intertwining of will" of the involved persons (Hua 14, 170). This intertwining is a specific "level of a general, super-individual, and yet personal, operating consciousness" (Hua 14, 200).

Social acts can constitute the unity of a communicative plurality of persons, an intentional unity of consciousness that "streams out" (*ausströmen*) of these persons and "streams through them" (*durchströmen*) consistently (Hua 14, 200). The subject of this connection is an *analogue* of an individual subject because it arises out of a multipolar structure, out of a plurality of subjects. However, this plural, constituted consciousness is said to "operate personally" because it manifests a unity and consistency despite its plurality and because it can lead to a unitary but plural action. The personal character of such associated plurality of persons consists of the position-takings that the association enacts and of the corresponding commitment of its members to endorse them. The bearer of this constituted will, which is distributed among the individuals and founded on their social acts, is the plurality of persons. The intentional structure of this super-individual social subject relies, according to Husserl, upon the enduring endorsement that its members require, if they wish to remain faithful to their commitment to enact the guiding position-taking of the plural subject.

Husserl's account is similar to Gilbert's *plural subject theory*. According to Gilbert, a plural subject is a super-individual, intentional grouping that is formed by acts of *joint commitment*. By endorsing a commitment, a person commits herself to self-consistency. If two or more people *jointly* commit themselves, they commit themselves to consistency to their *joint* endorsement, thereby forming a plural subject. The difference, however, from personal commitments is that joint commitments can, once endorsed, not be revoked by any single of the—jointly committed—individuals, but only, in turn, *jointly*, by the plural subject. Gilbert refers to this joint commitment as the *social atom* of sociality. This is the core of the plural subject, which is constituted through the grouping of the committed persons (cf. Gilbert 2003). By means of the concept of "plural subject," Gilbert aims to explain the emergence of collective intentions, representations, desires, and emotions, as well as complex structures such as language, responsibility, and political duty, without reducing them to a network of individual states. However, her account has been criticized because it can avoid individualism only by presupposing individuals that are capable of joint commitment prior to any form of socialization (Schmid 2005, 214). The individuals who then commit jointly are not part of a genuinely *social* ontology themselves, since their nature as individuals with mental properties (and a capacity for joint commitment) does not presuppose any concept of plural subjectivity (Gilbert 1989, 435).

Despite the fact that Husserl was often similarly criticized, his approach is more complex. It is true that he seems to operate with the concept of "personality of higher order" in an analogous fashion to Gilbert, but he claims that there are forms of personal connection that are not realized through active social acts. Accordingly, the accomplishment of active social acts is possible only against the background of pregiven communalities of life. If a plural subject has been enacted, the social acts that their members endorse according to their commitments toward it do not leave the ongoing life of these members unaffected. On the contrary, they are *affected* by these accomplishments: their individual, passive lives become partly socialized. These acts, then, sediment themselves in relative passivity and persist in the form of re-actualizable habitualities. Habitualities for Husserl are informed by the contents and goals of their enacting acts and can therefore become drivers for further re-enactments.[2] Yet, even if not actualized, such habits tend to influence tendencies of social drives and feelings, social needs, and affects. For instance, if Anna shares the values and convictions of an environmental group, she can decide to join it. Accordingly, she commits herself and takes part in planned, joint actions. Her engagement may reinforce her convictions and passions, which become strong dispositions, habits. Her experience as a campaigner for tackling climate change may induce her to take on new personal and joint actions. Moreover, her sensitivity to climate issues and environmental values may increase and lead to demanding further responsibility from her and her close friends. Indeed, a campaign to raise public awareness reaches its goal if the campaigners are able to spread their concerns, making their sensitivity become commonsensical, that is, if they are able to render their explicit awareness as sensible, as habitual, and as common as they can.

Husserl's concept of the common mind in fact ranges from the activity of plural subjects, such a well-organized joint action, to the passivity of shared sensibilities. At the active, personal level of communal life, intentionality goes beyond mere coordination and convergence and can reach coherence, consistency, and unity, while within passivity, a plurality of poles of action and affection interact with each other; at the active level of social acts, even if only episodically, these intentional poles can constitute "systems of poles" and corresponding unities of life (cf. Husserl 1997, 218), acting as one body.

Husserl distinguishes passive and active forms of communication. In passive communication, subjects develop horizons of communality and familiarity. They grow in communal frameworks of sense in a converging lifeworld (cf. Hua 39, 542). Beyond these communalities, they can enact "systems of poles" (Husserl 1997, 218), or, in Gilbert's term, "plural subjects," through the shared accomplishment of active position-takings. They can share this accomplishment passively or actively. They can follow the position-taking of a leader and passively accept his or her position (*Setzung*), or they can follow the sense of such a position-taking while assuming and endorsing it. Active, shared accomplishment (*aktiver Mitvollzug*) gives access to a further level of the social constitution of reality. It presupposes an active understanding of the content of shared belief (*nachverstehender Aktivität*) against the background of sense communalities. Through this active explication of the shared content, the previously implicit content is cast in a new, reflexive light and can eventually be personally endorsed or refused.

The enactment of a plural subject, therefore, requires for Husserl a personal commitment not only to the *jointness* of shared intentionality (commitment to be part of a plural subject), but also to its content (commitment to be responsible, i.e., consistently sensitive to what this content requires me to do). To join a plural subject also demands, contrary to Gilbert, a *personal* endorsement of its goals and values. Furthermore, Husserl claims that only through this endorsement is a subject able to develop personal character, because the constraints given by being part of a plural subject call its members to responsibility (Hua 14, 170f.). More radically, Husserl even suggests that self-reference as such can be enabled only by the personal endorsement (or rejection) of the shared point of view achieved in passive levels of communalities.

Husserl's plural subject theory is thus different from Gilbert's in a crucial respect: it does not presuppose non-social individuals that can commit themselves to become social. Husserl envisages intentional associations and socialization already at the level of passivity. At this level, a pre-reflexive, relational communality emerges and necessarily sediments itself in individual minds. But personal life arises only through the intentional medium of these communities and can be actively constituted through commitments and endorsements.

Now, how does this paradigm fit into the distinctions of the contemporary debate, which tries to localize collective intentionality in either 1. the subjects of intentional acts, 2. in a "We-mode," or 3. in the content of the respective intentions?

In answering this question, first, it is important to bear in mind that through the methodology of phenomenological bracketing (*epoché*), every reference that transcends experience has to be avoided. Therefore, no real object of intentionality can be made responsible for its collective nature. Husserl, because of his radical understanding of the intertwining of noematic and noetic intentionality, cannot localize the collective moment of intentionality in the content alone, in the subject alone, or in the mode. Following the distinction between the three main classes of intentional acts, i.e., between cognitive, volitive, and emotional acts, Husserl tries to offer an ideal typology of different types of groupings. He emphasizes the *dynamics of grouping* rather than the *structures of groups*.[3]

Cognitive acts associate multipolar systems of subjects, to which Husserl often refers with the term "intersubjectivity." Cognitive systems are unified by the overarching goal of gaining objectivity. As individuals can explore their environments through their senses, apperceptions, and enduring cognitions, so, similarly, a "communicative plurality of subjects" can explore its common environment (Hua 14, 197). Thus, this plural subject of cognition disposes of a plural system of sensibility and of enduring apperception constituted through communication. Its correlate is the objective world and its constitutive performativity is accomplished in each subject that takes part in its enactment. Each act of cognition directed to the objectivity of the world approximates to the constitutive operations of this ideal plural subject called intersubjectivity. The more demanding the task of objectivity the individual endorses, the broader the horizon of intersubjectivity the individual enacts. To the infinite task of universal knowledge corresponds the infinitively open structure of intersubjectivity. The community of knowing subjects associated in the task of open intersubjectivity is an ideal sociality that enables each of them to accomplish cognitive actions that are ideally *reliable for everyone*.

Husserl contrasts open intersubjectivity with concrete groupings unified by emotive and volitive acts. Intentionality is originally shaped socially in affective life (*Gemütsleben*). To be sure, others' views and arguments can lead me to form new beliefs. Yet, in order to grasp the motives of others' beliefs, I have to be able to understand them (through empathy, expressions, or signs), and *understanding* presupposes more basic forms of socialization (primary communalization, spoken and written language learning, etc.). Beyond the passive level of communalities and familiarities, active associations are enacted by volitive and affective joint intentionality. For instance, in the abovementioned case of the collective will of an environmental group, the concerned subjects commit themselves to the tasks necessary to the success of the awareness campaign. By grouping for acting, they group themselves in an associated plurality (*verbundene Vielheit*) as a "unity constituted in plurality" (*in Vielheit konstituierte Einheit*): as campaigners, they are unified by the campaign. Such a plural subject is conceptualized by Husserl as a personal substrate for acts and enduring acts. The acts and enduring unities of the plural subject are "unities of higher orders" founded in the corresponding acts of the individual subjects (Hua 14, 201). *Through the plural action, a higher-order personal being is founded by the unified will of the individuals.* A plural action, as the accomplishment of collective intentionality, does not *presuppose* a group as a plural subject, but, rather, *groups* the enacting subjects according to its own unity. In Husserl's view, a plural subject is more than a group: it is the enduring effect of grouping.

Husserl refers to social groupings that manifest personal traits as *personalities of a higher order* because he understands them as the expression of a *foundational relation*. The position-takings of the group are said to be unities of a higher order because they are founded in the acts of the subjects who endorse the position-taking of the group. The latter, therefore, is a *constituted object of higher order* because it is a founded object of the same class as the founding objects. Reassessing Husserl's mereology, Conni defines two forms of whole: *pregnant* and *emergent* ones. The pregnant whole is characterized through mutual foundation among its parts, while the emergent structure is characterized by a jointly immediate foundation of a novel whole (Conni 2005, 84). The emergent whole and the founding parts engage in a mutual foundation relation: the founding parts are *individuated* by the founded whole, being *interpenetrated* by its properties.

Accordingly, a *personality of higher order* is an emergent object. The individual persons as such are not the founding parts—they remain *autonomous parts*—but only some of their particular acts. Every personal act is a *non-autonomous part* of the individual person, but only those acts that are committed to the goals of the personality of higher order are individuated by it. Only the acts accomplished *as a campaigner* constitute the campaign and are constituted by it. The mutual foundation relation between parts and whole embraces, therefore, not individuals and associations, but only some non-autonomous parts of the individuals and the emergent structures they found (i.e., the campaigners' acts and the campaign). Therefore, the person who *jointly* endorses a position-taking (i.e., the person who campaigns) will be the bearer of the part of an *emergent* whole (i.e., will accomplish some campaign's acts and will bear some campaigner's habits). Thus, Anna will be implicated in the foundation of a plural subject (i.e., the campaign's organization), but she will not be simply absorbed by the latter, since she is not herself exclusively part of the whole: she is not like an organic member of the group, as the organ of an organism. Her life goes beyond the life of the plural subject. The life of Anna goes beyond her engagement as a campaigner.

For Husserl, enduring habits pertain essentially to the concept of person, since personal individuality is enacted through passions (volitive and emotive acts) and endures in habitual sentiments or dispositions (*Gesinnungen*). Personalities of a higher order are given only if jointly enacted and only if firm habitualities endure in their founding persons. The emergent whole, the personal plural subject, can endure only through an enduring endorsement of the bearers of the founding parts.

According to Husserl, the association through collective will is deeper if it is the effect of the bond of love. Love, as paradigmatic of affective intentionality, demands personal contact to the individuality of the beloved; it strives after attachment. Love, for Husserl, is striving after a community in life and striving for a community in which the life of the beloved is assumed and the beloved's will is endorsed. The lovers care for the realization of their mutual strivings and wills. If they group their inner passions, they live one in the other: "I live as an I in her and she in me" (Hua 14, 172). The inner perspective of the beloved becomes a habitual, implicit moment of the passions of the lover.

The community of lovers therefore attains an individuation and interpenetration of personal life that enacts a paradigmatic form of personality of higher order: love brings the lovers, in being intentional and habitual, one into the other (*Ineinandersein*). They carry each other, one in the other, in passive and active striving. They live an intimate, collective will, even if they are not always in actual contact (cf. Hua 14, 174, cf. Salice in this volume).

## 2 HUSSERL ON WE-INTENTIONALITY

Open intersubjectivity, plural subjects, and personalities of a higher order are characterized by different forms of grouping and accordingly by different grades of integration of personal life. A social personality is given, according to Husserl, only if a "form of I-centring" and an "enduring habituality" is enacted (cf. Hua 14, 405). There are many forms of social groupings that are not centered in such a way, but plural subjects and personalities of a higher order, in fact, are. They do not simply possess this property: they are enacted by forms of centering. Now, one might wonder whether the intentionality of grouping that is brought about by this form of I-centering should be understood *egologically*, i.e., as a collective I-mode. Were this the case, it seems that the specificity of we-intentionality, i.e., its irreducibility to I- or I-mode intentions, could not be properly addressed in Husserlian terms. However, Husserl does not attribute a simple egological form to we-intentionality. On the contrary, he describes it as a "form of *ego-alteri*":

> The communal subjectivity is a multi-headed subjectivity, a form of *ego-alteri*. Each communalized *ego* has not only his consciousness, but his consciousness as it is open to the access into the others', and as associated in the multi-headed subjectivity. As such this consciousness is open to the horizons of indeterminacy.
>
> (Hua 14, 218)

In other words, each head, as it were, of the "multi-headed subjectivity" has open horizons, "an open indeterminate plurality of others, beyond those that I can embrace and actually grasp in understanding" (ibid.). By the metaphor of the "multi-headed subjectivity," Husserl describes the plural horizons of experience that are given as members of an open, plural subject. Each member can fully understand only some of the other members; beyond that, however, one can still experience the indeterminacy of other possible members, as these are pre-delineated through the horizons of the concrete encounter with the closer members. Moreover, Husserl inquires into the *transcendental* relevance of this discovery: if the subject of experience is a socialized one, how does its sociality contribute to the constitution of its experience?

The intentional horizons of the experience of a socialized subjectivity bears not only the implicit structures that an individual ego has acquired, or can acquire, but also those intentional structures that are implicated by other socialized subjects:

> [. . .] therefore, it would be wrong to say that the transcendental reduction reduces me, my being and inner life only to my transcendental subjectivity. Since in my experience I always have another subjectivity, this or that concrete ones and, furthermore, a plurality of *alter ego*, it reduces me to a multi-headed transcendental subjectivity, which embraces, along with my own subjectivity, also everyone of these *alter ego*, with all their life, with all their phenomena, and intentional correlates.
>
> (Hua 35, 111)

In his 1922 *London Lectures*, Husserl emphasizes how crucial it is to make these very implications of socialized subjects phenomenologically explicit: "In the proper line of its explication lies the development of the originally, egological [. . .] phenomenology into a transcendental sociological phenomenology" (as cited in Schumann 1988, 56; cf. Hua 9, 539). The explication of the constitutive operations of subjectivity discloses to phenomenological analysis the constituting relevance of its sociality. Therefore, phenomenology will research the constitutive enactments (*Leistungen*) of the subject not in the framework of a transcendental egology, but in "every social form"

(Hua 6, 182), i.e., in the broader framework of a "transcendental sociology" (Lee 2005). Husserl does not abandon the idea of an egological centering of the constituting subjectivity, but this centering is consequently addressed in its relational dynamics, or in the process of socialization (in the form of *ego-alteri*). The so-called "Cartesian way" to phenomenology is accordingly modified, as "directly directed to the *ego cogito* and *nos cogitamus*" (Hua 8, 316).

The reduction to the We—i.e., its phenomenological discovery—can occur either within the framework of the static or the genetic method, depending on whether the *structure* of the socialized experience or the *process* of socialization are at the core of the phenomenological analysis. In the first case, it is the ontological structure of the lifeworld that is at stake. The guiding questions here are: how does the world appear *to us*? How can we experience it together and in our common sense as the same world? How can we describe its ontological structures, those which we commonly take as necessary and for granted? And how can the world appear in other modalities (i.e., not as necessary, but as questioned, or possible, etc.) (cf. Hua 15, 67)? For Husserl, these questions can be addressed only if the ontology of the lifeworld is analyzed as the world "for us," which claims to be and gives evidences for being, at its core, the world "as such." The clarification of the way from the "for us" to the "as such," usually interpreted as the distinction between epistemological and ontological questions, is for Husserl the main task of transcendental phenomenology.

Moreover, Husserl addressed the problem of socialization by elaborating a special form of phenomenological reduction and contrasting it with the previous questions:

> Instead of analysing the common modes of relativity through which our world is given to us, let's question back: the world of our experience is primarily the world of *my* experience. The Others, who are experiencing with me, are always worldly given to me, in different phenomena and subjective modes. I reduce to the I and to the *cogitations* out of which there is world for me and I question, *how* it is there. I reduce therefore directly to the primordial *ego* and I question then, how it becomes a social *ego*. How can a community continuously prove itself (*sich bewähren*) for this ego? How can every single person in this community be like me and take for granted the same, that I take for granted, and experience the communal world as I do?

(Hua 15, 66)

Husserl's attempt to answer to these questions led him to the infamous primordial reduction of the *Fifth Cartesian Meditation* (Hua 1, 91ff.). The aim of this reduction is to bracket or inhibit the validity of every constitutive enactment and effort that presupposes other subjects. By inhibiting the constitutive socialization of the subject, Husserl tries to clarify the very structure of socialization (*Vergemeinschaftung*), namely by investigating the special form of passive mental operation that leads to the constitution of pairs or groups. Husserl calls this passive synthesis *pairing* (*Paarung*) or *grouping* (cf. McIntyre 2012, 76). Two or more given objects pair or group themselves, i.e., they form a "similarizing association" (*verähnlichende Assoziation*) in the form of a pair or of a group, if, in their givenness, a configuration that is mutually founded in these objects passively emerges. Accordingly, trees are given in the row of a colonnade, stars as configured in a constellation, birds in a swarm, and so on. For the experiencing subject, these groupings are given prior to their parts, since they emerge passively and manifest qualities that are irreducible to their founding components.

In social grouping, however, the subject is itself involved in the pairing: the synthesis is elicited by the embodied habits of a similar body. Another body pairs and other bodies group within the embodied experience of the subject. This synthesis enables a mutual constitution of pairs and groups of situation-bound and bodily-centered habits. The most general form of correlation, *ego-alteri*, consists of these habits. The iteration of such basic socialization culminates in the structure of we-intentionality:

> I, in the centre, the others around me—not as objects, but as actors. In this way I have my others, but each of these others has me and its others around it, *eccentrically*, while each centre is there as a subject of interests, as a first person, while the others are second and self-mediating persons.
>
> (Hua 39, 385)

Within the structure of we-intentionality, the others are given eccentrically because each centering excludes the centering of the others. But their horizons become constitutive parts of *my* horizon: *our* horizons "compenetrate" and merge in a socialized horizon, centered around me. This is the formal structure of we-intentionality, according to Husserl. The description of a We-mode of experience or the postulation of a capacity for we-intentionality is only the point of departure of a complex phenomenological analysis: "discovering the We" means, for Husserl, to uncover the sedimentation of the most basic associations or groupings that enable the constitution and the development of a *common* world.

It is only against the background of socialized horizons that *collective* (or *individual*) position-takings that require a commitment to self-coherence become possible. If collective motives and themes are understood and followed, if the subject lives through a community, participates and cooperates in its life, some of the traits of communal life that were actually accomplished by the subject can sediment and become habitual traits of its background. The new centering consists of the intertwining of these communal actualities and habitualities. Furthermore, each form of personal position-taking is influenced by the form *ego-alteri*, since each one can know its own self only through the others and as their other (Hua 14, 418). For these reasons, it is implausible to assume the existence of two separate capabilities, of I-intentionality and we-intentionality, between which each individual can switch. Rather, it seems more plausible to understand the I and the We as two different foci of the same first-person perspective. As if "zooming out," the subject can simply focus within the horizon of the common world of familiar counterparts, can tend to the wide horizon offered by the structure of open intersubjectivity, or else can focus primarily on its own personal realm.

According to Husserl, then, the enrichment and broadening of intentional horizons in the process of socialization should be studied, genetically, step by step, and, importantly, with regard to the different types of intentional acts, not only cognitive but also, and foremost, with regard to volitive and affective ones (cf. Chelstrom, Vendrell Ferran, Krueger, and Salice, in this volume). The specific field of study of a crucial part of phenomenology, namely of constitutive or transcendental sociology (Lee 2005), ought to take all these dimensions and stages of sociality into account. Finally, the convergence of undefined horizons, at the limits of the idea of open intersubjectivity (cf. Zahavi 2001), should not only be deduced from, or statically constructed by, the analysis of the experience of objectivity, but should rather be clarified genetically, in its very emergence (cf. Caminada 2011).

## CONCLUSION

Husserl discusses social groupings both within an ontological framework and within a genetic, phenomenological account of the passive synthesis of grouping. Both sides are intricately intertwined.

Following the distinction between the three main classes of intentional acts (cognitive, volitive, and emotional acts), I distinguished between the structures of open intersubjectivity, plural subjects, and personalities of a higher order.

I emphasized the *dynamics of grouping* rather than the *structures of groups* in Husserl's account: a plural action, as the accomplishment of collective intentionality, does not *presuppose* a group as a plural subject, but, rather, *groups* the enacting subjects according to its own unity. A plural subject is more than a group: it is the enduring effect of grouping. Further, I defended an ontological reading of the idea of plural subject and of personality of higher order on the basis of Husserl's own mereology.

Finally, I stressed the way in which Husserl in his genetic phenomenology does not abandon the idea of an egological centering of the constituting subjectivity, but consequently addresses this centering in the process of socialization. Therefore, I claim that it is implausible to assume the existence of two separate capabilities, of I-intentionality and We-intentionality, between which each individual can switch. Rather, it seems plausible to understand the I and the We as two different foci of the same first-person perspective.

## ACKNOWLEDGMENTS

I would like to thank Alex Englander and Thomas Szanto for their helpful suggestions on an earlier version of this text.

## NOTES

1 On the systematic relevance of this concept for Husserl's phenomenology, see Caminada (forthcoming).
2 On the role of habits, both in Husserl's social epistemology and social ontology, see Caminada (forthcoming).
3 The main argument of the following presentation of Husserl's typology corresponds to Toulemont's distinction between *simple intersubjectivité*, *systemes de poles*, and *synthèse de pôles* (cf. 1962, 311ff.). Similarly, Szanto (2015) distinguishes four types of shared intentionality: intersubjective, social, communal, and collective intentionality.

## REFERENCES

Berger, Peter L., & Luckmann, Thomas (1966). *The Social Construction of Reality*. Garden City, NY: Anchor Books.
Caminada, Emanuele (2011). "Husserls intentionale Soziologie". In: V. Mayer, C. Erhard, & M. Scherini (Eds.). *Die Aktualität Husserls*. Freiburg/München: Alber.
——— (2014). "Joining the Background: Habitual Sentiments Behind We-Intentionality". In: A. Konzelmann Ziv, & H. B. Schmid (Eds.). *Institutions, Emotions, and Group Agents Contributions to Social Ontology*. Dordrecht: Springer.
——— (forthcoming). "Die Relevanz der Entdeckung des Gemeingeistes für die phänomenologische Philosophie". In: J. Brudzińska, & D. Lohmar (Eds.). *Phänomenologie des Menschen und die Grundlagen einer modernen Sozialtheorie. Neuere Beiträge zur Phänomenologie und Anthropologie des Sozialen*. Dordrecht: Springer.
——— (forthcoming). *Plurale Habitūs. Zur Sozialisierung der phänomenologischen Philosophie*.
Conni, Carlo (2005). *Identità e Strutture Emergenti*. Milano: Bompiani.
Garfinkel, Harald (1967). *Studies in Ethnomethodology*. Englewood Cliffs, NJ: Prentice-Hall.
Gilbert, Margaret (1989). *On Social Facts*. London/New York: Routledge.
——— (2003). "The Stucture of the Social Atom: Joint Commitment as the Foundation of Human Social Behavior". In: F. P. Schmitt (Ed.). *Socializing Metaphysics*. Oxford: Rowman & Littlefield.
Husserl, Edmund (1997). "Wert des Lebens. Wert der Welt. Sittlichkeit (Tugend) und Glückseligkeit <Februar 1923>". In: *Husserl Studies* 13, 201–235.
——— (1950) [=Hua 1]. *Cartesianische Meditationen und Pariser Vorträge*. Ed. by S. Strasser. Den Haag: Martinus Nijhoff.
——— (1952) [=Hua 4]. *Ideen zur einer reinen Phänomenologie und phänomenologischen Philosophie. Zweites Buch: Phänomenologische Untersuchungen zur Konstitution*. Ed. by M. Biemel. Den Haag: Martinus Nijhoff.
——— (1976) [=Hua 6]. *Die Krisis der europäischen Wissenschaften und die transzendentale Phänomenologie. Eine Einleitung in die phänomenologische Philosophie*. Ed. by W. Biemel. Den Haag: Martinus Nijhoff.

―――― (1959) [=Hua 8]. *Erste Philosophie (1923/4).* Zweiter Teil: Theorie der phänomenologischen Reduktion. Ed. by Rudolf Boehm. Den Haag: Martinus Nijhoff.
―――― (1968) [=Hua 9]. *Phänomenologische Psychologie. Vorlesungen Sommersemester. 1925.* Ed. by W. r Biemel. Den Haag: Martinus Nijhoff.
―――― (1966) [=Hua 11]. *Analysen zur passiven Synthesis. Aus Vorlesungs- und Forschungsmanuskripten, 1918–1926.* Ed. by M. Fleischer. Den Haag: Martinus Nijhoff.
―――― (1973a) [=Hua 14]. *Zur Phänomenologie der Intersubjektivität.* Texte aus dem Nachlass. Zweiter Teil. 1921–28. Ed. by Iso Kern. Den Haag: Nijhoff.
―――― (1973b) [=Hua 15]. *Zur Phänomenologie der Intersubjektivität.* Texte aus dem Nachlass. Dritter Teil. 1929–35. Ed. by I. Kern. Den Haag: Nijhoff.
―――― (1984) [=Hua 19]. *Logische Untersuchungen. Zweiter Teil. Untersuchungen zur Phänomenologie und Theorie der Erkenntnis.* Ed. by U. Panzer. Den Haag: Martinus Nijhoff.
―――― (2002) [=Hua 35]. *Einleitung in die Philosophie. Vorlesungen 1922/23.* Ed. by B. Goossens. Dordrecht: Kluwer.
―――― (2008) [=Hua 39] *Die Lebenswelt. Auslegungen der vorgegebenen Welt und ihrer Konstitution. Texte aus dem Nachlass (1916–1937).* Ed. by R. Sowa. New York: Springer.
Lee, Nam-In (2005). "On the Future of Phenomenological Sociology". In: S. Geniusas, D. Lavoie, & N. Patnaik (Eds.). *On the Future of Husserlian Phenomenology.* https://www.newschool.edu/nssr/husserl/Future/Part%20One/Lee.html [14. 01. 2015]
Luckmann Thomas, & Schütz, Alfred (1974). *The Structures of the Life-World.* London: Heinemann.
McIntyre, Ronald (2012). "We-Subjectivity: Husserl on Community and Communal Constitution." In: C. Fricke, & D. Follesdal (Eds.). *Intersubjectivity and Objectivity in Adam Smith and Edmund Husserl: A Collection of Essays.* Frankfurt: Ontos.
Perreau, Laurent (2013). *Le monde social selon Husserl.* Dordrecht: Springer.
Reinach, Adolf (1913). "Die apriorischen Grundlagen des bürgerlichen Rechtes". *Jahrbuch für Philosophie und phänomenologische Forschung* 1, 685–847.
Schmid, Hans Bernhard (2000). *Subjekt, System, Diskurs. Edmund Husserls Begriff transzendentaler Subjektivität in sozialtheoretischen Bezügen.* Dordrecht: Springer.
―――― (2005). *Wir-Intentionalität. Kritik des ontologischen Individualismus und Rekonstruktion der Gemeinschaft.* Freiburg/München: Alber.
Schmid, Hans Bernhard, & Schweikard, David (2009). "Einleitung: Kollektive Intentionalität. Begriff, Geschichte, Probleme". In: Schmid, Hans Bernhard/Schweikard, David (Eds.). *Kollektive Intentionalität. Eine Debatte über die Grundlagen des Sozialen,* Frankfurt: Suhrkamp.
Schuhmann, Karl (1988). *Husserls Staatsphilosophie.* Freiburg, München: Alber.
Schütz, Alfred (1932). *Der sinnhafte Aufbau der sozialen Welt. Eine Einleitung in die verstehende Soziologie.* Wien: Springer.
―――― (1957). "Das Problem der transzendentalen Intersubjektivität bei Husserl". *Philosophische Rundschau* 5, 81–107.
―――― (1959). "Husserl and the Social Sciences". In: *Edmund Husserl. 1859–1959. Recueil commémoratif publié à l'occasion du centenaire de la naissance du philosophe.* Den Haag: Springer, 86–98.
―――― (1971). *Das Problem der Relevanz.* Frankfurt, a.M.: Suhrkamp.
―――― (1975). *Collected Papers III. Studies in Phenomenological Philosophy.* Ed. by I. Schütz. Den Haag: Springer.
Srubar, Ilja (1988). *Kosmion: die Genese der pragmatischen Lebensweltheorie von Alfred Schütz und ihr anthropologischer Hintergrund.* Frankfurt, a.M.: Suhrkamp.

Szanto, Thomas (2015). "Husserl on Collective Intentionality." In: A. Salice & H. B. Schmid (Eds.). *Social Reality: The Phenomenological Approach*. Dordrecht: Springer.

Szanto Thomas, & Moran, Dermot (Eds.) (forthcoming). *Empathy and Collective Intentionality. The Social Philosophy of Edith Stein.Human Studies* (Special Issue).

Toulemont, René (1962). *L'essence de la société selon Husserl*. Paris: Presses Universitaires de France.

Welton, Donn (2000). *The Other Husserl: The Horizons of Transcendental Phenomenology*. Bloomington: Indiana University Press.

Zahavi, Dan (2001). *Husserl and Transcendental Intersubjectivity: A Response to the Linguistic-Pragmatic Critique*. Athens, OH: Ohio University Press.

# 18 Collectivizing Persons and Personifying Collectives
## Reassessing Scheler on Group Personhood

*Thomas Szanto*

## 1 INTRODUCTION

Can a group of persons constitute a group person? From Plato's notorious analogy between the *polis* and the human soul in the *Republic*, to Hobbes's concept of artificial personhood and Locke, Hume, and the following modern discussion of personal identity, the idea that personhood is no natural kind, and that persons may come in different scopes and sizes, transgressing the boundaries of the human organism, looms large. Centuries later, a number of philosophers would press Plato's analogy further (Parfit 1986, 211; Korsgaard 1989; Rovane 1998). The question of whether individual persons can integrate into a single personal unit that differs from ordinary, human-sized persons is not only pre-figured in the debate on diachronic and synchronic personal identity, but has also been extensively discussed in the German and British legal theory traditions of the 19th and 20th centuries (cf. Runciman 1997). Most recently, the issue has been fueled by the analytic debate on collective intentionality and group agency.[1] Similarly, in times of ever more concentrated corporate power, one can also witness a growing interest in the respective normative and political questions. For example, it has been argued that corporate persons, lacking certain essential capacities for moral conduct and accountability, such as affectivity and empathy, exhibit all the features of 'psychopaths' (Bakan 2004). Meanwhile, some have inquired whether we have proper obligations towards group persons, or whether they have, above and beyond moral accountability (French 1979; Manning 1984), any moral or political rights of their own, such as the right to protection, the right to persist (Ozar 1985), and the right to freedom of speech (Stoll 2005; List & Pettit 2011; Briggs 2012; Hess 2013; Hindriks 2015).[2]

What is less known is that many phenomenologists, including Husserl (e.g., 1952, 1973), have complex accounts of group personhood, or have critically engaged in the debate on the possibility of such entities.[3] Scheler is certainly the figure of the phenomenological movement who not only makes the most use of the notion, but also has elaborate conceptual requisites, firmly embedded in his personalist value ethics, for dealing with the ontological, and especially the normative, implications of group personhood.

The present chapter aims to reassess Scheler's account, and with particular attention paid to the intricate issue of intentional and normative collectivism. In doing so, I wish to show that Scheler's account, however ambiguous it is at times, is not only equipped to fulfill those central requirements for group personhood that I argue any theory of group persons must account for (see section 2), but, on the most charitable reading, it also navigates the thin line between merely summative and all-too-collectivist accounts of group persons. Ultimately, I hope that in sketching this Schelerian path (see sections 3 and 4), and by pointing to the strengths and weaknesses of his account (see section 5), we get a better grip of what really is, ontologically and normatively, at stake when one collectivizes persons, or personifies collectives.

## 2 FOUR REQUIREMENTS FOR GROUP PERSONS

To begin with, consider the following general requirements that I contend any adequate theory of group persons (GPs) must fulfill:

(1) *Plurality Requirement*: GPs, qua *group* persons, must be so construed as to account for the fact that they 'comprise' (at some given time[4]) a *plurality* of individuals, allowing also for a certain 'intentional variation' in their mental lives.[5]

(2) *Integrity Requirement*: GPs, qua group *persons*, must be so construed as to account for the fact that they not only form a collection or multiplicity of individuals, but have an integrity as a distinctive person. Moreover, GPs must enjoy a certain autonomy vis-à-vis the individuals who are their members or constituents, and vice versa.

(3) *Normativity, or Moral Accountability, Requirement*: given (2) and the commonly held specific normative status of individual persons, GPs should as well have some normative or axiological status, i.e., moral right or value of their own, and/or should be morally accountable in their own right.[6]

(4) *Anti-Collectivism Requirement*: given (1) and certain standard, normative requirements for individual personhood (autonomy, etc.), GPs must not (normatively or intentionally) 'override' or 'outflank' the individuals they comprise (cf. Pettit 1993; 2014).

While the first requirement should be fairly obvious—no group person without a group of persons—and while the second and third are expounded in detail in one or the other abovementioned accounts, rather strikingly, very few current GP-accounts discuss (4), i.e., the normative and non-normative (intentional-psychological) relation of GPs to individuals. With a view to this task, Scheler is a good starting point, to say the least.

Furthermore, however obvious the plurality requirement may be, some may question it by, rightly, assuming the possibility of there being one single individual who bears or instantiates the properties of a group person. This indeed is a real possibility, especially for Scheler, as we shall see. Thus, we need to slightly qualify the above requirement to the effect that, first, for any GP, there must be, at one point or another, a *collective* of individuals who constitute it and, secondly, once constituted, and even if eventually instantiated by only a single individual, GP-properties must stand in some relation to and allow for a variety of intentional properties of a plurality of individuals.

With these preliminaries in place, in the following, I shall show that Scheler's account of GPs does fulfill all four of these requirements—however ambivalent Scheler may be at times, and however much (1)–(4) may prima facie conflict with one another.

## 3 SCHELER'S CONCEPT OF *GESAMTPERSON*

One of the fundamental claims concerning personhood that virtually all phenomenologists agree upon concerns its social nature. According to this view, personhood has intrinsically and irreducibly social aspects. Few phenomenologists, and few philosophers in general, have been more explicit and adamant about this than Scheler. One of Scheler's central claims is that (individual or communal) persons have an irreducible social aspect, such that even hypothetical Robinson Crusoes are from birth essentially embedded in social relations and have both a non-social, or "intimate sphere" and a "social sphere" as their equal co-constituents (Scheler 1926a, 548ff.; 1926b, 228ff.). Moreover, Scheler argues for an irreducible, socio-ontological correlation between individual and 'plural' subjects. He maintains not only that "the I is but a 'part' ('*Glied*') of the We and We an essential part of the I" (1926b, 225), but that the We, "genetically" viewed, and regarding its "reality" and "specific content," precedes the I (1926c, 52, 57). Going even further than this, Scheler argues that it is an a priori feature of personhood that every person is a member of a social unity, and that, indeed, insofar as every individual person *has* a non-individual, or communal, person as her essential part, she, in turn, *is* and *experiences* herself as a member of a "communal person" (*Gesamtperson*) (henceforth: CP)[7] and, eventually, as a member of a set of such communal persons.

Now, one may wonder why Scheler employs the notion of CP in the first place. However, the answer is rather clear: for Scheler, communities have intrinsic values. Values, according to his ethical personalism, are founded upon and can only be borne by persons. And, since the highest social values belong to certain forms of communities, they belong not to persons *simpliciter*, but to *communal* persons (1926a, 514). Hence, for Scheler, the attribution of personhood to communities, more than for any other reason, clearly is born out of considerations regarding persons as bearers of values. Accordingly, the concept of CP is not simply a moral- or social-psychological epistemology (in the sense of 'group minds' (*Gruppengeist*), as Scheler employs that concept in his sociology of knowledge; cf. 1926c, 54f), nor is it merely a social-ontological concept. It is just as much an axiological, or properly ethical, concept.

Two central features—an axiological and an epistemological-*cum*-ontological one—characterize personhood for Scheler. First, persons are the "ultimate" (*letzte*) and, at the same time, the "highest" (*höchste*) values, and bearers of values (1926a, 103ff., 499, 514). Secondly, the very ontological nature of persons, apart from being bearers of values, is to be unique "centres of experiencing" (*Aktzentrum des Er-lebens*) (1926a, 103, 382–92). Accordingly, the proper role of personhood, for Scheler, consists of the integration of mental and practical acts. Communal persons, in turn, are first and foremost yet more complex integrates of such integrations.

In order to understand Scheler's concept of CP, it is crucial to bear in mind what CPs are not. First, they are neither opposed to, nor in any proper sense contrasted with, individual persons, nor are they simply a collection or an aggregate thereof. Furthermore, they are not a synthesis, composition, or some fusion of individual persons. Scheler would also reject the currently dominant view of collective intentionality, according to which the (plural) subjects of group agency are constituted by collective agreement, or joint commitment (e.g., Gilbert 1989; Searle 1995; Tuomela 2007; cf. Scheler 1926a, 512f., 521). Lastly, being a CP most certainly is not a matter of scope. A CP, Scheler explicitly tells us, is not some individual of a "wider scope" (1926a, 513).

How, then, are CPs constituted, and what is their socio-ontological status? Most generally viewed, CPs are not supra-individuals or macro entities. Rather, they are complex matrices of different levels and depths of the social integration of intentional and phenomenal experiences, volitions, and actions. CPs are "social unities" as well as "experienced realities" (*erlebte Realität*; 1926a, 511f.). They are *constituted by* and *experienced in* those specific intentional acts that Scheler calls mutual co-experiencing or co-living (*Miteinandererleben, Miteinanderleben*). It is easy to misunderstand these acts. Their distinctive feature is not some specific type of phenomenal quality, some 'feeling of togetherness' built into them, nor are co-experiences constituted merely by shared *types* of individuals' experiences. Furthermore, it is not essentially a matter of some 'we'-intentional mode, like for example, Tuomela's (2007) "We-mode," or some Searlean 'I *we*-experience x.' Neither is it simply a matter of the intentional directedness to some shared intentional object or goal that makes such acts constitutive of communal persons. Rather, for Scheler, the fact that a subject S is co-experiencing something is a matter of S's experiencing something and, at the same time, experiencing herself as a member of a community for which, and for whose members, S bears specific relations of *solidarity* and *co-responsibility* (*Mit-Verantwortlichkeit*). That is to say that, for Scheler, the experiential and normative properties of such social integrations of experiences are inseparably and constitutively tied together. CPs, then, are constituted, and their personhood essentially consists of, more than anything else (e.g., autonomous, intentional agents), being "act-centres of experiencing within the co-experiencing of persons" (1926, 512), as well as of being centers of co-responsibility, or solidarity.

Importantly, not only is a CP not a matter of scope, but there is no *one* ultimate, maximum-sized, or all-encompassing CP. Given that CPs are "varieties of centers of experiencing (*mannigfache Zentren des Er-lebens*) within the endless totality of co-experiencing-with-one-another," precisely by being "never-ending" integrations and re-integrations of social unities, CPs "essentially" are, like concentric circles, contained as social unities within one another. In other words: every CP essentially has other CPs as its members, without there being *one* single 'meta-CP' who would contain all other CPs within itself (1926a, 510, 521).[8] As examples of CPs, Scheler typically mentions nations (but not peoples), states, "cultural circles/regions" (*Kulturkreise*), and, in its highest and purest form, the church (Scheler 1915/16, 380; 1916b, 336f.; 1926a, 533–48).

CPs would be not *persons* for Scheler, if they would not be just as individual as individual persons. In fact, they bear an individuality of their own. However, a CP is not an entity of which *one* single subject or person can be predicated. But again, and this is the very gist of Scheler's argument, even if not a 'single subject' (*Einzelperson*), CPs not only have individuality, but they *are* individuals: "the communal person [. . .] is as much a spiritual (*geistig*) *individual* as the individual person" (1926a, 514). CPs are not merely the phenomenal content of individual persons' social or communal experiences, i.e., simply *given in* such experiences. They are more than that: like individuals, they are themselves centers of intentional and experiential acts and, more particularly, they constitute a "unity of *spiritual* act-centers" (1926a, 531). And, precisely as centers of acts of co-experiencing, they are the proper (formal) subjects of such communal experiences (1926a, 511). Moreover, being essentially spiritual entities, CPs have, above and beyond their experiential reality and their individuality, their own volitional and intentional reality. They are experiential unities as well as subjects of whom practical intentionality and agency can be predicated (*pace* Kelly 2011, 6).

CPs also have an intentional "'consciousness-of' that is *different from* and *independent of* the consciousness-of of the *individual* persons" (1926a, 512). Although the intentional content of the consciousness of a CP does transcend individuals' consciousness—as individuals' experiences do not "encompass" the total experiential content of a CP—what we have here is not some "mysterious" collective consciousness, transcending altogether the "kind" of consciousness that individuals have. For, even if in co-experiencing there is an excess of intentional content relative to any individual's experiences—no CP is "fully" (*ganz*) given in any single individual's experiential life, in much the same way as, for Husserl, physical objects are not fully given in single instances of perception—co-experiencing is still an affair of individuals. It takes place 'within' mutually interrelated but individual persons. Moreover, CPs are "given in" and "given for" each and every one of its members, irrespective of their standing within the system of co-experiencing. In this respect, experiential transcendence notwithstanding, "the consciousness-of of the communal person is *always contained* in the consciousness of a total finite person as *act-direction* [and] is not something transcendent to it" (1926a, 512f.). Indeed, what makes an individual's experiencing mutual co-experiencing, and eventually part of a CP's communal experiencing is, over and above the mutual awareness of the respective persons co-experiencing, the recognition that there is an excess of intentional contents vis-à-vis the individual, upon whose co-experiences those communal ones, nevertheless, supervene. At the same time, individuals need not be reflectively aware of (all) the specifically co-experiential, intentional content. However, individuals are (pre-reflectively) aware of essentially being members of one or more CPs (1926a, 522). To put it more succinctly: the intentional and phenomenal, or experiential, consciousness of CPs is *trans*-individual, but not, properly speaking, *collective* or *supra*-individual.[9]

Now, what exactly individuates group persons, for Scheler? Unlike most contemporary authors writing on the topic (notably, French 1979, Korsgaard 1989, Rovane 1998, and Mathiesen 2003), Scheler fails to provide any clear-cut epistemic, practical/agential, or normative criteria of individuation for CPs. Given Scheler's general axiology and his account of ethical personalism, there seems to be a plausible candidate nonetheless. On the face of it, the most obvious candidate seems to be the respective centers of co-experiencing. This fails to be sufficient to mark off CPs from one another, however, for centers of co-experiencing, according to Scheler, are essentially, as we have seen, embedded in "the endless totality of co-experiencing-with-one-another" (1926a, 510). Rather, given Scheler's idea of the essential incommensurability of individuals in terms of their values, and in terms of their radical separateness as individual bearers of values, here, we seem to have a criterion of individuation for CPs. Surely, one and the same (token or type of) bearer of values may well bear different values. Hence, one and the same (type of) CP may instantiate different values. Conversely, however, Scheler maintains that, precisely as *individuals*, and as individual *persons*, two different CPs cannot instantiate the same value. Now, if one takes into account that, for Scheler, there is an intrinsic correlation between persons and values, it is easy to see that the mentioned axiological difference establishes a corresponding difference in the corporate identity of a CP.

What about the relation of CPs to their individual members? The ontological relation between the concrete individuals (*Einzelpersonen*) and CPs is a relation of—relative—independence. Just as most institutional collectives are, regarding their persistence, more or less immune to membership changes, depending, obviously on their statutory, functional, etc. nature, CPs are, regarding their personhood and their individuality, independent of the intentional acts of any concrete individual, or of individuals taken separately or summatively. Conversely, one and the same individual may stand in membership relations to different CPs at the same time. For example, someone may be a member of the Catholic Church and a member of the Prussian State. In modern terms, CPs are multiply realizable, or, as Scheler puts it, "freely variable" vis-à-vis their members (1926a, 513). However, they are not independent of persons as such. On the contrary, as Scheler pointedly remarks: "It is [. . .] *in* the person that the mutually related *individual person* and *communal person* are differentiated, and the idea of the one does not represent the 'foundation' of the other" (1926a, 512). Crucially, this does not mean that persons or personhood properties would somehow multiply within persons, or that persons divide into a number of some homuncular persons, only by virtue of their entertaining social relations or relations to collectives. Moreover, it is vital to recognize that the relation between communal and individual persons is not a foundational relation of any sort, but rather a genuine correlation.[10] Consider also that the relations between individuals and CPs cannot be understood as exemplifications of part-whole type membership, or mereological containment, nor any other ordinary sort of membership relation (cf. 1923/24, 124). That is not to say that Scheler would deny that CPs have members at all and that they have individual persons as their members. On the contrary: "Indeed, it belongs to the essence of all communal persons to have persons as member-persons (*Gliedpersonen*), who are *also* individual persons" (1926a, 513). However, persons qua members are not simply *parts* of other persons, namely of CPs. Rather, they are complete and autonomous personal unities in their own right, who entertain mutual membership relations, including their very membership to a certain CP. The phenomenal (i.e., living- and co-experiencing-together) and normative (i.e., solidarity and co-responsibility) aspects of enjoying and maintaining such person-to-person membership relations define also the essence of the relations between individual and communal persons—rather than mereological containment.

Scheler, however, is not always immune to a sort of a compositional fallacy, according to which, regardless of how cohesive the respective personal properties of a set of individuals engaging in some joint endeavor may be, it would nevertheless be wrong to infer the existence of one vehicle or bearer of such properties. This becomes particularly manifest when he characterizes CPs—*nota bene* precisely contra Ryle's (1949) famous category mistakes examples—by drawing an analogy between, for instance, CPs becoming "macroscopically visible" in communal experiences such as war, or "someone flying in a balloon [who] would, all of a sudden, see [the] one city that is somehow mysteriously contained in the streets, people [. . .] carriages, or goods" (1916a, 274). Moreover, Scheler tells us that "all societal connections of individuals A, B, C, or groups G, $G_1$, $G_2$ occur *only* if A, B, C, or G, $G_1$, $G_2$ belong at the same time to another totality (*Ganzem*) G of a community—one that is not formed by A, B, C, or G, $G_1$, $G_2$, which, however, contains them as its members" (1926a, 521).

Similarly, Scheler's talk of infinite containment, or of one CP being nested in another, must be taken literally. Scheler holds that every CP is "essentially always *also* a member of another CP which encompasses a collective of CP" (1926a, 531). Moreover, Scheler maintains that it is part of the a priori nature of CPs that there is a multiplicity of types and instantiations, or tokens, thereof (1926a, 541). He presents us with a rather bewildering taxonomy of CPs, not only in terms of the mereological interlacement and hierarchies of lower- and higher-order CPs, but also in terms of different types of CPs. There are three main types of CPs that are associated with different functions (such as the establishment and regulation of systems of laws, rights, etc., and the furtherance of individual and communal well-being, welfare, etc.) and different values ("values of rights," "of power," and "of welfare"): (i.) "pure spiritual CP" (*reine geistige*), or "cultural CP," in particular, nations and so-called "cultural regions" (*Kulturkreise*); (ii.) the state (as distinct from both peoples and nations); and, finally, as a sort of synthesis, or 'coincidence' of (i.) and (ii.), (iii.), the "perfect spiritual CP," i.e., the "state-nation", the "cultural nation" and, as the highest-ranked CP of all, the church, viewed as the universal "community of love," in which all spiritual, individual persons partake (1926a, 531, 545).[11]

Notice a further stratification: as we have seen, in Scheler's social phenomenology of personhood, individual persons are, irreducibly, interrelated and, accordingly, there is an interlacement of different strata and different types of personhood (social, intimate, communal)—notwithstanding the fact that persons are individuated solely by themselves, and also have their, though purely axiological, essences 'in' themselves (1926b, 44). Now consider that the distinction between the social and intimate spheres of persons is orthogonal to the distinction between individual and communal persons. The former distinction applies just as much to communal as to individual persons: CPs have their own intimate spheres, which is relative to either other CPs, with whom they entertain social relations (1926a, 549), or the community of CPs, or a higher-order CP, of which the given CP is a member. Take, for instance, a UN member state's socio-economic or political life, which may be independent of specific UN policies.

Furthermore, the concept of the CP is also embedded in a network of conceptual distinctions with regard to the ontological, axiological, and normative structure of social reality. Scheler employs, for example, the well-known distinction made by Tönnies between society and community for marking four distinct types of "social unities" (1926a, 517; 1926c, 33). Without going into the details here (cf. Vendrell Ferran's contribution in this volume), suffice it to say that in the context of these distinctions, Scheler refers to a CP as a "personalist system of solidarity of autonomous, self- and co-responsible individuals," or as "the personal-solidarity association of non-representable (*unvertretbar*) individuals" (1926c, 33, 45). What primarily distinguishes CPs from other non-personal collectives is that only the goal-directed volitions or intentional actions of the former bear any autonomy and sovereignty over the particular interests of their individual, or even communal, members (1926a, 531).

The difference in accountability also corresponds to a difference in the respective principle of solidarity: in life-communities, the "principle of representable solidarity" reigns. Individuals are hereby interchangeable, for every individual is considered to be co-responsible only for some communal value. In CPs, on the other hand, we have the principle of "non-representable solidarity" (*unvertretbar*), according to which each and every individual is responsible for herself (self-responsibility) as well as co-responsible for all other members and their total integration in the CP. With this distinction, we enter the normative dimension of CPs, and face the issue of collectivism versus anti-collectivism.

## 4 BEYOND COLLECTIVISM AND ANTI-COLLECTIVISM?

So far, I aimed to show that Scheler's concept of the CP fulfills the above plurality, integrity, and the above stated normativity requirements (1)–(3). Though CPs are constituted by the co-experiences and co-solidarity of a plurality of incommensurable individuals, they enjoy relative independence and autonomy vis-à-vis their members and are, as persons, also morally accountable. Now, what about the further normative implications and, in particular, the anti-collectivism requirement? In the remainder, I shall argue that, despite any ambiguities and occasional collectivistic undertones, Scheler's concept of the CP is ultimately anti-collectivist in spirit, or, at the very least, compatible with anti-collectivism.

Recall that anti-collectivism is the view that individual personhood is not compromised, outflanked, or overridden by collectives—that the respective individuals belong to as members or not—and the intentional and normative laws governing such collectives. Notice that the normative version of anti-collectivism does not necessarily amount to a view that List and Pettit call "normative individualism," according to which "whether or not a group person should exist, and whether it should function within this or that regime of obligation, should be settled by reference to the rights or benefits of the individuals affected, members and non-members alike" (List & Pettit 2011, 182).[12] Although not incompatible with such normative individualism, Scheler's normative anti-collectivism is certainly not identical to it.

Consider the following claims, which formulate different aspects and strengths of (normative and non-normative) anti-collectivism:

(i.) The personhood of individuals is co-constituted by their intersubjective and membership relations to CPs (and the CP's personhood properties).
(ii.) Individuals bear certain normative relations of accountability and co-responsibility to CPs (and possibly vice versa).

(iii.) The personhood of individuals is derived from and/or reducible to the relations in (i.).

(iv.) The axiological status, or value, of individual persons is derived from the CP they belong to, and/or from the function they have for promoting those CPs, and for which they are exclusively accountable.

Notice that (i.) formulates a version of social holism[13] regarding non-normative (intentional-psychological or otherwise) relations between individuals and CPs, while (ii.) and (iii.) target their normative and axiological relations. Accordingly, we may distinguish *intentional* from *normative* collectivism. Furthermore, (iii.) resonates with Scheler's ideas on "value collectivism" (*Wertkollektivismus*), according to which a person's value is to be measured against his contribution to a collective, and on "causal collectivism" (*Kausalkollektivismus*), according to which a person's value is to be measured against the value of the historical development of communities (1926a, 495f.). Scheler rejects both versions, to be sure. Contrary to (iii.), then, Scheler holds that the criterion for measuring the value of a community (and of history) is the extent to which it promotes the 'ontic value' (*Seinswert*) of the maximum number of (individual and communal) persons of the highest value (1926a, 495). Notice how this, even if not incompatible, rubs up uncomfortably against normative individualism.

Obviously, various combinations of (i.) to (iv.) will result in different strengths of (anti-)collectivism. Thus, (i.) and (ii.), taken either in conjunction or disjunctively, are compatible with a robust anti-collectivism, while (iii.) and/or (iv.) are not and, taken together, amount to the strongest form of collectivism. I take Scheler to endorse precisely (i.) and (ii.)—neither more, nor less.

However, even though he certainly does not embrace collectivism head-on anywhere in his work, it is no coincidence that reading Scheler often strikes a (quasi)collectivist chord. Thus, even with a view to the largely non-normative issue of whether the personhood of individuals is only co-constituted by (i.) or rather, derived from their membership relation to collectives or to CP (iii.), Scheler is far from offering a clear-cut explanation. On the one hand, he argues that persons essentially have both an intimate as well as a social sphere and, hence, that their very personhood is (holistically) co-constituted by *inter*personal relations. Moreover, he holds that persons are, in part, what they are by means of their irreducible membership in communities and, ultimately, in CPs. On the other hand, Scheler time and again insists on the irreducible individuality and the normative and non-normative incommensurability of individual persons. He could not be more precise about rejecting collectivism with regard to any alleged constitutional or axiological hierarchy between individual and communal persons when he writes that "every person is with *equal* originality (gleich*ursprünglich*) both an individual person and (essentially) a member of a communal person, and one's own value (*Eigenwert*) as an individual is independent of one's value as a member" (1926a, 514).

And, yet, nowhere is Scheler's oscillation between collectivism and anti-collectivism clearer than in passages of his notorious essay, "War as Communal Experience" (1916a). Three claims, which prima facie are in tension with one another, stand out here: (1) there are communal experiences (*Gesamterlebnis*), as in a "national experience" of the Great War, which a.) are not a "highly complex aggregation (*Zusammensetzung*) of individual experiences, enriched with common knowledge or presumption," but the co-experiencing of one and the same (token) of experience, and which b.) may not only be by far larger, but also "more colourful and richer" than either any contingent individual experience thereof or the summation of all individual experiences (1916a, 273; cf. 1926a, 516; 1926b, 23f.). (2) A CP, e.g., the state, can, and indeed, *ought* to, lay certain claims (*fordern*) on individuals for its own sake and prosperity, especially since a CP's existence typically outlives the lifespan of its members. (3) Finally, however, CPs ought to lay claim on individuals only if they "respect" individuals' intrinsic, and indeed "eternal," value (1916a, 280f).

Now, on closer scrutiny, the tension is easily resolved. For while (2) is simply normatively conditional upon (3), both are normative considerations that do not affect there being (or not being) certain irreducible, collective, intentional and/or phenomenal patterns of communal experiences. In other words, the tension dissolves once we properly distinguish between *normative* and *intentional* (anti-)collectivism.

At first glance, a similar tension seems to presents itself when one considers Scheler's intricate concept of co-responsibility and, in particular, his concept of "communal guilt" (*Gesamtschuld*). Thus, on the one hand, Scheler suggests a strongly collectivist interpretation of the principle of solidarity—the "highest axiom of social ethics and social philosophy" (1926b, 209f.)—by claiming that, due to this principle, and the original co-responsibility of individuals for one another that it entails, every individual person bears and partakes in, in addition to her individual accountability, "communal merit" or guilt, which, to be sure, "cannot be added up by the sum of the merit or guilt of the respective individuals" (1926a, 488f). Moreover, though a given individual S is not (collectively or individually) responsible for any concrete, collective action, unless S has in fact been "causally and volitionally involved" in the given action (1926a, 522), S's overall co-responsibility for others and for some CP is grounded in the very nature of there being an ethical community of persons, rather than in S's complicity or concrete action. On the other hand, and in contrast to the strongly collectivist principle of (representable) solidarity in life-communities, insofar as individual and communal persons are concerned, self- and co-responsibility are co-original and always co-instantiated. Hence, it is not the case that an individual's self-responsibility is derived from or founded upon her co-responsibility for others, or for a CP:

> In marked contrast to the life-community where the bearer of *all* responsibility is the communal reality, and the individual is only *co*-responsible, in the communal person, each individual as well as the

communal person are *self*-responsible (responsible for oneself), and at the same time, every individual is also co-responsible for the communal person (and for every individual 'in' the communal person), just as the communal person is co-responsible for *each* of its members. Hence, co-responsibility between individual and communal person is *mutual* and does not preclude self-responsibility on the part of both [. . .] there is *neither* an ultimate responsibility of the individual to the communal person, as in the case of life-community, *nor* an ultimate responsibility of the communal person to the individual (or to the sum or a majority of individuals), as in the case of society. (1926a, 522; cf. 548)

Moreover, as Scheler continues this passage, the co-originality of self- and co-responsibility is evidenced by Scheler's onto-theological claim that "both the communal person and the individual person are responsible to the person of all persons, to God, and indeed in terms of self-responsibility as well as co-responsibility" (ibid.). Furthermore, since every CP is essentially also a member of other CPs, every CP is just as co-responsible for other CPs (same-level as well as higher-level ones) as for its own individual members (1926a, 531).

Consider also that the principle of non-representable solidarity precludes any fusion of individuals in a community or any identification of individuals and community. Indeed, the very concept of co-responsibility, the responsibility of an individual for a CP and the responsibility of the CP for the individual, presupposes that CPs and individual persons neither coincide, nor are fused (cf. Henckmann 1998, 131). Otherwise, obviously, talk of *co*-responsibility would not make sense, and self-responsibility would be the appropriate concept. Analogously, Scheler lays particular stress on the fact that 'pure' sympathy (*reines Mitfühlen*), as well as re- or co-experiencing another's mental life (*Mit-fühlen, Mit-erleben*), is only possible if there is neither emotional contagion, nor mere reproduction, nor, importantly, emotional fusion or identification (*Einsfühlung*) of the respective persons' experiences (1926b, 23ff., 48ff., 75).[14]

At times, Scheler even ponders whether moral consciousness, conscience, sense of duty, or moral phenomena in general would still exist were there no sociality (*Sozietät*), or whether moral phenomena are necessarily and exclusively social phenomena. Interestingly, Scheler explicitly denies that (1926b, 83). He also cautions against an overtly holistic socialization of conscience when he remarks that our very ethical being is not affected by any suggestive power, to the effect that an individual would become culpable just because she internalizes some social verdict about her culpability (1926b, 18).

Lastly, consider also Scheler's nuanced opposition to Durkheimian 'sociologism' (*Soziologismus*), social determinism, and conventionalism. Analogous to his concept of *co*-responsibility in his sociology of knowledge is Scheler's advocacy of a *co*-determination between mind, knowledge, and society. Thus, he argues that society and its "dominant perspective of social interests" only "co-determine" (*mitbedingt*) the "forms" of cognition, perception, and knowledge (i.e., the intentional psychology) and "the *selection* of objects of knowledge"—not, however, as sociologism, a "pendant of psychologism," would have it, the epistemic content, let alone the epistemological validity of thoughts or theories (1926c, 57f.).

## 5 CONCLUSION

What are the merits of Scheler's account of group persons, and where does it run the risk of overextending the concept? Three features of the theory stand out positively, especially against standard, contemporary accounts: (1) its internal differentiation, providing, if not a fully worked-out taxonomy, at least an account of layers, sedimentations, or grades of integrations of corporate personhood within the social reality of individuals; (2) its phenomenological or experiential qualities; and, (3) finally, its normative or axiological dimension. Notice that all this complies especially well with the integrity and moral accountability requirements and is, as I have argued, not incompatible with the anti-collectivism requirement to say the least (and, *a fortiori*, complies with the plurality requirement).

Again, for Scheler, the experiential, or phenomenal, and normative aspects of the process of integrating centers of (co-)experiencing into one another, and into a communal center of such, viz. a CP, are inseparably and constitutively tied together. This is both an advantage—the account thus yields a phenomenologically richer conception of group identification—but it certainly bears some risks. To be sure, as CPs, for Scheler, are tightly embedded in systems of co-experiences and co-responsibility, the argument that corporate entities lack certain essential capacities for moral conduct, such as empathy and affectivity, and that corporate persons would, hence, typically exhibit 'psychopathic' behavior (Bakan 2004), loses its force. And, even if the Schelerian construal is not committed to any arguably unjustified form of collective (phenomenal) consciousness to GPs (cf. Szanto 2014), or some strong version of collectivism, Scheler's account does reinforce certain normative questions, in ways that might strain all too many political sensibilities today.

It is precisely Scheler's insistence on a particularly strong form of social holism—i.e., his insistence on an irreducible and ineliminable correlation between individual and corporate personhood—that makes his account at once phenomenologically, and indeed metaphysically, plausible, but also vulnerable to troubling normative concerns. For, if Scheler is right, it seems that one must bite the bullet and concede certain moral rights to or obligations towards CPs. For example, one will have to be prepared to hold that corporate persons, in principle, will have just the same rights to respect, esteem, and protection as individual persons, or even the moral right to persist (Ozar 1985). At the most extreme, we might end up with a view that the British political pluralist and contemporary of Scheler, Figgis, pointedly formulated—with a view to the church, and congenial to Scheler's onto-theological underpinning of the concept—according to which the denial of the personality of (some) corporations equals the "tyrannical and unjust" denial of human personality in "slavery" (Figgis 1913, 42). But this seems too big a socio-political price to pay just for being socio-ontologically plausible. Or is it? We may decide in the end, however, that Scheler's account of CPs can, I submit, serve as one of the most instructive philosophical case studies on how intricate the relation between the autonomy of individuals, the integrity of group persons, and the threat of collectivism ultimately is.

## NOTES

1 For different stances on group personhood within this paradigm, see esp. Rovane (1998), Mathiesen (2003), Sheehy (2006), Tollefsen (2003), List & Pettit (2011), and Huebner (2014); see also Szanto (2015b).
2 This is particularly pertinent since the recent *Citizens United v. Federal Election Commission* (2010) U.S. Supreme Court ruling, according to which corporations are entitled to free speech rights under the First Amendment; http://www.supremecourt.gov/opinions/09pdf/08-205.pdf; cf. Hess (2013).
3 Most critical of all phenomenologists were Schütz (esp. 1957, 114f.) and Kaufmann (1944, 163f.; 1930, 307). We find more balanced, though still skeptical, views in Stein (1920), Hildebrand (1930), Walther (1923), and Hartmann (1926), but also somewhat different tone with regard to Scheler in Schütz (1958), esp. 500f., and 1953, 38f.; on the former, see Salice's contribution to this volume; on the latter, see Caminada (2014); on Husserl and on Stein, see Szanto (2015a) and Szanto (forthcoming), respectively.
4 This qualification should allow for cases where there is a group person (at a given time $t_2$) constituted by a plurality of persons at $t_1$, even though at $t_2$ no such plurality, but maybe only one last single member (a 'last Mohican') exists.
5 Cf. also Gilbert (1989), Mathiesen (2003), and Chelstrom (2013).
6 See, however, Hess's (2013) criticism of the entailment of moral agency and personhood.
7 Because of its summative connotations, I shall not use the standard translation for *Gesamtperson*, 'collective person.' Consider also that Scheler uses the attribute 'collective,' e.g., in combination with collective values (*Kollektivwerte*), to refer to *societal* and not *communal* social relations (1926a, 119f.).
8 It should be noted, though, that Scheler is highly ambivalent about the dialectical role or teleological status of the "highest" "cultural CP," i.e., the church; thus, he sometimes suggests that all other CPs are somehow 'synthesized' by the church's alleged unitary bond of solidarity (*solidarische Einheit*) into one whole "pure and perfect CP" (*reine vollkommene*), cf., e.g., 542–544.
9 See more on this in Chelstrom (2013) and Szanto (2014, 2015a).
10 In this respect, Scheler's *Gesamtperson* significantly differs from Husserl's otherwise rather similar concept of 'higher order persons'; cf. Szanto (2015a).
11 Similarly, for the conservative Scruton (1989), the paradigm corporate person is the church.
12 Cf., critically, Hindriks (2015) and Kusch (2014).
13 On the holism issue, see also the formulation in the introduction of this volume.
14 On the affective dimension of CPs, and on Scheler's theory of emotions, see Mulligan (2008), Vendrell Ferran's and Krueger's contributions in this volume, as well as Vendrell Ferran (2008), and on Scheler's theory of empathy, see Zahavi (2010).

## REFERENCES

Bakan, Joel (2004). *The Corporation. The Pathological Pursuit of Profit and Power.* New York: The Free Press.
Briggs, Rachael (2012). The Normative Standing of Group Agents. *Episteme* 9 (3), 283–291.
Caminada, Emanuele (2014). "Joining the Background: Habitual Sentiments Behind We-Intentionality." In: A. Konzelmann Ziv, & H. B. Schmid (Eds.). *Institutions, Emotions, and Group Agents. Contributions to Social Ontology.* Dordrecht: Springer, 195–212.
Chelstrom, Erik (2013). *Social Phenomenology: Husserl, Intersubjectivity, and Collective Intentionality.* Lanham: Lexington.
Figgis, John N. (1913). *Churches in the Modern State.* London: Longmans, Green.
French, Peter A. (1979). "The Corporation as a Moral Person." *American Philosophical Quarterly* 16 (3), 207–215.
Gilbert, Margaret (1989). *On Social Facts.* London/New York: Routledge.
Hartmann, Nikolai (1926). *Ethik.* Berlin: de Gruyter.
Henckmann, Wolfhart (1998). *Max Scheler.* München: Beck.
Hess, Kendy M. (2013). "'If You Tickle Us. . .': How Corporations Can Be Moral Agents Without Being Persons." *The Journal of Value Inquiry* 47 (3), 319–335.
Hildebrand, Dietrich von (1930). *Metaphysik der Gemeinschaft.* Augsburg: Haas & Grabherr.
Hindriks, Frank (2015). "How Autonomous Are Collective Agents? Corporate Rights and Normative Individualism." *Erkenntnis.* doi: 10.1007/s10670–014–9629–6.
Huebner, Bryce (2014). *Macrocognition. A Theory of Distributed Minds and Collective Intentionality.* Oxford: Oxford University Press.
Husserl, Edmund (1952). *Ideen zu einer reinen Phänomenologie und phänomenologischen Philosophie. Zweites Buch: Phänomenologische Untersuchungen zur Konstitution.* Ed. by Mary Biemel. Den Haag: Nijhoff.
—— (1973): *Zur Phänomenologie der Intersubjektivität. Texte aus dem Nachlaß. Zweiter Teil: 1921–1928.* Ed. by Iso Kern. Den Haag: Nijhoff.
Kaufmann, Felix (1930). "Soziale Kollektiva." *Zeitschrift für Nationalökonomie* 1, 294–308.
—— (1944). *Methodology of the Social Sciences.* Oxford: Oxford University Press.
Kelly, Eugene (2011). *Material Ethics of Value: Max Scheler and Nicolai Hartmann.* Dordrecht: Springer.
Korsgaard, Christine M. (1989). "Personal Identity and the Unity of Agency: A Kantian Response to Parfit." *Philosophy & Public Affairs* 18 (2), 101–132.
Kusch, Martin (2014). "The Metaphysics and Politics of Corporate Personhood." *Erkenntnis* 79 (9), Suppl., 1587–1600.
List, Christian, & Pettit, Philip. (2011). *Group Agency. The Possibility, Design, and Status of Corporate Agents.* Oxford: Oxford University Press.
Manning, Rita C. (1984). "Corporate Responsibility and Corporate Personhood." *Journal of Business Ethics* 3 (1), 77–84.
Mathiesen, Kay (2003). "On Collective Identity." *Protosociology* 18–19, 66–86.
Mulligan, Kevin (2008). "Max Scheler. Die Anatomie des Herzens, oder was man alles fühlen kann." In: H. Landweer, & U. Renz (Eds.). *Klassische Emotionstheorien von Platon bis Wittgenstein.* Berlin: de Gruyter, 589–612.
Ozar, David T. (1985). "Do corporations have moral rights?" *Journal of Business Ethics* 4 (4), 277–281.
Parfit, Derek (1986). *Reasons and Persons.* Oxford: Oxford University Press.
Pettit, Philip (1993). *The Common Mind. An Essay on Psychology, Society and Politics.* Oxford: Oxford University Press.

—— (2014). "Three Issues in Social Ontology." In: J. Zahle, & F. Collin (Eds.). *Rethinking the Individualism-Holism Debate*. Cham: Springer, 77–96.
Rovane, Carol (1998). *The Bounds of Agency. An Essay in Revisionary Metaphysics*. Princeton: Princeton University Press.
Runciman, David (1997). *Pluralism and the Personality of the State*. Cambridge: Cambridge University Press.
Ryle, Gilbert (1949). *The Concept of Mind*. Chicago: University of Chicago Press.
Scheler, Max (1915/16). "Absolutsphäre und Realsetzung der Gottesidee." In: M. Scheler (Ed.). *Zur Ethik und Erkenntnislehre. Gesammelte Werke, Vol. 10, Schriften aus dem Nachlaß, Vol. 1*. Bern: Francke 1957, 179–255.
—— (1916a). "Der Krieg als Gesamterlebnis." In: *Politisch-Pädagogische Schriften. Gesammelte Werke, Vol. 4*, Ed. by M.S. Frings. Bern: Francke 1982, 267–282.
—— (1916b). "Der allgemeine Begriff von 'Nation' und die konkreten Nationalideen." *Schriften zur Soziologie und Weltanschauungslehre. Gesammelte Schriften, Vol 6*. Ed. by M. Scheler. Bern: Francke 1960, 334–347.
—— (1923/24). "Über die Nationalideen der großen Nationen." In: M. Scheler (Ed.). *Schriften zur Soziologie und Weltanschauungslehre. Gesammelte Schriften, Vol. 6*. Bern: Francke 1960, 121–130.
—— (1980) [1926]. *Der Formalismus in der Ethik und die material Wertethik. Neuer Versuch der Grundlegung eines ethischen Personalismus*. Bern: Francke.
—— (1982) [1926c]. *Probleme einer Soziologie des Wissens*. In: *Die Wissensformen und die Gesellschaft. Gesammelte Werke, Vol. 8.*, Ed. by M. Scheler. Bern: Francke, 15–190.
—— (2005) [1926]. *Wesen und Formen der Sympathie. Gesammelte Werke, Vol. 7.*, Ed. by M.S. Krings. Bonn: Bouvier.
Schütz, Alfred (1957). "Das Problem der transzendentalen Intersubjektivität bei Husserl." *Philosophische Rundschau* 5, 81–107.
—— (1958). "Max Scheler's Epistemology and Ethics II." *The Review of Metaphysics* 11 (3), 486–501.
—— (1970) [1953]. "Husserl's *Ideas* volume II." In: A. Schütz. *Collected Papers III: Studies in phenomenological philosophy*. The Hague: Nijhoff, 15–39.
Scruton, Roger (1989). "Corporate Persons." *Proceedings of the Aristotelian Society, Suppl. Vol.* 63, 239–274.
Searle, John R. (1995). *The Construction of Social Reality*. London: Penguin.
Sheehy, Paul (2006). *The Reality of Social Groups*. Aldeshot: Ashgate.
Stein, Edith (1920). *Beiträge zur philosophischen Begründung der Psychologie und der Geisteswissenschaften. Edith Stein Gesamtausgabe, Vol. 6*. Wien/Basel/Köln: Herder 2010.
Stoll, Mary L. (2005). "Corporate Rights to Free Speech?" *Journal of Business Ethics* 58 (1–3), 261–269.
Szanto, Thomas (2014). "How to Share a Mind: Reconsidering the Group Mind Thesis." *Phenomenology and the Cognitive Sciences* 13 (1), 99–120.
—— (2015a). "Husserl on Collective Intentionality." In: A. Salice, & H.B. Schmid (Eds.). *Social Reality. The Phenomenological Approach*. Dordrecht: Springer.
—— (2015b). "Do Group Persons have Emotions?" In: S. Rinofner-Kreidl, & H. Wiltsche (Eds.). *Analytical and Continental Philosophy: Methods and Perspectives*. Berlin/Boston: de Gruyter.
—— (forthcoming). "Collective Emotions, Normativity, and Empathy: A Steinian Account." *Human Studies*, doi. 10.1007/s10746-015-9350-8.
Tollefsen, Deborah P. (2003). "Participant Reactive Attitudes and Collective Responsibility." *Philosophical Explorations* 6 (3), 218–234.
Tuomela, Raimo (2007). *The Philosophy of Sociality. The Shared Point of View*. Oxford: Oxford University Press.

Vendrell Ferran, Íngrid (2008). *Die Emotionen. Gefühle in der realistischen Phänomenologie*. Berlin: Akademie.

Walther, Gerda (1923). "Zur Ontologie der sozialen Gemeinsachten." In: *Jahrbuch für Philosophie und phänomenologische Forschung* 6, 1–158.

Zahavi, Dan (2010). "Max Scheler". In: A. Schrift (Ed.). *History of Continental Philosophy III*. Edinburgh: Acumen, 171–186.

# 19 Brothers in Arms
## Fraternity-Terror in Sartre's Social Ontology

*Nicolas de Warren*

"Que faire contre l'ouragan de fraternité et de joie?"

Victor Hugo

## "THE DAY WE LOST OUR BROTHERS..."

No one who was there will ever forget the clarity of the day the towers fell. Wherever one happened to be, whatever one happened to be doing, each spontaneously found themselves in an elected sense of unity, compassion, and defiance. The skies shone blue as never seen before, people wandered in confusion and disbelief, seeking each other in speech and silence, in a constant circulation of moved solidarity. "We are all Americans," it was proclaimed the day after in an editorial of *Le Monde*. And indeed, 'American' then came to exemplify humanity *tout court*, transcending all national affiliation and cultural heritage. Politicians extended hands in demonstration of non-partisan unity. Firefighters, police officers, medical workers, and others, regardless of gender, creed, or identity, stood arm in arm. A new age was sensed to have been born in mourning and resolve in the face of terror. Common individuals were called to poetry, as with one of the many now lingering in the digital commonplace: "But our hearts carry the scars and we will always remember, / The day we lost our brothers ... the eleventh day of September!"[1]

Those who were there will also never forget: kneeling down in animal pens, exposed to the sun in bright orange suits, hands tied behind their backs, and isolated from the world in suspended animation. Forbidden to speak with each other in a zone between bare survival and death, 'terror suspects' and 'confirmed terrorists' were placed on an island beyond the pale. Is Hell prior to evil, or is evil prior to Hell? As Terry Holdbrooks, a U.S. soldier who served at Guantanamo, recalls, his commanding officer took his company prior to their deployment to Ground Zero and told them, "When we get down to Guantanamo, men, remember the 3,000 lives that we lost here. Remember what Islam did to us here."[2]

The pathos of the lament, "Why did they do this to *us*?" is indeed directly proportional to the force of "What did we do to *them*?" At first glance, fraternity would seem diametrically opposed to evil. In fraternity, a common front against evil is formed through a reciprocal solicitude for the death of others. Within the bond of fraternity, each is touched, and hence partakes, in the death of the Other. You are not alone in your hour of need: even if we each must die our own death, we are not abandoned to die alone, without the protest, succor, and companionship of what Jorge Semprún named *Mit-Sein-zum-Tod*. Evil in this light appears as the complete eclipse of fraternity in the relegation of its victims to a death denied any succor from another, or witness by the other, or grave, or name bequeathed to remembrance. Fraternity internalizes a relation towards the death of others that brings together individuals into a common front against the absolute separation of evil.

The line demarcating the bond of fraternity from the separation of evil is, however, not absolute. As Marc Crépon observes, "C'est du coeur même de la fraternité, de la façon dont elle est circonscrite et exclusive, des frontières, réelles et symboliques qui la divisent que le mal peut faire irruption"[3] (Crépon 2008, 129). This ambivalence of fraternity and evil—whether it defines an inviolable line separating fraternity from evil or whether it circumscribes a space for evil in fraternity—renders more urgent a meditation on Malraux's observation: "Je cherche la région cruciale de l'âme, où le Mal absolu s'oppose à la fraternité"[4] (Malraux 1996, 788). For if fraternity and absolute evil are not simply opposed, but are liable of passing into each other, what hope is there for fraternity, or any form of Being-with, against evil? Or is the "crucial region" of the soul where absolute evil and fraternity *oppose each other* in truth the source of their tacit complicity and conjunction?

In this chapter, my aim is to further contribute to Malraux's search—a search taken up in turn by Semprún, Ricouer, and Crépon—by exploring the institution of fraternity in pledging and the bond of "Fraternity-Terror" (*fraternité-terreur*) in Sartre's *Critique of Dialectical Reason*. Under the heading of "fraternity-terror," Sartre proposes to understand a dialectical relation that underpins the formation of social groups in establishing inner bonds of reciprocity ("fraternity) against external threats. In so doing, I seek to understand Sartre's insight that man is "violent—throughout History right up to the present day [. . .]—to the anti-human (that is to say, to any other man) and to his Brother in so far as he has the permanent possibility of becoming anti-human himself" (Sartre 2004, 186).

## GROUP IN FUSION

Sartre's analysis of the pledge is situated within his discussion of the "statutory group"—a group of individuals bound to each other through an act of allegiance, pledge, or oath to the group as such, and hence to others in the group. Within the *Critique*'s investigation of the dialectical progression from "groups to history," the statutory group represents a decisive transitional stage between what Sartre terms "the group in fusion" (*groupe en fusion*) and "the organization." The former represents the primordial crystallization of collective agency in which individuals are reciprocally bound to each other through a genuinely free, common *praxis*. Individuals recognize each other as acting in concert with each other according to a common objective and interest. A group in fusion (misleadingly rendered in the English translation of the *Critique* as a "*fused* group"—my emphasis—which, however, wrongly suggests a *finished* state) is characterized by intrinsic volatility, since its cohesion as a group is still in flux. Since Sartre considers that *praxis* "constitutes itself as an opening made in the future, and sovereignly affirms its own possibility—simply through the emergence of the undertaking itself" (Sartre 2004, 405), a group in fusion can be seen as creating an alternative social future against entrenched forms of social existence and their defining shape of time.

A group in fusion comes into being through the spontaneous emergence of a concerted *praxis* of individuals in view of a common objective. Every group in fusion disrupts "seriality," that is, a form of social existence in which individuals act without a unifying common interest. In Sartre's classic example, individuals standing in line for the bus share a similar goal (getting on the bus), yet the conduct of each remains determined by self-interest (me getting on the bus), individual purpose (me needing to get home), and potential conflict with others; hence, the jostling, cutting in line, and other forms of behavior that indicate the absence of any cooperating praxis and genuinely common objective. Viewed from afar, a bus line appears to behave as something of a unity (it slowly moves forward, it makes room for an elderly person); yet, this appearance of concerted action is the result of an aggregate harmonization of discrete (i.e., "serialized") individuals. Should the bus run behind schedule or not arrive at all, the disruption of individual habit (i.e., my daily routine) and public transportation (i.e., scheduled stops, reliability, etc.) *might* provide a catalyst for the crystallization of a common interest and "totalizing" group *praxis* that would thereby modify (restructure) the relationship of individuals vis-à-vis each other, transforming the serial line into a veritable group in fusion, or collective agency. Such a disruption of seriality thus reconfigures its 'neither/nor' form of collective existence—neither genuine collective agency nor complete absence of concerted movement—into a group in fusion that, in Hegelian fashion, both suppresses and transcends seriality into a new social configuration.

A recent example of a group in fusion is the Occupy Wall Street movement of 2011. Individuals from different professions, social backgrounds, and ethnic affiliations, who (for the most part) did not previously know each other or enjoy direct social contact, spontaneously came together at Zuccotti Park in protest of the economic and social injustice fostered by Wall Street. These individuals discovered each other through a unifying praxis (setting up camp, pitching tents, distributing flyers, etc.) against an external threat (the institution of Wall Street) and, more broadly, against a certain social arrangement of reality. This reactive motion in the thrust of a nascent social movement is modeled in Sartre's thinking on the paradigmatic status of revolutionary action, which seeks to reorganize a field of action (and possibilities) along with a reconfiguration of social existence: its *free* praxis attempts to the break with an impossibility ("that things cannot change," the status quo, etc.) in the creation of a novel horizon of possibility. A group in fusion is thus baptized as a collective violence against an established status quo, vested interest, or established social necessity (some form of the "practico-inert"). A group in fusion is "a free violence of men against misery and the impossibility of living," and since "misery and the impossibility of living" are always the products of *other men*, their institutions, and a material field, the constitutive violence of a group in fusion is directed against *another social organization, i.e., other men.*

Given this reactive catalyst, the unity of a group in fusion is *negatively* determined (united *against* Wall Street); yet, this external threat becomes in Sartre's parlance "interiorized" within the group as individual constituents come to recognize each other as belonging to a unified group on the basis of acting in concert. This interiorization of an external threat shapes the "totalization" (or "synthetic unification") of different actions (setting up tents, attending open lectures, etc.) into a common praxis, but it does so only through the freedom of each individual's *praxis*. As Sartre observes, the active and passive elements in the formation of a group in fusion are often impossible to differentiate, that is, whether the group differentiates itself internally or in reaction to an external threat continually pass into each other ("dialectical mediation"). Although the unity of a group in fusion is reactive to an external threat, it is proactive in the sense that it is through the free *praxis* of individuals that the group in fusion comes into being. As significantly, genuine freedom is experienced in the group in fusion through reciprocal action that enhances individual freedom *through* the free praxis of others. This concatenation of two centers of freedom—mine and yours—means that an individual experiences his or her freedom as genuinely *his or hers* only in concert with the freedom of another. Whereas in seriality, the individual acts under the illusion of genuine freedom, without any concert with others, in a group in fusion, the individual experiences *his or her own freedom* in participating in a collective agency with others likewise acting in their own freedom. Interiorization is a granular concept in Sartre's thinking; it adds considerable granularity to his account of the constitution of the group in fusion by denoting three distinct, yet inseparable dimensions: the psychological interiorization of a common objective and reciprocal recognition of other individuals, the sociological interiorization as a group that delimits itself from other groups, and the material interiorization within a field of action, for example, in the example of the Occupy Wall Street movement, the territorialization of a physical space (Zuccotti Park).

Each of these declinations of interiorization demarcates a line between "us and them."

Each individual within a group in fusion is a self-determining individual (determined by his or her own motivation, personal history, initiative, etc.), yet each individual also determines him or herself as what Sartre calls "the third" (*le tiers*). Within the broader vision of the *Critique*, the "the third" founds a cornerstone to Sartre's social ontology. As Sartre observes, "it is a common error of many sociologists [. . .] to treat the group as a binary relation (individual-community), whereas, in reality, it is a ternary relation" (Sartre 2004, 374). With this critique, Sartre rejects a variety of sociological approaches to the constitution of groups, from the theory of social contractualism popular among the French Republican tradition, to theories of moral sentiment (natural sympathy for social existence), to Comte's positivistic notion of society as a natural entity, or reality. Sartre is especially critical of Durkheim's conception of collective consciousness. As Sartre remarks in his 1961 Rome Conference, "Ce qui nous offre la possibilité de comprendre en quoi la subjectivité est indispensable pour la connaissance dialectique du social. C'est parce qu'il n'y a que des *hommes*, qu'il n'y a pas de grandes formes collectives, comme Durkheim et d'autres l'ont imaginé, et que ces hommes sont obligés d'être la médiation entre eux de ces formes d'extériorité qu'est, par exemple, l'être de classe" (Sartre 1993, 35).[5]

Insofar as I see myself as part of a group, I determine myself from the point of view of the group, or as "the third." As Sartre stresses, this unification, or "totalization," is *practical* insofar as I realize a common *praxis* through my own individual *praxis*. Adopting a phenomenological distinction (albeit dialectically recast), the relationship between the individual and the group is structured through a tension of "transcendence-immanence" (Sartre 2004, 409)/ Immanence is the sense that I have interiorized a common interest, means, and an objective into my individual praxis, such that the group acts "in" me, *is* me, much like the savvy U.S. Army recruiting slogan, "Army of One." Transcendence in the sense that the group and its common *praxis* transcend my individual praxis. It is because of this transcendence of the group in me that a group can establish regulatory controls over itself as well as adopt an internal, critical distance. No individual in particular "is" the group, not even all of the members added together arithmetically, yet the group does not act as nobody, as an anonymous or serialized formation. Due to the condition of immanence, an individual incorporates the third without thereby realizing a complete fusion with the group.

Rather than characterize the constitutive "transcendence-immanence" tension of the group in fusion as a form of intentionality (or consciousness), Sartre thinks in terms of the dialectical intelligibility, or rationality, of common praxis. As with its phenomenological provenance, the dialectical structure of transcendence and immanence is grasped by Sartre as a founded-founding relationship: transcendence *in* immanence. As Sartre writes, the group "is that of a *constituted reason*, of which the dialectic of free individual *praxis* is the *constituent reason*" (Sartre 2004, 411). Individual *praxis* remains *free and constitutive* of social existence even as it is entirely mediated by social relations with others. By the same argument, Sartre guards against Durkheim's collective consciousness and a Marxism (in its virulent Stalinist form) committed to an impersonal or anonymous historical determinism. There is only *one* group in fusion that acts with unified purpose; this unity is constituted by a *multiplicity* of individual actions, deliberations, etc. Paradoxically, or better: *dialectically*, the unity of the group *transcends* the aggregate of individual efforts (the whole is greater than its parts), although the multiplicity of individuals is *irreducible* to the unity of the group as such.

The volatility of a group in fusion reflects its essential instability as a unity in the making. With the Occupy Wall Street movement, its eventual disintegration was not only caused by the violence of police operations ("counter-finality," i.e., an objective against the group's own objective), it was in equal measure (dialectically speaking) *self-induced* given its failure (or inability) to transform itself from a group in fusion into a statutory group. In fact, the Occupy Wall Street movement understood itself to be a movement in perpetual motion without any defining platform. It committed itself to sustaining an *atmosphere* rather than to instituting a substantial form of social existence and political praxis. When viewed from Sartre's dialectic rationality, it is precisely this lack of self-constituting permanence—this failure to become a statutory group—that accounts for the movement's disintegration: whether through the intrinsic disintegration of its unstable dialectical tension or through an unbearable increase of external violence, *or both*, a group in fusion collapses, and the brief window of its free praxis becomes shut. As Slavoj Žižek cautioned the movement in a Sartrean premonition, "There is a danger. Don't fall in love with yourselves. We have a nice time here. But remember, carnivals come cheap. What matters is the day after, when we will have to return to normal lives. Will there be any changes then?"[6]

## THE PLEDGE GROUP

The Occupy Wall Street movement is an exemplary instance of a group in fusion that faltered due to its failure to transform itself into a statutory group. Žižek's caution went unheeded. In a Sartrean register of expression, the disintegration of the movement resulted in individuals returning to a serialized social existence: the revolution did not happen, the dream is over. The dialectical organization of a group in fusion is defined by the interiorization of common praxis in individual praxis and the exteriorization of individual praxis through common praxis. Rather than achieve an inertial stability, a group in fusion, however, *tends* towards disintegration. This unstable tension between "immanence" and "transcendence" can best be illustrated with the perennial challenge for any nascent social group of securing an individual's resolve and commitment to the group. As Sartre remarks (with this kind of example in mind), "My courage and endurance, during my lonely watch, will be proportional to the *permanence within me* of the group as a common reality" (Sartre 2004, 41; my emphasis). "Permanence within me" is here the critical notion. The transformation of a group in fusion into a statutory group produces permanence within the group as well as within individuals: individuals are bound to each other, to the group, as well as to themselves in manner than is inviolable or, at least, violable with severe cost and consequence. The significance of this transition to permanence is ontological. The incarnation of the common reality of the group in me becomes my veritable *substance*: *I* am *an American, I* am *a New England Patriots fan*, etc. It is only by virtue of producing an "internal inertia through itself in mediated reciprocity" that individuals become bound to the group—and hence each other—in a manner whose violation amounts to an ontological catastrophe. It is likewise only through such an ontological substantialization of a group and congealing of individuals into the group that individuals are motivated and called to sacrifice themselves for the group, for each other, and in a manner that can equally be rationalized as for *themselves.*

A statutory group is ontologically instituted through an act of pledging: taking an oath, swearing allegiance, pledging to uphold, etc. "[It] goes without saying," as Sartre observes, "that pledges can take very different forms [. . .]," and Sartre's purpose is by no means to provide an inventory of all possible variants of pledging, nor to describe *exhaustively* the constituting act of pledging (Sartre 2004, 419). The aim is instead to identify the pledge as the originary constituting praxis of a statutory group, which underlies any further progression of groups into organizations and institutions (not discussed in this chapter). This significance of pledging for the constitution of social permanence is widely portrayed in the dramatization of national myths of origin: the Tennis Court Oath in the French Revolution, the American Declaration of Independence, the distribution of the Eagles with Napoleon, and, more infamously, Hitler's *Reichswehreid*.

A pledge is not to be confused with a social contract or other presumed basis for society, since Sartre's is not a claim concerning the *origin* of society as such, but a claim regarding how a group binds itself, thus producing its own regulatory inertia. Although Sartre does not characterize the pledge explicitly in these terms, he implicitly understands the pledge as a performative speech act and, more precisely, as falling under what Austin called "commissives." As Austin explains, "commissives are typified by promising or otherwise undertaking; they *commit* you to doing something, but include also declarations or announcements of intention, which are not promises, and also rather vague things which we may call espousals, as for example, siding with" (Austin 1975, 152). Sartre himself speaks of the pledge as a "practical device" and an "immediate praxis" of mediated reciprocity.[7] Sartre in fact grants a wide scope to the performative manifestation of pledging: a pledge need not be uttered (it might be made in silence and in private, as with a novice's vow, or symbolically and publically, as with the French painter David's painting *Distribution of the Eagle Standards*). Different forms of pledging are tethered to different forms of "securing uptake" as well as different "conventional consequences" (to import here Austin's expressions).

The pledge equally institutes a normative social order or, in short, a self-regulating form of social existence. A pledge is a performative speech act of mediated reciprocity and recognition that institutes a self-regulatory social object: the statutory group. When an individual, as free praxis (i.e., not coerced), pledges, the individual swears before others, where other individuals (in the group) stand as both witness (as an individual) *and* recipient (as "the third"), even though, in the instance of the individual as a mediating third, no individual *is* the group as such. Pledging is a mediated and reciprocal act, and in cases where future members join a statutory group, it is as if every member of the group receives the pledge of a newly adhering individual. As Sartre explains, "I give my pledge to all the third parties, as forming the group of which I am a member, and it is the group which enables everyone to guarantee the statute of the permanence to everyone" (Sartre 2004, 421). It is before you as "the third" that I pledge myself, and in thus pledging myself to the group, you—and all others—become the objective guarantee for my pledge: I am bound to certain obligations, duties, and norms of the group. If we suspend the diversity of possible empirical content to the norms and obligations that bind members of a statutory group, the foundational ontological significance of pledging consists, according to Sartre, of establishing an objective guarantee from the other that protects and inhibits me from becoming *Other*, that is, from exiting and/or betraying the group.

The pledge is ontologically more consequential than Austin's speech act, since it is by virtue of the pledge that a new social object is created, or instituted, thus transforming the relationship of individuals to each other within a group in fusion—to wit, a group in fusion becomes reconfigured into a statutory group. The pledge is in fact double-edged in its ontological significance. The pledge "interiorizes" a permanent community within me so as to give me substance (as constituent of the group) as well as "exteriorizes," or objectifies, my own praxis—the pledge—into the veritable substance of the group. The group only exists by virtue of pledged individuals *to* the group. The pledge is the group directed towards itself as the object of its own self-fashioning. But, if the pledge thus forecloses the possibility of my exit from the group, it by the same token creates that very possibility. As Sartre remarks, "[T]he guarantee of permanence provided by the oath of the Others produces itself in me as the objective impossibility (in interiority) that alterity should come to me from outside; but at the same time, it is the possibility that I should make myself Other (by betraying, fleeing, etc.) which is underlined as a possible future coming from me to the Others" (Sartre 2004, 422). In pledging myself to a group, I also implicitly create for myself the possibility of exiting or betraying the group, since the word that binds to the other is *my word* freely given and hence, is free to be withdrawn. This possibility of betrayal is intimately mine, against which the objective guarantee of others protects me. The freedom of pledging binds me to the group, yet it also transcends the word that is our bond since "it reproduces itself as a freedom to transcend (to change, to betray) the pledge if circumstances change" (Sartre 2004, 423).

This double-edged significance of the pledge highlights a central aspect of social existence. Although social groups vary considerably in composition, function, and purpose, every social group is defined by mechanisms and rituals of expulsion and admission. Every statutory group is circumscribed by "points of rupture"—points at which individuals can break with the group. As a performative speech act, the instituting pledge reciprocally *gives voice* to the individuals within the group: it is the first act of speech that legitimates the voice of an individual within a group. With these two aspects of "exit" and "voice," Sartre masterfully anticipates a central insight in Albert O. Hirschman's classic of sociology, *Exit, Voice and Loyalty* (Hirschman 1970). Within a statutory group (a group constituted through a reflexive and regulatory mechanism of inclusion and exclusion), dissatisfied individuals may either improve their own lot by "exiting" the group (and pay the price of exit: social stigma, financial loss, etc.) or seek to alter the common praxis of the group through the exercise of voice only granted them as (pledged) members of the group. As Hirschman explored, the strategy of exit may reduce the manifestation of dissenting voice within an organization; likewise, leaders within an organization may foster either a responsiveness to voice or an encouragement of exit. In Sartre's own analysis, it is crucial that a statutory group—a group of mutually recognizable and legitimate "voices" circumscribed by points of rupture—integrates a constitutive function of *conflict*. Whereas a group in fusion is caught in the perpetual birth of revolution, marked by an unstable tension between "immanence" and "transcendence," a statutory group incorporates this tension into a positive and self-sustaining function. On the one hand, the group receives substance through self-regulating mechanisms of inertial motion guaranteeing the continued existence of the group as such. On the other hand, the group is defined by a dialectical tension between the centrifugal and centripetal forces of exit and voice. Whereas the inertial motion of the group continually runs the risk of promoting institutional stupidity—the subsumption of a group's *best* interests to an interest in preserving the group as an end in itself—the tension of exit and voice allows for the production of a group's critical intelligence and creativity.

This dialectical tension between exit and voice accounts for the constant presence of a coercive force and force of constraint (Sartre speaks of a *groupe en contrainte*) within the group *as well as* the need for a self-sustaining regulative idea that becomes assimilated by the group. The latter functions as an interior norm, or *ethos*, of the group: an idea or value (freedom, Allah, etc.) expressed and symbolized in oaths and pledges (Stack 1977, 120). As Sartre notes, however, whether a pledge appeals to a transcendent entity, its signifier, or symbol (God, Nation, etc.), is immaterial to the basic function of the pledge as instituting the "absolute power of man over man." In a religious community, God is the symbolic displacement for this exercise of absolute power; in a secular community, other idols, for example, the idea of Humanity, or the cult of man, may be instituted. The perimeter and contour of entry and exit (as well as the topography of voice) map differently on different kinds of groups, and can be seen as expanding in scope and deepening in ontological purchase over the evolution of the group until one reaches the level of "nationhood" and "humanity." The *ethos* of a group—its core investment in itself—does not merely function as a regulative idea, but, in Sartre's thinking, functions as the institution of a *political* ontology in the sense of establishing an existential distinction and demarcation between us and them.

Although individual free praxis *constitutes* the "constituted" rationality of the group and its collective agency, individuals are in turn "substantialized"— given substance *as individuals belonging* to a group: each individual subsists in the permanent being of the group. The ontological force of this "social substantialization" of the individual is directly proportional to the degree of violence exercised against traitors. Those who violate the regulatory norms and *ethos* of a group are "unforgivable." Something *primordial* in our social existence *is* violated with betrayal, as, for example, reflected in the contaminated presence of the traitor as an "evil" eliciting a reaction of disgust. The one who betrays the group fundamentally threatens *from within* the distinction between inside and outside, us and them. Hence, the not-untypical association of traitors, double agents, and individuals operating both for and against a group as "slimy," "slippery," and, in general, ontologically amorphous.

The pledge institutes a framework for the cultivation of trust and solidarity within a statutory group that reflects a pervasive sense of collective and concerted free praxis. The fundamental dynamic of the pledge is as a reflected action upon itself: the group acts on itself. The aim is to protect the common interest, yet in the absence of a real threat from outside, the group must produce from within a pressure on its members by establishing a "reign of absolute violence over its members." The pledge institutes a reign of violence: "Everyone's freedom demands the violence of all against it and against that of any third party as its defense against itself [. . .] To swear is to say, as a common individual: you must kill me if I secede" (Sartre 2004, 431). In this manner, as Sartre argues, "the fundamental statue of the pledged group is Terror" (Sartre 2004, 433).[8]

## FRATERNITY-TERROR

Within this order of co-existence, the statutory group solidifies itself into a social, psychological, and material field of action in which individuals foster trust and solicitude for each other. This inclusiveness can rapidly flip into an unmitigated release of violence against an individual member, should s/he become Other in betraying or abandoning the group. As Sartre notes, "this [*pledge*] guarantee is everyone's solicitude for everyone, but this solicitude is a bearer of death" (Sartre 2004, 435). How quickly we turn on others once they become Other in breaking the word and the world that binds us together. The trust, solidarity, and reciprocity that sustain a statutory group is marked by an undertone of terror. It is not a perceptible or discernable terror, as with manifest coercion, nor an imposing form of terror, as with Hobbes' *Leviathan*. It is the *latent* threat that each represents for the other the bearer of death should an individual ever betray the group. The being of the group is sustained *in* terror, not *through* terror.

The statutory group is founded in a mediated reciprocity that is both concrete and practical. It is concrete because "the third" recognizes individuals not as abstract individuals, but as belonging concretely to the group. Expressed more emphatically, individuals are *constituted* as members of a common *species*. As Sartre writes, group members are the "sworn members of a particular species—a species which is connected with concrete circumstances, with objectives, and with the pledge" (Sartre 2004, 435). Sartre charges the term "species" with an ontological purchase. The statutory group institutes the mutual recognition of members as belonging to a species *as if* belonging to a *natural kind*. It is *my* being, *our* being that is sustained by the narrative of the group's history, its founding myth of origin, and, most significantly, a common *hexis*, or texture of habitualities: bodily gestures, patterns of speech, social customs, etc. The statutory group is the materialization of a temporal social object: the creation of a certain past (official histories, etc.) and future. This substantialization of the group *in* individuals is manifest in affects (pride in being an American, a fan of the New England Patriots, etc.) as well as materially in the uniforms, clothing, etc., that mark membership. Gang tattoos are perhaps one of the clearest examples of how the body becomes physically inscribed—and hence incorporated—into a social group. The tattooed body becomes the material referent for the group, along with its exploits, narrative, and symbolic system. As Sartre writes, "We are *the same* because we emerged from the clay at the same date, through each other and through all others; and so we are, as it were, an individual species, which has emerged at a particular moment through a sudden mutation; but our specific nature unites us in so far as it is freedom" (Sartre 2004, 437). The paradoxical (or better: dialectical) underpinning of a statutory group is that although it is based on the contingency of circumstances and freedom of individual *praxis*, it institutes a normative space and medium of social existence that is viscerally *experienced* as Nature such that any violation against the group's permanence is perceived as a violation of nature.

It is with this ontological significance of the "species" character of social existence that Sartre introduces and understands the notion of fraternity. The statutory bond of common individuals is constituted in a fraternity:

"he and I *are brothers.*" As Sartre further comments, "And this fraternity is not based, as is sometimes stupidly supposed, on physical resemblance expressing some deep identity of natures [. . .] We are brothers in so far as, following the creative act of the pledge, we *are our own sons*, our common creation" (Sartre 2004, 437). Fraternity is the "real bond" between individuals within a statutory group, since each individual lives "*his being*" as well as the being of others in the form of the "untranscendable," not only, it must be stressed, in terms of the obligations and duties that commonly define us (and gives us voice), but also in terms of an ontological threshold beyond which there is death and the "anti-human."

This ontological emphasis on a common identity created "from the same clay" can be illustrated with the use of biological and familial notions in the discourse of national identity. Every town and village in France, for example, is dotted with monuments commemorating the First World War on which we read: "La commune de [. . .] à ses enfants morts pour la France" (or "pour la Patrie").[9] This common designation of soldiers as "children" connotes a *biological* and hence natural relationship between "France" and its constituent individuals, as if France had given birth to her sons and daughters. The term "children" suggests an *innocence* to the soldiers, assigning their death the status of victimhood while at the same time recognizing their deaths as the "supreme" sacrifice for the Nation and its *future* children. With the outbreak of the war in August 1914, different political parties in France coalesced into *L'union sacrée*. As the Prime Minister René Viviani declared, "Dans la guerre qui s'engage, la France [. . .] sera héroïquement défendue par tous ses fils, dont rien ne brisera devant l'ennemi l'union sacrée."[10]

The ontological incorporation of individuals into a statutory group institutes a line of demarcation between us and them. Individuals who betray the group represent an existential ontological catastrophe *against* which the group must re-substantialize itself. Those who betray the group become *unforgivable*—beyond the possibility of reconciliation and re-integration. To be unforgivable is, in this sense, to be granted *more voice* at the price of an irresolvable ambiguity of authority, or voice: the whistleblower is both unforgivable and unexpulsable as s/he speaks both from within and from without (as with the current predicament of Edward Snowden). In this regard, the traitor is categorically different from the enemy, since the traitor, by virtue of having been a brother, and hence having been "interiorized," is in a liminal zone between us and them. It is perhaps for this reason that the traitor, or potential traitor, instills a heightened sense of paranoia and anxiety (e.g., the McCarthy hearings in the 1950s or the perniciousness of the association of Jews with the *Dolchstoßlegende*). The traitor is neither "in" nor "out," and thus will always suffer from being an exception to an exception. As Sartre remarks, "[T]he traitor is not excluded from the group; indeed he cannot extricate himself from it. He remains a member of the group in so far as the group—threatened by betrayal—reconstitutes itself by annihilating the guilty member, that is to say, by discharging *all its violence* onto him" (Sartre 2004, 438). This form of "fraternity-terror" expresses an *internalization* of fraternity and "evil" *within* a band of brothers, who, once one of their own becomes Other, discharge an unforgiving violence against those who have betrayed them.

The folding of fraternity *into* terror is not only "interiorized" (within the group against one of its own species); it can also be "exteriorized" against what Sartre calls the "anti-man"—those others who pose an existential threat to the group. In both directions—centrifugally against an alien species and centripetally against one of its own (who has become Other)—the function of terror is double-edged, for Sartre contends that "everyone feels at one with everyone in the practical solidarity of the risks run and of the common violence. I am a brother in violence to all my neighbours: and it is clear that anyone who shunned this fraternity would be suspect" (Sartre 2004, 439). As Sartre writes, "[T]hrough socialized matter and through material negation as an inert unity, man is constituted as Other than man. Man exists for everyone as *non-human man*, as an alien species" (Sartre 2004, 130). The double-edged performative of the pledge institutes a form of *Manichaeism*: if not my friend, my enemy, and whoever threatens the group in an existential manner *is* an alien-species. As Sartre remarks, the "non-humanity" of the Other is "objectively" expressed in *praxis* by "the perception of evil as the structure of the Other" (Sartre 2004, 132). The ethical imperative is thus destructive: evil must be destroyed.

## ACKNOWLEDGEMENTS

My thanks to William Remley and Basil Vassilicos for their helpful comments and discussion while writing this chapter.

## NOTES

1 *The Day The Towers Fell* by Carroll D. Jones. Available at: http://www.poemhunter.com/poem/the-day-the-towers-fell (accessed August 29, 2014
2 https://news.vice.com/video/guantanamo-black-out-bay-full-length (accessed September 8, 2014).
3 "It is at the very heart of fraternity, in the manner in which fraternity is circumscribed and exclusive through boundaries, whether real or symbolic frontiers that divide it, that evil can irrupt."
4 "I am searching for that crucial region of the soul where absolute evil stands opposed to fraternity."
5 "This offers us the possibility of understanding how subjectivity is indispensable for the dialectical knowledge of the social. It is because there are only *men* that there are large collective forms, as Durkheim and others have understood them, and that men are necessarily the mediation amongst themselves of these exterior forms, as for example, the entity of class."

6 http://www.imposemagazine.com/bytes/slavoj-zizek-at-occupy-wall-street-transcript (accessed August 30, 2014).
7 Individuals may pledge in different temporal sequences, yet the structure of a pledge implies that each individual who pledges, pledges to every other individual (in the group) who likewise pledges.
8 Every member runs the risk of death, and here it is critical to stress that "death" in this context of discussion includes "social death." Violence is a statutory structure: "in this sense, being-in-the-group as an untranscendable limit produces itself as the certainty of death should the limit be transcended" (Sartre 2004, 432). But whereas with Hobbes, it is by virtue of violence that individuals form into the Leviathan, with Sartre's notion of the statutory group, individuals come together in freedom, yet paradoxically submit themselves to an internal violence in the form of fear.
9 "The community of [. . .] to its children who died for France" (or "for the nation").
10 "In the war now beginning, France will be heroically defended by all of its sons; nothing will break the sacred union in front of the enemy."

## REFERENCES

Austin, J.L. (1975). *How To Do Things With Words*. Cambridge, MA: Harvard University Press.
Crépon, Marc (2008). *Vivre avec*. Paris: Hermann
Hirschman, Albert O. (1970). *Exit, Voice, and Loyalty: Responses to Decline in Firms, Organizations, and States*. Cambridge, MA: Harvard University Press.
Malraux, André (1996). *Le miroir des limbes*. In: *Œuvres complètes, Vol. III*. Paris: Gallimard.
Sartre, Jean-Paul (1993). "Conférence de Rome de 1961." *Les Temps Modernes* 49 (560), 11–39.
——— (2004). *Critique of Dialectical Reason, Vol. 1*. Transl. by A. Sheridan-Smith. London: Verso.
Stack, George J. (1977). *Sartre's Philosophy of Social Existence*. St. Louis: Warren H. Green.

# Contributors

**Emanuele Caminada** is a Postdoctoral Researcher and Mentor in the a.r.t.e.s Graduate School of the University of Cologne. His publications include, among others, the articles "Higher-order persons: an ontological challenge?" (*Phenomenology and Mind* 1, 2011), and "Husserls intentionale Soziologie" (in V. Mayer et al. (Eds.): *Die Aktualität Husserls*. Freiburg: Alber 2011). Recently, he also co-edited the Special Issue of *Norms, Values, Society: Phenomenological and Ontological Approaches* (*Phenomenology and Mind* 3, 2012). Currently, he is finishing a book manuscript on phenomenology and social ontology (forthcoming).

**Havi Carel** is a Senior Lecturer in Philosophy at the University of Bristol and also teaches at Bristol Medical School. She is currently a British Academy Fellow and is writing a monograph for Oxford University Press, provisionally entitled "Phenomenology of Illness." She has written on the embodied experience of illness, well-being within illness, and patient-physician communication in *The Lancet*, *BMJ*, the *Journal of Medicine and Philosophy*, *Theoretical Medicine and Bioethics*, *Philosophia*, and in edited collections. She is the author of the monographs "Illness" (Acumen, 2008, 2013), and of "Life and Death in Freud and Heidegger" (Rodopi, 2006), and co-edited *Health, Illness and Disease* (Acumen, 2012), *What Philosophy Is* (Continuum, 2004) and *New Takes in Film-Philosophy* (Palgrave, 2010). She recently co-edited a special issue of *Philosophy* on "Human Experience and Nature." From 2009 to 2011, she led an AHRC-funded project on the concepts of health, illness, and disease and from 2011 until 2012, she was awarded a Leverhulme Fellowship for a project entitled "The Lived Experience of Illness."

**Eric Chelstrom** is an Assistant Professor of Philosophy at St. Mary's University in San Antonio, Texas. He is author of *Social Phenomenology: Husserl, Intersubjectivity, and Collective Intentionality* (Lexington, 2013), as well as a contributor to the forthcoming collection, *Phenomenology and Virtue Ethics*. His research has focused on collective intentionality and horizon intentionality from within the tradition of Husserlian phenomenology, and is currently shifting to consider implications of collective intentionality debates on the nature of art.

**Steven Crowell** is a Professor of Philosophy and the Joseph and Joanna Nazro Mullen Professor of Humanities at Rice University. He is the author of two books, *Normativity and Phenomenology in Husserl and Heidegger* (Cambridge University Press, 2013) and *Husserl, Heidegger, and the Space of Meaning: Paths Toward Transcendental Phenomenology* (Northwestern University Press, 2001), in addition to numerous articles on phenomenology and continental philosophy. He recently edited the *Cambridge Companion to Existentialism* (2012) and, with Jeff Malpas, *Transcendental Heidegger* (Stanford University Press, 2007). Crowell has served as executive co-director of the Society for Phenomenology and Existential Philosophy, and he is currently co-editor of *Husserl Studies*.

**Nicolas de Warren** is a Professor of Philosophy at the Institute of Philosophy at KU Leuven. He is the author of the book *Husserl and the Promise of Time: Subjectivity in Transcendental Phenomenology* (Cambridge University Press, 2009). His most recent publications include "Husserl and Phenomenological Ethics" for the *Cambridge History of Moral Philosophy* and a forthcoming volume on the legacy of neo-Kantianism (Cambridge University Press). He is currently writing a book on the unforgivable.

**Jo-Jo Koo** is a Postdoctoral Fellow at Mount Holyoke College (South Hadley, Massachusetts). He received his PhD at the University of Pittsburgh in 2011 with a dissertation about the social constitution of the human individual and its ramifications for social ontology. Before coming to Mount Holyoke College he was Visiting Assistant Professor at Concordia University (Montreal, Canada), Dickinson College (Carlisle, Pennsylvania), and Skidmore College (Saratoga Springs, New York). His main areas of research interest and publications include work in 19th and 20th-century European philosophy (especially theories of recognition, phenomenology, existentialism, hermeneutics), social ontology (including theories of collective intentionality), theories of practices (including later Wittgenstein on normativity), the philosophy of the social sciences, and the philosophy of race and gender.

**Joel Krueger** is a Lecturer in Philosophy at the University of Exeter. He works on various issues in phenomenology, philosophy of mind, and cognitive science, with a particular focus on empathy and social cognition. He also works on Asian and comparative philosophy, philosophy of music, and pragmatism. His recent publications include the journal articles "Ontogenesis of the socially extended mind" (*Cognitive Systems Research* 25/26, 2013); "Seeing mind in action" (*Phenomenology and* the *Cognitive Sciences* 11, 2012); (with John Michael) "Gestural coupling and social cognition: Möbius Syndrome as a case study" (*Frontiers in Human Neuroscience* 6, 2012); and "Extended cognition and the space of social interaction" (*Consciousness and Cognition* 20, 2011).

Felipe León is a PhD Fellow at the Center for Subjectivity Research at the University of Copenhagen. In 2015 he was a Visiting Research Scholar in the Philosophy Department of the University of California, Berkeley. His current research focuses on issues within the fields of collective intentionality and social cognition. His most recent and forthcoming publications include: "Shame and selfhood" (*Phänomenologische Forschungen*, 2012); "Experiential other-directness: to what does it amount?" (*Tidsskrift for Medier, Erkendelse og Formidling*, 1, 2013); "Reflexión, objetivación, tematización: sobre una crítica heideggeriana de Husserl" (forthcoming in *Investigaciones Fenomenológicas*); and, co-authored with Dan Zahavi, "Phenomenology of experiential sharing: The contribution of Schutz and Walther" (forthcoming in: A. Salice and H.-B. Schmid (Eds.). *Social Reality: The Phenomenological Approach*. Dordrecht: Springer).

Sophie Loidolt is an Assistant Professor in the Department of Philosophy at the University of Vienna. She was a visiting researcher in Paris, Leuven, New York, and Copenhagen. In 2010, she was a visiting scholar at the New School for Social Research and from 2010 to 2011, an APART Fellow of the Austrian Academy of Science. She has published numerous articles on phenomenology, is the author of two monographs, *Anspruch und Rechtfertigung. Eine Theorie des rechtlichen Denkens im Anschluss an die Phänomenologie Edmund Husserls* (Springer, 2009), and *Einführung in die Rechtsphänomenologie. Eine historisch-systematische Darstellung* (Mohr Siebeck, 2010), and co-editor of *Das Fremde im Selbst. Transformationen der Phänomenologie: Intersubjektivität, Alterität, Politik* (Königshausen & Neumann, 2010), and *Urteil und Fehlurteil* (Turia+Kant, 2011). Currently, she has a further monograph under review, entitled *Phenomenology of Plurality. Hannah Arendt and the Phenomenological Tradition*.

Dermot Moran is a Professor of Philosophy (Metaphysics and Logic) at University College Dublin and a Member of the Royal Irish Academy, which also awarded him the "Gold Medal in the Humanities." From 2013 until 2018, he is heading the International Federation of Philosophical Societies as its president. Prof. Moran has published extensively on the history of philosophy, medieval philosophy, the philosophy of the 20th century and, in particular on phenomenology. Among his numerous monographs and edited volumes are: *Introduction to Phenomenology* (Routledge, 2000); *The Phenomenology Reader* (co-edited with Tim Mooney, Routledge, 2002), *Phenomenology. Critical Concepts in Philosophy*, 5

Volumes (co-edited with Lester Embree; Routledge, 2004); *Edmund Husserl: Founder of Phenomenology* (Polity 2005), *Routledge Companion to Twentieth Century Philosophy* (ed., Routledge, 2008); *The Husserl Dictionary* (co-edited with Joseph Cohen, Bloomsbury-Continuum, 2012), and *Edmund Husserl's Crisis of European Sciences: An Introduction* (Cambridge University Press, 2012).

**Cathal O'Madagain** is a Postdoctoral Researcher in the Department of Developmental and Comparative Psychology at the Max Planck Institute for Evolutionary Anthropology in Leipzig, where he works with Michael Tomasello. His work focuses on the philosophy of language and mind, and particularly on social issues that arise in these areas, such as how the meanings of words in shared languages are fixed by social interaction, and what effects social interaction has on the cognition of individuals. His article "Can Groups have Concepts? Semantics for Collective Intentionality" is forthcoming in *Philosophical Issues*.

**Matthew Ratcliffe** is a Professor of Philosophy at the University of Vienna, Austria. Most of his recent research has addressed issues in phenomenology, philosophy of psychology, and philosophy of psychiatry. He is the author of *Rethinking Commonsense Psychology: A Critique of Folk Psychology, Theory of Mind and Simulation* (Palgrave, 2007) and *Feelings of Being: Phenomenology, Psychiatry and the Sense of Reality* (Oxford University Press, 2008). The topics he is currently working on include empathy, the experience of depression, and the nature of auditory verbal hallucinations.

**James Risser** is a Professor of Philosophy at Seattle University. He is the former executive co-director of the Society for Phenomenology and Existential Philosophy, and currently serves on the board of directors for the Collegium Phaenomenologicum and for the North American Society for Philosophical Hermeneutics. His published works include *Hermeneutics and the Voice of the Other: Re-reading Gadamer's Philosophical Hermeneutics* (1997), and *The Life of Understanding: A Contemporary Hermeneutics* (2012). He is the editor of *Heidegger Toward the Turn: Essays on the Work of the 1930s* (1999), the co-editor of *American Continental Philosophy* (2000), and the associate editor of the journal *Research in Phenomenology*.

**Alessandro Salice** is a Lecturer in Philosophy at University College Cork (Ireland). Previously, he was a Postdoctoral Fellow at the Center for Subjectivity Research at the University of Copenhagen. He has also worked and taught at the University of Graz, Basel and Vienna and was visiting professor at the State University for the Humanities in Moscow. His main research interests are on phenomenology and social ontology. On these and related topics he has published extensively. Some of his most recent publications include: *La visione delle idee. Il metodo del realismo fenomenologico* (ed. with S. Besoli, Quodlibet, 2008), *Urteile und Sachverhalte. Ein Vergleich zwischen Alexius Meinong und Adolf Reinach* (Philosophia, 2009), *Intentionality* (editor, Philosophia, 2012), and an special issue on *Social Facts: Metaphysical and Empirical Perspectives* (ed. with Luca Tummolini), which is forthcoming in the journal *Phenomenology and the Cognitive Sciences*.

**Christian Skirke** is a Lecturer in Metaphysics at the University of Amsterdam. He has published on existential phenomenology and the Frankfurt School in the *European Journal of Philosophy*, *Inquiry* and *Zeitschrift für philosophische Forschung*, among others. He wrote the *Oxford Online Bibliographies* entry on Jean-Paul Sartre.

**Thomas Szanto** is currently a Postdoctoral Research Fellow at the Center for Subjectivity Research (CFS) at the University of Copenhagen, where he is collaborating with Dan Zahavi. From 2016 until 2018, he will be working at the CFS witihin the framework of his Marie Curie Individual Fellowship project "SHARE: Shared Emotions, Group Membership, and Empathy." Before coming to Copenhagen, he was a Postdoctoral Research Fellow at University College Dublin (2012–2013), where he worked with Dermot Moran on the Irish Research Council project "Discovering the 'We': The Phenomenology of Sociality." Previously, he has also held Adjunct Lecturer positions at the universities of Vienna, Graz, and Klagenfurt. His recent publications include articles in the journals *Phenomenology and the Cognitive Sciences* and *Human Studies*, the monograph "Bewusstsein Intentionalität und Mentale Repräsentation: Husserl und die Analytische Philosophie des Geistes" (de Gruyter, 2012) and the forthcoming *Human Studies* Special Issue *Empathy and Collective Intentionality: The Social Philosophy of Edith Stein* (co-edited with Dermot Moran).

**Joona Taipale** is an Advanced Researcher at the University of Jyväskylä (Finland) within the framework of a KONE Foundation research project focusing on questions concerning self/other differentiation and interpersonal understanding from the point of view of phenomenology, psychoanalysis, and social ontology. Previously, he was a postdoctoral research fellow at the Center for Subjectivity Research at the University of Copenhagen (2013–2015). He is also an adjunct professor in the Philosophy Section of the University of Tampere (Finland). Taipale has published extensively on phenomenology, the philosophy of the mind, and psychoanalysis; his focal topics have been empathy, intersubjectivity, and embodiment. His recent publications include the monograph "Phenomenology and Embodiment. Husserl and the Constitution of Subjectivity"

(Northwestern University Press, 2014), as well as the articles "Beyond Cartesianism: Body-Perception and the Immediacy of Empathy" (*Continental Philosophy Review*, 2015), "Facts and Fantasies: Embodiment and the Early Formation of Selfhood" (edited volume *The Phenomenology of Embodied Subjectivity*, Springer, 2013), and "Twofold Normality: Husserl and the Normative Relevance of Primordial Constitution" (*Husserl Studies*, 2012). Taipale has also recently co-edited, with Dan Zahavi, a special issue on phenomenology for the *Continental Philosophy Review* (2015).

**Íngrid Vendrell Ferran** is an Assistant Professor of Theoretical Philosophy at the University of Jena (Germany). She has been an Assistant Professor at the Philipps Universität Marburg (Germany), Postdoctoral Researcher at the Universidad Complutense de Madrid, the Université de Genève (CISA), the Universität Luzern, and at the Freie Universität Berlin (Cluster Languages of Emotion). Her research interests are primarily in the philosophy of the mind, phenomenology, value theory, and epistemology. She is the author of the book *Die Emotionen. Gefühle in der realistischen Phänomenologie* (Akademie Verlag, 2008) and she is currently preparing her second book on *Erkenntnis und Fiktion*. She has translated and edited the works of Max Scheler and Aurel Kolnai into Spanish and edited (together with Christoph Demmerling) the book *Wahrheit, Wissen und Erkenntnis in der Literatur. Philosophische Beiträge* (Akademie Verlag, 2014).

**Richard Wolin** is a Distinguished Professor of History, Political Science, and Comparative Literature at the Graduate Center of the City University of New York. Among his numerous books, which have been translated into ten languages, are *Heidegger's Children: Hannah Arendt, Karl Löwith, Hans Jonas, Herbert Marcuse* (Princeton University Press, 2001); *The Seduction of Unreason: The Intellectual Romance with Fascism From Nietzsche to Postmodernism* (Princeton University Press, 2004); *The Frankfurt School Revisited and Other Essays on Politics and Society* (Routledge, 2006), and *The Wind from the East: French Intellectuals, the Chinese Cultural Revolution, and the Legacy of the 1960s* (Princeton University Press, 2010), which was recently listed by the *Financial Times* as one of the best books of 2012. He frequently writes on intellectual and political topics for the *New Republic*, *The Nation*, and *Dissent*.

# Index

affectivity 3, 15, 13, 15–16, 49, 217, 221, 230, 259, 273, 296, 308; shared 7, 8; *see also* emotions; affective intentionality
affordance 71–73
agency collective 17, 279, 315, 316, 322 *see also* joint action
alterity 2, 46, 71, 100–102, 150, 320
*Angst* 86
Apel, Karl-Otto 5, 57
apperception 193, 286; analogizing 71–72; typifying 151
apperceptive transfer 71
appresentation 132–134
Arendt, Hannah 9–13, 42–55, 260
Aristotle 33, 36, 39, 252, 256
Austin, John L. 77, 235, 238, 319–320
authenticity 47, 87, 95, 104; *see also* Eigentlichkeit

Barnes, Julian 210
being-for-one-another (*Füreinandersein*) 107, 114
being-in-the-world 46, 61, 93–94, 103, 108–109, 113
being-with 1, 3, 12, 38, 85, 87, 93, 99–100, 103, 249, 314; *see also* Mitsein
being-with-one-another 29, 31, 33, 35, 38; *see also* Miteinandersein
Berger, Peter L. 19
body social 174, 177
Bratman, Michael 1, 159, 248–249, 254, 256, 257–258
Brentano, Franz 116, 227, 231
Buber, Martin 11–13, 30, 34, 93, 99–100, 123
Burckhardt, Jacob 63

Caillois, Roger 120
Call (*Ruf*) Heidegger 85–88
Canguilhem, George 182–83
Cavarero, Adriana 43
Cohen, Hermann 30
collective intentionality 3, 5–7, 13–17, 217, 231, 232, 248, 252, 254, 260, 263, 269, 273, 281–283, 286–287, 293, 296, 299; *see also* We-intentionality
collectivism 17, 282, 297, 304–306
Collingwood, R. G. 1
communication 31, 59, 66, 74–75, 112, 114, 117, 121, 176, 235, 237, 240–241, 243, 285–286
community 29–30, 38, 47, 52–53, 64, 84–86, 108, 115, 116, 118, 169, 219, 224–227, 231, 241, 249–251, 257, 270, 283, 286, 288, 290–291, 299, 302–303, 317, 320, 322 (*see also Gemeinschaft*); moral 84–86, 88
Conni, Carlo 287
conscience 58, 70; Heidegger 85–88; Levinas 84–85; *see also* Call (*Ruf*) Heidegger
Crépon, Marc 314

Damasio, Antonio 258
Darwall, Stephen 10, 12, 70, 74–86, 88
*Dasein* 1, 30–31, 38, 45, 85–88, 93, 95
Davidson, Donald 13, 127–39
DeNota, Tia 266
dialogue 31, 40, 72, 79
Didion, Joan 207
Dilthey, Wilhelm 57–60, 115
Dubose, J. Todd 212
Durkheim, Emil 63, 307, 317–318, 325
Dutt, Carsten 33

## Index

*Eigentlichkeit* 47, 85; *see also* authenticity
*Einfühlung* 3, 4, 96, 109–111, 119; *see also* empathy
*Einsfühlung* 8, 307; *see also* fusion
emotional contagion 15, 188, 199, 224–225, 307
emotions collective 7–9, 257, 260–261, 269, 273; shared 7, 8, 16, 263, 266–270; *see also* affectivity; regulation
empathy 3, 7, 8, 12, 14, 15, 29, 36, 38, 71, 74–75, 80, 82, 84, 96, 109–111, 122, 143–156, 165, 173, 178–180, 182, 187–200, 211, 219, 221, 231, 242, 253–255, 259; *see also Einfühlung*; *Nachfühlen*
ethics 9, 26, 42, 70, 101, 102, 227, 231, 282, 296, 306

false-belief 135–138
fellow feeling 15, 187–188, 196, 199–200, 224–225; *see also Mit-fühlen*
Feuerbach, Ludwig 30, 38
first-person perspective 2, 12, 44, 47, 49, 162, 292; plural 2, 10, 13
Foucault, Michel 63
Fraternity-terror 313, 314, 322–325
Freud, Sigmund 59
friendship 36, 39, 252, 256
fusion 8, 249–50, 252, 257, 259, 260, 299, 307; *see also Einsfühlung*; group in fusion

Gadamer, Hans-Georg 11, 12, 29–41, 59–60, 115
Garfinkel, Harald 281
*Gemeinschaft* 64, 108, 116; *see also* community
*Gesamterlebnis* 306
*Gesamtperson* 19, 220, 251, 298, 309; *see also* collective person; group personhood
*Gesellschaft* 64; *see also* society
Gilbert, Margaret 1, 18, 159, 248–249, 252, 254, 256–260, 284–286
Goldie, Peter 207, 231
grief 202–214, 270–273
Gross, James J. 264, 266, 268
group in fusion Sartre 314–321; *see also* fusion
group personhood 18, 297, 309; *see also* collective person; *Gesamtperson*

Gubser, Michael 9
guilt 9, 82–85, 257, 306
Gurwitsch, Aron 1, 7, 11, 14, 16, 157, 248–60

Haas, Willy 230
Habermas, Jürgen 10, 11, 12, 56–68, 77, 81, 102
Heidegger, Martin 1, 11, 12, 13, 30–31, 37, 38, 43, 45–46, 58, 60, 61, 70, 82, 85–88, 93–96, 98–104
Hemon, Aleksandar 208, 210
Henrich, Dieter 231
Henry, Michel 220
hermeneutics 58–66
Hildebrand, Dietrich von 7, 9, 11, 16, 231, 235, 236, 239–244, 245, 281
Hobbes, Thomas 296, 323, 326
holism 5, 7–8, 76, 305, 308
Honneth, Axel 8
Hugo, Victor 313
Hume, David 58, 75, 230, 296
Humphrey, Helen 211
Husserl, Edmund 1, 2, 3, 5, 9, 10, 11, 12, 13, 17, 18, 29, 43, 45, 46, 49, 50, 51, 54, 56–57, 60–64, 68, 70–72, 74–75, 96, 104, 107–124, 127–28, 132–139, 146–151, 155, 174, 178, 187, 190–195, 199, 213, 219–220, 231, 233, 240, 245, 255, 281–293, 296, 300, 309

I-Thou relation 12, 13, 15, 30, 34–39, 100, 167, 178, 241
illness, experience of 15, 173–185
incommensurability 78, 81, 301, 305
individualism 2, 5, 9, 281, 282, 284, 304–305
*Ineinandersein* 13, 107–123, 288
intentionality, affective 16, 219–231
interactionism 159, 170; *see also* social interaction
intercorporeality 121, 178
*l'interlacs* 107, 113
*l'intermonde* Merleau-Ponty 112, 122
interpersonal relations 4, 10, 12, 14, 15, 203, 271, 305
intersubjectivity 2, 10, 13, 15, 30, 31, 33, 34, 35, 39, 43, 47–49, 51, 52, 64, 66, 71, 93, 96–104, 108, 112, 113–19, 123, 173, 175–178, 187, 213, 219, 220, 231, 286, 288, 292

Jacobi, Friedrich 30
Jaspers, Karl 68
joint action 160, 263, 285 (see also collective action); attention 6, 130, 137–138, 198, 200; commitment 3, 7, 258, 261, 284, 299
Jones, Karen 256
Jones, Paul W. 183

Kern, Iso 108
Korsgaard, Christine M. 77

Lacan, Jacques 120
language 33, 35–36, 137, 143, 155
*Lebensgemeinschaft* 251; see also life-community
*Lebenswelt* 56, 61, 111; see also lifeworld
Levinas, Emmanuel 11, 13, 70–73, 76, 79, 83–85, 88, 93, 99, 101–105, 220
Lévi-Strauss, Claude 120, 123
Lévy-Bruhl, Lucien 120
life-community 225–226, 306–307; see also *Lebensgemeinschaft*
lifeworld 12, 57, 60–68, 281, 285, 290; see also *Lebenswelt*
Locke, John 58, 133, 296
love 15, 16, 36, 114, 205, 221, 223–226, 228–230, 233–235, 237, 239–243, 245, 256, 270, 288
Löwith, Karl 11, 12, 29–39
Luckmann, Thomas 19, 60, 281
Lyotard, Jean-François 11, 70, 78–81, 87

McLeod, Carolyn 256
Malraux, André 314
*Man, das* 85, 95, 103, 104
Marx, Karl 59, 66
Marxism 1, 9, 10, 18, 56–57, 318; phenomenological 56
Meinong, Alexius 229
Merleau-Ponty, Maurice 3, 7, 9, 11, 13, 56, 61, 93, 96–99, 101, 102, 103, 104, 107–124, 143, 147–149, 153, 155, 174, 178, 182, 184, 187, 212, 213, 219, 220
metaphysics 231, 235, 239; descriptive 77
Miller, Seumas 248
*Mit-fühlen* 224, 307; see also fellow feeling
*Miteinandersein* 31, 45–47, 93; see also being-with-one-another

moods 228, 249, 267
morality 75, 78, 258
Mulligan, Kevin 232

*Nachfühlen* 8, 16, 242, 243; see also empathy; vicarious feeling
Niedenthal, Paula 265
Nietzsche, Friedrich 84
normativity 16, 95, 182, 297, 304

Oates, Joyce Carol 206
objectivity 13, 49, 51, 59, 66, 68, 91, 127–139, 174, 176, 178, 184, 223, 286, 292
ontology 31, 42–43, 70–74, 81–82, 87, 101, 119, 124; social 3–10, 13–14, 17–18
orientation: type– 145, 147, 150, 152; token– 145–147, 150, 152
Ortega y Gasset, José 219, 220, 221
other, the 29, 32–39, 46, 71–76, 79–84, 97–102, 120–122, 133–134, 137, 143–156, 160, 189–194, 212, 224–226, 242–243, 253–255, 270–73, 288–89, 320–325

Paci, Enzo 9, 19, 56
Parfit, Derek 296
participation 1, 35–36
Patočka, Jan 9
Pavlov, Ivan 129
Peirce, Charles S. 59
perceptual crossing 160, 164–169
person collective 220, 226, 209; communal 298, 300–302, 305–307; see also first-, second-, and third-person perspective; *Gesamtperson*
Pettit, Philip 1, 18, 309
Pfänder, Alexander 220, 221, 227–231, 232
Plato 31, 62, 245, 296
plurality 29, 42–53, 116, 250, 283–287, 289, 297–298, 304, 309; actualized 12, 42–53
plural subject 5, 284–289, 292
pragmatics 67, 78–79
pre-reflective self-awareness 81, 99
presentification 190–196, 242
Prinz, Jesse 258
psychology: belief-desire 15, 202–203, 213; developmental 127, 138, 162, 202

Ranke, Friedrich 59
Ratcliffe, Mathew 9, 14, 15, 202–214
re-living (*Nachleben*) 225
reciprocity 29, 67, 74, 167–168, 177, 212, 254, 314, 319–320, 323
recognition 34, 37, 39, 156, 166, 177, 320; mutual 13, 76, 78, 82, 323; reciprocal 74, 166, 316; self- 30, 189–191
Reddy, Vasudevi 163
Rees, Dewi W. 209
regulation 8, 16, 57, 74, 163–164, 268, 272–273; co- 17; self- 263–270
Reinach, Adolf 11, 16, 220, 225, 231, 235–239, 241–242, 245
responsibility 12, 72–76, 82–83, 87, 225, 226, 284–285, 304, 306–307; co- 299–300, 302, 306–308
Ricoeur, Paul 54, 61, 314
Riley, Denise 210–212
Rinofner-Kreidl, Sonja 200
Rosenzweig, Franz 30
Rovane, Carol 1, 18
Ryle, Gilbert 302

Sartre, Jean-Paul 3, 9, 11, 13, 17, 18, 48, 56, 70, 71–73, 82, 83, 93, 99–100, 103, 104, 112, 173–174, 176–178, 187–191, 194–196, 199, 208, 313–326
Scheler, Max 1, 3, 7, 8, 9, 11, 16, 17, 18, 19, 123, 188–189, 199, 213, 219–227, 231, 242–243, 249, 251, 270, 272, 273, 274, 281, 296–309
Schmid, Hans Bernhard 3, 8, 10, 282
Schütz, Alfred 3, 9, 10, 11, 16, 19, 57, 60, 64, 151–153, 157, 219, 220, 221, 252, 262, 281, 309
Searle, John 1, 3, 159, 160, 237, 260
second-person perspective 1–2, 12, 74, 84, 162, 178; plural 2, 13
second-person phenomenology 10, 12, 70–74, 76–78, 81–82, 84–86
self 38, 46–51, 73, 83, 98, 102–103, 107, 118, 193–200, 206, 212, 225, 227–230, 245, 249, 256; *see also* pre-reflective self-awareness
Semprún, Jorge 314
sentiments 16, 220, 221, 227–232, 249, 254, 282–283, 288

shame 7, 9, 14, 15, 48, 73, 82–84, 99, 187–200
shared life 29, 31–33, 35, 37
shared world 12, 32, 39, 96, 109, 110, 114, 198, 204
sharing 1, 5, 9, 13, 30–37, 93–103, 159–160, 167–169, 224, 226, 228, 269; emotional 6, 16
Simmel, Georg 63
*Sittlichkeit* (ethical life) 67–68
Skirke, Christian 9, 14, 15, 187–200
Slatman, Jenny 184
social acts 3, 16, 50, 220–221, 225, 235–241, 243, 283–285
social interaction 1, 5, 6, 13–15, 49, 51, 96, 132, 147, 160–169, 177–178; theory 160–169, 184, 202, 271; *see also* interactionism
social philosophy 4, 9, 10, 11, 14, 306; Husserl's 282
social stance 239–44
society 42, 52–53, 63–64, 66, 123, 219, 228, 250, 257, 303, 307; *see also* Gesellschaft
solidarity 29, 37, 39, 63, 67, 225–226, 299–300, 302–304, 306–307, 313, 323, 325
solipsistic subject 38, 71, 72, 98, 121, 219
statutory group 315–323
Stein, Edith 3, 7, 9, 11, 12, 29–30, 116, 147, 149, 191–193, 195, 199, 211, 219, 227, 228, 231, 281, 309
Strauss, Leo 36
subjectivity 2, 13, 33–34, 47–49, 53, 62, 64, 72, 96, 110–111, 119–121, 124, 174, 177–178, 184, 189, 191, 195, 197, 267, 289–90, 292, 325; plural 284; *see also* plural subject
*sunesis* 36–37
sympathy 15, 188, 199, 220, 224, 307, 317

Theunissen, Michael 13, 93, 99, 100, 103, 104
third-person perspective 44–46, 63, 162
Thompson, Evan 254–255, 258
togetherness 2, 17, 50, 52–53, 249, 257, 299
Tomasello, Michael 168
Toombs, S. K. 176, 179, 182, 184

Trân Duc Thao 9, 19, 56
Tuomela, Raimo 1, 248, 299
typification 7, 14, 143–57, 252–253, 256–257, 280

*Umwelt* 111–112, 120

*Verständigung* 32, 67
*Verstehen* 56–60, 242
vicarious feeling 16, 224, 226, 242–243; *see also Nachfühlen*
Voigtländer, Else 230
*Vorhandensein* 44–46; *see also Zuhandensein*

Waldenfels, Bernhard 9, 10
Walther, Gerda 7, 11, 16, 221, 227, 228–229, 231, 232, 250, 281

We 1–2, 9, 10, 17, 18, 47, 48, 51–53, 81, 249, 250 259; affective 263; -communities 241; experience 165, 167, 299; -intentionality 281, 288–93, 299; -mode 299; -world 3, 5, 13, 91, 107
Weber, Max 61, 63, 66, 281
Welton, Donn 259, 261
Whybrow, Peter 205
Winch, Peter 1
Wittgenstein, Ludwig 1, 54, 68, 149, 159
Wright, Georg Henrik von 1, 5, 57

Zahavi, Dan 139, 199, 200, 213
*Zuhandensein* 84; *see also Vorhandensein*